5000 EPISODES AND NO COMMERCIALS

THE ULTIMATE GUIDE TO TV SHOWS ON DVD 2007

DAVID HOFSTEDE

BACK STAGE BOOKS
NEW YORK

Executive Editor: Mark Glubke
Project Editor: Ross Plotkin
Cover Designer: Elizabeth Elsas Mandel
Interior Designer: Jay Anning, Thumb Print
The principal typefaces used in the composition
of this book were ITC Weidemann and Helvetica Neue

First published in 2006 by Back Stage Books,
An imprint of Watson-Guptill Publications,
A division of VNU Business Media, Inc.,
770 Broadway, New York, NY 10003
www.wgpub.com

Library of Congress Control Number: 2006928029
ISBN-13: 978-0-8230-8456-2
ISBN-10: 0-8230-8456-6

Printed in the United States

First printing, 2006

1 2 3 4 5 6 7 8 9 / 14 13 12 11 10 09 08 07 06

Contents

Acknowledgments

Special thanks go out to Robert Berg, Craig Byrne, and Jack Condon for their expertise and writing contributions on some of the series listed in this volume. My own research was aided immeasurably by the many studios that provided DVD sets for review, and by the staff at the Museum of Television and Radio in Los Angeles. I am grateful to Mark Glubke at Watson-Guptill for his suggestions on how to create a guidebook of this scope from scratch.

Introduction

When the DVD was introduced in 1998, no one could have foretold the role that television would play in its success. The original goal was to replace videocassettes with a digital format that could hold a movie plus extra features, at a price that would make buying the DVD a tempting alternative to renting the film at the video store. And though movie sales have been brisk, it has been collections of television series that have shocked industry watchers with their popularity. Fans are routinely paying anywhere from $30 to $120 for full-season sets of their favorite shows.

For the first time in the medium's history, television has become a collectible commodity. This is wonderful news, especially for those old enough to remember when the only access we had to favorite episodes of favorite TV series was when they aired in syndication. Back then, we were lucky to be reunited with these old friends once or twice in a year. But today, thanks to DVD, we can watch Lucy work in the chocolate factory, the Monkees sing "Daydream Believer," and Ross and Rachel get together (or break up) whenever we choose.

Since May 2000, when first-season sets of *The X-Files* and *Sex and the City* became the first series to be collected on DVD, more than 400 other sets have reached the market. According to *Video Store Magazine*, sales of TV DVDs are outpacing all other categories, surpassing $2 billion in 2004. "What once seemed a niche market is now firmly entrenched in the mainstream and contributes big bucks to the bottom line of various studios," reports the *Los Angeles Daily News*.

Sales are spread across the full spectrum of television programming. Recent shows that play daily in syndication, such as *Friends* and *The Simpsons*, sell well. Shows that appeal to younger audiences, such as *Buffy the Vampire Slayer*, rank with the format's top sellers. Collectors appreciate that no television library is complete without the all-time classics, including *The Dick Van Dyke Show* and *The Honeymooners*. Even short-lived shows that failed in their primetime runs, such as *Sports Night* and *Freaks and Geeks*, have found an enthusiastic following on DVD.

What You'll Find in This Book . . . And What You Won't

5,000 Episodes and No Commercials: The Ultimate Guide to TV Shows on DVD lists and rates on a 0–5 star scale every prominent show released on DVD, whether in season sets, individual episodes, or "best of" compilations. The objective is to let TV fans know what is out there, and whether it's worth picking up.

Different fans have different expectations from the format. Most are just delighted to add their favorite shows to a home entertainment library, but some will refuse to buy a series if the audio is Dolby Digital 2.0, rather than 5.1. While it would be wonderful to have each DVD set released with the highest-quality picture and sound achievable in the format, the majority of consumers don't have a home entertainment system capable of telling the difference. But buyers do have a right to expect that the video and audio quality of their DVDs should be equal or superior to how the series looked when originally broadcast, and it is by that standard that they are judged here.

Music rights is another ongoing issue. As television networks could not have foreseen the possibility that their shows would be packaged for the retail market, no effort was made to secure the rights to the music played in some series beyond their original and syndicated runs. This is a particularly thorny issue for shows that incorporate a variety of popular songs, such as *21 Jump Street*, *Moonlighting*, and *WKRP in Cincinnati*. In some cases an effort was made, often at great expense, to preserve the original music, while other studios opted to delete the more expensive soundtrack in favor of a generic equivalent. These instances have been cited here in the text, so the potential buyer can make an informed decision.

While many fans might let the studios slide on a few song substitutions, there is one practice that could constitute a deal breaker, and that is the use of syndicated-episode cuts. One might expect this from the public-domain releases, slapped together by quick-buck distributors who had neither the budget nor the inclination to do the job right. But this egregious practice has also made its way into the mainstream, on such high-profile series as *Roseanne* and *The Cosby Show*. If DVD is to be regarded as an archival format for the television medium, there is no excuse for the release of incomplete shows.

The A-Team (1983–1987)

Season 1 (14 episodes on 4 discs): ★ ★ ★ ½
Season 2 (22 episodes on 3 discs): ★ ★ ★
Season 3 (25 episodes on 3 discs): ★ ★ ★
Season 4 (22 episodes on 3 discs): ★ ★

Universal Home Video
Video: Full-Frame; Audio: Dolby Digital 2.0

How do you schedule an R-rated action movie in the family hour? Stephen J. Cannell found a solution with *The A-Team*: crash cars, blow up stuff real good, and spray all the bullets you want from automatic weapons; just make sure nobody's hurt when the battle's over. The result was ludicrous, and in some ways more offensive than more graphic portrayals of violence, where the consequences aren't as unrealistic. Still, it was entertaining if you didn't think too much.

Stories followed a formula that rarely changed: Hannibal, Face, B.A., and Murdock, wrongly accused Vietnam vets on the run, offer their services to people in trouble, while avoiding the pursuit of Colonel Decker. They were joined in the first season by Amy Allen, an investigative reporter looking to expose the team, who wound up joining them on their missions. Allen, played by Melinda Culea, was written out of the series halfway through Season 2.

The DVD sets offer little in the way of extras, but any excuse to bask once again in the wonder that was Mr. T is worth the investment, and it's a treat to see the original pilot, with Tim Dunigan cast as Templeton Peck.

GREAT MOMENTS: Season 1: Murdock rescues the team from a cult leader played by John Saxon in "Children of Jamestown"; the Team busts up a Big Apple protection racket in "The Out-of-Towners"; the camaraderie and the cockroaches in "Black Day at Bad Rock"; Season 2: Former *Battlestar Galactica* star Dirk Benedict is reunited with a Cylon in "Steel"; Judy Strangis, a.k.a. Dynagirl, guests in "In Plane Sight"; Season 3: Murdock's guise of "Fireman Fred" in "Fire"; B.A.'s in love in "Skins."

FAST-FORWARD: Season 2: The *Dukes of Hazzard* knockoff "Pure-Dee Poison"; the flashback episode "Curtain Call."

EXTRAS: Like the A-Team, the DVDs are shooting blanks.

ABC After School Specials (1974–1986)

Collector's Set (26 episodes on 13 discs): ★ ★ ★ ½
Volume 1 (1974–1976) (4 episodes on 1 disc): ★ ★ ★ ★
Volume 2 (1976–1977) (4 episodes on 1 disc): ★ ★ ★
Volume 3 (1978–1979) (4 episodes on 2 discs): ★ ★ ½
Volume 4 (1979–1980) (4 episodes on 2 discs): ★ ★ ★ ½
Volume 5 (1981–1982) (4 episodes on 2 discs): ★ ★ ★ ½
Volume 6 (1982–1986) (4 episodes on 2 discs): ★ ★ ★ ★

BCI Eclipse

Video: Full-Frame; Audio: Dolby Digital 2.0

The ABC network wanted to be every kiddy's pal in the 1970s. If they weren't teaching disco-era tykes how to multiply by nine or identify an adverb in *Schoolhouse Rock*, they were cautioning America's youth about teenage pregnancy, peer pressure, and coping with loss in a series of *After School Specials.* These achingly sincere dramas were well intentioned and may have straightened out a few adolescents in their day, but they seem pretty sappy now; sometimes it's so hard to get past the feathered hair and designer jeans that the life lessons are missed completely. That said, the price is right at fifteen bucks a volume, and if you're of the generation that originally watched these after school, there's a nostalgic kick in seeing them again. Even the Trapper-Keeper packaging on Volumes 1 and 2 can stir up dormant anxiety over a pop earth-science quiz. The *Collector's Set* contains everything in the individual volumes, plus two never-before-released specials.

GREAT MOMENTS: Volume 1: Lance Kerwin faces the school bully in "Psst! Hammerman's After You"; Brady kids Chris Knight and Eve Plumb costar in "Sara's Summer of the Swans"; Volume 4: "Schoolboy Father," with Rob Lowe, Dana Plato, and Nancy McKeon; Volume 6: "Did You See What Happened to Andrea?", the winner of five Emmy Awards.

FAST-FORWARD: The 1940s period piece "Thank You, Jackie Robinson" (Volume 3).

EXTRAS: Collector's Set: Highlight clips; National Public Radio interview with creator Martin Tahse.

The Abbott and Costello Show (1951–1953)

Volume 1 (4 episodes on 1 disc): ★ ★ ★
Volume 2 (4 episodes on 1 disc): ★ ★ ★
Volume 3 (4 episodes on 1 disc): ★ ★ ★
Volume 4 (4 episodes on 1 disc): ★ ★ ★
Volume 5 (4 episodes on 1 disc): ★ ★ ★
Volume 6 (4 episodes on 1 disc): ★ ★ ★
Volume 7 (4 episodes on 1 disc): ★ ★ ★
Volume 8 (4 episodes on 1 disc): ★ ★ ½
Volume 9 (4 episodes on 1 disc): ★ ★ ½
Volume 10 (4 episodes on 1 disc): ★ ★
Volume 11 (4 episodes on 1 disc): ★ ★ ½
Volume 12 (4 episodes on 1 disc): ★ ★
Volume 13 (4 episodes on 1 disc): ★ ★ ½

Shanachie Home Video (Volumes 1 & 2, 7–13); Koch International (Volumes 3–6)
Video: Full-Frame; Audio: Dolby Digital 2.0

When the roll call is taken of classic 1950s comedies, *The Abbott and Costello Show* is too often overlooked. Perhaps that's due to its being rarely rebroadcast in the past half-century; or perhaps because the show originally aired in syndication, or lasted only two seasons, or that its burlesque shenanigans harkened back to an earlier era, rather than embracing the new genre of TV situation comedy. Ironically, the show now seems more progressive than many of its contemporaries. As with *Seinfeld*, the episodes were less about plot than about the eccentricities of the characters and the incorporation of clever wordplay and stand-alone comic moments. Season sets would have rated higher than the individual volumes, which cost too much and gobble up shelf space.

GREAT MOMENTS: Volume 1: The legendary "Who's on First?" routine in "Actor's Home"; Volume 7: The famous "Niagara Falls" vaudeville routine in "Jail."

FAST-FORWARD: Nothing.

EXTRAS: None.

Absolutely Fabulous (1992–2004)

Series 1 (6 episodes on 1 disc): ★ ★ ★ ★
Series 2 (6 episodes on 1 disc): ★ ★ ★ ★ ½
Series 3 (6 episodes on 1 disc): ★ ★ ★
Series 4 (6 episodes on 2 discs): ★ ★ ★
Series 5 (7 episodes on 2 discs): ★ ★ ★
Absolutely Special (2 episodes on 1 disc): ★ ★
The Complete DVD Collection (18 episodes on 4 discs): ★ ★ ★ ★

BBC Video
Video: Full-Frame; Audio: Dolby Digital 2.0

There are many reasons to love *Absolutely Fabulous*, and bravery in the face of political correctness ranks near the top of the list. Just as we're being lectured about how some self-destructive behavior is no longer funny, along comes a series about two unrepentant, self-absorbed, boozing, drugging, sex-starved trollops, staggering through life in search of the next party. The first two series are as fabulous as the title implies, while the next two coast on the chemistry of stars Joanna Lumley and Jennifer Saunders. Series 5 was an unexpected and terrific return to form, but the DVD set has both scenes and music cut from the original broadcasts. The *Complete DVD Collection* gathers just the first three seasons, with a few extras not available in the individual series releases.

GREAT MOMENTS: Series 1: Edina isn't happy about turning forty in "Birthday"; the editorial meeting in "Magazine"; Series 2: Eddy drops in on her father's funeral—literally—in "Death"; Saffron is sold into white slavery in "Morocco"; Patsy's sister Jackie spoils a party plan in "Happy New Year"; Series 5: Emma "Baby Spice" Bunton plays one of Eddy's disgruntled clients in "Cleanin'."

FAST-FORWARD: Nothing.

EXTRAS: Series 1–3: Outtakes; Series 4: Commentary by Jennifer Saunders; outtakes; "Mirror Ball" special; Series 5: Commentary by Jennifer Saunders; outtakes; *Absolutely Special*: Outtakes; *The Complete DVD Collection*: The original *AbFab* skit from *French and Saunders*; highlights/outtakes collection; "How to Be Absolutely Fabulous" featurette; celebrity cameo appearance guide.

Adam-12 (1968–1975)

Season 1 (26 episodes on 2 discs): ★ ★ ★

Universal Home Video

Video: Full-Frame; Audio: Dolby Digital 2.0

No reading of the credits was necessary to identify *Adam-12* as a product of the Jack Webb school of drama. The series, which followed the daily routine of LAPD cops Reed and Malloy, had the same poker-faced leads, the same awkward insertions of humor when there was down time at the station, and the same "Don't mess with authority" message as Webb's signature series, *Dragnet.* Universal took the same no-nonsense approach to the DVDs: no surprises, no extras.

GREAT MOMENTS: Malloy reconsiders quitting in the pilot, "Log 1"; Barry Williams, just prior to landing *The Brady Bunch*, appears in "Log 152."

FAST-FORWARD: Nothing.

EXTRAS: None.

The Adventures of Brisco County Jr. (1993–1994)

The Complete Series (26 episodes on 8 discs): ★ ★ ★ ★

Warner Bros. Home Video

Video: Full-Frame; Audio: Dolby Digital 2.0

As *Star Wars* adapted storytelling elements from Westerns, *The Adventures of Brisco County Jr.* incorporated science fiction into its nostalgic western tale of a square-jawed bounty hunter on a quest to find the men who murdered his father. The mix proved too quirky for most viewers but as with every project starring Bruce Campbell, a cult following was inevitable. Warner Bros. took its time with the DVDs, though the results are worth the wait: you get the full series, including the two-hour pilot and a saddlebag full of extra features. They even let fans vote on the cover design of the DVD box.

GREAT MOMENTS: Wickwire rides a phallic rocket car into a town populated only by women in "No Man's Land"; the multiple con games in "Riverboat"; Sheriff Aaron Viva, the Old West's first Elvis impersonator, debuts in "Hard Rock."

FAST-FORWARD: Nothing.

EXTRAS: Commentary on the pilot by series creator Carlton Cuse and star Bruce Campbell; featurettes "A *Brisco County* Writer's Room," "The History of *Brisco County Jr.*," "A Reading from the Book of Bruce," and "Tools of the Trade."

A

The Adventures of Jonny Quest (1964–1965)

Season 1 (26 episodes on 4 discs): ★ ★ ★ ★ ½

Warner Home Video

Video: Full-Frame; Audio: Dolby Digital Mono

What's great about *Jonny Quest*? You mean, besides the jazzy Hoyt Curtin theme and the richly detailed animation supervised by Doug Wildey, and the jetpacks, because there's still nothing cooler than jetpacks? Here's the answer—what's really great about *Jonny Quest* is it's the only Hanna-Barbera cartoon with a body count. There were no fatalities on *The Flintstones*, no fiery crashes on *Wacky Races*, but here, in the very first episode ("Mystery of the Lizard Men") more than twenty bad guys are wiped out by Jonny and Race Bannon. The series doesn't glorify violence, but it's honest about the consequences of one's actions, and that in itself was a revelation for a 1960s family-hour cartoon. There hasn't been a better animated adventure since, even given the ongoing annoyance of Bandit's near-constant yappin'.

Hanna-Barbera bills the collection as Season 1, but it's really the entire series—this was all the classic *Quest* that was made, and the less said about the 1986 revival, the better. All in all a splendid package, but it's a shame that Tim Matheson, who voiced Jonny, is a no-show in the special features.

GREAT MOMENTS: The first appearance of Jade in "Double Danger"; Dr. Zin's creepy spider robot in "The Robot Spy"; the thrilling hilltop siege in "A Small Matter of Pygmies."

FAST-FORWARD: "Werewolf of the Timberland": a search for petrified wood in the "exotic" land of Canada.

EXTRAS: "Adventures in Animation" featurette; fun facts and trivia; a vintage Jonny Quest P.F. Flyer commercial.

The Adventures of Pete & Pete (1993–1994)

Season 1 (8 episodes on 2 discs): ★ ★ ★ ½

Season 2 (13 episodes on 2 discs): ★ ★ ★

Paramount Home Video

Video: Full-Frame; Audio: Dolby Digital 2.0

The thing about whimsy is it's sometimes hard to know when to stop. Some shows have just a dash of this silly, surreal quality, while others dive in and wallow. Of these, only a few get it right. *The Adventures of Pete & Pete* joins *Rocky & Bullwinkle* near the top of TV's whimsical wonders, though as with the moose and squirrel, most of its more bizarre conceits were probably wasted on a preteen audience. Though the video quality could be much better, here's a chance to get acquainted (or reacquainted) with Nickelodeon's most subversive series.

GREAT MOMENTS: Season 1: Little Pete tries to set a no-sleep record in "The Nightcrawlers"; Big Pete confronts his eccentric shop teacher in "Tool and Die"; Season 2: The boys encounter a haunted pay phone in "The Call"; Big Pete battles the Pumpkin Eaters to save Halloween in "Halloweenie."

FAST-FORWARD: The front-loaded promos for other Paramount releases.

EXTRAS: Season 1: Two *Pete & Pete* shorts and four bonus specials; commentaries on three episodes by series co-creators Will McRobb and Chris Viscardi, and director Katherine Dieckmann; Season 2: Commentaries; five *Pete & Pete* shorts; *Pete & Pete* special "Space Geeks and Johnny Unitas."

The Adventures of Superman (1951–1957)

The Complete First Season (26 episodes on 5 discs): ★ ★ ★ ½
The Complete Second Season (26 episodes on 5 discs): ★ ★ ★
Seasons 3 & 4 (26 episodes on 5 discs): ★ ★ ★

Warner Home Video
Video: Full-Frame; Audio: Dolby Digital 2.0

If one can overlook the primitive special effects, television's first Superman series still holds up as grand entertainment. The DVD release of the first season will be especially well received by fans, as these episodes haven't been syndicated as often due to their violent content. For some this will be the first opportunity to view an uncut version of the infamous episode "The Evil Three," more than fifty years after its original broadcast.

GREAT MOMENTS: Season 1: The familiar origin story is retold in "Superman on Earth"; Superman vows to clean up organized crime in Metropolis in the atmospheric "Crime Wave"; Season 2: "Panic in the Sky" is a series highlight; Seasons 3 & 4: "The Wedding of Superman," Noel Neill's favorite episode, features a poignant dream sequence in which Lois and Supes tie the knot; Jack Larson plays a dual role as both Jimmy Olsen and mobster Kid Collins in "Jimmy the Kid."

FAST-FORWARD: The Professor Pepperwinkle episodes.

EXTRAS: Season 1: The theatrical film *Superman and the Mole Men* is George Reeves's first appearance as the Man of Steel; vintage George Reeves short;

"From Inkwell to Back Lot" retrospective; original Kellogg's Cereal commercials; episode commentaries by Superman experts; Season 2: Commentaries by costars Noel Neill and Jack Larson; documentary "The First Lady of Metropolis"; "Stamp Day for Superman" featurette.

Airwolf (1984–1986)

Season 1 (11 episodes on 2 discs): ★

Universal Home Video

Video: Full-Frame; Audio: Dolby Digital 2.0

Anyone who traveled through Europe in the 1990s had to contend with two perpetual annoyances: a lousy exchange rate and *Airwolf*. From Paris to Vienna, our allies across the pond inexplicably embraced this ridiculous action show starring Jan-Michael Vincent, Ernest Borgnine, and a black-ops helicopter. A series about a new American superweapon would probably get a chillier reception these days. Admittedly, the show can be fascinating in its dreadfulness; every aspect of the production—dialogue, characters, stories, acting, costume design, even the incidental music—works in perfect cohesion to create a work of complete and utter cheese. The pilot's name is "Stringfellow Hawke," for heaven's sake! The line between *Airwolf* and *Airplane!* is so paper-thin that an objective viewer might have trouble figuring out which one is the intentional parody.

GREAT MOMENTS: Shannen Doherty's guest appearance in "Bite of the Jackal."

FAST-FORWARD: Just about all of it, unless you're watching for laughs.

EXTRAS: None.

ALF (1986–1990)

Season 1 (25 episodes on 4 discs): ★ ½

Season 2 (26 episodes on 4 discs): ★ ½

Lions Gate

Video: Full-Frame; Audio: Dolby Digital 1.0 (Season 1); Dolby Digital 2.0 (Season 2)

1980s pop culture welcomed a furry new icon when ALF dropped in from the planet Melmac. ALF (short for Alien Life Form) was adopted by the Tanner family, who spent most of the series hiding their new alien houseguest from friends and neighbors, particularly the Kravitz-like Ochmoneks. The family also had to keep ALF from eating their family cat, Lucky.

Whatever the show's merits (and they are indeed questionable), the first- and second-season DVD sets earned the ire of consumers by landing on DVD in syndicated prints. Sure, to some the less ALF, the better, but fans of the orange alien were rightfully peeved.

MENU screens, featuring ALF describing the episode you're about to watch, are a treat, and the set also offers a gag reel and the unaired pilot, which contains additional scenes and an alternate series logo. It's unfortunate that Lions Gate didn't devote the same time and attention to recovering the original episode prints.

GREAT MOMENTS: Season 1: ALF stars in a music video in "Don't It Make My Brown Eyes Blue?"; Season 2: Bob Denver, Alan Hale, Russell Johnson, and Dawn Wells visit ALF in "Gilligan's Island Special."

FAST-FORWARD: If you don't like edited shows, all of it.

EXTRAS: Season 1: Gag reel; unaired pilot; Season 2: Episodes of *ALF's Animated Adventures* and *ALFTales.*

Alfred Hitchcock Presents (1955–1965)

Season 1 (39 episodes on 3 discs): ★ ★ ★ ★

Universal Home Video

Video: Full-Frame; Audio: Dolby Digital 1.0

A few episodes of Alfred Hitchcock's suspense anthology series had previously turned up in DVD collections of the director's film classics, but Season 1 is the first release devoted solely to the television show, and the best place to begin one's collection. The story quality was not as consistently head spinning as *The Twilight Zone*, but when the material was there, as in the show's many adaptations of classic short stories, Hitchcock presented some very memorable tales indeed. And his droll introductions alone are nearly worth the purchase price.

GREAT MOMENTS: Joseph Cotten plays a businessman who hates to show emotion, which causes him to be presumed dead after he is paralyzed in a car accident, in "Breakdown"; the twist at the end of "Back for Christmas"; "The Creeper" lives up to its title.

FAST-FORWARD: The overly sentimental holiday tale "Santa Claus and the Tenth Avenue Kid."

EXTRAS: Season 1: "Alfred Hitchcock Presents: A Look Back" documentary.

Alias (2001–)

The Complete First Season (22 episodes on 6 discs): ★ ★ ★ ½
The Complete Second Season (22 episodes on 6 discs): ★ ★ ★ ★
The Complete Third Season (22 episodes on 6 discs): ★ ★ ★
The Complete Fourth Season (22 episodes on 6 discs): ★ ★

Buena Vista Home Entertainment
Video: Full-Frame; Audio: Dolby Digital 2.0

Lost creator J.J. Abrams launched Jennifer Garner into superstar, dream-girl, and Bennifer v.2 status with this spy/intrigue series about a college student who moonlights as a secret agent. The show's first three years include cliffhangers at the end of nearly every episode, but the show adopted a more self-contained format with Season 4, which didn't sit well with many fans. Sydney Bristow's school and personal life were also phased out as the series progressed.

In addition to Garner's appeal, *Alias* boasted outstanding performances from Ron Rifkin as the duplicitous Arvin Sloane and Victor Garber as Sydney's "spy daddy," Jack Bristow. The second season introduced Lena Olin as Sydney's mother, Irina Derevko, the most intriguing character of the series. DVD commentaries and gag reels show off the lighter sides of the actors that you never see from their characters. The *Alias* sets also boast some of the best MENU screens for a TV series on DVD.

GREAT MOMENTS: Season 2: Sydney, Jack, and Irina go on a mission together in "The Passage, Parts 1 & 2"; the series changes forever as SD-6 is taken down in "Phase One."

FAST-FORWARD: Most of Season 4 is forgettable; out of twenty-two episodes, only five or six measure up to the standard set in earlier seasons, despite a return appearance by Lena Olin in the season finale.

EXTRAS: All season sets offer featurettes, gag reels, and episodic commentaries; Season 3 includes a special *Alias* animated feature that takes place during Sydney's "missing years."

All Creatures Great and Small (1978–1980; 1988–1990)

Series 1 (13 episodes on 4 discs): ★ ★ ★ ★ ★
Series 2 (14 episodes on 4 discs): ★ ★ ★ ★
Series 3 (14 episodes on 4 discs): ★ ★ ★ ★ ½
Series 4 (10 episodes on 3 discs): ★ ★ ★
Series 5 (12 episodes on 4 discs): ★ ★ ★

The Specials (2 episodes on 1 disc): ★ ★ ★ ½

BBC Video

Video: Full-Frame; Audio: Dolby Digital 2.0

Based on a beloved series of books by British country veterinarian James Herriot, these bucolic World War II–era stories set in the Yorkshire Dales are an Anglophile's dream. They drifted further away from the books as the series progressed, finally abandoning them altogether for new tales when viewers demanded more episodes after the source material ran out. While the cast and creative team perfectly recaptured Herriot's gentle tone and subtle wit, the later seasons were hurt by the recasting of Lynda Bellingham as Helen Herriot, replacing the much-loved Carol Drinkwater.

GREAT MOMENTS: Series 1: James's courting of Helen Alderton; Series 2: The cake judging in "Merry Gentlemen"; Series 3: James and Seigfried leave their beloved Darrowby to defend England in World War II in "Big Steps and Little 'Uns."

FAST-FORWARD: Nothing.

EXTRAS: Series 1: Documentary on James Herriot; Series 3: Commentary by actors Robert Hardy, Peter Davison, and Carol Drinkwater, and directors Christopher Barry and Michael Hayes; featurette on the James Herriot museum in Thirsk, Yorkshire; Series 4: Interviews with Christopher Timothy and John McGlynn; *The Specials*: On-location featurette.

All in the Family (1971–1992)

The Complete First Season (13 episodes on 3 discs): ★ ★ ★ ★ ★

The Complete Second Season (24 episodes on 3 discs): ★ ★ ★ ★ ★

The Complete Third Season (24 episodes on 3 discs): ★ ★ ★ ★ ★

The Complete Fourth Season (24 episodes on 3 discs): ★ ★ ★ ★

The Complete Fifth Season (25 episodes on 3 discs): ★ ★ ★ ★

Columbia Tristar Home Video

Video: Full-Frame; Audio: Dolby Digital Mono

How many thirty-year-old shows still run a risk of being edited for content in our anything-goes era of broadcasting? Only *All in the Family*, with its frank discussions on racism, homosexuality, class envy, and the generation gap, which seem more daring now than they did when Nixon was in the White House. Political correctness, with the best of intentions, has eradicated from today's television much of what made this series so important and so entertaining. But creator Norman Lear knew that the best way to combat

A

antiquated ideas was to hold them up to the light, rather than pretend they didn't exist. True, there were those who claimed Archie Bunker as a working-class hero, but even that was okay for in Lear's universe, as in the real world, no one—liberal or conservative—has an exclusive claim to virtue.

The episodes look great on DVD, but commentaries would have been appreciated, especially on such a groundbreaking series. It also might have been appropriate to include an episode of the British series *Till Death Do Us Part*, on which *All in the Family* was based. But all you get are the original, uncut shows; and that's enough.

GREAT MOMENTS: Season 1: The extraordinary pilot "Meet the Bunkers," which probably caused plenty of dishes to drop in suburban America; the family pulls together after Gloria loses a baby in "Gloria's Pregnancy"; the first appearance of Louise Jefferson (Isabel Sanford) in "The First and Last Supper"; Season 2: TV's funniest interracial kiss, courtesy of Archie and Sammy Davis, Jr., in "Sammy's Visit"; Bea Arthur's debut as Maude in "Maude"; Archie's pro-gun editorial in "Archie and the Editorial"; Season 4: Archie's conversation with God in "Archie in the Cellar"; Season 5: The highlights episode hosted by Henry Fonda.

FAST-FORWARD: Season 4: "Gloria's Boyfriend."

EXTRAS: They've been stifled.

Ally McBeal (1997–2002)

Ally on Sex and the Single Life (6 episodes on 2 discs): ★ ★ ★ ½

20th Century-Fox

Video: Full-Frame; Audio: Dolby Digital 2.0

Only a few TV series reach a level of cultural significance that earns them the cover of *Time* magazine. *Ally McBeal* joined that select company in 1998, when a new round of sociological debate about working women was inspired by Calista Flockhart's complex portrayal of a smart and sexy but neurotic attorney. While all five seasons of this edgy David E. Kelley legal dramedy are already available in boxed sets throughout the UK and Europe, those of us in Ally's nation of origin must content ourselves with a sampler disc of six first-season episodes. That means no Ling and no Nell, but at least the dancing baby makes an appearance.

GREAT MOMENTS: The famous dancing baby debuts in "Cro-Magnon."

FAST-FORWARD: Nothing.

EXTRAS: The music video for Vonda Shepard's series theme, "Searchin' My Soul."

The Amanda Show (1999–2002)

Volume 1: Amanda, Please! (4 episodes on 1 disc): ★ ★ ½
Volume 2: The Girls' Room (4 episodes on 1 disc): ★ ★

Paramount Home Video
Video: Full-Frame; Audio: Dolby Digital 2.0

Amanda Bynes appears well on her way to a substantive career in film and television, which will surprise no one who discovered her in this popular Nickelodeon series. While most of the sketches will fall flat for anyone over the age of nine, Bynes's ebullience and enthusiasm shine through the weakest of material.

GREAT MOMENTS: Volume 1: Substitute teacher Mr. Gullible; Volume 2: The *Dawson's Creek* parody "Moody's Point."

FAST-FORWARD: The Hillbilly Moments.

EXTRAS: Volumes 1 and 2: Outtakes and a behind-the-scenes featurette.

The Amazing Race (2001–)

Season 1 (12 episodes on 4 discs): ★ ★ ★ ★
The Seventh Season (12 episodes on 4 discs): ★ ★ ★ ★

Paramount Home Video
Video: Full-Frame; Audio: Dolby Digital 2.0

Emmy wins and rave reviews have imbued *The Amazing Race* with a classier reputation than most reality shows. The frenetic globe-hopping pace, bickering duos of contestants, and clever challenges can be addicting, though many of the great wonders of the world are dashed by too quickly for viewers expecting a travelogue. Season 7 was released before 2–6 because of the infamous antics of Rob and Amber, former *Survivor* contestants who probably should have won the Race, were it not for a still controversial airport moment in the season finale.

GREAT MOMENTS: Season 1: Team Guido!; The Seventh Season: Rob Mariano's underhanded tactics and the scorn they engendered in other teams, especially Lynn and Alex; the visit to the African orphanage.

FAST-FORWARD: Nothing.

EXTRAS: Both sets offer contestant commentaries, featurettes, and enough deleted scenes to fill three more episodes.

American Dreams (2002–2005)

Season 1—Extended Music Edition (25 episodes on 7 discs): ★ ★ ★

Universal Home Video

Video: Full-Frame; Audio: Dolby Digital 5.1

Stories of the Pryor family coping with times that were a-changin' in 1960s America were pleasant, if not particularly compelling. What made *American Dreams* a borderline hit was its inspiration of casting contemporary singers as their classic-rock counterparts, for performances on *American Bandstand.* The Season 1 DVD set wisely boasts extended versions of the musical numbers, and how nice that Universal popped for a 5.1 track, given that the studio has become synonymous with 2.0 on its DVDs. Unfortunately, the show also aired in both widescreen and full-screen formats, and while series creator Jonathan Prince lobbied for the former, the Season 1 set was released full-screen.

GREAT MOMENTS: Michelle Branch as Lesley Gore in "The End of the Innocence"; Usher as Marvin Gaye in "Cold Snap"; India.Arie as Nina Simone in "Heartache."

FAST-FORWARD: Ashanti as Dionne Warwick in "Silent Night."

EXTRAS: Dick Clark remembers the superstars of *American Dreams*; episode commentaries by Clark and the series' cast; music video featuring Stacie Orrico and the cast.

American Gothic (1995–1996)

The Complete Series (22 episodes on 3 discs): ★ ★

Universal Home Video

Video: Full-Frame; Audio: Dolby Digital 2.0

When releasing a cult show on DVD, it's never wise to incur the wrath of the hardcore fans. They don't ask much, just an acceptable level of picture and sound quality and such no-brainer basics as listing the episodes in their proper order. Unfortunately, Universal went zero for two with *American Gothic*, a one-season-and-out suspense series about strange doings in a South Carolina town.

GREAT MOMENTS: Carter learns it's not wise to say no to Sheriff Buck in "Damned if You Don't"; Lucas and Caleb square off in "Requiem."

FAST-FORWARD: Nothing.

EXTRAS: Pilot-episode commentary; deleted and extended scenes.

American Idol (2002–)

American Idol: The Search for a Superstar: ★ ★ ★

The Search for a Superstar—Exclusive Two-Disc Set: ★ ★

The Best of Seasons 1–4: ★ ★ ★

The Worst of Seasons 1–4: ★

Respond 2

Video: Full-Frame; Audio: Dolby Digital 2.0

It figured *American Idol* would be a nightmare to get to DVD because of music-rights issues, which is why after four series we only have three highlights collections in the home-video market. *The Search for a Superstar* holds fifteen songs from Season 1 contestants Kelly and Justin and Nikki, among others. The two-disc set would figure to offer more of what's missing, but instead the extra disc is devoted to such features as "A Day in the Life of Justin Guarini," and profiles of the judges.

The "best of" collection gathers memorable performances from all the *Idol* winners and runners-up, as well as other memorable contestants who fell short of the prize. The music makes it a worthy purchase, but it's beyond me why anyone would want to buy the "Worst of" release. A little William Hung goes a long way.

GREAT MOMENTS: *Search for a Superstar*: Tamyra Gray sings "A House Is Not a Home"; Kelly Clarkson's "You Make Me Feel Like a Natural Woman," and her tearful "A Moment Like This" in the season finale; *Best of*: Performances by Clay Aiken, Ruben Studdard, Fantasia Barrino, Carrie Underwood, and Bo Bice.

FAST-FORWARD: The early auditions of losers who couldn't carry a tune in a suitcase are only funny once.

EXTRAS: *Search for a Superstar*: A variety of featurettes, including "When Judges Attack" and "Inside the *Idol* Mansion"; *Best of*: Interviews; featurettes on the judges and the *American Idol* phenomenon; *Worst of*: Clip packages of judge and contestant reactions; "How Not to Dress for Your Audition" featurette.

America's Funniest Home Videos (1990–)

Animal Antics: ★ ★
Deluxe Uncensored: ★ ★ ★
Family Follies: ★ ★ ½
Home for the Holidays: ★ ★
Volume 1 (12 episodes on 4 discs): ★ ★ ★ ½

Shout! Factory (Volume 1 and *Home for the Holidays*); E-Realbiz (*Animal Antics*, *Deluxe Uncensored*, and *Family Follies*)

Video: Full-Frame; Audio: Dolby Digital 2.0

Sure, watching guys take a Wiffle ball in the crotch is hilarious the first time, but is it still funny after several repeat viewings? Yeah, actually, it is. Thank you, people of America, for taping your stupidest moments for posterity. The E-Realbiz discs date from the Bob Saget era of the series, while Volume 1 offers the more contemporary take on pet and baby high jinks with host Tom Bergeron. Actually, Volume 1 is probably all the funny home videos anybody needs, as it includes a couple of "greatest hits" collections that pull the best moments from more than a dozen years of episodes. Of the individual releases, *Deluxe Uncensored* is the most interesting, as it offers the clips that ABC either refused to show, or aired with the naughty bits covered.

GREAT MOMENTS: People in pain, cute kids being cute.

FAST-FORWARD: The animal sex footage in *Deluxe Uncensored* could have stayed censored.

EXTRAS: Volume 1: Two shows celebrating the 300th episode that showcase the best of twelve years' hilarious footage.

Andromeda (2000–2005)

Season 1 (22 episodes on 10 discs): ★ ★
Season 2 (22 episodes on 10 discs): ★ ★
Season 3 (22 episodes on 5 discs): ★ ★ ½
Season 4 (22 episodes on 5 discs): ★ ★ ½
Seasons also available as individual five-volume sets. All: ★ ★

A.D. Vision

Video: Anamorphic Widescreen; Audio: Dolby Digital 2.0

Not content with creating a sci-fi saga so popular it has practically become the official idealization of mankind's distant future, Gene Roddenberry also dreamt up this alternative take on man's space-faring exploits, as a more

cynical sequel to *Star Trek. Andromeda* took more than twenty-five years to find its way to television, by which time the Great Bird of the Galaxy was already gone. He didn't miss much. As Captain of the starship Andromeda, Kevin Sorbo is no William Shatner, or even Scott Bakula, but the visual effects are nice and some of the stories will appeal to less discriminating sci-fi buffs.

GREAT MOMENTS: Season 3: The ship is attacked by a metal-eating maggot in "For Whom the Bell Tolls."

FAST-FORWARD: Season 1: Rommie falls for an android in "Star-Crossed."

EXTRAS: All individual volumes and season sets contain character profiles, alternate takes, and image galleries; many also offer cast interviews, and commentaries on selected episodes by Kevin Sorbo and Allan Eastman.

The Andy Griffith Show (1960–1968)

The Complete First Season (32 episodes on 4 discs): ★ ★ ★ ★ ½
The Complete Second Season (31 episodes on 5 discs): ★ ★ ★ ★ ★
The Complete Third Season (32 episodes on 5 discs): ★ ★ ★ ★ ★
The Complete Fourth Season (32 episodes on 5 discs): ★ ★ ★ ★ ★
The Complete Fifth Season (32 episodes on 5 discs): ★ ★ ★ ★ ½
The Complete Sixth Season (30 episodes on 5 discs): ★ ★ ★ ★

Paramount Home Video
Video: Full-Frame; Audio: Dolby Digital 2.0

To the extent that all classic TV programs are security blankets for those who grew up on them, there's still something more profound in the comfort derived from an episode of *The Andy Griffith Show.* Maybe it's the town of Mayberry, which can seem like the most idyllic place on Earth after enduring the daily inconsiderations of modern life. Even the city-bred among us who would go stir crazy in a small town can indulge vicariously in church picnics, fishing holes, and chicken and dumplings for Sunday dinner.

Griffith played Sheriff Taylor more broadly in the first season, though he had already toned down the character's more spiteful edge from his debut in an episode of *Make Room for Daddy*, which would have made a nice extra with the first-season set. In subsequent seasons, Griffith further dialed down the portrayal to become Mayberry's voice of reason, as the series evolved into an ensemble sitcom featuring Barney and Gomer and Floyd and other folks from the friendliest fictional place on Earth.

GREAT MOMENTS: Season 1: Andy outwits a big-city police force in "The

Manhunt"; the jailhouse concert in "Guitar Player"; the "half-a-boy" conversation between Andy and Opie in "Opie's Charity"; Season 2: Aunt Bee's pickles cause problems for Andy and Barney in "The Pickle Story"; Barney is revealed as a tone-deaf deputy in "Barney and the Choir"; Season 3: Andy thinks Opie's friend Mr. McBeevee is imaginary—but is he? in "Mr. McBeevee"; three lady crooks take Barney and Floyd hostage in "Convicts-at-Large"; Gomer Pyle makes his first appearance in "The Bank Job"; Season 4: The classic "Opie the Birdman" may be the series' best episode; the pilot for the spin-off series *Gomer Pyle, U.S.M.C.*; Season 5: Ernest has a crush on Helen in "The Education of Ernest T. Bass."

FAST-FORWARD: Season 1's "Irresistible Andy" has the normally levelheaded sheriff acting more like his flustered, over-suspicious deputy.

EXTRAS: Seasons 2 and 3: Original sponsor spots.

The Andy Milonakis Show (2005–)

The Complete First Season (8 episodes on 2 discs): ZERO

Paramount Home Video

Video: Full-Frame; Audio: Dolby Digital 2.0

This show is crap. Count how many DVD sets are listed in this book, and then add up how many received a zero-star rating. Yes, it's just this one. Hopefully, that won't provide this moronic series with enough notoriety to prompt any curiosity in those with a taste for the bizarre. As horrible as Milonakis is, however, I must begrudgingly give the idiot credit for one idea—the inclusion of a scathing commentary track by *New York Daily News* reporter Richard Huff, who hates the show as much as I do.

GREAT MOMENTS: Ha!

FAST-FORWARD: All of it.

EXTRAS: Commentary track by Andy, Larry, Ralphie, and Rivka; a separate track by reporter Richard Huff; a collection of twenty-five unaired bonus skits; cast interviews, outtakes, extended scenes, and the featurette "Andy Goes to Hollywood."

Angel (1999–2004)

The Complete First Season (22 episodes on 6 discs): ★ ★ ★ ★ ★
The Complete Second Season (22 episodes on 6 discs): ★ ★ ★ ★ ½
The Complete Third Season (22 episodes on 6 discs): ★ ★ ★ ★ ½
The Complete Fourth Season (22 episodes on 6 discs): ★ ★ ½
The Complete Fifth Season (22 episodes on 6 discs): ★ ★ ★ ★ ★

20th Century-Fox

Video: Full-Frame (Season 1) Anamorphic Widescreen (Seasons 2–5); Audio: Dolby Digital 2.0

Much as *Buffy* fans respected Joss Whedon's storytelling skills, the idea of spinning hunky vampire Angel into his own series was met with skepticism. We should have known better. *Angel* proved to be nearly the equal of its predecessor. David Boreanaz found heretofore unknown dimensions to the brooding vampire with a soul, Cordelia Chase became a real person rather than a caricature of every high school's queen bitch, and if there's a character that has taken a more provocative dramatic journey over the course of two television series than Wesley Wyndham-Pryce, I've never met him. Sadly, but not surprisingly, Alexis Denisof's amazing performance was so thoroughly ignored by the Emmys that he probably couldn't get into the awards show with a ticket.

After three superb seasons, the series took a dramatic dive with the arrival of Vincent Kartheiser as Connor, Angel's whiny, moronic teenage son. The addition of James Marsters as Spike revitalized the series in its final year, when *Angel* was cancelled, arguably at the height of its creativity.

GREAT MOMENTS: Season 1: Spike's first crossover appearance in "In the Dark"; the evil Angelus reemerges in "Eternity"; Season 2: The Pylea trilogy, an inter-dimensional adventure featuring Krevlornswatch of the Deathwok clan, which introduces Amy Acker as bookworm babe Fred, and reveals the first glimpse of Wesley's dark side; Season 3: Darla's unnatural childbirth in "Quickening"; Season 5: Angel becomes a Muppet in "Smile Time," the series' funniest episode; the heartbreaking conclusion of "A Hole in the World."

FAST-FORWARD: The icky Connor-Cordelia romance arc in Season 4.

EXTRAS: All five seasons include commentaries by the cast and the writers, the best of which are by creator Joss Whedon, as well as featurettes that are interesting, but light on cast contributions. Outtakes are added from Season 3 on.

Angels in America (2003)

The Complete HBO Production (2 discs): ★ ★ ★ ★ ★

HBO Home Video

Video: Anamorphic Widescreen; Audio: Dolby Digital 5.1

Tony Kushner's remarkable play, justifiably hailed as the theatrical achievement of his generation, is adapted with care by Mike Nichols and an extraordinary cast, almost all of whom were Emmy nominated. Cuts were made from the original six-hour play, which was usually performed over two nights, but the HBO production feels true to the spirit of the work, and still boasts a scope and grandeur rarely achieved not just in television but any entertainment medium.

GREAT MOMENTS: Though it's all mesmerizing, the moments shared between Al Pacino and Meryl Streep are especially memorable.

FAST-FORWARD: Nothing.

EXTRAS: None, a particular disappointment here.

Animaniacs (1993–1998)

Volume 1 (25 episodes on 5 discs): ★ ★ ★ ★

Warner Bros. Home Video

Video: Full-Frame; Audio: Dolby Digital 5.1

Proving that smart cartoons didn't die in the '80s, this Steven Spielberg–produced series combined all the best elements from an earlier generation of Warner Bros. 'toons—sarcasm, cruelty, irresponsible behavior—with a modern-day sensibility. Once again, kids could laugh at the antics of silly characters, while their parents back on the couch would roar at the references that whizzed over junior's head.

GREAT MOMENTS: "Yes, Brothers Warner We," "Wakko's America Song."

FAST-FORWARD: Nothing.

EXTRAS: Comedian Maurice LaMarche interviews "the cast" in "Animaniacs Live!"

Anne of Green Gables (1985–1998)

The Complete Miniseries: ★ ★ ★ ★ ½

Anne of Green Gables: The Sequel: ★ ★ ★ ★

Anne of Green Gables: The Continuing Story: ★ ★

Sullivan Entertainment

Video: Full-Frame; Audio: Dolby Digital 2.0

The challenege for the actors is to pull a viewer's eyes away from the gorgeous scenery in this collection of miniseries, partly filmed on Canada's Prince Edward Island. Megan Follows is superb as Anne Shirley, opposite Colleen Dewhurst and Richard Farnsworth as her adopted guardians. Both the original series and the sequel remain faithful to the books of L.M. Montgomery, but the final entry departs drastically from the source material, and substitutes manufactured melodrama for the wit and innocent charm of its predecessors.

GREAT MOMENTS: *Green Gables*: Matthew buys Anne a dress; Gilbert pays a price for calling Anne "Carrots" in school; just about every scene set on the Island. *The Sequel*: Anne's speech before the teacher's college.

FAST-FORWARD: For Montgomery purists, all of *The Continuing Story.*

EXTRAS: Commentary by director Kevin Sullivan and alternate takes are included with each volume. The original miniseries set also contains Megan Follows's screen test.

The Apprentice (2003–)

The Complete First Season (15 episodes on 5 discs): ★ ★ ★

Universal Home Video

Video: Full-Frame; Audio: Dolby Digital 5.1

Shelf life is always an issue with reality TV, and *The Apprentice* may be especially vulnerable, as the search for a corporate executive is not as flashy as the battles waged on *Survivor* or *American Idol*, particularly on repeat viewing. However, Donald Trump junkies will enjoy the generous amount of previously unaired footage from the tasks, the boardroom, and the taxicabs included with the Season 1 DVD. Universal, which usually deserves a Trump-trademarked "You're fired" for its lack of extras on most sets, delivered the goods here.

GREAT MOMENTS: Ereka and Nick in the boardroom; Omarosa gets fired.

FAST-FORWARD: The theme song, since it's not the one originally heard on the series.

EXTRAS: Deleted and extended scenes; contestants' audition tapes; seven featurettes; interview with Donald Trump; job advice from George and Carolyn.

Archie Bunker's Place (1979–1983)

The Complete First Season (24 episodes on 3 discs): ★ ★ ★

Sony Pictures Home Entertainment
Video: Full-Frame; Audio: Dolby Digital Mono

In 1979, Jean Stapleton, Rob Reiner, and Sally Struthers were ready to move on from *All in the Family*, but Carroll O'Connor couldn't say goodbye to Archie Bunker, hence the transformation into a workplace sitcom, in which America's favorite bigot becomes co-owner of the neighborhood tavern. The first season will appeal most to *All in the Family* fans, given the occasional appearances of Stapleton as Edith, and the holiday-reunion shows with Reiner and Struthers.

GREAT MOMENTS: Mike (Rob Reiner) and Gloria (Sally Struthers) return for Thanksgiving in "Thanksgiving Reunion, Parts 1 & 2"; Archie is reunited with Sammy Davis, Jr., in "Sammy Returns"; Jerry Stiller and Anne Meara appear in "Veronica's Ex."

FAST-FORWARD: Nothing.

EXTRAS: None.

Are You Being Served? (1972–1985)

The Complete Collection—Series 1–10 (69 episodes on 4 discs): ★ ★ ★ ★
The Complete Collection—Series 1–5 (34 episodes on 7 discs): ★ ★ ★ ★ ½
The Complete Collection—Series 6–10 (36 episodes on 7 discs): ★ ★ ★
Volumes 1–13 (each: 6 episodes on 1 disc): ★ ★ ★ ½
Christmas (4 episodes on 1 disc): ★ ★

BBC Video
Video: Full-Frame; Audio: Dolby Digital 2.0

Proving the sophisticated Brits weren't above the lowest of lowbrow humor, *Are You Being Served?* was a popular import in the 1980s when it crossed the pond via PBS, having already earned enormous ratings in its homeland

over ten seasons. Critics hated the scatological humor, the silly sex jokes, and the effeminate portrayal of Mr. Humphries by John Inman, but as usual nobody cared. Few series could get more laughs out of funny costumes or a racy double-entendre.

The first five seasons feature the original and best cast; the retirement of Mr. Grainger (Arthur Brough) in Season 6 prompted a rotating lineup of menswear clerks, and the subsequent departure of Mr. Lucas (Trevor Bannister) after Season 7 was the beginning of the end. Still, *The Complete Collection* is the way to go, as the later shows still have their moments and the collection of extras, including three marvelous cast profiles, are all worth a look. And remember, the sleeves will ride up with wear.

GREAT MOMENTS: Season 1: Mr. Grainger's Churchill impression in "Camping In"; Joanna Lumley plays a sexy perfume seller in "His and Hers"; Season 3: The folk dance in "German Week"; Season 5: The moving mannequins of Mr. Humphries and Mrs. Slocombe in "It Pays to Advertise."

FAST-FORWARD: Season 5: The staff takes over the Grace Bros. toy department in "A Change Is As Good As a Rest"; Season 7: Captain Peacock's boxing match in "The Hero"; every appearance of Mr. Spooner.

EXTRAS: *Complete Collection*: Featurettes on John Inman, Mollie Sugden, and Wendy Richard; "Celebrating Mollie Sugden" special; "best of" featurette; the "Are You Being Confused?" feature translates British expressions into American.

Arrested Development (2004–)

Season 1 (22 episodes on 3 discs): ★ ★ ★ ★ ½
Season 2 (18 episodes on 3 discs): ★ ★ ★ ★ ½

Fox Home Entertainment
Video: Widescreen; Audio: Dolby Digital 2.0 Surround

"Now the story of a wealthy family who lost everything, and the one son who had no choice but to keep them all together." Former teen idol Jason Bateman plays the "one son" in a family full of crazy characters. Narrating the story is Executive Producer Ron Howard, no stranger himself to the world of the TV sitcom.

Episodes involve shady dealings inside the Bluth company after patriarch George's arrest; son Buster's avoidance and later romance with the "other Lucille" (Liza Minelli); Tobias and his insistence on leaving his practice in order to become an actor; Segway-riding magician and least favorite son Gob; and young

A

George-Michael's infatuation with his cousin, Maebe. A majority of the action takes place under the roof of a model home owned by the Bluth company.

Arrested Development on DVD is incredibly addictive, and will no doubt be a new experience to the general public who have steadfastly ignored the series while it collects critical and industry raves.

GREAT MOMENTS: Season 1: Henry Winkler makes a familiar gesture to a mirror in "Altar Egos"; it's a comedy of errors as Gob learns his girlfriend may be cheating on him in "Marta Complex"; Season 2: Henry Winkler jumps a shark in "Motherboy XXX"; the meta-textual humor of Michael Bluth questioning a reduced order from twenty-two to eighteen houses, a reference to FOX making the same order adjustment in Season 2 episodes, in "The Sword of Destiny."

FAST-FORWARD: Season 1: Fans may be disappointed with the Museum of Television and Radio cast panel discussion. Rather than including the entire segment, only certain clips were used, and some actors were rarely seen or heard on what made it to the disc.

EXTRAS: Season 1: Extended pilot; commentary by creator Mitchell Hurwitz, directors Joe Russo and Anthony Russo, and actors Jason Bateman, Portia de Rossi, Will Arnett, Tony Hale, Michael Cera, Alia Shawkat, Jessica Walter, Jeffrey Tambor, and David Cross; "Behind the Scenes" and TV Land "Future TV Classic" featurettes; selections from a Museum of Television and Radio cast panel discussion.

As Time Goes By (1992–2002)

The Complete Original Series (64 episodes on 11 discs): ★ ★ ★ ★
Complete Series 1 & 2 (13 episodes on 2 discs): ★ ★ ★ ★ ½
Complete Series 3 (10 episodes on 2 discs): ★ ★ ★ ★
Complete Series 4 (10 episodes on 2 discs): ★ ★ ★ ★
Complete Series 5 (7 episodes on 1 disc): ★ ★ ★ ½
Complete Series 6 (7 episodes on 1 disc): ★ ★ ★ ½
Compete Series 7 (7 episodes on 1 disc): ★ ★ ★
Complete Series 8 & 9 (10 episodes on 2 discs): ★ ★ ★ ½
You Must Remember This (3 episodes on 1 disc): ★ ★ ★

BBC Video

Video: Full-Frame; Audio: Dolby Digital 2.0

The punch lines won't knock you on your backside, but the smiles roused by Judi Dench and Geoffrey Palmer in *As Time Goes By* last a very long time. Dench, best-known in the US for her Oscar-winning film work, elevates the very form of the situation comedy with her consummate portrayal of Jean Pargetter, a career woman in—let's say late middle-age—who is unexpectedly reunited with a soldier she briefly knew and loved thirty years earlier. Lionel Hardcastle (Palmer) has become something of a curmudgeon over the years, but a second chance with Jean reawakens the romantic within. A perceptive, sweet, and altogether charming series.

GREAT MOMENTS: Series 1: Lionel and Jean find their old Buckinghamshire haunts have changed in Episode 3; Series 3: Rocky's wedding in Episode 2; Series 6: Lionel surprises Jean in Episode 7.

FAST-FORWARD: The shows that spend too much time on Harry and Sandy.

EXTRAS: *Complete Series*: Cast interviews; excerpts from the BAFTA Tribute to Judi Dench, featuring Geoffrey Palmer.

The Avengers (1961–1969)

1963, Sets 1–4 (each: 6 episodes on 2 discs): ★ ★ ½

1964, Sets 1 & 2 (each: 6 or 7 episodes on 2 discs): ★ ★ ½

1965, Sets 1 & 2 (each: 6 or 7 episodes on 2 discs): ★ ★ ★ ★ ★

1966, Sets 1 & 2 (each: 6 or 7 episodes on 2 discs): ★ ★ ★ ★ ★

1967, Sets 1–4 (each: 6 or 7 episodes on 2 discs): ★ ★ ★ ★ ★

1968, Sets 1–5 (each: 6 or 7 episodes on 2 discs): ★ ★

The Complete Emma Peel Megaset (51 episodes on 16 discs): ★ ★ ★ ★ ★

A&E Home Video

Video: Full-Frame; Audio: Dolby Digital 2.0

There have been countless crime-solving couples since Agatha Christie introduced Tommy and Tuppence Beresford. Television has given us *Hart to Hart*, *Moonlighting*, *Remington Steele*, and a hundred other variations on the theme, but even after forty years *The Avengers* remains enchantingly unique. The impeccable chemistry between Patrick Macnee as John Steed and Diana Rigg's Emma Peel sparkles over smart, quirky stories that bask in the aristocratic breeding of the characters, while simultaneously stepping outside to laugh at the foibles of the spoiled upper class.

Steed had partners before and after Mrs. Peel, but only the Macnee-Rigg shows remain essential. *The Complete Emma Peel Megaset* includes all the Rigg episodes at a price lower than buying the yearly sets individually. Commentary tracks (or any extra material) is sorely missed. The Cathy Gale era (1963–1964) has its moments, but the 1968 Tara King shows are recommended only for hardcore *Avengers* enthusiasts.

B

GREAT MOMENTS: *1965, Set 2*: Steed and Mrs. Peel infiltrate a dating service in "The Murder Market"; the wine-tasting showdown in "Dial a Deadly Number"; Steed receives a Christmas card from Cathy Gale in "Too Many Christmas Trees"; *1966, Set 2*: Emma beats up a military regiment in "The Danger Makers"; Mrs. Peel goes undercover (but not much cover) as the Queen of Sin in "A Touch of Brimstone"; *1967, Set 1*: Steed and Emma take a journey through the past in "Escape in Time"; *1967, Set 3*: Steed and Emma switch bodies in "Who's Who?"

FAST-FORWARD: Just about all the Tara King shows (in the 1968 sets) can be safely skipped.

EXTRAS: None, except for a photo gallery.

Baa Baa Black Sheep (1976–1978)

Volume 1 (11 episodes on 2 discs): ★ ★ ★ ½

Universal Home Video

Video: Full-Frame; Audio: Dolby Digital 2.0

And the Creative Packaging award goes to Universal for finding a way to collect *Baa Baa Black Sheep*, a series that lasted two years and thirty-seven episodes, into three premium-priced box sets. That said, this World War II–era drama about maverick Marine flyer Pappy Boyington and his famous Black Sheep Squadron is a heady mix of military action and camaraderie, ably led by Robert Conrad, one of TV's toughest badasses.

GREAT MOMENTS: The two-hour pilot, "Flying Misfits"; the machismo showdown between Robert Conrad and Charles Napier in "Best Three out of Five."

FAST-FORWARD: Nothing.

EXTRAS: Vintage interviews with the real Greg "Pappy" Boyington.

Babylon 5 (1993–1999)

The Complete First Season (22 episodes on 6 discs): ★ ★ ★

The Complete Second Season (22 episodes on 6 discs): ★ ★ ½

The Complete Third Season (22 episodes on 6 discs): ★ ★ ★ ½

The Complete Fourth Season (22 episodes on 6 discs): ★ ★ ★ ½

The Complete Fifth Season (22 episodes on 6 discs): ★ ★ ½

The Gathering/In the Beginning (2 episodes on 1 disc): ★ ★
The Movie Collection (5 episodes on 5 discs): ★ ★ ★

Warner Home Video
Video: Anamorphic Widescreen; Audio: Dolby Digital 5.1

B

Political intrigue at a busy space station was the focus of J. Michael Straczynski's *Babylon 5*, a series envisioned from its inception with a specific beginning and a specific end. Unfortunately, real-world intrusions into Straczynski's carefully crafted storylines, not the least of which was fear of cancellation after nearly every season, prompted a regrettable number of changes and rushed resolutions. The result is an uneven pace through many of the story arcs, which seem either stretched or accelerated depending on the status of network negotiations. Ironically, the series hit its stride when it was at its most vulnerable, in the "Shadow War" epic of Seasons 3 & 4. The excellent DVD collections, overseen by Straczynski, finally give *Babylon 5* the attention it never received during the original run.

GREAT MOMENTS: Season 1: *Star Trek*'s Walter Koenig embraces the dark side in "Mind War"; "Signs and Portents" sets many of the series' principal plots in motion; Season 2: John Sheridan arrives in "Points of Departure"; the pivotal "In the Shadow of Z'Ha'Dum"; Season 3: Babylon 5 secedes from the Earth Alliance in "Severed Dreams"; the two-part adventure "World Without End"; Season 4: The preparations for war in "Into the Fire" and "No Surrender, No Retreat"; Season 5: The Neil Gaiman–scripted "Day of the Dead," featuring magicians Penn and Teller.

FAST-FORWARD: Season 1: The alien boxing match in "TKO"; Season 3: "Grey 17 is Missing."

EXTRAS: Season 1: Introduction and commentaries by creator J. Michael Straczynski; "The Making of *Babylon 5*," "Back to *Babylon 5*," and "Stations Tour" featurettes; Season 2: Cast/crew episode introductions and commentaries; "Shadows and Dreams: Honors of *Babylon*" featurette; Season 3: Cast/crew episode introductions and commentaries; Season 4: Introductions and commentaries, plus "Celestial Sounds" featurette; personnel files, data files, and gag reel; Season 5: Episode introductions and commentaries; "Digital Tomorrow" and "Beyond *Babylon 5*" featurettes; gag reel; *The Movie Collection*: Episode introductions and commentaries by J. Michael Straczynski.

B

Ballykissangel (1996–2001)

Complete Series 1 (6 episodes on 2 discs): ★ ★ ★ ★
Complete Series 2 (8 episodes on 3 discs): ★ ★ ★ ★ ★
Complete Series 3 (11 episodes on 3 discs): ★ ★ ★ ½
Complete Series 4 (12 episodes on 3 discs): ★ ★ ½

BBC Video
Video: Full-Frame; Audio: Dolby Digital 2.0

Maybe Irish villages like Ballykissangel exist only in fiction, but that doesn't make a visit any less delightful. English priest Peter Clifford (Stephen Tompkinson) feels the same way, even after meeting its population of colorful eccentrics. Peter's friendship with feisty pub owner Assumpta Fitzgerald (Dervla Kirwan) takes on more intriguing layers throughout the first three series. Tompkinson and Kirwan fell in love and left BallyK soon after, leaving a void from which the show could not recover. Many fans will never forgive series creator Kieran Prendiville for how he resolved their story. (I won't either.) Series 4 is worth a look for the appearance of Colin Farrell in the recurring role of roguish Danny Byrne.

GREAT MOMENTS: Series 1: The modern confessional in "Trying to Connect You"; an old flame returns for Assumpta in "The Power and the Glory"; Series 2: The BallyK slave auction in "For One Night Only"; the beauty contest in "Only Skin Deep"; Series 3: Father Clifford finally shares his feelings with Assumpta in "The Reckoning."

FAST-FORWARD: Nothing.

EXTRAS: Series 1: Beware of the behind-the-scenes doc, which reveals plot details of later seasons; Series 3: "On the *Ballykissangel* Trail" featurette; a tour of the village where the series was filmed.

Baretta (1975–1978)

Season 1 (12 episodes on 3 discs): ★ ★ ★ ★
The Best of Baretta (3 episodes on 1 disc): ★ ★ ½

Universal Home Video
Video: Full-Frame; Audio: Dolby Digital Mono

Let's skip the Robert Blake "Don't do the crime if you can't do the time" jokes and just revel in this tasty slice of '70s counterculture. With its antisocial rule-breaking detective, who lived in a fleabag hotel and whose best friend was a cockatoo named Fred, *Baretta* wasn't your dad's kind of cop show. The guy lived for his work and got results, often through the most unorthodox of methods. Created by Stephen J. Cannell before cop shows got all serious with *Hill Street Blues*, *Baretta* was an enormous hit that has rarely surfaced since its original run. Sadly, it also appears to be another victim of the underselling Season 1 jinx, which is a particular shame here as the show only got better the longer it ran. But it's been four years since the first DVDs, and if that's all the *Baretta* we get, then it's better than nothing. And that, as the man himself would say, is the name of that tune.

GREAT MOMENTS: Baretta interrogates snooty aristocrats in "This Ain't My Bag"; Margot Kidder plays a mobster's moll in "The Secret of Terry Lake."

FAST-FORWARD: Baretta goes undercover as an African-American in a fake Afro and blackface in "Woman in the Harbor."

EXTRAS: None.

B

Barney Miller (1975–1982)

The First Season (13 episodes on 2 discs): ★ ★ ★

Columbia Tristar Home Video

Video: Full-Frame; Audio: Dolby Digital 2.0

The cop show that most cops say best captures the less-than-glamorous reality of their profession is *Barney Miller*, which substitutes scenes of office work for the urban shoot-outs more common to TV's men in blue. The detectives at New York's Twelfth Precinct are featured in a no-frills Season 1 set that reminds us why the show ranked among the more-respected comedies of the late 1970s, and also how, in its first thirteen shows, the series was still struggling to find its way. With the title character being played by Hal Linden, the best-known cast member at the time, there was an understandable tendency to build the show around Barney's quiet, professional demeanor, relegating Fish and Yemana and Harris and Wojo to supporting roles. But as the series progressed it became more of an ensemble piece, and all the better for it. Fans who hoped for another look at the series' little-seen 1974 pilot, "The Life and Times of Captain Barney Miller," will be disappointed that it was not included with the set. It might still turn up in a subsequent collection, depending on first-season sales.

GREAT MOMENTS: Linda Lavin plays Detective Wentworth in "Ms. Cop"; Lawyer-from-hell Arnold Ripner debuts in "The Experience." Wojo's weakness for fallen women is first revealed in "Snow Job."

FAST-FORWARD: Scenes of Barney at home with wife Barbara Barrie, which would be dropped in subsequent seasons.

EXTRAS: None.

B

Batman Beyond (1999–2001)

Batman Beyond: The Movie (6 episodes on 1 disc): ★ ★ ★ ½
School Dayz/Spellbound (6 episodes on 1 disc): ★ ★ ½
Tech Wars/Disappearing Inque (5 episodes on 1 disc): ★ ★

Warner Home Video
Video: Full-Frame; Audio: Dolby Digital 2.0

Set in the future, after Bruce Wayne has given up the mantle of Batman and a biker gang called "the Jokerz" terrorizes Gotham City, *Batman Beyond* introduced a new Caped Crusader in Terry McInnis, a teenager whose life was changed by tragedy. (Apparently that's a prerequisite for the job.) Kevin Conroy, who voiced Batman in *The Animated Series*, reprises his role as an older and wiser Bruce Wayne.

The initial *Batman Beyond: The Movie* release features five episodes from the show's first season, including the series premiere, and is definitely the most recommended of what's available thus far. Hopefully, Warner Home Video will release full-season sets in the future.

GREAT MOMENTS: *The Movie*: "Rebirth" introduces Terry McInnis.

FAST-FORWARD: Some later episodes don't match the sense of wonder exhibited in the series premiere.

EXTRAS: None.

Batman: The Animated Series (1992–1995)

The Legend Begins (5 episodes on 1 disc): ★ ★ ½
Tales of the Dark Knight (5 episodes on 1 disc): ★ ★
Out of the Shadows (4 episodes on 1 disc): ★ ★
Secrets of the Caped Crusader (4 episodes on 1 disc): ★ ★
Adventures of Batman & Robin: Poison Ivy/The Penguin (4 episodes on 1 disc): ★ ★
Adventures of Batman & Robin: The Joker/Fire & Ice (4 episodes on 1 disc): ★ ★
Volume 1 (28 episodes on 4 discs): ★ ★ ★ ½

Volume 2 (29 episodes on 4 discs): ★ ★ ★
Volume 3 (29 episodes on 4 discs): ★ ★ ★
Volume 4 (24 episodes on 4 discs): ★ ★ ★

Warner Home Video
Video: Full-Frame; Audio: Dolby Digital 2.0

B

In the wake of diminishing returns at the movie box office, Batman was reinvented for a 1990s audience in this popular animated series that mixed the best elements of past Caped Crusader lore into a cohesive cartoon suitable for all ages. The retro-style animation and top-tier voice talent, including Mark Hamill (as the Joker), Melissa Gilbert (as Batgirl), Malcolm McDowall, Adam West, and Ed Asner probably had more than a few adults watching over their kids' shoulders.

The series went by several titles throughout its run, among them *The Adventures of Batman & Robin*, *The New Batman/Superman Adventures*, and *Batman: Gotham Knights.* Its most significant addition to the Batman mythos was the creation of villainess Harley Quinn, who has since become a mainstay in the comics.

GREAT MOMENTS: Volume 2: "Robin's Reckoning" tells the origin of the comics' most famous sidekick; Volume 4: "Legends of the Dark Knight" adapts artistic styles from Batman as rendered in the 1950s through Frank Miller's "Dark Knight Returns"; any episode featuring the Joker and/or Harley Quinn ranks among the series' best.

FAST-FORWARD: Nothing.

EXTRAS: Multi-episode volumes include creator commentaries and bonus featurettes.

Battlestar Galactica (1978–1980)

The Complete Epic Series [Cylon Head Packaging]
(24 episodes on 6 discs): ★ ★ ½
The Complete Epic Series [Unlimited Packaging Edition]
(24 episodes on 6 discs): ★ ★ ½
Battlestar Galactica: ★

Universal Home Video
Video: Full-Frame; Audio: Dolby Digital 5.1

While this series deserves its reputation as a silly *Star Wars* clone, the special effects were a breakthrough for television at the time, and with a cast of beautiful people including Richard Hatch, Maren Jensen, Dirk Benedict, and Laurette Spang, there was eye candy aplenty to take everyone's mind off the dull adventures of a ragtag fugitive fleet, pursued by the evil robotic Cylons, searching for a paradise planet called Earth.

B

The Cylon head package is either pretty cool or a pain in the butt depending on one's perspective; store it next to the Homer Simpson head package for *The Simpsons*' sixth season and let the two of 'em stare at each other.

The individual release *Battlestar Galactica* is the European theatrical version of the pilot show "Saga of a Star World," but is actually shorter than the version that aired in two parts in the US.

GREAT MOMENTS: "War of the Gods," a two-part adventure that's as good as *Galactica* got; the *Shane*-inspired "The Lost Warrior."

FAST-FORWARD: "Conquest of the Earth," featuring disc jockey Wolfman Jack; Boxey and that K-9 wannabe daggit.

EXTRAS: The series box sets contain identical extras: a "making of" featurette, interviews with the cast and creator Glen A. Larson, deleted scenes, commentaries by cast and crew, and featurettes on the show's special effects and music.

Battlestar Galactica (2003–)

Season 1 (14 episodes on 5 discs): ★ ★ ½

Season 2 (10 episodes on 3 discs): ★ ★ ½

The Miniseries: ★ ★

Universal Home Video

Video: Anamorphic Widescreen; Audio: Dolby Digital 5.1

To have transformed the foolishness that was the original *Battlestar Galactica* into something that approximated credible science fiction is undeniably impressive. Trouble is, they overcompensated on the serious side, resulting in one of the most dour space adventures ever devised. The only laughs arise from the characters' repeated use of the word "frack" as substitute profanity for a word you still can't say on basic cable. That said, Mary McDonnell gives a splendid, Emmy-worthy performance as a politician way down the presidential food chain that must take the oath of office after the government is wiped out. She's so good she almost makes this worth picking up. Almost.

The miniseries is included in the Season 1 set, along with a plethora of extras that should please any *Galactica* fan, except for loyalists to the original show who won't accept Starbuck as a girl.

GREAT MOMENTS: Season 1: Dr. Baltar's role in the Cylon invasion is revealed in "Six Degrees of Separation"; the cliffhanger-heavy "Kobol's Last Gleaming, Part 2."

FAST-FORWARD: Season 1: Too many Baltar dream sequences with Six.

EXTRAS: Season 1: Commentary by director Michael Rymer and executive producers David Eick and Ronald D. Moore; deleted scenes; eight behind-the-scenes featurettes; documentary "*Battlestar Galactica*: The Series Lowdown"; Season 2: Commentaries and deleted scenes.

Beavis and Butt-Head (1992–1997)

The "Best of" Series (43 episodes on 3 discs): ★ ★ ½

MTV's Beavis and Butt-Head Do Christmas (2 episodes on 1 disc): ★ ½

The Final Judgment (7 episodes on 1 disc): ★ ★

The Mike Judge Collection (40 episodes on 3 discs): ★ ★ ★

Time-Life (*"Best of" Series*); Sony Music (*Beavis & Butt-Head Do Christmas* and *The Final Judgment*); Paramount/MTV Home Video (*The Mike Judge Collection*)

Video: Full-Frame; Audio: Dolby Digital 2.0

For a while it seemed all we'd ever get from *Beavis and Butt-Head* DVDs was half a show. What made the series an unlikely MTV hit was the combination of the cartoon stories and the footage of B&B watching and reviewing music videos, playing air guitar with the metal bands they worshipped, and savagely shredding everything else. But for the usual reasons (music rights, etc.), all we got were the cartoons, and without the video respites the dimwitted duo's animated adventures become awfully repetitive.

The Mike Judge Collection is a step in the right direction, as it includes eleven music videos complete with B&B commentary, but it's still not the same as releasing the episodes as they originally aired. Unlike in *South Park*, the writing here is rarely clever enough to pull one's attention from Judge's stiff animation. Heh, heh—we said "stiff."

GREAT MOMENTS: The appearances from Beavis's alter ego, Cornholio; *Final Judgment*: "No Laughing," one of the more unique outings.

FAST-FORWARD: The tired Scrooge pastiche in "Christmas."

EXTRAS: *The Mike Judge Collection*: Music videos with B&B commentary; director's cuts; B&B appearances and interviews; "Taint of Greatness: The Journey of Beavis and Butt-Head" featurette.

The Ben Stiller Show (1992–1993)

The Complete Series (12 episodes on 2 discs): ★ ★ ★ ★

Warner Home Video

Video: Full-Frame; Audio: Dolby Digital 2.0

B

Often the best comedy emerges from actors writing and performing material they think is funny, without concern for whether the viewers at home will be along for the ride. That's what Ben Stiller, Janeane Garofalo, Andy Dick, and Bob Odenkirk did with *The Ben Stiller Show*, and though they only got away with it for twelve episodes, the results outstrip every sketch-comedy series to debut since. Within the space of one show, they matched the inspired pop-culture satire of the genre's standard-bearers, *SCTV* and early *Saturday Night Live*. But FOX, the network with a heart, scheduled the show on Sundays at 7 PM, opposite *60 Minutes*. And this was back when most people didn't even know FOX *was* a network. Chances are you knew someone who watched it and loved it, but by the time they convinced you to check it out the show was cancelled. And then they said, "I told you so," a lot when the series scored a surprise Emmy win for Best Writing. Here's a chance to see what the fuss was about.

GREAT MOMENTS: The Oliver Stone Amusement Park; "Tom Cruise—The Musical"; the *Cops* parodies set in various historic eras.

FAST-FORWARD: "The Grateful Dead insurance salesman"—a rare misfire.

EXTRAS: Cast commentaries; unaired sketches; outtakes; an *E! Behind the Scenes Special*; *A Brief History of* The Ben Stiller Show, featuring alternate versions of the pilot.

The Benny Hill Show (1955–1977)

Benny Hill: Golden Classics (2 discs): ★ ★ ½

Benny Hill: Golden Greats (2 discs): ★ ★ ★

The Best of Benny Hill: ★ ★

Complete and Unadulterated: The Naughty Early Years, Set 1 (11 episodes on 3 discs): ★ ★ ★

Complete and Unadulterated: The Naughty Early Years, Set 2 (10 episodes on 3 discs): ★ ★ ★

Complete and Unadulterated: The Naughty Early Years, Set 3 (10 episodes on 3 discs): ★ ★ ★

The Lost Years: ★ ★ ½

HBO Home Video (*Golden Classics*, *Golden Greats*); BBC Video (*The Lost Years*); Anchor Bay (*The Best of Benny Hill*); A&E Home Video (*Complete and Unadulterated: The Naughty Early Years*, Sets 1–3)

Video: Full-Frame; Audio: Dolby Digital 1.0

In 1979, edited versions of *The Benny Hill Show* proved nearly as popular in America as they were in bawdy olde England. Mixing clever song parodies, slapstick, and countless sketches built around Hill leering at a cute bird's cleavage, the shows clearly owed a debt to the *Carry On* films and the Three Stooges, but there was more to the portly pervert than sexual-harassment humor. Watching the shows in their entirety, as one can finally do now that they're on DVD, it's evident that Benny Hill deserves his place in the pantheon of British comedy legends.

There's some repeat material between the HBO, Anchor Bay, and A&E releases. The *Complete and Unadulterated* sets offer the most Benny for the buck, but at typically lofty A&E prices. *The Lost Years* is a collection of Benny's BBC highlights, before he was lured away by Thames Television into the series that established him as an international sensation.

GREAT MOMENTS: The silent slapstick chases, set to the addictive strains of "Yakety Sax"; the many careers of Fred Scuttle; *Complete and Unadulterated, Set 1*: "The Girls of the Sousa-Bar," one of Benny's best songs; "Fun in the Kitchen with Johnny and Cranny Faddock."

FAST-FORWARD: Musical numbers by the Ladybirds and Trisha Noble in the *Complete and Unadulterated* sets.

EXTRAS: *Golden Greats*: "Benny Hill: The World's Favorite Clown" documentary (note: this feature also appears on Set 1 of *The Naughty Early Years*; *The Lost Years*: Previously unreleased sketches; *Complete and Unadulterated, Set 2*: "Benny Hill: Laughter and Controversy" episode of A&E's *Biography*.

The Bernie Mac Show (2001–2005)

Season 1 (22 episodes on 4 discs): ★ ★ ★

20th Century-Fox

Video: Full-Frame; Audio: Dolby Digital 2.0

A post-millennium family sitcom, which means the adults and the kids spend their days engaged in open warfare. But if you're going to fill thirty minutes with cruel put-downs they should at least be funny, and Bernie Mac delivers.

GREAT MOMENTS: Season 1: Bernie discovers to his chagrin that he's about to inherit his sister's three kids in the pilot episode; Bernie puts Vanessa in charge of her siblings in "The King and I."

FAST-FORWARD: Nothing.

EXTRAS: Commentary on the pilot by Bernie Mac, writer Larry Wilmore, and director Ken Kwapis; "TVography": Bernie Mac; TV's *Family Man* special from the A&E Network.

The Best of Ernie Kovacs (2000)

The Complete Series (5 episodes on 2 discs): ★ ★ ★ ★

White Star

Video: Full-Frame; Audio: Mono

Many legendary comedians played on television in its golden age, but only Ernie Kovacs played *with* television, exploring the comic possibilities of the medium with a bottomless bag of audio and visual tricks. Here is blackout gag comedy before *Laugh-In*, surrealism before Monty Python, snark before David Letterman. This "best of" compilation, introduced by Jack Lemmon, was a five-part series that originally aired on PBS. Though it hits all the high points and unearths some rare, forgotten treasures, there's no rhyme or reason to the presentation of the clips. Probably just the way Kovacs would have liked it.

GREAT MOMENTS: The Nairobi Trio; Edie Adams's impersonation of Marilyn Monroe singing "The Ballad of Davy Crockett"; the wordless "Eugene" skits.

FAST-FORWARD: "Mack the Knife." (You'll know it when you hear it.)

EXTRAS: None.

Beverly Hillbillies (1962–1971)

20 Classic Episodes (20 episodes on 2 discs): ★
4-Pack (8 episodes on 2 discs): ★
The Beverly Hillbillies (10 episodes on 2 discs): ★
The Beverly Hillbillies (10 episodes on 5 discs): ★
The Ultimate Collection, Volume 1 (26 episodes on 4 discs): ★ ★ ★
The Ultimate Christmas Collection (3 episodes on 1 disc): ★ ★ ½
Volume 1 (10 episodes on 1 disc): ½
Volume 2 (10 episodes on 1 disc): ½

BCI Eclipse (*20 Classic Episodes*, *Volume 1*, *Volume 2*); GoodTimes Entertainment (*4-Pack*); Madacy Entertainment (*The Beverly Hillbillies* sets); MPI Home Video (*Ultimate Collection* and *Ultimate Christmas Collection*)

Video: Full-Frame; Audio: Dolby Digital 1.0; Dolby Digital 2.0 (*Ultimate Collection* and *Ultimate Christmas Collection*)

Sometimes a classic show can't catch a break on DVD. After a cement pond-ful of public-domain releases, each lousier than the last, MPI Home Video finally stepped up with a *Beverly Hillbillies* set prepared with the participation of series creator Paul Henning's family; *The Ultimate Collection* sports original music, restored picture and sound, and a wonderful assortment of extras. It's also missing ten of the thirty-six first-season shows. Maybe they counted on Jethro's fourth-grade education to do the cipherin'. The MPI release is still the best of a miserable lot, but complete season sets would be nice.

B

GREAT MOMENTS: *Ultimate Collection*: The Clampetts load up the truck and move to Beverly (Hills, that is) in the pilot episode; Flatt and Scruggs make their first series appearance, along with the unforgettable Joi Lansing as Gladys Flatt, in "Jethro Throws a Wingding"; Jesse White plays a con man who sells Jed the Hollywood Bowl, Griffith Park, and the Hollywood Freeway in "Jed Buys the Freeway"; the Clampetts show off their sharp-shooting skills in "Jed Becomes a Banker."

FAST-FORWARD: *Ultimate Collection*: Anytime Max Baer, Jr., plays Jethrene.

EXTRAS: *Ultimate Collection*: Introduction by Linda Kaye Henning; original cast commercials; "Paul Henning and the Hillbillies" documentary; variety show appearances by Buddy Ebsen and Irene Ryan; unaired pilot with extra footage.

Bewitched (1964–1972)

The Complete First Season [black-and-white]
(36 episodes on 4 discs): ★ ★ ★ ★ ★
The Complete First Season [color] (36 episodes on 4 discs): ★ ★ ★ ★
The Complete Second Season [black-and-white]
(36 episodes on 5 discs): ★ ★ ★ ★ ★
The Complete Second Season [color] (36 episodes on 5 discs): ★ ★ ★ ★
The Complete Third Season (33 episodes on 4 discs): ★ ★ ★ ★ ½

Sony Pictures Home Entertainment
Video: Full-Frame; Audio: Dolby Digital 2.0

The best of the fantasy-inspired 1960s sitcoms, *Bewitched* remains every bit as charming today as it was forty years ago. Who doesn't adore Elizabeth Montgomery? Who doesn't look forward to every visit from Serena and Dr. Bombay, and Aunt Clara and Uncle Arthur? Only people who don't love television, and they're not reading this book.

Fans may have some minor quibbles; Sam's father is called "Victor" rather than Maurice in the liner notes, and why is Paul Lynde pictured on one of the four Season 1 discs when his only appearance that year was a guest spot as a driving instructor? Hey, Sony, where's the Larry Tate love?

B

But the most egregious misstep was the decision to produce colorized sets when most DVD customers prefer to purchase every show as it was originally broadcast. It will be a surprise if the color box sells half of what the black-and-white does, though some major retailers stacked the deck by not offering both. Someone oughta twitch their noses and turn them into artichokes.

GREAT MOMENTS: Season 1: Endora's brief but beautiful monologue on the nature of witches ("We live on the wind, and in the sparkle of a star") in "Be It Ever So Mortgaged"; Darrin meets Endora for the first time in "Mother Meets What's His Name"; Sam flies problem-child Billy Mumy to the North Pole to meet Santa Claus in "A Vision of Sugar Plums"; Darrin is temporarily granted the power of witchcraft in "A Is for Aardvark"; Season 2: Paul Lynde makes his first appearance as Uncle Arthur in the hilarious "The Joker Is a Card"; Darrin is placed under a truth-telling hex in "Speak the Truth"; Tabitha is born, and Elizabeth Montgomery plays Serena for the first time in "And Then There Were None"; Season 3: Darrin discovers that Tabitha's a witch in "The Moment of Truth"; Aunt Clara conjures up Ben Franklin in "My Friend Ben."

FAST-FORWARD: Season 1: Arte Johnson's guest appearance as the family elf in "Cousin Edgar" is surprisingly light on laughs; Season 3: "Soapbox Derby" is an inferior remake of the Season 1 episode "Little Pitchers Have Big Fears."

EXTRAS: Season 1: "The Magic Unveiled" and "Magic and Mishaps" featurettes; Season 2: "Bewitched, Bewildered, and Be-Bloopered" featurette.

The Big Valley (1965–1969)

Season 1 (30 episodes on 5 discs): ★ ★ ★ ½

20th Century-Fox

Video: Full-Frame; Audio: Dolby Digital Mono

Premiering just as television's obsession with the Western had passed, *The Big Valley* introduced audiences to Lee Majors before he was bionic, Linda Evans before she was Krystle, and Richard Long before he met Nanny. But the show's best casting coup was Hollywood legend Barbara Stanwyck, who specialized in tough dames and created a memorable one in matriarch Victoria Barkley. An essential pickup for any Western DVD collection.

GREAT MOMENTS: "Boots With My Father's Name" is a powerful showcase for Barbara Stanwyck.

FAST-FORWARD: Nothing.

EXTRAS: None.

A Bing Crosby Christmas (1999)

DVD Collection: ★ ★ ★ ½

Questar

Video: Full-Frame; Audio: Mono

B

Highlights from fifteen of Bing Crosby's annual Christmas specials are collected in this salute hosted by Gene Kelly and Kathryn Crosby. More full performances would have been preferable to the clip packages—Bing starts "Do You Hear What I Hear?" twice and doesn't get to finish either time. But this is a nice holiday slice of sentimental nostalgia with great music and guest stars (Fred Astaire, Jackie Gleason), and it's fun to watch Mary Crosby grow up from age seven into the woman who would shoot J.R.

GREAT MOMENTS: Bing's now-legendary duet with David Bowie on "Little Drummer Boy/Peace on Earth"; a montage of Bing's "White Christmas" performances.

FAST-FORWARD: Bing trading *Hee Haw* jokes with Roy Clark.

EXTRAS: Film clips from Crosby's performances in *Holiday Inn* and *The Bells of St. Mary's*; additional clips featuring Frank Sinatra, Bob Hope, Louis Armstrong, and Rosemary Clooney.

Black Adder (1983–1989)

The Complete Black Adder Set (25 episodes on 5 discs): ★ ★ ★ ★ ½
Black Adder I (6 episodes on 1 disc): ★ ★ ★
Black Adder II (6 episodes on 1 disc): ★ ★ ★ ★ ½
Black Adder III (6 episodes on 1 disc): ★ ★ ★ ½
Black Adder IV: Black Adder Goes Forth (6 episodes on 1 disc): ★ ★ ★ ★
Black Adder V: Back and Forth: ★ ★ ★

BBC Video

Video: Full-Frame; Audio: Dolby Digital 2.0

An ingenious concept, following generations of a family of scoundrels and reprobates over four centuries of British history, who all have "a cunning plan" for every occasion, and all of whom are played by the brilliant Rowan Atkinson. *The Complete Black Adder Set* is the only way to go here, as half the fun is the contrasts in Atkinson's different portrayals of Black Adder. As skewered as these takes on history by creator Richard Curtis may seem, a lot of accurate factual references do make their way into the stories. They're still no substitute for homework but they're a lot more entertaining.

B

GREAT MOMENTS: *Black Adder I*: Peter Cook plays King Richard III in "Foretelling"; *Black Adder II*: Miranda Richardson's portrayal of Queen Elizabeth I; Black Adder hires a deranged pirate, played by *Doctor Who*'s Tom Baker, in "Potato"; *Black Adder III*: Black Adder impersonates the Scarlet Pimpernel in "Nob and Nobility"; *Black Adder IV*: The torture scenes in "Private Plane"; *The Complete Set*: The shocking and hilarious "Black Adder's Christmas Carol" features guest stars from each previous era.

FAST-FORWARD: Nothing.

EXTRAS: *The Complete Black Adder Set*: "Who's Who in *Black Adder*" featurette; "What's What—Interactive Guide to Historical Figures and Events"; *Black Adder's Christmas Carol*; "*Black Adder* in the Cavalier Years"; Richard Curtis Interview; *Back and Forth*: "Making of" featurette.

The Bob Hope Show (1950–2000)

The Ultimate Collection: ★ ★ ★ ½
Hope for the Holidays: ★ ★ ★

Respond 2
Video: Full-Frame; Audio: Dolby Digital 2.0

The Ultimate Collection is a compilation of highlights from fifty years of Bob Hope specials, including the annual Christmas shows and footage from his performances for military audiences around the world. Preserving broadcasts in their entirety is always preferable, especially with vintage material, but as clip packages go this one's hard to beat, given the appearances of almost everyone who's ever been famous since 1950. *Hope for the Holidays* repeats some material from the *Ultimate Collection*, but one can never have too many heartwarming holiday memories.

GREAT MOMENTS: *Ultimate Collection*: If you have any favorite actors or singers that predate the Reagan administration, chances are they're here; the Vietnam-era shows; *Hope for the Holidays*: Bob's annual rendition of "Silver Bells"; duets with everyone from Gale Storm to Olivia Newton-John.

FAST-FORWARD: *Ultimate Collection*: Bob always thought a little too much of Brooke Shields's comedic talents.

EXTRAS: *Ultimate Collection*: An excerpt from the 1995 special "Bob Goes to War"; a collection of short subjects filmed by Hope in the 1930s, and Bob's first radio broadcast, from 1935; a Hope biography and photo album; *Hope for the Holidays*: Bloopers.

The Bob Newhart Show (1972–1978)

The Complete First Season (24 episodes on 3 discs): ★ ★ ★ ★ ½
The Complete Second Season (24 episodes on 3 discs): ★ ★ ★ ★ ★
The Complete Third Season (24 episodes on 3 discs): ★ ★ ★ ★

20th Century-Fox
Video: Full-Frame; Audio: Dolby Digital Mono

It's hard to believe anybody went out on Saturday nights in the 1970s, when television offered such treasures as *M*A*S*H, The Mary Tyler Moore Show, All in the Family, The Carol Burnett Show,* and *The Bob Newhart Show.* Or maybe that just applied to those of us who couldn't get dates. If so, here's a chance for the popular kids to discover what they missed.

The Bob Newhart Show is another stellar sitcom from the *MTM* stable, and in psychologist Robert Hartley the series provided a perfect showcase for Newhart's subdued comic gifts. The home-front humor shines brightest thanks to the repartee of Newhart with screen-wife Suzanne Pleshette, but the office scenes are equally memorable, particularly the group-therapy sessions attended by manic-depressive Elliot Carlin. When a phone rings, at home or at the office, get ready for comedy gold, as no one ever managed a funnier one-sided phone conversation than Bob Newhart. Technical credits on the DVDs are what you'd expect for a '70s show, but since there are no extras on the Season 1 set you can amuse yourself, as the dateless did during the original run, by counting the number of "Hi, Bob!"s per episode.

GREAT MOMENTS: Season 1: Emily tries to overcome her fear of flying, with little help from stewardess Penny Marshall, in "Fly the Unfriendly Skies"; *Monday Night Football* drives a rift between the Hartleys in "Don't Go to Bed Mad"; the Oom-Pah-Pahs in "Let's Get Away From It, Almost"; Season 2: Bob becomes jealous when Emily scores higher on an IQ test in "Mr. Emily Hartley"; the "mod" '70s fashions in "The Modernization of Emily."

FAST-FORWARD: Season 2: "Emily in for Carol" recycles an old *Dick Van Dyke Show* plot, and not particularly well; Season 3: Too much Howard and Moosie in "Sorry, Wrong Mother."

EXTRAS: Season 2: Episode commentaries by Bob Newhart, Jack Riley, Marcia Wallace, and David Davis.

B

Bonanza (1959–1973)

Best of Bonanza, Volume 1 (8 episodes on 1 disc): ★ ★ ★
20 Episode Set (20 episodes on 5 discs): ★ ★
8 Episodes (8 episodes on 2 discs): ★ ½
4-Pack (4 episodes on 4 discs): ★
Box Set, Volumes 1–5 (5 episodes on 5 discs): ★

BCI Eclipse (*20 Episode Set*, *8 Episodes*); GoodTimes Entertainment (*4-Pack*); Madacy Entertainment (*Box Set, Volumes 1–5*); Artisan Entertainment (*Best of Bonanza*).

Video: Full-Frame; Audio: Dolby 1.0 (*Best of Bonanza*: Dolby Digital 2.0)

Few series have been victimized by as many shoddy DVD collections as *Bonanza*. Numerous public-domain releases have flooded the market, containing anywhere from one to twenty episodes, with no effort made to boost the audio and video quality near DVD standards. I've ignored the several single and two-episode disc packages, as should you. The larger sets will please only those who want the episodes any way they can get them.

In 2003, Artisan Entertainment finally stepped up with a collection worthy of the series, with hopefully more to come. Though season sets are still preferable, at least fans can finally return to the Ponderosa with uncut shows, digitally remastered picture and sound, and episodes worthy of the "best of" declaration.

GREAT MOMENTS: *Best of Bonanza, Volume 1*: Howard Duff guest-stars as Mark Twain in "Enter Mark Twain"; "Any Friend of Walter's"—one of the long-running series' best comic outings.

FAST-FORWARD: Nothing, if you bought the right set.

EXTRAS: None.

Boomtown (2002–2003)

Season 1 (18 episodes on 5 discs): ★ ★

Artisan Home Entertainment

Video: Anamorphic Widescreen; Audio: Dolby Digital 2.0 Surround

Boomtown won a Peabody Award but was ignored by the Emmys. Typical. It was ignored by viewers as well, resulting in cancellation after just twenty-four episodes. Why, then, did Artisan release only the eighteen shows that comprise the first season, omitting the six remaining episodes that wrapped up the series? Even in its video afterlife, *Boomtown* can't catch a break.

For those who never watched (which judging by the ratings would be just about all of you), this was a cutting-edge urban drama that aimed for *Sopranos*-

level sophistication in its edgy storytelling, within the more restricted confines of network television. The gimmick was in relating the events of an L.A. crime-and-punishment story from the varying perspectives of its participants—the cops, the crooks, the press, and the politicians. The large cast, led by Donnie Wahlberg and Mykelti Williamson, and the stories that continued from one episode to the next, required a measure of viewer loyalty that the series could not sustain.

B

GREAT MOMENTS: McNorris battles his alcoholism in "Blackout"; Ray gets fed up with a condemned convict's attitude in "Execution."

FAST-FORWARD: The chat with the ghost in "Fearless."

EXTRAS: Cast and crew commentaries; featurettes "Building *Boomtown*" and "The *Boomtown* Shuffle."

Boston Legal (2004–)

Season 1 (17 episodes on 5 discs): ★ ★ ★ ★

Fox Home Entertainment

Video: Anamorphic Widescreen; Audio: Dolby Digital 5.1

Creator David E. Kelley filled his *Practice* spin-off with young, pretty lawyers, but we only had eyes for veteran scene-stealers William Shatner and James Spader, whose efforts to out-mug each other were more memorable than any of the women they seduced or the cases they argued.

GREAT MOMENTS: Shatner's self-aggrandizing introductions—"Denny Crane"; Candice Bergen debuts as Crane's nemesis/ex-lover in "Schmidt Happens."

FAST-FORWARD: Any scene without Shatner or Spader.

EXTRAS: Cast/writer interviews; commentary on "Death Be Not Proud"; featurette "Court Is Now in Session."

Boy Meets World (1993–2000)

The Complete First Season (22 episodes on 3 discs): ★ ★ ★

The Complete Second Season (23 episodes on 3 discs): ★ ★ ½

The Complete Third Season (22 episodes on 3 discs): ★ ★ ½

Buena Vista Home Entertainment

Video: Full-Frame; Audio: Dolby Digital 2.0 Surround

Ben Savage, younger brother of *The Wonder Years*' Fred Savage, starred in this 1990s ABC Friday-night staple. Ben played young Cory Matthews, who was introduced as a sixth-grader, and through the magic of television aging was married to his elementary-school sweetheart Topanga by series' end. A constant thorn in his side was William Daniels, adding more gravitas than the series deserved as Cory's principal and next-door neighbor, Mr. Feeney.

B

Picture and sound are as good as you'd expect, but it's not fair that this is already on DVD while we still wait for *The Wonder Years.*

GREAT MOMENTS: Season 1: Cory meets Topanga for the first time in "Cory's Alternative Friends."

FAST-FORWARD: Bowing down to parent company Disney, the show, like many of its ABC counterparts in the mid-'90s, predictably takes things to Disney World in Season 3's "The Happiest Show on Earth."

EXTRAS: Season 1: Episode audio and video commentaries with the cast; bonus Season 4 episode.

The Brady Bunch (1969–1974)

The Complete First Season (25 episodes on 4 discs): ★ ★ ★ ½
The Complete Second Season (24 episodes on 4 discs): ★ ★ ★ ½
The Complete Third Season (23 episodes on 4 discs): ★ ★ ★ ★ ½
The Complete Fourth Season (23 episodes on 4 discs): ★ ★ ★ ★ ★
The Complete Fifth Season (21 episodes on 4 discs): ★ ★ ★ ½

Paramount Home Video
Video: Full-Frame; Audio: Dolby Digital 2.0

No other family-based sitcom has been as lovingly embraced by several generations of fans as *The Brady Bunch.* To those who judge a series' merit only by its writing, acting, and other technical credits, the Brady phenomenon must be inexplicable. Why does this particular show resonate so deeply with those who grew up with it?

Surely some of this affection can be attributed to its comforting portrayal of a happy marriage and six cheerful, well-adjusted children. There are no "very special episodes" in which something dire happens to a Brady. Dad goes to work, Mom goes shopping, the kids go to school, and Alice cooks dinner. The idealized American family may only exist on television, but their home is still a reassuring place to visit. And even those fans who have every episode memorized will see a few moments in these uncut shows that haven't been broadcast in decades, like the game of "Ha!" in "The Slumber Caper" or the tag scene in "The Un-Underground Movie."

Paramount should have taken advantage of the cast's willingness to embrace their Brady past, by including them in more commentaries and interviews. The episodes, however, look terrific. You can even spot individual blades of plastic grass in the Astroturf backyard.

GREAT MOMENTS: Season 1: Mike installs a pay phone in the Brady home in "Sorry, Right Number"; Season 2: Jan's first neurotic meltdown in "The Not-So-Ugly Duckling"; Mom's favorite vase is broken in "Confessions, Confessions"; Greg's "mod" wardrobe in "Our Son, the Man"; Season 3: Peter's still-funny Bogart imitation ("Pork chops and applesauce") in "The Personality Kid"; Jan's "Marcia, Marcia, Marcia!" lament in "Her Sister's Shadow"; Marcia stalks a Monkee in "Getting Davy Jones"; Season 4: The season's opening Hawaii trilogy; the Family Night Frolics performances in "The Show Must Go On?"; Marcia gets beaned with a football in "The Subject Was Noses"; the Silver Platters performance in "Amateur Night"; Season 5: Joe Namath guests in "Mail Order Hero"; Greg's career as a pop idol collapses in "Adios Johnny Bravo."

FAST-FORWARD: All the skippable stuff is in Season 5, including the Cousin Oliver appearances, the lame twin story "Two Petes in a Pod" and the attempted spin-off episode "Kelly's Kids."

EXTRAS: Season 1: Two episode commentaries by Barry Williams, Christopher Knight, and Susan Olsen; commentary on the pilot by series creator Sherwood Schwartz; featurette "The Brady Bunch—Coming Together Under One Roof."

The Brady Bunch Hour (1977)

The Brady Bunch Variety Hour (2 episodes on 1 disc): ★

Rhino

Video: Full-Frame; Audio: Dolby Digital 2.0

A disastrous show, but one possessed of a compelling polyester Day-Glo horror that's difficult to ignore. It won't pollute your house like moldy cheese but there's definitely a risk of lowered social standing if a copy is found on your shelf. Even the legions of Brady fans can't stomach too much of this all-singing, all-dancing, all-terrible variety spectacular, which star Barry Williams described as "the worst show in television history."

GREAT MOMENTS: You're kidding, right?

FAST-FORWARD: Any moments with Brady ringer Geri Reischl, a.k.a. Fake Jan.

EXTRAS: Interview with Susan Olsen and Mike Lookinland.

Buck Rogers in the 25th Century (1979–1981)

The Complete Epic Series (37 episodes on 5 discs): ★ ★ ★

B

Universal Home Video

Video: Full-Frame; Audio: Dolby Digital 2.0

Once described as "*Logan's Run* on laughing gas," *Buck Rogers in the 25th Century* offers both the kitschy delights and cringe-inducing stupidity that characterized American sci-fi TV in the 1970s.

Despite being saddled with the cute robot that every sci-fi franchise required after *Star Wars*—in this case, the Mel Blanc–voiced Twiki (all together now—"Bee-dee-bee-dee-bee-dee, way to go, Buck!"), Gil Gerard and Erin Gray tried to play the material straight, which of course only made the results more amusing. Handsome Gerard certainly had the all-American hero look to him, and the shiny spandex uniforms that were spray-painted on Gray's Colonel Wilma Deering provided a bigger ratings boost than any contribution from the series' writers.

Season 2 brought wholesale changes to the format, none of which could be considered improvements: gone were Princess Ardala and her metal bikinis, the Draconians, Dr. Theopolis, and Wilma's self-respect as she was transformed from officer to drudge. The series focused on outer-space adventures, as Buck and crew left Earth to explore the galaxy, accompanied by the new character of Hawk, a jump-the-shark addition if there ever was one.

Fans will be disappointed to learn that Gil Gerard and Erin Gray both offered to record commentary tracks for selected episodes, only to be rebuffed. Those tracks, or extras of any kind, would have helped Universal justify its original $89.99 ticket price.

GREAT MOMENTS: The two-hour pilot episode, which played in movie theaters before being re-cut for television; Buster Crabbe, the original Buck Rogers, appears in "Planet of the Slave Girls"; Princess-in-heat Ardala's repeated attempts to seduce Buck, in such episodes as "Escape from Wedded Bliss" and "Ardala Returns."

FAST-FORWARD: The vapid title song by Kipp Lennon (no relation to John, but that's obvious after one listen); Gary Coleman's appearance as Hieronymous Fox in "Cosmic Whiz Kid"; Buck travels to Musicworld to stop a world-threatening performance from the cosmic rock band Andromeda in "Space Rockers"; just about all of Season 2.

EXTRAS: None.

Buffalo Bill (1983–1984)

The Complete First and Second Seasons (26 episodes on 3 discs): ★ ★ ★ ★

Lions Gate

Video: Full-Frame; Audio: Dolby Digital 2.0

B

Situation comedies centering on unsympathetic characters are always a tough sell. *Fawlty Towers* pulled it off, and so did *Buffalo Bill*, but only one of those shows got the credit it deserved. Dabney Coleman's talk show host Bill Bittinger was a true TV original: arrogant, lecherous, vindictive, insensitive, and at his best utterly hilarious. Coleman was surrounded by a terrific ensemble cast, including Geena Davis, Joanna Cassidy, John Fiedler, and Charles Robinson. *Buffalo Bill* was a hit with critics and audiences, though NBC almost seemed embarrassed to claim the credit, given the controversial nature of the series (Bill's Zulu dream sequence would never get on the air now). *The Complete First and Second Seasons* is actually the complete series, and though a few extras would have been nice, it's great to have the chance to just view these groundbreaking episodes once again.

GREAT MOMENTS: Bill's dream in "Hit the Road, Jack"; the station is overrun by fifty Jerry Lewis impersonators (one of them played by Jim Carrey) in "Jerry Lewis Week."

FAST-FORWARD: Nothing.

EXTRAS: None.

Buffy the Vampire Slayer (1997–2003)

Season 1 (12 episodes on 3 discs): ★ ★ ★ ★ ★
Season 2 (22 episodes on 6 discs): ★ ★ ★ ★ ★
Season 3 (22 episodes on 6 discs): ★ ★ ★ ★ ★
Season 4 (22 episodes on 6 discs): ★ ★ ★ ★
Season 5 (22 episodes on 6 discs): ★ ★ ★ ★
Season 6 (22 episodes on 6 discs): ★ ★ ★ ★ ½
Season 7 (22 episodes on 6 discs): ★ ★ ★ ★
The Complete Series (144 episodes on 40 discs): ★ ★ ★ ★ ★

20th Century-Fox

Video: Full-Frame; Audio: Dolby Digital 2.0

At it's best, *Buffy the Vampire Slayer* was better than anything else on television. At its worst, the series was still better than ninety-five percent of everything on television. It was that good.

B

Creator Joss Whedon adapted his misfired motion picture of the same name into a masterpiece of horror, humor, drama, action, and adolescent angst. As with a series like *The Simpsons*, there are some who will never get past the surface trappings to see the genius beneath; yes, it's a silly title, and it's sometimes a show about bug monsters and high school students battling demonic possession between classes. But Whedon populated a slasher movie premise with intelligent characters who not only fight back, but who contend with bigger problems than the monster outside the door. The writing was brilliant, the cast superb. No description can adequately describe the depth and delights of the Buffyverse to the uninitiated. To those who missed it the first time around—if you're willing to take a chance, you won't be disappointed.

The DVD sets are light on special features, and video quality on the first couple of seasons is hit-and-miss, though that's to be expected as they were shot on the cheap in 16 mm. A few scenes, such as those set in the hallways of Sunnydale High after dark, look like they were shot through a dirty screen door. The technical credits improve significantly from Season 3 on.

GREAT MOMENTS: Season 1: Angel's origin is revealed in "Angel"; Buffy's "I'm sixteen years old, I don't want to die" speech in "Prophecy Girl"; Season 2: The introduction of Spike and Drusilla in "School Hard"; Angel turns evil after a romantic night with Buffy in "Innocence"; the tragic fate of Jenny Calendar in "Passion"; Buffy sends Angel to hell in "Becoming, Part 2"; Season 3: The fight scene in "Anne"; Faith debuts in "Faith, Hope, and Trick"; Spike returns in "Lover's Walk"; the students of Sunnydale High honor Buffy's heroism at "The Prom"; Season 4: The silent killers in "Hush"; Buffy and Faith switch bodies in "Who Are You?"; Season 5: Buffy attempts to slay the greatest vampire of them all in "Buffy vs. Dracula"; the Buffy-Spike interaction in "Fool for Love"; Season 6: Buffy's confession to Spike about where she was during her "death" in "After Life"; the magnificent musical episode "Once More, with Feeling"; the battle against Evil Willow in "Two to Go" and "Grave"; Season 7: The superbly written and genuinely frightening "Conversations with Dead People"; the return of Faith and the debut of demonic preacher Caleb in "Dirty Girls."

FAST-FORWARD: Among the rare misfires: "Living Conditions" and "Restless" (Season 4) and "Him" (Season 7).

EXTRAS: Every season set offers commentaries, primarily from creator Joss Whedon and the writing staff; cast commentaries are a rarity (Seth Green in Season 4; Danny Strong, Tom Lenk, D.B. Woodside, James Marsters, and Nicholas Brendon in Season 7); the sets also contain brief behind-the-scenes featurettes that are nowhere near as ambitious or entertaining as the series they salute. An exception is the closer look at the Season 6 show "Once More, with Feeling."

The Bugaloos (1970–1972)

The Complete Series (17 episodes on 3 discs): ★ ★ ★ ★ ½

Rhino

Video: Full-Frame; Audio: Dolby Digital 2.0

You can't explain *The Bugaloos* to someone who's never watched it. Go ahead—try to describe a show about a quartet of British teenagers who portray singing bugs (one of whom is a ladybug, played by a guy) who live in a place called Tranquility Forest. Then mention their nemesis is a frustrated singer named Benita Bizarre, who lives in a jukebox with her henchman, a Nazi rat named Funky. Yes, kids, there was a time when imagination was more important than product placement on Saturday mornings. Martha Raye's delirious portrayal of Benita must be seen to be believed.

GREAT MOMENTS: The Bugaloos perform "The Senses of Our World" in "Firefly, Light My Fire"; I.Q. impersonates Benita in "Benita's Double Trouble."

FAST-FORWARD: The clip show "The Good Old Days."

EXTRAS: Cast interviews.

C

Cadfael (1994–1998)

Box Set 1 (4 episodes on 4 discs): ★ ★ ★ ★

Box Set 2 (3 episodes on 3 discs): ★ ★ ★ ★

Box Set 3 (3 episodes on 3 discs): ★ ★ ★ ★

Box Set 4 (3 episodes on 3 discs): ★ ★ ★ ½

Individual releases (A Morbid Taste for Bones, One Corpse Too Many, Rose Rent, Saint Peter's Fair, The Devil's Novice, The Holy Thief, The Leper of Saint Giles, The Pilgrim of Hate, The Potter's Field, The Raven in the Foregate, The Sanctuary Sparrow, The Virgin in the Ice): ★ ★ ★

Acorn Media

Video: Full-Frame; Audio: Dolby Digital 2.0

Fans of unique detective stories, and anyone who was mesmerized by Derek Jacobi's performance in *I, Claudius*, should enjoy *Cadfael*, in which Jacobi plays a monk in twelfth-century England, who solves crimes in an era that predates Sherlock Holmes by six hundred years. The BBC does its usual yeoman work in recreating the medieval world of the Ellis Peters novels.

GREAT MOMENTS: *Box Set 1*: "One Corpse Too Many" is an ideal introduction to the series; *Box Set 2*: Cadfael's heated confrontation with Undersheriff

Beringar in "Saint Peter's Fair; *Box Set 4*: A body is discovered in the Shrewsbury monastery in "The Potter's Field."

FAST-FORWARD: The liberties taken with Ellis's novel "The Pilgrim of Hate" (*Box Set 4*) may disappoint fans of the book.

EXTRAS: All sets include audio notes (but not episode commentaries) by star Derek Jacobi.

Caesar's Hour (1954–1957)

The Sid Caesar Collection: Creating the Comedy
(5 episodes on 1 disc): ★ ★ ★ ★
The Sid Caesar Collection: Inside the Writer's Room
(5 episodes on 1 disc): ★ ★ ★ ★
The Sid Caesar Collection: The Magic of Live TV
(5 episodes on 1 disc): ★ ★ ★ ★
The Box Set [Creating the Comedy, Inside the Writer's Room, and
The Magic of Live TV] (18 episodes on 3 discs): ★ ★ ★ ★ ½
The Sid Caesar Collection: Fan Favorites (3 discs): ★ ★ ★ ★ ½
The Sid Caesar Collection: Buried Treasures (3 discs): ★ ★ ★

Goldhil Media
Video: Full-Frame; Audio: Dolby Digital 1.0

Sid Caesar's equally inspired follow-up to *Your Show of Shows* found the great comic working once again with Carl Reiner, Imogene Coca, and Howard Morris, and the now-fabled writing staff that included Neil Simon, Larry Gelbart, Woody Allen, Mel Brooks, and Selma Diamond. Hopefully it's not sacrilege to say that each disc contains a few misfires along with the classics—comedy inspired by current events is bound to be dated fifty years later—but television's original sketch-comedy troupe set the gold standard to which Carol Burnett, *Saturday Night Live*, and *SCTV* hoped to aspire. Goldhil Media deserves special praise for its frame-by-frame labors in cleaning up the cloudy kinescopes.

GREAT MOMENTS: *The Box Set*: the Commuters sketches; "From Here to Obscurity," a takeoff on the film *From Here to Eternity*; *Fan Favorites*: Caesar effortlessly covers for a broken prop on live TV in the "Gallipacci" sketch; *Buried Treasures*: "Professor on Archaeology."

FAST-FORWARD: The Haircuts sketches, in which Caesar, Reiner, and Morris mock rock 'n' roll bands, haven't aged well.

EXTRAS: Each release includes bonus sketches, and interviews with either writers or cast members, including Sid Caesar, Carl Reiner, Nanette Fabray, Woody Allen, Mel Brooks, Larry Gelbart, and Neil Simon.

C

Candid Camera (1948–1999)

Five Decades of Smiles (44 episodes on 10 discs): ★ ★ ★ ★

Rhino

Video: Full-Frame; Audio: Dolby Digital Mono

Fifty years before anyone had coined the phrase "reality TV," *Candid Camera* was steering the man on the street into embarrassing situations for our amusement. Creator and host Allen Funt had a real genius for crafting outlandish scenarios that were just credible enough to take in his victims, yet there was an innocence to these elaborate pranks that is missing from such modern-day successors as *Punk'd*. Rhino has put together a terrific retrospective, though I wish the collection had focused more on the series' 1960s glory days, and devoted less time to the revivals of the 1980s and 1990s.

GREAT MOMENTS: Classic bits like the talking mailbox and the sneeze phone; Allen Funt takes hidden cameras into the Soviet Union without the government's permission, which could have landed him in a gulag.

FAST-FORWARD: The 1990s shows, hosted by Peter Funt and Suzanne Somers, aren't as consistently entertaining.

EXTRAS: "*Candid Camera* Through the Decades" featurettes; a "lost" episode from 1949; the twenty-fifth-anniversary and fortieth-anniversary "television specials."

The Captain and Tennille (1976–1977)

The Ultimate Collection (11 episodes on 3 discs): ★ ★ ★ ½

Respond 2

Video: Full-Frame; Audio: Dolby Digital 2.0

For anyone stuck in the '70s, the release of this short-lived variety series is manna from Heaven. Not only will you get live (though mostly lip-synched) versions of the Captain and Tennille's greatest hits, including "Love Will Keep Us Together," "Shop Around," "Lonely Night (Angel Face)," and, yes, even "Muskrat Love," the guest-star list is a who's who of the era. Among those who stop by to make fun of the Captain's hat are Leo Sayer, the soft-pop band

Bread, all three of Charlie's original Angels, the Sweathogs from *Welcome Back, Kotter*, and the cast of *Happy Days*. How groovy can you get?

GREAT MOMENTS: The performance of the pop classic "Love Will Keep Us Together"; Toni's duet with Dionne Warwick; the Bionic Watermelon.

FAST-FORWARD: Most of the comedy sketches, retro charms aside, are dreadful.

EXTRAS: The Captain and Tennille's national TV debut on *The Tonight Show*; music video for "Do That to Me One More Time"; a bonus CD single of the duo's 2005 Christmas song, "Saving Up Christmas."

C

Carnivale (2000)

Season 1 (12 episodes on 6 discs): ★ ★ ★ ★ ★

HBO Home Video

Video: Anamorphic Widescreen; Audio: Dolby Digital 5.1

"And to each generation was born a creature of light and a creature of darkness . . ." Although it gained a devoted cult following for its brilliant blend of fantasy and historic drama, *Carnivale* never became a mainstream hit and was cancelled after two twelve-episode seasons, with all of its major plotlines left dangling.

Set in the Dust Bowl during the Great Depression, the series detailed the parallel storylines of two characters with supernatural powers: a young ex-convict, Ben Hawkins (Nick Stahl), who worked in a traveling carnival filled with freaks and sideshow attractions, and a Methodist minister, Justin Crowe (Clancy Brown), both of whom came to discover the meaning and extent of their abilities over the course of the series. The show served up an intriguing web of complicated, tantalizing mysteries; strange symbolism; religious allusions; and complex characters.

HBO has provided fans with one of the finest video transfers ever produced for a television-series set. Each episode is a masterpiece of cinematography. The colors are flawless, and the detail so fine you can see the ever-present dust and grit on all of the characters' costumes. It was shot in HD, and it shows.

GREAT MOMENTS: The mysterious baggage cart in "After the Ball Is Over"; Ben controlling the storm in "Black Blizzard"; Justin and Iris's origin story in "The River"; Justin's second baptism in "Hot and Bothered"; the life-and-death climax of the season finale, "The Day That Was the Day."

FAST-FORWARD: *Carnivale* is a deliberately paced show, which tested the patience of many audience members and might inspire some viewers to fast-forward certain episodes. But each contains a different piece of a large puzzle, and patience is rewarded by Season 2.

EXTRAS: There are three insightful commentaries with the show's creative team, and a featurette that details how the set and costume designers so accurately re-created the 1930s Dust Bowl.

C

Chappelle's Show (2003–2005)

Season 1 Uncensored (12 episodes on 2 discs): ★ ★ ★ ★
Season 2 Uncensored (13 episodes on 3 discs): ★ ★ ★ ★ ½

Paramount Home Video
Video: Full-Frame; Audio: Dolby Digital 2.0

You'd win a lot of bets asking people to name the series with the best-selling TV-on-DVD sets in the brief history of the genre. To describe *Chappelle's Show*'s ascendance to this market domination as shocking is no knock on the show's quality, but how can one not be amazed that this Comedy Central series is outselling everything from *The X-Files* to *Seinfeld*?

Perhaps audiences have responded to Chappelle's audacity, with his edgy stand-up routines and sketches like "National Geographic's Third-World Girls Gone Wild." Though some of the scatological segments and the Make-A-Wish bit with the dying child cross the line of good taste, it's refreshing to have somebody who's not afraid to take those chances.

GREAT MOMENTS: Season 1: The "Real World" parody; "Ask a Gay Guy With Mario Cantone"; Season 2: The Racial Draft; Chappelle's road trip with Wayne Brady.

FAST-FORWARD: Season 2: Paul Mooney as soothsayer "Negrodamus."

EXTRAS: Season 1: Deleted scenes/gag reel; "Ask a Black Dude" with Paul Mooney featurette; Commentaries by Dave Chappelle and series co-creator Neal Brennan; Season 2: New stand-up material from Chappelle; deleted scenes/gag reel; Rick James interview.

Charles in Charge (1984–1990)

The Complete First Season (22 episodes on 3 discs): ★ ★ ★ ½

Universal Home Video
Video: Full-Frame; Audio: Dolby Digital 2.0

For a paycheck and a place to live, college student Scott Baio takes care of three kids with busy parents. The first year of *Charles in Charge* aired on network television, and had Charles looking after the Pembroke children. These episodes aren't as well remembered as the later syndicated shows, which introduced a different family and, more memorably, Nicole Eggert. Fortunately (or unfortunately, depending on whom you ask), Willie Aames's Buddy Lembeck is present for the entire series as Charles's constant sidekick.

GREAT MOMENTS: Charles juggles his first date with the beautiful Gwendolyn Pierce while trying to make sure Lila behaves in the pilot. The Season 2 premiere, "Amityville," is offered as a bonus feature.

FAST-FORWARD: "Make over your best friend" episodes had already gotten old by the time *Charles in Charge* got there, but "A Date with Enid" tried anyway. You can zoom by.

EXTRAS: "The Great '80s TV Flashback" featurette includes a brief interview with Julie Cobb (Jill Pembroke); bonus episode from Season 2.

Charlie Brown/Peanuts Specials

The Peanuts Classic Holiday Collection (6 episodes on 3 discs): ★ ★ ★ ★ ★
Be My Valentine, Charlie Brown: ★ ★ ★
A Charlie Brown Christmas: ★ ★ ★ ★
A Charlie Brown Thanksgiving: ★ ★ ★ ★
A Charlie Brown Valentine: ★ ★
I Want a Dog for Christmas, Charlie Brown: ★ ★ ½
It's the Easter Beagle, Charlie Brown: ★ ★ ★
It's the Great Pumpkin, Charlie Brown: ★ ★ ★ ★
It's the Pied Piper, Charlie Brown: ★ ★
Lucy Must Be Traded, Charlie Brown: ★ ★

Paramount Home Video
Video: Full-Frame; Audio: Dolby Digital Mono

The Classic Holiday Collection offers the three most-coveted shows: *A Charlie Brown Christmas*; *It's the Great Pumpkin, Charlie Brown*; and *A Charlie Brown Thanksgiving*, classics all, along with three later specials themed to the same holidays, which most will watch once and promptly forget. It's both confusing and disappointing that the below-average outing *I Want A Dog for Christmas* contains a behind-the-scenes look at the making of *A Charlie Brown Christmas*, featuring interviews with the show's original cast and producers. Obviously this is an extra that should have accompanied the actual show. The later specials lack the innocent charm of the early efforts, but kids will probably love them all.

GREAT MOMENTS: Linus explains "what Christmas is all about" in *A Charlie Brown Christmas*; Sally demands restitution in *It's the Great Pumpkin, Charlie Brown.*

FAST-FORWARD: *It's the Pied Piper, Charlie Brown*—any Peanuts show where adults talk rather than squawk just ain't canon.

EXTRAS: "The Making of *A Charlie Brown Christmas*" (*I Want a Dog for Christmas*); A Charles Schulz retrospective with an interview and a timeline tracing the development of the original comic strip is attached to *It's the Pied Piper, Charlie Brown.*

Charlie's Angels (1976–1981)

The Complete First Season (23 episodes on 5 discs): ★ ★ ★ ★

The Complete Second Season (26 episodes on 5 discs): ★ ★ ★ ★

The Best of Charlie's Angels (5 episodes on 1 disc): ★ ★ ★

Angels Under Cover (2 episodes on 1 disc): ★

See also: *The Greatest '70s Cop Shows*

Columbia Tristar Home Video

Video: Full-Frame; Audio: Mono

To some, *Charlie's Angels* symbolized the ultimate objectification of women; others felt the series empowered the female sex and broke new ground, in its portrayals of lady detectives who used both smarts and sexuality to solve their cases. But while the debate raged in the 1970s, everybody was watching. An overnight phenomenon, *Charlie's Angels* landed its trio of comely stars on the cover of *Time* magazine after fewer than a dozen episodes, its first season drawing ratings unequaled except by such special events as the Super Bowl.

What some defenders of virtue once criticized as sleazy looks positively wholesome now when compared to just about anything on MTV or the E! channel, and the show itself holds up well, a result of the eye-candy appeal and camaraderie of stars Jaclyn Smith, Kate Jackson, Farrah Fawcett, and, beginning with Season 2, Cheryl Ladd.

The episodes look and sound terrific on the two season sets released thus far. A couple of moments were snipped from the Season 2 opener, "Angels in Paradise," but thankfully none of them involved Cheryl Ladd in a bikini. The "best of" disc is an adequate sampler for those undecided about springing for the season sets, but since all five shows are from the first season, the "best" claim is dubious. *Angels Under Cover* offers two first-season shows, neither one representative of the series at its finest.

GREAT MOMENTS: Season 1: "Angels in Chains," set in a women's prison, remains the series' most famous episode. The clarity of the DVD image finally allows the more pathetic among us to freeze-frame the moment when one of Farrah's breasts is visible in an overhead shot; the skateboard chase in "Consenting Adults"; Season 2: the two-parter "Angels on Ice," featuring guest appearances by Jim Backus and Phil Silvers; the beauty pageant send-up "Pretty Angels All in a Row"; Kris's Swedish accent in "The Jade Trap."

C

FAST-FORWARD: "Game, Set, Death" and "Angel Blues," both from Season 2.

EXTRAS: Season 1: *Angels Forever* featurette.

Charmed (1998–)

The Complete First Season (22 episodes on 6 discs): ★ ★ ★
The Complete Second Season (22 episodes on 6 discs): ★ ★ ★ ½
The Complete Third Season (22 episodes on 6 discs): ★ ★ ★ ½
The Complete Fourth Season (22 episodes on 6 discs): ★ ★ ★
The Complete Fifth Season (21 episodes on 6 discs): ★ ★ ★

Paramount Home Video
Video: Full-Frame; Audio: Dolby Digital 2.0

Aaron Spelling had an impressive track record with shows about sexy trios (*Charlie's Angels, The Mod Squad*), so maybe it was only a matter of time before a producer credited with a magic touch created a series about three magical characters. *Charmed* may have started as *Buffy*-lite, but it quickly built a fan following that had been impatient for DVDs since 2003. But when Season 1 finally made it to market, the quality of the transfers took some heat from videophiles, and for such a recent series there was certainly every reason to expect better picture quality. Subsequent sets arrived looking slightly better.

Piper opens a nightclub in Season 2, opening the series to such musical guest stars as Dishwalla, the Cranberries, Paula Cole, and the Goo Goo Dolls; though Paramount might anger fans for its lack of extras and non-skippable trailers, at least they managed to keep all the original music.

GREAT MOMENTS: Season 1: Shannen Doherty acquires a split personality (insert your own joke here) in "Which Prue Is It, Anyway?"; Finola Hughes plays the witchy trio's mom in the time-travel adventure "That '70s Episode"; Season 2: The Cranberries perform in "She's a Man, Baby, a Man!"; Season 3: The Halliwells' supernatural secret is exposed in "All Hell Breaks Loose."

FAST-FORWARD: Season 2: The girls lose their powers, and Piper wonders if she's better that way, in "How to Make a Quilt Out of Americans."

EXTRAS: None.

Cheers (1982–1993)

Season 1 (22 episodes on 4 discs): ★ ★ ★ ★
Season 2 (22 episodes on 4 discs): ★ ★ ★ ★ ★
Season 3 (25 episodes on 4 discs): ★ ★ ★ ★ ½
Season 4 (26 episodes on 4 discs): ★ ★ ★ ★ ★
Season 5 (26 episodes on 4 discs): ★ ★ ★ ★ ★
Season 6 (25 episodes on 4 discs): ★ ★ ★ ½
Season 7 (22 episodes on 4 discs): ★ ★ ★

Paramount Home Video
Video: Full-Frame; Audio: Dolby Digital 2.0

It's a little ditty about Sam and Diane, and let's be glad *Cheers* came along at a time when the networks could still be patient with a new series, 'cause there wasn't anybody watching the first season. Critical acclaim and a slew of Emmy nominations brought the audience around, and once they pulled up a barstool they stayed for a decade. There will be those who will only collect the Diane Chambers years on DVD, and that's your privilege, but while *Cheers* didn't handle Diane's departure very well, the casting of Emmy-winner Kirstie Alley helped the series avoid that fatal shark jump.

GREAT MOMENTS: Season 1: Harry Anderson's first appearance as a con man in "Sam at Eleven"; Diane competes in a barmaid contest in "No Contest": Sam and Diane finally hook up with one of TV's most famous first kisses in "Show Down, Part 2"; Season 3: Diane returns to help Sam, who's started drinking again, in "Rebound, Parts 1 & 2"; Season 5: Diane's "derivative of Godard" documentary about Woody's life at Cheers in "Cheers: The Motion Picture"; Season 6: Norm and Rebecca bond in "Paint Your Office"; Season 7: Woody performs "The Kelly Song" in "The Gift of the Woodi."

FAST-FORWARD: Every appearance of Nick Tortelli.

EXTRAS: Season 1: Ted Danson interview; Season 2: Gag reel; Season 3: "Nicholas Colasanto: His Final Season" features tributes from Ted Danson, George Wendt, and Rhea Perlman; "Cheers Bar Tour" featurette. The first three season sets also contain themed clip packages that can be safely skipped.

Cheyenne (1955–1963)

The Complete First Season (15 episodes on 5 discs): ★ ★ ★ ½

Warner Bros. Home Video

Video: Full-Frame; Audio: Dolby Digital 1.0

C

What was the point of all those single-disc "Television Favorites" releases of vintage TV series? To help Warner Bros. gauge fan response on which shows deserved a more comprehensive treatment on DVD. Proving there's still an audience for classic Westerns, *Cheyenne* became the first of the "Favorites" to graduate to season sets. Clint Walker starred as Cheyenne Bodie, a quick-on-the-draw adventurer who wandered the West in the days following the Civil War, accompanied by his faithful sidekick, Smitty (L.Q. Jones). Don't get used to him—he's gone by Season 2.

GREAT MOMENTS: A mother and daughter compete for Cheyenne's affection in the twisted-revenge tale "The Storm Riders"; Michael Landon plays a young soldier in "Decision."

FAST-FORWARD: Nothing.

EXTRAS: Documentary "The Lonely Gunfighter: The Legacy of *Cheyenne*," featuring a new interview with Clint Walker.

The Cisco Kid (1950–1956)

Volume 1 (20 episodes on 4 discs): ★ ★
Volume 2 (20 episodes on 4 discs): ★ ★
Volume 3 (20 episodes on 4 discs): ★ ★
Volume 4 (20 episodes on 4 discs): ★ ★

MPI Home Video

Video: Full-Frame; Audio: Dolby Digital 1.0

Television's first successful syndicated series, *The Cisco Kid* was a Sunday-morning staple in many US markets for more than two decades after its original six-year run. The popular kiddy Western was filmed in color at a time when nobody had a color TV set, and the process was so primitive that the unrestored episodes now look washed out and blurry, even on DVD. The MPI sets each collect twenty episodes in no particular order, and any one is as good—or silly—as the next. Kudos to Leo Carillo, though, who played Pancho opposite Duncan Renaldo as Cisco, and did much of his own riding and many action scenes, having already passed his seventieth birthday.

GREAT MOMENTS: All anybody remembers are the opening narration ("Here's adventure! Here's romance!") and the fadeout exchange, "Oh, Pancho," "Ohhhhh, Ceeee-scooo!"

FAST-FORWARD: Nada.

EXTRAS: None.

C

Clarissa Explains It All (1991–1994)

Season 1 (15 episodes on 2 discs): ★ ★ ½
Season 2 (13 episodes on 2 discs): ★ ★

Paramount/Nickelodeon
Video: Full-Frame; Audio: Dolby Digital 2.0

From the first wave of SNICK shows, a Saturday Nickelodeon programming block that bridged the gap between the network's afternoon kids' series and Nick at Nite, *Clarissa Explains It All* quickly emerged as the most popular, though its appeal didn't extend beyond its target tweener demographic. Melissa Joan Hart was better than her material, but by paying homage to the trendy teen, the 1991 series now seems more dated in its clothing and pop-culture references than shows that left the air decades earlier. One oddity in the Season 1 set is the use of a later season's opening credits, in which Clarissa, Sam, and even little demon-spawn Ferguson look much older than they do in the actual episodes.

GREAT MOMENTS: Clarissa's asides to the viewers at home remain the most memorable aspect of the series.

FAST-FORWARD: Front-loaded trailers for other Paramount DVD releases; Ferguson's at his most obnoxious in "Brain Drain."

EXTRAS: Season 1: Melissa Joan Hart on *MTV Cribs*; vintage Nickelodeon bumpers.

Clerks: The Animated Series (2000)

Clerks: Uncensored (6 episodes on 1 disc): ★ ★ ★ ★

Buena Vista Home Entertainment
Video: Full-Frame; Audio: Dolby Digital 2.0

Cult-favorite director Kevin Smith gets animated in this underrated, short-lived spin-off from his *Clerks* movie franchise. Only two episodes aired on television before ABC pulled the plug. The animators later provided an extra short for Smith's *Clerks X* DVD, and an animated feature, *Clerks: Sell Out*, is still in the works.

GREAT MOMENTS: Episode 4: Jay and Silent Bob sue the Quick Stop after an accident; the Honorable Judge Reinhold presides; Episode 6: An all-nighter includes parodies of *Freaks* and *The Matrix*, plus ABC's special version of hell.

C

FAST-FORWARD: Episode 2: A flashback episode isn't that funny if you just watched the one that preceded it.

EXTRAS: DVD intros by Kevin Smith and Jason Mewes; episode commentaries with Smith, the stars, and producers offering often-hilarious anecdotes. Some names have been censored to protect the innocent.

Coach (1989–1997)

The First Season (13 episodes on 2 discs): ★ ★ ★

Universal Home Video

Video: Full-Frame; Audio: Dolby Digital 2.0

Future generations will enjoy spirited debates about how *Coach* lasted nine seasons, and will conclude that it had less to do with star Craig T. Nelson, engaging as he was in the title role, than with the folks around him. Second-banana Jerry Van Dyke deserved some good TV karma after he turned down *Gilligan's Island* for *My Mother the Car*, and Shelley Fabares is a national treasure. The first season was released in both a standard set and a limited-edition Playbook Package, which sports a pigskin-covered DVD box. C'mon, Universal, it's *Coach*. While it's nice to see you make the effort, especially since it doesn't happen very often, save the special stuff for shows that people are passionate about.

GREAT MOMENTS: Christine meets Hayden's ex-wife in "Parents' Weekend"; Hayden must choose between benching a player and a winning record for the season in "Whose Team Is It, Anyway?"

FAST-FORWARD: Nothing.

EXTRAS: The Season 2 episode "Homewreckers."

Columbo (1971–1993)

Season 1 (9 episodes on 5 discs): ★ ★ ★ ★ ★
Season 2 (8 episodes on 4 discs): ★ ★ ★ ★ ★
Season 3 (8 episodes on 2 discs): ★ ★ ★ ★ ★
Season 4 (10 episodes on 2 discs): ★ ★ ★ ★ ★

Universal Home Video
Video: Full-Frame; Audio: Mono (Season 1); Dolby Stereo (Seasons 2 & 3)

C

Of all the gumshoes that ever cracked a mystery on a TV series, only Columbo has earned the distinction as television's one true contribution to the detective genre, a character worthy to join the ranks of Holmes, Poirot, Dupin, and Ellery Queen. Created by Richard Levinson and William Link for the rotating anthology series *The NBC Mystery Movie*, the stories broke every rule right out of the gate by showing the criminal committing the crime in the first act; no mystery, no phony suspects, no false leads. The audience knows whodunit from the start, and then watches as Lieutenant Columbo, played by five-time Emmy-winner Peter Falk, tries to figure out what the audience already knows.

The formula worked because of the way the rumpled detective went about his job. He pesters his prime suspect, sometimes giving a false sense of security by playing the befuddled cop who just wants to wrap up the case and go home to his wife. We're not always sure exactly when Columbo knows he's got his man, but sometimes there's a moment when you see the flick of the light switch in the detective's eyes, and then the challenge for the viewer is to discover how Columbo put the pieces together. The unique story structure made for a devilishly difficult show to write, which makes the series' impressive track record of memorable cases all the more astonishing.

GREAT MOMENTS: Season 1: "Murder by the Book," written by Steven Bochco and directed by Steven Spielberg; Robert Culp and Ray Milland guest-star in the fiendishly clever "Death Lends a Hand"; Season 2: Columbo goes to London in "Dagger of the Mind"; Season 3: Johnny Cash plays a murderous minister in "Swan Song"; "Any Old Port in a Storm" might be *Columbo*'s finest moment; Season 4: Columbo solves a murder on a cruise ship in "Troubled Waters."

FAST-FORWARD: "Étude in Black," a ninety-minute script awkwardly stretched to fill a two-hour time slot (Season 2).

EXTRAS: Season 3 includes an episode of *Mrs. Columbo*, but that's it. A shame, as it would be fascinating to hear a Peter Falk commentary on his most famous creation.

Combat (1962–1967)

Season 1—Campaign 1 (16 episodes on 4 discs): ★ ★ ★ ★
Season 1—Campaign 2 (16 episodes on 4 discs): ★ ★ ★ ★
Season 2—Mission 1 (16 episodes on 4 discs): ★ ★ ★ ★
Season 2—Mission 2 (16 episodes on 4 discs): ★ ★ ★ ★
Season 3—Operation 1 (16 episodes on 4 discs): ★ ★ ★ ★
Season 3—Operation 2 (16 episodes on 4 discs): ★ ★ ★ ★
Season 4—Conflict 1 (16 episodes on 4 discs): ★ ★ ★ ★
Season 4—Conflict 2 (15 episodes on 4 discs): ★ ★ ★ ★
Season 5—Invasion 1 (13 episodes on 4 discs): ★ ★ ★ ★
Season 5—Invasion 2 (12 episodes on 4 discs): ★ ★ ★

Image Entertainment

Video: Full-Frame; Audio: Dolby Digital Mono

Mention *Combat* in a game of TV word association, and the response you'll probably get is "mud." No series splattered more of it in five years, as the men of King Company gave viewers a grunt's-eye view of the European Theater in World War II. Stalwart regulars Vic Morrow and Rick Jason were joined on their missions by an amazing lineup of guest stars. If you wanted to play cowboy in a good Western, you went to *Gunsmoke*; if you wanted to play soldier in an authentic military drama, you signed on for a tour of duty with *Combat*. Among those who answered the call were Robert Duvall, Lee Marvin, Charles Bronson, James Coburn, Mickey Rooney, and John Cassavettes.

Given the series' sporadic (at best) appearances in wide syndication over the past three decades, it's a pleasant surprise to find the DVD sets containing more than just the original shows. One drawback: the episodes seem to be time-compressed. Since this is DVD and there's no reason to cut their running time to squeeze in more commercials, the only explanation is the preferable print quality of these versions. It's a minor but not fatal irritant.

GREAT MOMENTS: Season 1—*Campaign 1*: the men of King Company prepare for the D-Day invasion in the pilot, "A Day in June"; *Season 2—Mission 1*: Lee Marvin plays a demolition expert in "Bridge at Chalon"; James Caan plays a German officer who matches wits with Sergeant Saunders in "Anatomy of a Patrol"; *Season 4—Conflict 2*: Hanley sets out on a particularly perilous mission in "Hills Are for Heroes."

FAST-FORWARD: Nothing.

EXTRAS: Each set offers a "Notes, Oddities, and Bloopers" feature, as well as commentary tracks by the cast, various guest stars, and creative personnel.

The "Memories of Combat" documentary, included in the *Season 1—Campaign 1* set, includes interviews with directors Robert Altman and Richard Donner.

C

The Commish (1991–1995)

Season 1 (21 episodes on 6 discs): ★ ★
Season 2 (22 episodes on 3 discs): ★ ★ ½
The Best of Season 1 (4 episodes on 1 disc): ★ ★

Anchor Bay
Video: Full-Frame; Audio: Dolby Digital 2.0

While it's not true that the only way to tell *The Commish* and *The Shield* apart is Michael Chiklis's hairline, there should be a statute of limitations on how many cops an actor can play in one career—and no peeps out of you either, Dennis Franz. The characters are certainly different—Tony Scali's a teddy bear compared to *The Shield*'s Vic Mackey, and isn't nearly as interesting as a result. Script quality varies widely, though the Season 2 shows fare better thanks to a more interesting supporting cast, led by Melinda McGraw.

GREAT MOMENTS: Season 1: Tony deals with a mysterious arson case and a beautiful widow in "Sex, Lies, and Kerosene"; Season 2: The race-against-time adventure "The Sharp Pinch."

FAST-FORWARD: Season 2: "Adventures in the Skin Trade," a clichéd primetime take on the film *Hardcore.*

EXTRAS: Season 1: Cast interviews.

The Cosby Show (1984–1992)

Season 1 (24 episodes on 4 discs): ★ ★
Season 2 (25 episodes on 4 discs): ★ ★ ★ ★ ★

Urban Works
Video: Full-Frame; Audio: Dolby Digital 2.0

One of the saddest cases of a five-star series sabotaged by a poor DVD treatment, hence the two-star rating. *The Cosby Show* deserves serious consideration as one of the ten best situation comedies in the history of the medium. The show shepherded NBC's rise to ratings dominance and the beginning of the "Must See TV" era that continued through *Seinfeld* and

Friends. Beyond smart writing and the magical presence of Bill Cosby, the series offered a matter-of-fact portrayal of a prosperous, professional African-American family at a time when such characters rarely appeared in primetime. The decision to release edited versions of the first-season episodes (contrary to the distributor's own press release) is as inexplicable as it is inexcusable. Fortunately, the situation was corrected by Urban Works with Season 2.

C

GREAT MOMENTS: Season 1: Cliff's Monopoly money discussion with Theo in the pilot episode remains the series' most famous scene; the funeral for Rudy's goldfish in "Mr. Fish"; Season 2: The classic "Night Time Is the Right Time" performance in "Happy Anniversary"; Stevie Wonder appears in "A Touch of Wonder."

FAST-FORWARD: Nothing.

EXTRAS: None.

Coupling (2000–)

The Complete First Season (6 episodes on 1 disc): ★ ★ ★ ★
The Complete Second Season (9 episodes on 2 discs): ★ ★ ★ ★ ½
The Complete Third Season (7 episodes on 2 discs): ★ ★ ★ ★
The Complete Fourth Season (6 episodes on 2 discs): ★ ★ ½

BBC Video
Video: Anamorphic Widescreen; Audio: Dolby Digital Stereo

It's a little bit *Friends* and a little bit *Sex and the City*, but *Coupling* also deserves praise for its own original take on the contemporary dating game. Viewers rightly rejected the NBC adaptation but should embrace the original BBC series, which benefits from expert casting and the innovative scripts of creator Stephen Moffat. It also helps that when dirty things are said with a British accent, to most Americans they sound endearing rather than vulgar.

It's arguable whether *Coupling* survived the fourth-season loss of Richard Coyle as Jeff, the one character out of the sextet of three guys and three girls that the series could least afford to lose. Jeff's off-kilter, *Seinfeld*-ian explorations of the mysteries of woman are such an inspired blend of writing and delivery that it's amazing the other cast members kept a straight face. The outtakes on the Season 3 set reveal how often the actors failed.

One unavoidable irritant in these sets is the scenes from each episode that play on the MENU screens, which are annoying for those who'd rather not have the sneak preview.

GREAT MOMENTS: Season 1: Steve's attempt to describe the plot of the porno flick *Lesbian Spank Inferno* in "Inferno"; Season 2: Jeff tries chatting up a girl on a train in "The Man with Two Legs"; Susan's dinnertime revenge on Steve in "Gotcha"; the mistaken identity farce "The End of the Line"; Season 3: The surprise revelation at the end of "Perhaps, Perhaps, Perhaps."

FAST-FORWARD: Outside of a *Reservoir Dogs* visual gag, Season 1's "Sex, Death, and Nudity" can be safely skipped; Jeff fans might want to forget Season 4 altogether.

EXTRAS: Season 1: cast interviews; Season 2: Cast and creator commentaries; Season 3: Commentaries and outtakes; Season 4: Outtakes; commentaries; interview with Richard Mylan; featurette "From Script to Screen."

Crime Story (1986–1988)

Season 1 (22 episodes on 5 discs): ★ ★ ½
Season 2 (22 episodes on 4 discs): ★ ★ ½
The Pilot: ★ ★ ½

Anchor Bay
Video: Full-Frame; Audio: Mono

Ask anyone about TV shows set in Las Vegas, and most will skip right from Dan Tanna in the '70s to the *CSI* team thirty years later. And in doing so they omit the one series that best captured Sin City in its halcyon, Mob-controlled 1960s heyday, when the Rat Pack ruled the Strip and the hotels didn't look like God's miniature golf course. *Crime Story*, Michael Mann's second series after a phenomenal debut with *Miami Vice*, put a sharkskin-suit-clad spin on *The Fugitive*, with its saga of relentless cop Mike Torello (Dennis Farina), and his obsession with apprehending ruthless gangster Ray Luca (Anthony Denison).

The show merits a four-star rating, but the DVD set, sadly, does not. Even if one overlooks the absence of chapter indexing and the incidental music changes on a series where music played a pivotal role (*Crime Story* returned Del Shannon's "Runaway" to the pop charts), audio and video border on the abysmal. Fans will want it anyway but this was a show that deserved better.

GREAT MOMENTS: Season 1: A then-unknown Julia Roberts plays an abused teenager in "Survivor"; the legendary Miles Davis appears as (what else?) a trumpet player in "The War"; "Pursuit of a Wanted Felon," the first episode set in Las Vegas; Season 2: Luca returns to Vegas in "Shockwaves"; Billy Zane and Laura San Giacomo appear in "Protected Witness."

FAST-FORWARD: Season 1: The season review show "Crime Pays."

EXTRAS: None.

CSI (2001–)

The Complete First Season (23 episodes on 6 discs): ★ ★ ★ ★
The Complete Second Season (23 episodes on 6 discs): ★ ★ ★ ★ ½
The Complete Third Season (23 episodes on 6 discs): ★ ★ ★ ★ ½
The Complete Fourth Season (23 episodes on 6 discs): ★ ★ ★ ★
The Complete Fifth Season (24 episodes on 7 discs): ★ ★ ★ ★

C

Paramount Home Video

Video: Full-Frame (Season 1); Anamorphic Widescreen (Seasons 2–5); Audio: Dolby Digital 2.0 (Season 1); Dolby Digital 5.1 (Seasons 2–5)

Many shows sport parental guidance cautions about mature language and behavior, but *CSI* deserves a special warning of its own: "Do not watch while eating." Set in Las Vegas before that became overdone, this series about crime-scene forensic investigators debuted with little support; CBS hoped it wouldn't scare too many viewers away from *The Agency*, the show the network was really excited about. But *The Agency* died quicker than one of Grissom's autopsy subjects, while *CSI* became the number-one show in the country. Nothing against William Petersen, but there hasn't been a series lead with such limited emotional range since Chuck Norris hung up his Ranger's badge. No matter—*CSI* was both well written and kinky from day one, and you don't go broke in television with either of those attributes.

GREAT MOMENTS: Season 1: The sordid saga of the Collins family in "Blood Drops"; a mysterious murder on an airplane en route to Vegas in "Unfriendly Skies"; Season 3: The tragic consequences of mob violence in "Blood Lust"; Season 4: "Turn of the Screws," an outstanding showcase for Marg Helgenberger; Season 5: "Grave Danger," written and directed by Quentin Tarantino.

FAST-FORWARD: The autopsy scenes, if you're squeamish; Season 4: "Bad Words"—kid-genius stories rarely work.

EXTRAS: Season 1: "People Lie . . . But the Evidence Never Does" featurette; "Who Are You?" music video; Season 2: Writer/producer/director commentaries; featurettes "*CSI* Shooting Locations," "Tools of the Trade," "The Making of a Hit"; Season 3: Writer/producer/director commentaries; featurettes "The *CSI* Tour: Police Station," "Making it Real," "The Writer's Room," and "*CSI* Moves Into Season 3"; Season 4: "The Evolution of an Episode from Concept to Completion" featurette.

CSI: Miami (2002–)

The Complete First Season (25 episodes on 7 discs): ★ ★ ★ ½

The Complete Second Season (24 episodes on 7 discs): ★ ★ ★ ½

Paramount Home Video

Video: Anamorphic Widescreen; Audio: Dolby Digital 5.1

The first attempt to franchise the *CSI* formula mixes the science-geek appeal of its Vegas predecessor with the sexy sights and sounds of South Beach. David Caruso returns to TV after his premature departure from *NYPD Blue*, having apparently attended the Don Johnson school of dramatic sunglasses removal. The casting of his fellow *Blue* alum Kim Delaney seemed like a good idea at the time, but she was gone before Season 1 was half over. With its sun-splashed setting and Emmy-winning cinematography, *CSI: Miami* is a show that always looks good—especially so on the widescreen DVD sets—even when the cases aren't as appealing as the photogenic forensic detectives who solve them.

GREAT MOMENTS: Season 1: Amber Tamblyn plays a juvenile delinquent far removed from *Joan of Arcadia* in "Camp Fear"; Season 2: The compelling first half of "Money for Nothing."

FAST-FORWARD: Nothing.

EXTRAS: Both seasons feature several brief featurettes on various aspects of the series, and audio commentaries by writers, producers, and crew.

CSI: NY (2004–)

The Complete First Season (24 episodes on 7 discs): ★ ★

Paramount Home Video

Video: Anamorphic Widescreen; Audio: Dolby Digital 5.1

The third installment in the *CSI* franchise tests the limits of one's interest in forensic science. There are only so many ways to make a corpse exciting, so you may find your thoughts wandering to other subjects, like how ideal Melina Kanakaredes would have been as Wonder Woman about ten years ago, and why a slumming Gary Sinise would forego his distinguished film work for this dull procedural. No more *CSI*s, please—just 'cause you can do an autopsy is no reason to beat a dead horse.

GREAT MOMENTS: The Yankees–Red Sox rivalry turns deadly in "The Closer."

FAST-FORWARD: Nothing.

EXTRAS: A set tour, and four featurettes.

Curb Your Enthusiasm (2000–)

The Complete First Season (10 episodes on 2 discs): ★ ★ ★ ½
The Complete Second Season (10 episodes on 2 discs): ★ ★ ★
The Complete Third Season (10 episodes on 2 discs): ★ ★ ★
The Complete Fourth Season (10 episodes on 2 discs): ★ ★ ★

HBO Home Video
Video: Full-Frame; Audio: Dolby Digital Stereo

C

For those who thought the *Seinfeld* characters were too kind and benevolent, here's *Seinfeld* creator Larry David playing himself, a wealthy and talented TV writer who has a life that anyone would envy but is mostly miserable in it. This is comedy that makes one squirm as much as laugh, especially during the multiple shouting matches in every episode. However, the casting of winsome Cheryl Hines as Larry's long-suffering wife gives hope to balding manic-depressives everywhere.

A "Your Mileage May Vary" series if there ever was one, *Curb Your Enthusiasm* is a show that will rank on some viewers' lists of top-ten sitcoms of all time, and be entirely bereft of laughs for others. Much is made of the *Seinfeld* connection, particularly during a Season 2 story arc in which Larry pitches a new show idea to Jason Alexander and Julia Louis-Dreyfus, but it's certainly possible to like *Seinfeld* and think *Curb* goes too far. However, they share one common trait in that none of the characters actually mature or learn anything, so one season, for good or ill, is much the same as the next.

GREAT MOMENTS: Season 1: The flirtation between Larry and Mary Steenburgen in "Ted and Mary"; Season 2: Larry debates the no-costume, no-candy rule of Halloween with two teenage delinquents in "Trick or Treat"; A Larry David–Richard Lewis kvetch-a-thon (plus Cheryl Hines in a bikini!) in "The Thong"; Season 4: Larry picks up a prostitute to help him beat the traffic in "The Car Pool Lane"; Jerry Seinfeld, Nathan Lane, and Anne Bancroft guest in "Opening Night."

FAST-FORWARD: "The Special Section" (Season 3) is tasteless even by *Curb Your Enthusiasm* standards.

EXTRAS: Season 1: Commentaries by Larry David, Cheryl Hines, Jeff Garlin, and Bob Weide; interview with Larry David from HBO's *On the Record*; Season 3: "Favorite Scenes" and "Stop and Chat" featurettes.

The Daily Show (1996–)

Indecision 2004 (10 episodes on 3 discs): ★ ★ ★ ½

Paramount Home Video

Video: Full-Frame; Audio: Dolby Digital 2.0

For decades, news and entertainment on television originated from separate entities with divergent agendas. But the wall between them had been crumbling for years until it finally collapsed in 1999, when Jon Stewart replaced Craig Kilborn as host of *The Daily Show. Indecision 2004* collects ten episodes from the nightly news—with a twist series that focused on the 2004 presidential campaigns of George Bush and John Kerry. Will such topical humor still be funny five years from now? Probably—if you're a Democrat.

GREAT MOMENTS: A feature on midterm elections modeled after *Schoolhouse Rock*; the interview with Senator John McCain; the coverage of the first Bush-Kerry presidential debate.

FAST-FORWARD: Nothing.

EXTRAS: Bonus segments; featurette "Requiem for a Show That Was Daily," by Stephen Colbert.

Dallas (1978–1991)

The Complete First and Second Seasons (29 episodes on 5 discs): ★ ★ ★ ★

The Complete Third Season (25 episodes on 5 discs): ★ ★ ★ ★ ½

The Complete Fourth Season (23 episodes on 4 discs): ★ ★ ★ ★

Warner Home Video

Video: Full-Frame; Audio: Dolby Digital 2.0

"A limited series with a limited future" was *Variety*'s assessment of *Dallas* in its first year; more than 350 episodes later, the series had not only become a global sensation but was influencing the medium as much as landmarks like *I Love Lucy* and *Hill Street Blues.* The "Who Shot J.R.?" cliffhanger gripped the nation in the summer of 1980 to an extent that it's hard to imagine any series achieving now. The DVD treatment is serviceable, if not befitting a billionaire Texas oil magnate, or a show that was *the* television phenomenon of its day.

GREAT MOMENTS: Seasons 1 and 2: Pamela meets the Ewings after marrying Bobby in "Digger's Daughter"; the first of the annual Ewing barbeques in

"Barbeque"; the fate of Julie Grey in "The Red File"; Season 3: J.R. meets Kristin (as played by Mary Crosby) in "The Silent Killer"; Barbara Bel Geddes received an Emmy Award for her moving work in the two-part episode "Mastectomy"; the season-finale cliffhanger is the most famous in TV history; Season 4: Kristin's fate is revealed in "Missing Heir."

FAST-FORWARD: Seasons 1 and 2: The romance between Ray Krebbs and a miscast Kate Mulgrew as country-singer Garnett McGee; Season 4: Skip the ongoing travails of Lucy's modeling career and the photographer with the fatal attraction.

EXTRAS: Seasons 1 and 2: "*Dallas* Reunion" featurette; commentaries by Larry Hagman, Charlene Tilton, and series creator David Jacobs; Season 3: "Who Shot J.R.?" featurette; commentaries by Patrick Duffy and Linda Gray.

The Dame Edna Experience (1987–1989)

The Complete Series 1 (6 episodes on 2 discs): ★ ★ ★ ★
The Complete Series 2 (7 episodes on 2 discs): ★ ★ ★ ★ ½
The Complete Collection (13 episodes on 5 discs): ★ ★ ★ ★ ½
The Christmas Collection (2 episodes on 1 disc): ★ ★ ★ ★

BBC Video
Video: Full-Frame; Audio: Dolby Digital 2.0

It's hard to explain Dame Edna to the uninitiated. She's an Australian housewife and megastar, with purple hair and glitter glasses who calls everyone "possum." She is portrayed by comedian Barry Humphries, but this is no Vegas-style drag routine. Edna Everage is a fully realized persona that exists entirely separate from her creator. Watching these hugely popular British talk shows, you'll forget within seconds about the man in the dress and just enjoy Edna's comic timing and devastating wit, as she cuts down A-list celebrity guests with a smile.

The "Audience with Dame Edna" shows are listed as an extra in the *Complete Series 1 & 2* and *The Christmas Collection*, but these sixty-minute specials are actually the gems of each DVD release. Facing a celebrity audience (though most of the celebs will be unknown to American viewers), Edna proves that there's nothing like a Dame.

GREAT MOMENTS: Series 1: Edna meets Charlton Heston; Series 2: Interviews with Lauren Bacall, Liza Minnelli, and Douglas Fairbanks, Jr.

FAST-FORWARD: Nothing, possums.

EXTRAS: Series 1: "An Audience with Dame Edna Everage" special; the talk show *Ester*, featuring Dame Edna; interview with Barry Humphries; archival footage; Series 2: "Another Audience with Dame Edna Everage"; interviews; an interview with Barry Humphries; *Christmas Collection*: The final "Audience with Dame Edna" special; Dame Edna's Christmas address.

Dark Angel (2000–2002)

Season 1 (21 episodes on 6 discs): ★ ★ ½
Season 2 (21 episodes on 6 discs): ★ ★

D

20th Century-Fox
Video: Full-Frame; Audio: Dolby Digital Surround

Dark Angel was branded as a *Buffy* clone before its first episode aired, and in retrospect that dismissal turned out to be too high a compliment. Creator-producer James Cameron had impeccable sci-fi credentials (*Aliens*, *Terminator 2: Judgment Day*) but his futuristic story of a genetically engineered hottie on the run from her creators never established a satisfying or even credible mix of character, action, and drama. As Max, gorgeous Jessica Alba had the smolder-and-pout aspects of the job down pat, but given her porcelain-doll face you'd never put smart money on her in a fight, even if the scripts had her winning.

Max's battles with the soldiers of Manticore, the government organization that created her, spanned the entire first season. The second and final year had Max taking on various creatures left over by *The X-Files*, but by then the show was already en route to cancellation. There's a cult following, as there is for any sci-fi property with a beautiful woman in the cast, and Fox has obliged with two bonus-packed season sets chockfull of commentaries.

GREAT MOMENTS: Season 1: The bar scene in "Heat," the season-ending cliffhanger in "And Jesus Brought a Casserole."

FAST-FORWARD: Season 2: The "It was all a dream!" episode, "Boo!"; any appearance by Dog-Boy Joshua.

EXTRAS: Season 1: Commentaries by Executive Producers Charles Eglee and Rene Echevarria, directors David Nutter and Jeff Woolnough, and star Jessica Alba; blooper reel; audition tapes; three behind-the-scenes featurettes; Season 2: Commentaries by Echevarria and Woolnough, plus writers Moira Kirkland Dekker, Jose Molina, and co-executive producer Kenneth Biller; deleted scenes; blooper reel.

Dark Shadows (1966–1971)

Collection 1 (40 episodes on 4 discs): ★ ★ ★ ★ ★
Collection 2 (40 episodes on 4 discs): ★ ★ ★ ½
Collection 3 (40 episodes on 4 discs): ★ ★ ★
Collection 4 (40 episodes on 4 discs): ★ ★ ★ ★ ★
Collection 5 (40 episodes on 4 discs): ★ ★ ★ ★ ★
Collection 6 (40 episodes on 4 discs): ★ ★ ★ ★ ★
Collection 7 (40 episodes on 4 discs): ★ ★ ½
Collection 8 (40 episodes on 4 discs): ★ ★ ★
Collection 9 (40 episodes on 4 discs): ★ ★ ½
Collection 10 (40 episodes on 4 discs): ★ ★ ★ ½
Collection 11 (40 episodes on 4 discs): ★ ★
Collection 12 (40 episodes on 4 discs): ★ ★ ★
Collection 13 (40 episodes on 4 discs): ★ ★ ★
Collection 14 (40 episodes on 4 discs): ★ ★ ★
Collection 15 (40 episodes on 4 discs): ★ ★
Collection 16 (40 episodes on 4 discs): ★ ★
Collection 17 (40 episodes on 4 discs): ★ ★
Collection 18 (40 episodes on 4 discs): ★ ½
Collection 19 (40 episodes on 4 discs): ★ ★ ½
Collection 20 (40 episodes on 4 discs): ★ ★
Collection 21 (40 episodes on 4 discs): ★ ★
Collection 22 (40 episodes on 4 discs): ★ ★
Collection 23 (40 episodes on 4 discs): ★ ★
Dark Shadows (Special Edition): ★ ★
Dark Shadows Reunion: Thirty-Fifth Anniversary Celebration: ★ ★ ★

MPI Home Video
Video: Full-Frame; Audio: Dolby Digital 2.0

If any daytime drama could achieve a full-run DVD release, it would be *Dark Shadows.* Its 1,200-plus episodes are already available on VHS, a testament to the enduring popularity of this thirty-five-year-old gothic soap. The MPI DVD collections begin not with the first episode, but with the arrival of Jonathan Frid as Barnabas Collins—the character that turned a series on the brink of cancellation into a daytime juggernaut that pulled in ten million viewers a day.

The time and money commitment required by the forty-episode MPI releases might seem daunting for newcomers; but if you're curious and sample the first batch of episodes, chances are you'll be hooked, at least through the 1795 story arc. Fans and completists will then go further, while the rest can safely stop, knowing they've enjoyed the best of *Dark Shadows.*

GREAT MOMENTS: *Collection 1*: Willie opens Barnabas's casket, the Collins family meet their cousin from England, and Barnabas terrorizes Maggie Evans; *Collection 3*: The beginning of the 1795 flashback, and the arrival of Lara Parker as Angelique; *Collection 4*: Barnabas is cursed by Angelique, and Josette plunges off Widow's Hill; *Collection 8*: The debut of warlock Nicholas Blair; *Collection 11*: "Quentin's Theme" is heard for the first time; *Collection 12*: The 1897 flashback begins; *Collection 19*: The parallel-time story, patterned after Daphne du Maurier's *Rebecca*.

FAST-FORWARD: The Leviathan story arc in *Collection 18* was the beginning of the end for *Dark Shadows*.

EXTRAS: Each collection features cast/crew interviews.

D

Dark Shadows (1991)

The Complete Revival Series (13 episodes on 3 discs): ★ ★ ★ ★

MGM Home Video

Video: Anamorphic Widescreen; Audio: Dolby Digital 2.0

It's difficult to attract viewers to a primetime soap opera when a network keeps pre-empting episodes for coverage of the first Gulf War, but that was the fate suffered by the second incarnation of *Dark Shadows*. By staying faithful to the original storylines and smartly casting the key roles (Ben Cross as Barnabas, Jean Simmons as Elizabeth, Barbara Steele as Dr. Hoffman), the revival captured the magic that imbued the daytime series, this time on a decent budget. For some reason, MGM opted for a widescreen DVD presentation of episodes that were originally broadcast full-frame.

GREAT MOMENTS: Barnabas steps into the sunlight to "prove" he's not a vampire in Episode 3; the reunion of Barnabas and Angelique in Episode 7; Victoria meets Josette in Episode 8.

FAST-FORWARD: Nothing.

EXTRAS: None.

The Darling Buds of May (1991–1993)

The Complete Series (20 episodes on 5 discs): ★ ★ ★ ★ ★

BFS

Video: Full-Frame; Audio: Dolby Digital Stereo

To American audiences, Catherine Zeta-Jones seemed to emerge fully formed (and what a form it was) in *The Mask of Zorro*, where her skirt-dropping courtship duel with Antonio Banderas made her a star. But she first captivated British audiences seven years earlier in *The Darling Buds of May*, an adaptation of a popular series of books by H.E. Bates. The series still ranks among England's most highly rated shows, and Zeta-Jones became the nation's "It" girl overnight. It's the story of the Larkin family: Pa the charming rogue, Ma the sweet eccentric, their six kids (including flirty oldest daughter Mariette, played by Zeta-Jones) and the parade of kind and wonderful souls with whom they pass the time on their bucolic farm in Kent, circa 1950. Simply put, it's the type of series for which the word "idyllic" was invented.

GREAT MOMENTS: Ma Larkin's fits of laughter at inappropriate times; the catfight between Mariette and Pauline in the strawberry patch; Charlie's marriage proposal to Mariette.

FAST-FORWARD: Not a single moment.

EXTRAS: Interviews with Catherine Zeta-Jones and David Jason; photo gallery; biographies; trivia.

Dastardly and Muttley in Their Flying Machines (1969)

The Complete Series (17 episodes on 3 discs): ★ ★ ★

Warner Home Video

Video: Full-Frame; Audio: Dolby Digital 2.0

I thought it strange that this *Wacky Races* spin-off would get the DVD treatment before better-known Hanna-Barbera properties like *Josie and the Pussycats*, until I learned that the snickering canine Muttley was one of the studio's most popular characters in other parts of the world. In Japan he's like Hasselhoff, the object of torrid adulation. So to the Muttley-lovers across the seas we say, here is your idol, in his second triumphant series. Set during World War I, *Dastardly and Muttley* has our heroes abandoning their double-zero racecar for a biplane, in a quest to stop Yankee Doodle Pigeon from delivering his messages. There are seventeen episodes, each with two separate stories, which explains why some sources list thirty-five shows in the set. Though Dastardly's fellow Vulture Squadron members Klunk and Zilly aren't as memorable as the Ant Hill Mob or the Slag Brothers, the chases and crashes are still fun.

GREAT MOMENTS: Muttley takes command of the squadron in "Sky-Hi IQ"; Muttley loses his medals in "Medal Muddle."

FAST-FORWARD: Dastardly gets amnesia in "Who's Who?"

EXTRAS: Ten episode commentaries by designers Iwao Takamoto and Jerry Eisenberg, and Scott Awley and Scott Jeralds of Warner Bros. Animation; highlights featurette "The Vulture Squadron's Greatest Misses"; a spin-offs retrospective.

D

Dawson's Creek (1998–2003)

The Complete First Season (13 episodes on 3 discs): ★ ★ ★ ★
The Complete Second Season (22 episodes on 4 discs): ★ ★ ★
The Complete Third Season (23 episodes on 4 discs): ★ ★
The Complete Fourth Season (23 episodes on 4 discs): ★ ★
The Complete Fifth Season (23 episodes on 4 discs): ★ ½
The Complete Sixth Season (23 episodes on 4 discs): ★ ★
The Series Finale—Extended Cut (2 episodes on 1 disc): ★ ★ ★ ★

Columbia Tristar Home Video
Video: Full-Frame; Audio: Dolby Digital 2.0

Dawson's Creek was one of the fledgling WB Network's first "coming of age" television series, and the one that continues to inspire variations on the same theme from the same network: a group of teenagers, most played by actors in their mid-twenties, overanalyze life a bit more than they need to, using very big words in the process.

That said, *Dawson's*, at least at its start, was rife with fresh dialogue and smart pop culture references, and tackled taboo characters and situations rarely explored on television. Through the course of six seasons, character interactions and relationships changed; there were sexual dalliances involving a high school teacher; and one of the main characters "came out" as a homosexual.

Much of the show's early success can be attributed to its original show runner and creator, Kevin Williamson (*Scream*). After his departure following Season 2, the characters began running in circles; not good for a series that hoped to break away from predictability and escape the "Peach Pit," as Pacey Witter commented in the first year, a reference to *Beverly Hills 90210*.

Be warned that the series' pop-music track has been changed for the DVD sets. Beginning with the third season, even Paula Cole's familiar "I Don't Want to Wait" theme has been excised. Also disappointing is Columbia Tristar's insistence on cramming as many episodes as possible on each disc, resulting in less-than-stellar quality on some tracks.

GREAT MOMENTS: Season 1: Dawson, Joey, Pacey, and Jen stay after school, *Breakfast Club*–style, in "Detention"; the series finale is the type of ambitious episode that fans of the show's first two years had given up hope of seeing again.

FAST-FORWARD: The later seasons are only recommended for diehard fans. However, things start picking up again in Season 6 as the show nears its conclusion.

EXTRAS: Producer commentaries; retrospectives. *The Season Finale—Extended Cut* DVD includes deleted scenes, commentary, and several alternate scenes from the series' original pilot-episode presentation.

Deadwood (2004–)

Season 1 (12 episodes on 6 discs): ★ ★ ★ ★

HBO Home Video

Video: Anamorphic Widescreen; Audio: Dolby Digital 5.1

John Wayne never talked like that. And that's the point, says *Deadwood* creator David Milch, former head writer of *NYPD Blue*. Milch would argue the authenticity of the language is important, even if it contradicts what we've known of Westerns for the past half-century. Nobody claims real cowboys were paragons of virtue, but their deportment in *Deadwood* is still a shock to the system for those generations that grew up with a more honorable archetype. This is wholesale reinvention of a genre, and while any successful revival of the Western should be cause for celebration, does it really prove anything to use a word that starts with "c" and ends in "sucker" thirty-eight times in one scene? Sometimes restraint is a good thing. But for those who don't flinch at the F-word, *Deadwood* is otherwise brilliant.

GREAT MOMENTS: Hickok plays in his famously fatal poker game in "Here Was a Man"; Calamity Jane cuts loose in "Bullock Returns to the Camp"; Swearengen has a bad day in "Mr. Wu."

FAST-FORWARD: Nothing, unless you're put off by profanity. In that case, everything.

EXTRAS: Featurettes "Making *Deadwood*: The Show Behind the Show," "The Real Deadwood," "An Imaginative Reality," and "The New Language of the Old West"; commentaries by David Milch and cast members; an interview with Milch and star Keith Carradine.

The Dean Martin Show (1965–1974)

The Best of the Dean Martin Variety Show, Volume 1: ★ ★ ★

D

Guthy-Renker

Video: Full-Frame; Audio: Dolby Digital 2.0

Available only via mail-order subscription series, *The Best of the Dean Martin Show* collects memorable moments from one of television's best (and least-syndicated) variety shows. A great era in show business has been captured in these clips, but until they're sold in stores instead of by infomercial, they'll never reach their full potential audience. Hopefully, as with the *Tonight Show* collection that started out the same way, the "best of" volumes will eventually be released through retail channels as well. Better yet, let's start from scratch and go with season sets—this is great stuff that deserves to be archived as originally broadcast.

GREAT MOMENTS: Dean's duets with Ann-Margret, Frank Sinatra, and Ella Fitzgerald.

FAST-FORWARD: Nothing.

EXTRAS: None.

Degrassi Junior High (1987–1991)

Season 1 (13 episodes on 4 discs): ★ ★ ½

Season 2 (13 episodes on 3 discs): ★ ★ ½

Season 3 (16 episodes on 3 discs): ★ ★

WGBH Boston

Video: Full-Frame; Audio: Dolby Digital 2.0

Degrassi Junior High originated in Canada and found a loyal audience on US public television. The show handled teen issues in a serious way in the days before *90210*, but unlike that series *Degrassi* cast actors that were actual teenagers, complete with bad skin, bad hair, and braces. They spent three seasons in junior high before matriculating to high school for the series' final two years.

The DVD sets are perfect for those who simply wish to relive their PBS Sunday-afternoon past; just don't look for any incredible special features.

GREAT MOMENTS: Season 1: Long-running characters such as Joey Jeremiah are first introduced in "Kiss Me Steph"; Season 2: Spike learns the responsibility of carrying around an egg as if it is her child.

FAST-FORWARD: Canadian teen melodrama must never be fast-forwarded.

EXTRAS: All season sets offer "Degrassi Talks" videos and printable materials for educators.

D

Degrassi: The Next Generation (2001–2006)

Season 1 (15 episodes on 3 discs): ★ ★ ★ ½
Season 2 (22 episodes on 4 discs): ★ ★ ★
Jay and Silent Bob Do Degrassi: Unrated (3 episodes on 1 disc): ★ ★ ★ ½
Jay and Silent Bob Do Degrassi (Vanilla version; 3 episodes on 1 disc): ★ ★ ½

Funimation
Video: Full-Frame; Audio: Dolby Digital 2.0

In the original *Degrassi* series, Christine "Spike" Nelson became a teen mother in the eighth grade. Nearly fifteen years later, Spike has a teenager of her own, in a series that is just as much a sequel to its predecessor as its own entity.

Degrassi: The Next Generation starts with a reunion of several members of the original cast, and quickly moves on to a new, younger set of friends surrounding Spike's daughter, Emma. Joey Jeremiah is a car salesman with a little girl and a stepson of his own; Caitlin Ryan has had her own talk show, and "Snake" is now the kids' Media Immersion teacher, Mr. Simpson. Episodes include stories on the dangers of meeting someone on the Internet, drug use, child abuse, teenage homosexuality, and abortion.

PBS must have passed on a return to Degrassi, as the Canadian series reached the US this time through Nickelodeon's Noggin channel. Several episodes, however, were censored for content.

In 2005, director Kevin Smith (*Clerks*) appeared in a three-episode story arc playing himself during the show's fourth season. Those episodes are collected in the *Jay and Silent Bob Do Degrassi* DVD, released in both censored and unrated versions.

GREAT MOMENTS: Season 1: Jimmy and Spinner learn that pranks on a teacher aren't always funny in "Friday Night"; Season 2: Joey's troubled stepson, Craig, makes his first appearance in "When Doves Cry, Part 1"; *Jay and Silent Bob*: Alanis Morissette makes a cameo as the principal of a Canadian high school.

FAST-FORWARD: The on-again, off-again relationship of Ashley and Jimmy in the show's first season becomes a bore, and is easily skipped. Likewise, the Jay and Silent Bob arc is more palatable when you go right to the scenes involving Kevin Smith.

EXTRAS: Season sets include cast auditions, bloopers, Degrassi karaoke, photo galleries, dozens of deleted scenes, and more; there's a commentary by director Kevin Smith and actors Jason Mewes and Stacie Mistysyn on the unrated *Jay and Silent Bob Do Degrassi* discs.

D

Designing Women (1986–1993)

Best of Designing Women (5 episodes on 1 disc): ★ ★ ★ ½

Columbia Tristar Home Video

Video: Full-Frame; Audio: Dolby 1.0 Mono

Designing Women is certainly worthy of the season-set treatment, at least for its 1986 through 1991 campaigns, before Emmy-nominated costars Delta Burke and Jean Smart left the fold, to be inadequately replaced by Julia Duffy and Jan Hooks. The admittedly well-chosen episodes in this single-disc collection are a reminder of how fresh and witty and bold this Southern-based sitcom was, especially in its exploration of such serious issues as racism and homophobia. More, please.

GREAT MOMENTS: The witty battle-of-the-sexes debate in "Reservations for Eight"; Mary Jo discovers the difference a stuffed bra can make in "Big Haas and Little Falsie"; Julia dresses down a client who believes AIDS is God's punishment on gays ("If God was giving out sexually transmitted disease to people as punishment for sinning, then you would be at the free clinic all the time!") in "Killing All the Right People."

FAST-FORWARD: Nothing.

EXTRAS: Again, none.

Desperate Housewives (2004–)

The Complete First Season (24 episodes on 6 discs): ★ ★ ★ ★

Buena Vista Home Entertainment

Video: Anamorphic Widescreen; Audio: Dolby Digital 5.1

None of us knew how much we missed high-camp primetime soaps like

Knots Landing, until writer Marc Cherry revived the genre, with a postmodern comical twist, with the instant hit *Desperate Housewives*. TV-on-DVD had become an established commodity by 2004, so it was obvious someone was planning ahead for *Housewives*' inevitable home-video release, given the abundance of extra features in the Season 1 set. Note to future TV producers: don't throw anything away.

GREAT MOMENTS: Susan is a reluctant streaker down Wisteria Lane in "Pretty Little Picture"; many secrets are revealed, and Bob Newhart guest-stars, in "Children Will Listen."

D

FAST-FORWARD: The premature flashback episode "Sorting Out the Dirty Laundry."

EXTRAS: Unrated, exclusive extended episodes; "Making of Season 1 Finale" featurette, with alternate endings; Marc Cherry's favorite episodes with commentary; cast commentaries with Marc Cherry; "Desperate Housewives Around the World" and "Dressing Wisteria Lane" featurettes; "Secrets of Wisteria Lane" interactive neighborhood tour; behind-the-scenes documentary hosted by Meredith Vieira.

Dharma & Greg (1997–2002)

Season 1 (23 episodes on 3 discs): ★ ★ ★

Fox Home Entertainment

Video: Full-Frame; Audio: Dolby Digital Stereo

Hippie chick meets Harvard attorney, and it's love at first sight in this comedy of clashing cultures and dueling in-laws. It's Jenna Elfman's show all the way, and when she works her Goldie Hawn-esque charm *Dharma & Greg* rises above its labored high concept and earns its classic sitcom wings.

GREAT MOMENTS: The "do-over" nuptials in "And Then There's the Wedding"; the revelations unearthed by a government security check in "He Ain't Heavy, He's My Father"; the country-club dance in "Spring Forward, Fall Down."

FAST-FORWARD: Nothing.

EXTRAS: Commentaries by stars Jenna Elfman, Mimi Kennedy, and Alan Rachins; featurette "When Worlds Collide: The *Dharma & Greg* Story."

The Dick Cavett Show (1969–1974)

Rock Icons (3 discs): ★ ★ ★ ½

The Ray Charles Collection (2 discs): ★ ★

The John Lennon & Yoko Ono Collection (2 discs): ★ ★

Comic Legends (4 discs): ★ ★ ★ ½

Shout! Factory

Video: Full-Frame; Audio: Dolby Digital Mono

At a time when talk shows were more than celebrity-plug machines, Dick Cavett was a master of the lively art of conversation, even if he sometimes focused more on himself than on his remarkable array of guests. For its Cavett compilation DVDs, Shout! Factory made the debatable but probably correct decision to include episodes in their entirety, which means you'll sit through guests who have nothing to do with the theme of each release, such as film critic Rex Reed in the *Comic Legends* collection, and silent-screen star Gloria Swanson sharing the stage with Janis Joplin in *Rock Icons*.

GREAT MOMENTS: *Rock Icons*: Jefferson Airplane is joined by David Crosby on "Somebody to Love," in an episode taped one day after Woodstock; *Ray Charles Collection*: Ray's performance of "America the Beautiful"; *Comic Legends*: Dick interviews Groucho Marx.

FAST-FORWARD: *The John Lennon & Yoko Ono Collection*: When Yoko sings—but you knew that already.

EXTRAS: Each collection features new episode introductions by Dick Cavett; *John Lennon & Yoko Ono Collection*: New interview with Dick Cavett; *Comic Legends*: Outtakes; the 1969 special *Here's Dick Cavett*; Cavett's 1966 appearance on *The Ed Sullivan Show*; a new Dick Cavett interview.

The Dick Van Dyke Show (1961–1966)

Season 1 (30 episodes on 5 discs): ★ ★ ★ ★ ★

Season 2 (32 episodes on 5 discs): ★ ★ ★ ★ ★

Season 3 (32 episodes on 5 discs): ★ ★ ★ ★ ★

Season 4 (32 episodes on 5 discs): ★ ★ ★ ★ ★

Season 5 (32 episodes on 5 discs): ★ ★ ★ ★ ★

The Complete Series (158 episodes on 25 discs): ★ ★ ★ ★ ★

The Best of the Dick Van Dyke Show, Volumes 1–5
(single discs with 4 episodes each). All: ★ ★ ★ ★

Image Entertainment

Video: Full-Frame; Audio: Dolby Digital 2.0

The Dick Van Dyke Show may be forty years old, but it hasn't aged at all. Replace Sally's typewriter with an iMac and the scenes in the *Alan Brady Show* writers' office could take place in any network writers' room today. And the impromptu comedy and music performances at the Petries' New Rochelle home offer a glimpse into an idealized suburban lifestyle to which many of us still aspire. Smart and sophisticated, but never too sophisticated for a master class in baggy-pants slapstick, the series remains one of the standards by which excellence in situation comedy should be judged.

And so, rather than expound any further on the merits of the series, let's turn our attention to five DVD season sets that are actually worthy of the brilliant show they collect. The picture quality of the 158 episodes is as sharp and vivid as black-and-white television has ever looked. The extra features go beyond the standard commentary tracks and cast interviews to include some unique items that would never see the light of day anywhere else. These include series creator Carl Reiner's original pilot, *Head of the Family*, in which Reiner himself played Rob Petrie; Emmy Award telecast clips; a cast appearance on the obscure game show *Pantomime Quiz*; and an episode of *The Danny Thomas Show* in which Morey Amsterdam reprised his role as Buddy Sorrell. Even the photo galleries contain some hidden treasures, including rare color shots of the Petrie living room and the *Alan Brady Show* office.

Don't bother with "best of" collections, which just whet the appetite for the season sets. Yes, they're pricey, but with thirty-plus episodes in each season and a variety of additional delights, they're worth the investment.

GREAT MOMENTS: Season 1: "Where Did I Come From?"—the best of the many flashback episodes; the two-part introduction of Rob's brother Stacy (played by Dick's brother Jerry) in "I Am My Brother's Keeper"; Season 2: Under hypnosis, Rob acts drunk every time he hears a bell in "My Husband Is Not a Drunk"; the sci-fi dream sequence in "It May Look Like a Walnut"; Season 3: The surprise twist in "That's My Boy"; Rob's amnesia-induced trip to Red Hook in "Who and Where Was Antonio Stradivarius?"; Season 4: Don Rickles tries to rob the Petries in an elevator in "4 ½"; Rob and Laura's romantic getaway goes awry in "Never Bathe on Saturday"; Season 5: the Laura–Alan Brady confrontation in "Coast to Coast Big Mouth"; Rob, Buddy, and Sally must retrieve an expletive-filled script before their boss reads it in "Obnoxious, Offensive, Egomaniac, Etc."

FAST-FORWARD: Season 1: "The Bad Old Days" is the series' only skippable episode; Season 4: an attempt to promote racial harmony in "A Show of Hands" plays as (no pun intended) heavy-handed.

EXTRAS: Each season set has cast interviews and commentaries, and surprisingly none are particularly compelling. Fortunately, there's plenty of other good stuff.

Season 1 offers the *Head of the Family* pilot and original commercials and promo spots with the cast; Season 2 contains a behind-the-scenes featurette on the classic episode "It May Look Like a Walnut"; in Season 3, there's some rare rehearsal footage, the *Danny Thomas Show* with Morey Amsterdam, and a clip of Mary Tyler Moore's appearance on Dick Van Dyke's 1975 variety series *Van Dyke and Company*; Season 4 has clips from TV Land's *The Alan Brady Show*, the CBS special *The Dick Van Dyke Show Remembered*, an episode of *Diagnosis Murder* with a guest appearance from Rob Petrie, Van Dyke's performance of the series' theme song at a 2001 Hollywood Bowl production, and never-before-seen rehearsal footage shot by Roddy McDowall; guest star Don Rickles provides commentary on his episodes in Season 5, which also contains *The Dick Van Dyke Show* cast reunion at 1992's *Comic Relief*, a clip from *Dick Van Dyke and the Other Woman* featuring Mary Tyler Moore, and a sketch from a Cass Elliot special. What more could any fan want?

Diff'rent Strokes (1978–1986)

The Complete First Season (24 episodes on 3 discs): ★ ★ ★

The Complete Second Season (26 episodes on 4 discs): ★ ★ ★

Sony Pictures Home Entertainment

Video: Full-Frame; Audio: Dolby Digital 2.0

Those of us who grew up in the Chicago area and first met Gary Coleman in a series of Harris Bank commercials knew that the kid was destined. With so much talent and timing, charisma, and natural charm, it was only a matter of time before he was cast in something more significant. That turned out to be *Diff'rent Strokes*, an adequate showcase for his precocious personality, now tainted by the sad legacies of its child-star trio. Season 1 is a reminder of happier times (the Janet Jackson, Dixie Carter, and Nancy Reagan sightings are several years later), but be warned that syndicated prints were used for two sixty-minute episodes: "The Retrospective" and "The Trip." Since the latter was a crossover with the ill-fated McLean Stevenson series *Hello, Larry*, perhaps that's for the best.

GREAT MOMENTS: The first "whatchoo talkin' 'bout?" in "Movin' In"; the *Facts of Life* pilot "The Girls School," with the debuts of Kim Fields as Tootie and Lisa Whelchel as Blair.

FAST-FORWARD: *Sanford and Son*'s LaWanda Page plays yet another annoying distant kin in "The Relative"; Season 2: Muhammad Ali guest-stars in "Arnold's Hero."

EXTRAS: Two featurettes, one on the show ("A Look Back at *Diff'rent Strokes*") and one on Gary Coleman ("Whatchoo Talkin' 'Bout?"). Coleman is a no-show, but there are new interviews with Conrad Bain, Todd Bridges, and Charlotte Rae; episode commentaries with writer Paul Rubin.

A Different World (1987–1993)

Season 1 (22 episodes on 4 discs): ★ ★
Season 2 (22 episodes on 4 discs): ★ ★ ★ ½

D

Urban Works
Video: Full-Frame; Audio: Dolby Digital 2.0

The *Cosby Show* spin-off built around college-bound Denise Huxtable (Lisa Bonet) blossomed following her departure, when the spotlight shifted to supporting characters Whitley (the sly Jasmine Guy) and Dwayne Wayne (Kadeem Hardison). Urban Works put out a stellar Season 1 set, with all the TLC and intriguing extras that *The Cosby Show* still hasn't received.

GREAT MOMENTS: Season 1: Rudy visits big sister Denise, but pays more attention to Whitley in "Rudy and the Snow Queen"; Denise and Dwayne go on a date in "If Only for One Night"; Season 2: the first hints of Dwayne and Whitley's mutual affection in "Dream Lover"; Diahann Carroll debuts as Whitley's mother in "For She's Only a Bird in a Gilded Cage."

FAST-FORWARD: "Porky de Bergerac" is typical of too many unfocused first-season shows.

EXTRAS: Season 1: Cast interviews; outtakes; "lost" episode featuring Tupac Shakur and Jada Pinkett; The E! Network special "*A Different World*: I Was a Network TV Star."

Dr. Quinn, Medicine Woman (1993–1998)

Season 1 (17 episodes on 5 discs): ★ ★ ★ ★
Season 2 (24 episodes on 7 discs): ★ ★ ★ ★
Season 3 (25 episodes on 8 discs): ★ ★ ★ ★ ½
Season 4 (27 episodes on 8 discs): ★ ★ ★ ★
Season 5 (26 episodes on 7 discs): ★ ★ ★ ½
Season 6 (22 episodes on 6 discs): ★ ★ ½

A&E Home Video
Video: Full-Frame; Audio: Dolby Digital 2.0

Westerns were headed for the last roundup on TV before Dr. Michaela Quinn rode into Colorado Springs. The premise of a female doctor in the Old West was intriguing on its own, but *Dr. Quinn, Medicine Woman* progressed far beyond its feminist hook in an impressive six-year run that allowed its characters to grow, change, and move forward with their lives. Stories dealing with racism, science versus religion, and the treatment of Native Americans were more ambitious than one might expect from a "feel-good" family show, but if you watched only for the sigh-worthy romance between Jane Seymour and Joe Lando as the Cheyenne mountain man Sully, that's fine too.

GREAT MOMENTS: Season 1: The racism-themed "Portraits"; Season 2: Mike returns to Boston and is romanced by a handsome doctor in "Where the Heart Is"; Season 3: Mike and Sully get married in "For Better or Worse"; Season 4: Mike leads an all-woman team up Pike's Peak in "Expedition"; Season 5: Poet Walt Whitman creates a stir in Colorado Springs in "The Body Electric"; Also, the Christmas and other holiday-themed episodes from each season are always a special treat.

FAST-FORWARD: Nothing.

EXTRAS: Season 1: The *Biography* episode *Jane Seymour: Hollywood's English Rose*; interactive tour of nineteenth-century Colorado Springs; Season 2: Cast and crew interviews; commentary by Joe Lando; Season 3: Commentary by Jane Seymour and Joe Lando; "Highlights" featurette; Season 4: "Favorites" featurette; Season 5: Commentary by Shawn Toovey and Chad Allen; Season 6: Commentary by Jane Seymour and James Keach.

Doctor Who (1963–1989; 2005–)

The Aztecs (4 episodes on 1 disc): ★ ★ ★ ★
The Dalek Invasion of Earth (6 episodes on 2 discs): ★ ★ ★ ½
Tomb of the Cybermen (4 episodes on 1 disc): ★ ★ ★
The Mind Robber (5 episodes on 1 disc): ★ ★ ½
The Seeds of Death (6 episodes on 2 discs): ★ ½
Spearhead from Space (4 episodes on 1 disc): ★ ★ ★ ★
The Three Doctors (4 episodes on 1 disc): ★ ★ ★ ½
Carnival of Monsters (4 episodes on 1 disc): ★ ★ ½
The Green Death (6 episodes on 1 disc): ★ ★ ★ ½
The Ark in Space (4 episodes on 1 disc): ★ ★ ★
Pyramids of Mars (4 episodes on 1 disc): ★ ★ ★ ★ ½
The Robots of Death (4 episodes on 1 disc): ★ ★
The Talons of Weng-Chiang (6 episodes on 2 discs): ★ ★ ★ ½

The Horror of Fang Rock (4 episodes on 1 disc): ★ ★ ½

The Key to Time Collection (contains the following six discs comprising the entire Season 16; see individual listings for ratings)

- The Ribos Operation (4 episodes on 1 disc): ★ ★ ★
- The Pirate Planet (4 episodes on 1 disc): ★ ★ ★ ½
- The Stones of Blood (4 episodes on 1 disc): ★ ★ ½
- The Androids of Tara (4 episodes on 1 disc): ★ ★
- The Power of Kroll (4 episodes on 1 disc): ★ ½
- The Armageddon Factor (6 episodes on 1 disc): ★ ★ ★

D

The Leisure Hive (4 episodes on 1 disc): ★ ★ ★

The Visitation (4 episodes on 1 disc): ★ ★

Earthshock (4 episodes on 1 disc): ★ ★ ★ ½

The Five Doctors Special Edition (1 episode on 1 disc): ★ ★ ★

Resurrection of the Daleks (4 episodes on 1 disc): ★ ★ ★

The Caves of Androzani (4 episodes on 1 disc): ★ ★ ★ ★

Vengeance on Varos (2 episodes on 1 disc): ★ ★

The Two Doctors (3 episodes on 2 discs): ★ ★ ★

Remembrance of the Daleks (4 episodes on 1 disc): ★ ★

Ghost Light (3 episodes on 1 disc): ★ ½

The Curse of Fenric (4 episodes on 2 discs): ★ ★

Season 1 (13 episodes on 5 discs): ★ ★ ★ ★ ½

BBC Video

Video: Individual releases: Full-Frame; Season 1: Anamorphic Widescreen; Audio: Individual releases: Dolby Digital 2.0; Season 1: Dolby Digital 5.1

The only science-fiction franchise on television to rival *Star Trek* in quality, innovation, and worldwide following (oh, be quiet, *Farscape* fans), *Doctor Who* was a fixture on the BBC for twenty-six years. After a hiatus, the series returned in 2005, more popular than ever. Ten different actors have played the Doctor, a time-traveler who wanders the galaxy in a vintage blue London police box. And each has left his own distinct imprint on the role. Joined by an ever-changing assortment of plucky companions (most of whom have been young, female, and cute, though the Doctor has always been above hanky-panky), the series has transported viewers to countless worlds and exciting encounters with Daleks, Cybermen, Sontarans, and alien monsters that look like they were assembled by a junior high art class. Once again the sci-fi fan gets soaked price-wise—for the pre-revival episodes the BBC has released each multi-part story individually rather than in season sets, but at least there are always a few extras to soften the blow.

GREAT MOMENTS: "The Aztecs" is a prime example of the William Hartnell era; "The Dalek Invasion of Earth" features the famous sequence of a parade of

Daleks crossing London Bridge; "Spearhead from Space," Jon Pertwee's first adventure, is a good introduction for new fans; "The Green Death" offers one of the show's most emotional moments, once you get past the low-budget maggot effects. The most memorable era for many fans—and the one that established the series in America, was that of actor Tom Baker. "Pyramids of Mars" is a superb outing, and also features one of the Doctor's most beloved companions, Sara Jane Smith. "The Pirate Planet" was penned by famed sci-fi author Douglas Adams; "The Caves of Androzani," was the last and best story to feature Fifth Doctor Peter Davison. The "Three Doctors" and "Five Doctors" stories offer special treats for fans; Season 1: The Doctor is reunited with one of his classic enemies in "Dalek"; the Doctor and Rose play futuristic versions of *Big Brother* and *The Weakest Link* in "Bad Wolf."

D

FAST-FORWARD: The low-budget look of later episodes, particularly those during the Sylvester McCoy era (1987–1990), may distract. Of course the budget was even lower on the shows from ten to twenty years earlier, but as with *Star Trek*, the quality of the writing and performance made the nickel-and-dime (or in this case, shilling-and-tuppence) special effects less critical. New special effects created for "The Curse of Fenric" are a treat, but they don't make the story any better.

EXTRAS: Almost all *Doctor Who* DVDs feature informational text offering episode trivia; stars and crew from the shows provide commentary with varying success. Season 1: Cast/crew commentaries; an interview with Christopher Eccleston; behind-the-scenes featurettes; a preview of the first story featuring David Tennant as the new Doctor.

Doogie Howser, M.D. (1989–1993)

The Complete First Season (26 episodes on 4 discs): ★ ★ ★ ★
The Complete Second Season (25 episodes on 4 discs): ★ ★ ★ ½
The Complete Third Season (24 episodes on 4 discs): ★ ★ ★
The Complete Fourth Season (22 episodes on 4 discs): ★ ★ ½

Anchor Bay
Video: Full-Frame; Audio: Dolby Stereo

After creating *Hill Street Blues* and *L.A. Law* for NBC, Steven Bochco signed a $50 million development deal with the struggling ABC network. His first offering was *Doogie Howser, M.D.*, a minor hit that still outclassed his second effort, the infamous *Cop Rock*.

Neil Patrick Harris, who will be Doogie for life even if he wins more Oscars than Tom Hanks, was perfectly cast as the sixteen-year-old whiz kid who finished high school in nine weeks, and graduated from Princeton at ten en route to serving as a resident at the Eastman Medical Center. Even if you buy the fanciful premise in this age of medical malpractice, it's still hard to swallow the friendship between Doogie and goombah-in-training Vinnie, who was always getting his genius buddy in trouble. The reactions of Doogie's patients are always fun, and I always liked Nurse Curly, who was more sympathetic to the problems a teenage doctor would face than was Doogie's whiny girlfriend, Wanda.

Included with the Season 1 set is a booklet from Doogie's personal journal, a nod to the familiar closing scene from each episode when Doogie would type his thoughts into a stone-age computer, like Carrie Bradshaw without the shoe fetish. It's always a nice bonus when a DVD set is put together by someone who actually watched the show.

GREAT MOMENTS: Season 1: Doogie is forced to examine Wanda when she suffers an appendicitis attack during a date in "A Stitch Called Wanda"; guest star Josie Bissett makes Wanda jealous in "Attack of the Green-Eyed Monster"; Season 2: Doogie deals with losing a patient in "To Live and Die in Brentwood"; Season 3: To win a bet with Vinnie, Doogie takes a job in a fast-food joint in "Double Doogie with Cheese"; Season 4: The Emmy-winning episode "Doogie Got a Gun."

FAST-FORWARD: Season 1: "The Ice Queen Cometh," an odd and creepy choice for the first post-pilot episode, in which one of Doogie's older hospital colleagues asks the sixteen-year-old to be her sperm donor; Doogie and Vinnie are held hostage in a convenience store, only to later have dinner with their would-be assailant, in "Use a Slurpy, Go to Jail."

EXTRAS: Season 1: Interviews with Steven Bochco and Neil Patrick Harris; "Doogie's Personal Journal"; Season 2: Interviews with Neil Patrick Harris and Max Casella; Season 3: Interviews with Neil Patrick Harris and James B. Sikking; Season 4: Interviews with Lawrence Pressman and Kathryn Layng.

The Doris Day Show (1968–1973)

Season 1 (28 episodes on 4 discs): ★ ★ ★

Season 2 (26 episodes on 4 discs): ★ ★ ★ ½

MPI Home Video

Video: Full-Frame; Audio: Dolby Digital 2.0

The premise of *The Doris Day Show* changed almost every season. The series {family ranch. But the rural life apparently didn't agree with Doris, as by

Season 2 she had taken a job with a San Francisco magazine. The transition from family sitcom to workplace comedy continued over the next two seasons, and by the fifth year Doris's children had been Chuck Cunningham-ed out of existence. One constant: the "Que Sera Sera" theme song, and for legions of Doris Day fans that's reason enough to buy the season sets.

This is MPI's best work on a DVD collection since the *Dark Shadows* series. What a pleasant surprise that a show that's been out of syndication for decades has been collected with so many wonderful extras, including new cast interviews (not with Doris, sadly), outtakes, and Day's two appearances on the game show *What's My Line?*

GREAT MOMENTS: Season 1: "The Flyboy" features Doris at her spunkiest, and garbed in the memorable outfit she wore in the film *Lover Come Back*.

FAST-FORWARD: Nothing.

EXTRAS: Season 1: Interviews; two 1968 promotional greetings by Doris Day; outtakes; *What's My Line?* clips; Season 2: Cast interviews; rehearsal footage; blooper reel; commercials and promos.

D

Dragnet (1952–1959)

Collector's Edition (3 episodes on 1 disc): ★ ½
Volume 1 (5 episodes on 1 disc): ★ ★ ½
Volume 2 (4 episodes on 1 disc): ★ ★ ★
Volume 3 (4 episodes on 1 disc): ★ ★
Volume 4 (4 episodes on 1 disc): ★ ★

Eclectic DVD (Collector's Edition); Alpha Video (Volumes 1–4)
Video: Full-Frame; Audio: Mono

Public-domain releases of the original *Dragnet* series are all over the market. Here's just the facts: the picture's bad, the sound's bad, but the episodes are superb police procedurals that have influenced every cop show of the last fifty years. Worth picking up if they're cheap enough, I suppose, but hopefully someone will eventually release them properly.

GREAT MOMENTS: Volume 2: The figurine of the infant Jesus is stolen from a church on Christmas Eve in "The Christmas Story."

FAST-FORWARD: Nothing.

EXTRAS: None.

Dragnet '67 (1967–1970)

Season 1 (17 episodes on 2 discs): ★ ★ ★ ½

Universal Home Video

Video: Full-Frame; Audio: Dolby Digital 2.0

It's not fair that the original *Dragnet* series is regarded a classic, while *Dragnet '67* gets the blame for transforming Jack Webb's stalwart Sergeant Joe Friday into a caricature. Sure, it's easy to laugh at the drug stories, played out at a fever pitch not seen since *Reefer Madness*, and Friday's square demeanor and out-of-touch attempts to relate to the counterculture (grilling one drug suspect: "You're pretty high and far out, aren't ya?"); and yet, there's a sincerity and conviction to Friday that very few other TV characters can touch. So iconic was Webb's portrayal that the real Los Angeles Police Department retired his badge number—704—as a tribute.

The DVDs look and sound terrific, but even a cop as sharp as Friday would have trouble figuring out the logic behind Universal's packaging: fourteen episodes on the first disc, three on the second, and none on the third, which contains an episode of the *Dragnet* radio series.

GREAT MOMENTS: "The Big LSD" is the infamous "Blue Boy" episode; Friday's speech about a cop's life to an officer suspected of wrongdoing (played by *Adam-12*'s Kent McCord) in "The Big Interrogation" is a series highlight.

FAST-FORWARD: The drunk scene in "The Big Bookie," the worst episode of the season, plays like a bad vaudeville routine in the middle of a serious undercover investigation.

EXTRAS: An episode of the *Dragnet* radio drama from 1954.

Due South (1994–1998)

Season 1 (22 episodes on 3 discs): ★ ★ ★

Season 2 (18 episodes on 3 discs): ★ ★ ½

Season 3 (14 episodes on 4 discs): ★ ★ ★

The Final Season (13 episodes on 4 discs): ★ ★ ★

Alliance Atlantis Home Entertainment

Video: Full-Frame; Audio: Dolby Digital 2.0

America doesn't import that many Canadian shows without the word Degrassi in the title, so it was a surprise to see this cross-cultural police story from the Great White North on the CBS primetime schedule. Even more surprising—it was a hit. Paul Gross played the Mountie whose dress reds stood out in Chicago like a Cardinals fan at Wrigley Field. He's teamed with a cynical streetwise cop—of course—and adventure ensues. The original pilot episode is included in the Season 3 set. Better late than never.

GREAT MOMENTS: Season 1: The ghost of Fraser, Sr., makes his first appearance in the Christmas story "Gift of the Wheelman"; Fraser meets a true love from the past in "Victoria's Secret"; Season 2: It's Ray's turn to have romance problems in "Juliet Is Bleeding"; *The Final Season*: Ray Vecchio returns in "Call of the Wild."

FAST-FORWARD: Nothing.

EXTRAS: *The Final Season*: Commentaries by Paul Gross.

The Dukes of Hazzard (1979–1985)

Season 1 (13 episodes on 3 discs): ★ ★ ★ ★
Season 2 (23 episodes on 4 discs): ★ ★ ★ ½
Season 3 (23 episodes on 4 discs): ★ ★ ★ ★
Season 4 (26 episodes on 9 discs): ★ ★ ★
Season 5 (22 episodes on 8 discs): ★ ½
Television Favorites (3 episodes on 1 disc): ★ ★ ½

Warner Home Video
Video: Full-Frame; Audio: Dolby Digital 2.0

"Just two good old boys, never meaning no harm . . ." *The Dukes of Hazzard* brought the Southern-fried fast-cars-versus-corrupt-law genre made famous by *Smokey and the Bandit* to the television screen, with more crashes and less cussing. John Schneider, Tom Wopat, and Catherine Bach played hell-raisin' cousins Bo, Luke, and Daisy Duke, but it was their orange 1969 Dodge Charger—the General Lee—that drove the series into legend, and now outpolls Adam West's Batmobile as TV's most famous car.

The series' first season, half of which was filmed in rural Georgia, featured more mature themes and bawdier humor than the family-friendly episodes that followed. Plots tended to all run together (out-of-town crooks pull robbery, Duke boys blamed, spend the rest of the hour clearing their names, the General Lee flies and squad cars crash), but fans never tired of watching the easy chemistry within the cast.

Despite the use of double-sided discs for the first three season sets, the episodes look good, and the Dolby Digital audio captures every tire screech, Dixie-playin' car horn, and country song from the famous victims of Boss Hogg's celebrity speed trap, including Loretta Lynn and Roy Orbison. Beware of Season 5, when Schneider and Wopat left over a contract dispute, and new Duke cousins Coy (Byron Cherry) and Vance (Christopher Mayer) slid into the General. Thankfully, the dispute was settled and Bo and Luke returned for the final four episodes.

GREAT MOMENTS: Season 1: "Mary Kaye's Baby" proves you don't need the General Lee for an entertaining show; Roz "Pinky Tuscadero" Kelly appears in "Luke's Love Story"; Season 2: "Days of Shine and Roses" is a favorite of many cast members and fans; Loretta Lynn guest-stars in "Find Loretta Lynn"; Season 3: The two-part "Carnival of Thrills" features a knockdown, drag-out fight between Bo and Luke; Season 4: *Star Trek*'s Jonathan Frakes beams down to Hazzard to romance Daisy in "Mrs. Daisy Hogg"; Daisy heats up the swimsuit competition in "Miss Tri-Counties"; Season 5: Coy and Vance leave (hooray!) in "Welcome Back, Bo and Luke!"

FAST-FORWARD: Fans of James Best's portrayal of Sheriff Rosco P. Coltrane may skip several Season 2 episodes in which he is replaced by rotating "guest sheriffs" like Dick Sargent; Season 4: "Pin the Tail on the Dukes" is silly even by Hazzard standards; Season 5: All the Coy and Vance shows.

EXTRAS: Season 1: Commentary on the series' pilot episode with actors John Schneider and Catherine Bach; "Hazzard County Barbecue" cast reunion; Season 2: "DukesFest" featurette; screen tests for actors John Schneider and Tom Wopat; Season 3: Visual commentary with Tom Wopat, John Schneider, and Catherine Bach; Season 4: More cast interviews and another delightful video commentary from the three Duke cousins; Season 5: Commentaries; two featurettes.

Dynasty (1981–1989)

Season 1 (13 episodes on 4 discs): ★ ★ ★

20th Century-Fox

Video: Full-Frame; Audio: Dolby Digital 2.0

The idea was to make *Dallas*, then TV's reigning primetime soap, look like a Salvation Army picnic. *Dynasty* poured on the opulence, concerning itself more with the trappings of wealth than with what anybody did inside the mahogany walls of the Carrington mansion. While they managed to break some new ground with Steven Carrington, television's first non-stereotypical gay character, this is a series remembered more for its Bob Mackie gowns than for its social conscience.

Season 1 gets bogged down in a ho-hum feud between the filthy-rich Carringtons and the working-class Blaisdels. That first year *Dynasty* barely scratched the Top 20; it was Season 2, with its introductions of Joan Collins as Alexis and Heather Locklear as Sammy Jo, plus the softening of Blake's rougher edges, that launched the series into the top ten where it remained for the next four seasons. Tech credits on the DVDs are just slightly above average, particularly the audio.

GREAT MOMENTS: The wedding of Blake and Krystle in "Oil, Part 3"; Blake attacks Steven's lover in "The Separation"; the climactic courtroom scene in the season finale that sets up Season 2.

FAST-FORWARD: Nothing.

EXTRAS: Commentaries by co-creator Esther Shapiro and star Al Corley; interviews with Corley and Pamela Sue Martin; "Family, Furs, and Fun: Creating *Dynasty*" and "Character Profiles" featurettes.

E

The Ed Sullivan Show (1948–1971)

Rock and Roll Classics 1: ★ ★ ★ ★
Rock and Roll Classics 2: ★ ★ ★
Rock and Roll Classics 3: ★ ★ ★
Rock and Roll Classics 4: ★ ★ ★ ½
Rock and Roll Classics Collection (9 discs): ★ ★ ★ ★ ½
Ed Sullivan Presents the Beatles: ★ ★ ★ ★
The Very Best of the Ed Sullivan Show, Volume 1: ★ ★ ★
The Very Best of the Ed Sullivan Show, Volume 2: ★ ★ ★
Great Moments in Opera from the Ed Sullivan Show: ★ ★ ★ ★

Rhino; Goodtimes Entertainment (*Very Best of . . .*); Kultur (*Great Moments in Opera*)

Video: Full-Frame; Audio: Dolby Digital 5.1 (*Rock and Roll Classics*): Dolby 2.0 (*Very Best of . . ., Great Moments in Opera*)

The individual volumes are pleasant enough samplers, but anyone with an interest in the history of rock 'n' roll, or who just wants to hear great songs performed on TV in an era before lip-synching became the exception rather than the standard, should pick up the *Rock and Roll Classics Collection*: nine discs holding more than 140 songs from the greatest singers and bands of rock music's first era. From Paul Anka to Janis Joplin, from Elvis to the Carpenters, and of course the Beatles, Beach Boys, and the Rolling Stones.

The Very Best of compilations are more of a grab bag, with performances from rock legends, Broadway shows, pop singers, and comedy sketches. For better or worse, they more accurately recapture the hodgepodge nature of a typical Sullivan show. The *Opera* collection, despite appearing to be hastily assembled with no performance dates or other information, will delight opera fans with rare performances from such greats as Beverly Sills, Lily Pons, Maria Callas, and Joan Sutherland.

GREAT MOMENTS: *Rock and Roll Classics 1*: "Monday, Monday" by the Mamas and the Papas; "Ruby Tuesday" by the Rolling Stones; *2*: "Proud Mary" by Creedence Clearwater Revival; *4*: Elvis Presley's now-legendary first appearance; *Great Moments in Opera*: "Vissi d'arte" by Leontyne Price.

FAST-FORWARD: *Rock and Roll Classics 1*: "I'm a Fool" by Dino, Desi & Billy.

EXTRAS: *Rock and Roll Classics Collection*: Interview with Ed Sullivan and his wife, Sylvia; interview with series director John Moffitt.

Eerie, Indiana (1991–1992)

The Complete Series (19 episodes on 5 discs): ★ ★ ★ ½

BMG

Video: Full-Frame; Audio: Dolby Digital 5.1

You'd think thirteen-year-old Marshall Teller (played by Omri Katz, best-remembered as J.R.'s son on *Dallas*) would have figured something wasn't quite kosher about a town named Eerie, Indiana. But when he meets Elvis on his paper route, he knows he's not in New Jersey anymore. With best friend Simon, Marshall embarks on a quest to investigate the town's hidden secrets, and to collect artifacts for the day when they'll expose their midwestern twilight zone to the rest of the world.

Though this 1991 series was short-lived and rarely rebroadcast, obviously there was still a following for *Eerie* in 2003, when BMG released a few DVD sets and then pulled the plug over distribution issues. Within weeks, the sets that got out were hitting $400 on eBay. But the series is available everywhere now at a much lower price. It seems BMG didn't spend much time on the project, as there's no evidence of clean-up in picture or sound, and even the box carries a couple of misprints. But fans will be glad to have the shows anyway, especially the final episode, "Broken Record," which never aired in the original run.

GREAT MOMENTS: The supernatural spin on Tupperware in "Foreverware"; Tobey Maguire guests as a mysterious boy who needs Marshall's help in "Dead Letter"; the surreal parallel universe in "Reality Takes a Holiday."

FAST-FORWARD: The clichéd capitalism condemnation of "Zombies in P.J.s."

EXTRAS: None.

The Electric Company (1971–1977)

The Best of The Electric Company (20 episodes on 4 discs): ★ ★ ★ ★

Shout! Factory

Video: Full-Frame; Audio: Dolby Digital 2.0

Too much Lorelei Chicken, not enough Julia Grownup. No Julia Grownup at all, actually, which suggests these twenty episodes from the landmark Children's Television Workshop series were not as well chosen as some would like. Sure, we get Letterman and Spider-Man, Fargo North, Easy Reader and Jennifer of the Jungle, but where's "Sweet, Sweet Sway," the best Short Circus song ever? Or such classics as "Billy Lick a Lolly," "N-Apostrophe-T," and "My Name is Kathy"?

Such lofty expectations may not have greeted this still-welcome set had it not been released by Shout! Factory, which has distinguished itself on several DVD compilations. Here the episode selection seems more random than motivated by outstanding content, and a trivia screen devoted to Short Circus singer Irene Cara, mistakenly accompanied by a picture of Cara's band-mate Melanie Henderson, indicates a sloppiness in research one wouldn't expect from Shout!

The show is brilliant, making this a warts-and-all must-buy, but unless there's a *Best of, Volume 2*, a lot of us won't be throwing out our Noggin tapes just yet.

GREAT MOMENTS: The "Fargo North, Decoder" sketches; the Cinderella segments with Rita Moreno and Judy Graubart; the "Punctuation" song in Episode 1; the performance of "Randy" in episode 379.

FAST-FORWARD: "Springing on a Sponge," in Episode 437, proves that not all the *EC* songs were gems.

EXTRAS: Episode introductions by Rita Moreno; outtakes; interviews with Rita Moreno, June Angela, writer Tom Whedon, and creator Joan Ganz Cooney; series trivia.

Ellen (1994–1998)

The Complete Season 1 (13 episodes on 2 discs): ★ ★ ★ ½
The Complete Season 2 (24 episodes on 3 discs): ★ ★ ★ ★
The Complete Season 3 (25 episodes on 3 discs): ★ ★ ★ ★ ½

A&E Home Video
Video: Full-Frame; Audio: Dolby Digital 2.0

Sometimes alteration makes sense, as in A&E's decision to release all of *Ellen*'s seasons under the same title, rather than resurrecting the original Season 1 title *These Friends of Mine*. Purists would understandably have preferred that the original credits run on the episodes themselves, though it's unfair to blame this entirely on A&E as the same change had already been made for the series' syndication run.

E

By whatever name, *Ellen* was one of the most successful variations on the *Seinfeld* model, though it had less of an edge than its progenitor, a result of its Southern California setting and the gentler humor of Ellen DeGeneres. The series found inspired ways to play to Ellen's rambling, stream-of-consciousness comic style, but in her struggles with a ballet bar and a water-cooler bottle she displayed skills as a physical comedian that equaled her verbal virtuosity. Season 4 featured Ellen Morgan's big coming-out party, an important TV moment that also proved too potent for the series to sustain, as every subsequent episode became more about Ellen's sexuality than about her everyday life.

GREAT MOMENTS: Season 1: Adam's cowardice prevents him from helping a gorgeous mugging victim, played by Mariska Hargitay, in "The Mugging"; Season 2: Ellen's laughing gas–induced confessions to her dentist in "The Dentist"; Ellen conjures memories of a classic *I Love Lucy* episode in "Ballet Class"; Season 3: The ever-changing introductions; Ellen hopes to meet John Travolta at his birthday party, but has to settle for Ron Palillo in "Horshack's Law"; Mary Tyler Moore guest-stars in "Lobster's Diary."

FAST-FORWARD: Nothing.

EXTRAS: Season 1: Commentary by costars Holly Fulger and Arye Gross; Season 2: Commentary by costars Joely Fisher and David Anthony Higgins; Season 3: Outtakes.

Elvis—'68 Comeback Special, Deluxe Edition (1968)

Three-Disc set: ★ ★ ★ ★ ★

BMG

Video: Full-Frame; Audio: Dolby Digital 5.1

In which the once and future King of Rock 'n' Roll, having been shoved aside by the British Invasion after tarnishing his own legacy with more crappy movies than any of us care to remember, dons a black leather jumpsuit and reminds the planet that he is still Elvis bleeping Presley. BMG's three-disc set presents the entire *Comeback Special* uncut for the first time on home video, with awesome picture and sound plus enough extras to exhaust even the most rabid Elvis fan. As befits a broadcast of such historic import, the set includes a booklet that details every aspect of the additional footage.

GREAT MOMENTS: The jam session with Scotty Moore and D.J. Fontana; the "Guitar Man" production number.

FAST-FORWARD: The throwaway treatment of "Love Me Tender," one of the King's best ballads, is the show's only misstep.

EXTRAS: All the raw footage from the concerts and taped segments from which the Special was assembled, including rehearsals and full alternate takes, as well as the false starts and technical glitches; "If I Can Dream—Special Music Video 2004" mixes various performances of "If I Can Dream."

Emergency! (1972–1977)

Season 1 (12 episodes on 2 discs): ★ ★ ★ ½

Season 2 (21 episodes on 3 discs): ★ ★ ★ ★

Universal Home Video

Video: Full-Frame; Audio: Dolby Digital 2.0

Jack Webb (*Dragnet*), the no-nonsense cop of TV's golden age, honors another branch of America's civil servants in this series set at the Squad 51 Fire Station. It's a straightforward look at professionals at work, often at the service of an indifferent or outright hostile public. Randolph Mantooth and Kevin Tighe became the breakout stars as Paramedics Gage and DeSoto, but re-watching the series on DVD one discovers renewed appreciation for the contributions of the Rampart staff, particularly Robert Fuller as Kelly Brackett, who is too often overlooked when lists of memorable TV doctors are made—even if his solution to almost every medical emergency is, "Start an I.V. with ringers lactate."

GREAT MOMENTS: Season 1: The original TV movie, *The Wedsworth-Townsend Act*, a fact-based, almost documentary-style look at the establishment of the L.A. Paramedic program, over the objections of some doctors who argued that firemen shouldn't be trusted with emergency medicine; Season 2: The lives of both paramedics and doctors are threatened in "Virus."

FAST-FORWARD: Some of the fire-station high jinks during downtime are pretty silly, proving once again that a Jack Webb series had no clue when it came to humor.

EXTRAS: None.

E

Entourage (2004–)

The Complete First Season (8 episodes on 2 discs): ★ ★ ★

HBO Home Video

Video: Full-Frame; Audio: Dolby Digital 2.0

At first glance *Entourage* seemed like a series that was too show-biz-inside to find an audience, even in our current celebrity-obsessed culture. But it turns out there's something universal about the pitfalls of success and the vexation of deadbeat friends and relatives that transcends the movie business. As with almost every HBO series, *Entourage* is smartly written, shrewdly cast (Jeremy Piven finally gets a role worthy of his talent), and creative in its frequent use of profanity. Even those who don't embrace the premise might want to give the series one look for its diverse variety of guest stars.

GREAT MOMENTS: Jessica Alba invites the boys to a party in "The Review."

FAST-FORWARD: Nothing.

EXTRAS: Commentaries with creator Doug Ellin and Executive Producer Larry Charles; cast and crew interviews.

ER (1994–)

The Complete First Season (25 episodes on 4 discs): ★ ★ ★ ★ ★

The Complete Second Season (22 episodes on 4 discs): ★ ★ ★ ★ ½

The Complete Third Season (22 episodes on 6 discs): ★ ★ ★ ★ ½

The Complete Fourth Season (22 episodes on 6 discs): ★ ★ ★ ★ ½

Warner Home Video

Video: Anamorphic Widescreen; Audio: Dolby Digital 2.0

Every ten years or so another series comes along to revitalize one of television's foundation genres. In the 1990s, *ER* pumped new blood into the doctor show by staging its life-and-death dramas with a pace and intensity that would have left Dr. Kildare dizzy. It probably shouldn't still be on the air as of this writing—heavy cast turnover has resulted in diminishing returns since at least since Season 5—but in its early years *ER* was the best drama on television, and arguably the best medical series ever. The season sets offer a widescreen transfer on episodes originally aired full-frame, a controversial decision but one generally accepted as positive. Outstanding extras only deepen one's appreciation for watching these excellent episodes.

GREAT MOMENTS: Season 1: The pilot episode sets a new standard for multiple storytelling at a feverish pace; Dr. Green delivers tragic news in "Love's Labor Lost"; Season 2: Dr. Ross must save a boy trapped in a storm drain in the Emmy-winning "Hell and High Water"; Season 3: Carol is taken hostage in a drugstore in "The Long Way Around," guest-starring Ewan McGregor; Season 4: "Ambush," an episode that originally aired live.

FAST-FORWARD: Nothing, at least until the original *ER* staff begin dropping like flies in the later seasons.

EXTRAS: Season 1: "Making of" documentaries on the pilot episode and the first season; featurettes on the series' medical consultants and on the post-production process; commentaries by series creator Michael Crichton, writers, and directors; outtakes; deleted scenes; Season 2: Outtakes/gag reel; cast-and-crew episode commentaries; featurettes "On Call" and "Anatomy of an Episode"; Season 3: "The Nurse's Station" and "Fear of Flying" featurettes; commentaries; outtakes/gag reel; Season 4: "Anatomy of an Ambush" and "Live Post Show" featurettes; outtakes.

Everwood (2004–)

Season 1 (23 episodes on 6 discs): ★ ★ ★ ★

Warner Home Video

Video: Anamorphic Widescreen; Audio: Dolby Digital 2.0

With its soap-opera story arcs, its clichéd big-city-versus-small-town conflicts, and its ping pong-ing between scenes of mopey adolescent angst and the kind of forced whimsy that can sink a better show like *The Gilmore Girls*, *Everwood* has no business being so addictive. The WB gathered Gregory Smith and Mike Erwin from its Dawson Leery stud farm of teen heartthrobs, casting them as rivals for the hand of the lovely Amy (Emily VanCamp); but the series' central relationship remains the one between Andy Brown (Treat Williams) and his son, Ephram (Smith), two characters forced to confront their strained history after the passing of Andy's wife.

GREAT MOMENTS: The emotionally explosive "Is There a Doctor in the House?"; Ephram deals with the first Thanksgiving without his mother in "A Thanksgiving Tale."

FAST-FORWARD: Andy's conversations with his deceased wife were wisely forgotten as the season progressed.

EXTRAS: Cast and crew commentaries on four episodes; the featurette "In Search of Everwood"; gag reel.

E

Everybody Loves Raymond (1996–2005)

The Complete First Season (22 episodes on 5 discs): ★ ★ ★ ½
The Complete Second Season (25 episodes on 5 discs): ★ ★ ★ ★
The Complete Third Season (26 episodes on 5 discs): ★ ★ ★ ★ ★
The Complete Fourth Season (24 episodes on 5 discs): ★ ★ ★ ★ ★
The Complete Fifth Season (25 episodes on 5 discs): ★ ★ ★ ★
The Series Finale: ★ ★ ★ ★

HBO Home Video

Video: Full-Frame (Seasons 1–3); Anamorphic Widescreen (Seasons 4 & 5, The Series Finale); Audio: Dolby Digital 2.0

It was the little sitcom that could. *Everybody Loves Raymond* struggled in its early years against mediocre ratings and being overshadowed by NBC's "Must See TV" lineup of comedy juggernauts, until finally the general public caught up with the critics and embraced *Raymond* as an exemplar of a family sitcom in the classic tradition. The DVD sets boast beautiful transfers and a generous selection of extras. The series later followed *Friends*' lead in releasing its final episode just weeks after it was first broadcast.

GREAT MOMENTS: Season 1: Tommy Lasorda, Marv Albert, and figure-skater Katarina Witt appear in "Recovering Pessimist"; Season 2: Debra finally confronts Marie, albeit through the mail, in "The Letter"; Marie embraces Robert's new girlfriend, prompting a twisted sense of competition in Ray, in "Good Girl"; Season 3: The flashback to Ray and Debra's first meeting in "How They Met"; Ray considers a vasectomy in "Halloween Candy"; Season 4: Debra fools Ray into thinking she's enhanced her bust line in "Boob Job."

FAST-FORWARD: Season 1: Debra nags Ray about spending more time with the kids, though not as amusingly as she usually does, in "Captain Nemo."

EXTRAS: Season 1: Commentaries with Ray Romano and series creator Phil Rosenthal; three behind-the-scenes featurettes; Ray Romano's appearance on *The Late Show with David Letterman*, which inspired the series' creation; Season 2: Romano/Rosenthal commentaries, plus deleted scenes and a blooper reel; Season 3: Same as Season 2, plus the Museum of Television and Radio panel discussion with the cast and creator Phil Rosenthal; Season 4: Bloopers and deleted scenes, plus commentaries with Romano and Rosenthal, Patricia Heaton, and Brad Garrett; Season 5: Cast/crew commentaries; bloopers and deleted scenes.

The Facts of Life (1979–1988)

The Complete First and Second Seasons (29 episodes on 4 discs): ★ ★ ★ ½

Sony Pictures Home Entertainment

Video: Full-Frame; Audio: Dolby Digital Mono

Smart move to package Seasons 1 and 2 together, because *The Facts of Life* stumbled through an uninspired first year, with too many schoolgirls to keep track of, and too much focus on the spun-off-from-*Diff'rent Strokes* character of Edna Garrett (Charlotte Rae). But by Season 2, Eastland's fab four were in place—Blair, Tootie, Natalie, and new girl Jo—while Nancy and Sue Ann and Cindy and even Molly Ringwald were expelled for poor charisma.

GREAT MOMENTS: Mrs. Garrett discovers her birthday present is hot in "Shoplifting"; Jo is reunited with her ex-con father in "The Secret."

FAST-FORWARD: Two words—"Cousin Geri"; the spin-off attempt "Brian and Sylvia."

EXTRAS: Featurettes "After Facts" and "Remembering *The Facts of Life.*"

Faerie Tale Theatre (1982–1987)

The Complete Collection (26 episodes on 4 discs): ★ ★ ★ ½

Rapunzel: ★ ★ ½

Rumplestiltskin: ★ ★

Goldilocks and the Three Bears: ★ ★

Hansel and Gretel: ★ ★ ★

Jack and the Beanstalk: ★ ★

Little Red Riding Hood: ★ ★ ★

The Nightingale: ★ ★ ★

The Princess and the Pea: ★ ★ ★
Sleeping Beauty: ★ ★ ★ ½
The Tale of the Frog Prince: ★ ★ ★

Starmaker II
Video: Full-Frame; Audio: Dolby Digital 2.0

The appeal of *Faerie Tale Theatre*, besides the stories themselves, was the casting of top stars (Susan Sarandon, Matthew Broderick, Robin Williams, Vanessa Redgrave) in the roles of familiar storybook characters, and the contributions of such directors as Tim Burton, Francis Ford Coppola, and Roger Vadim.

GREAT MOMENTS: *Complete Collection*: "Sleeping Beauty," with Beverly D'Angelo, Bernadette Peters, and Christopher Reeve; "Little Red Riding Hood" with Mary Steenburgen and Malcolm McDowell; "The Snow Queen" with Melissa Gilbert, Lance Kerwin, and Lee Remick.

FAST-FORWARD: *Complete Collection*: "Rumplestiltskin," with Hervé Villechaize; "The Boy Who Left Home to Find Out About the Shivers."

F

EXTRAS: None.

Fame (1982–1987)

The Complete First Season (16 episodes on 4 discs): ★ ★ ★ ★

MGM Home Video
Video: Full-Frame; Audio: Dolby Digital 2.0

Who didn't want to attend New York's School of the Arts after watching *Fame*? No other school had students bursting into song in the cafeteria, a new school play every week, dancing on cars in the parking lot, and the coolest teachers since Mr. Kotter retired. *Fame*, with its two original musical performances in every episode, was one of the more ambitious weekly drama series ever attempted, and sold more records and concert tickets than any series since *The Monkees*. All the music is intact in the first-season set and that's reason enough to buy it, though some extras would be nice when they get to Season 2.

GREAT MOMENTS: A pre-*Nanny* Fran Drescher appears in "Metamorphosis"; Lydia's dance class humbles a football team in "Tomorrow's Farewell"; the performance of "Starmaker" in "A Special Place."

FAST-FORWARD: Any time Lori Singer tries to sing.

EXTRAS: None.

Family Affair (1966–1971)

Season 1 (30 episodes on 5 discs): ★ ★ ★ ★

MPI Home Video

Video: Full-Frame; Audio: Dolby Digital 1.0

While it's remembered as one of TV's most gooey-sweet sitcoms, *Family Affair* opens in a very dark place—the sudden orphaning of six-year-old siblings and their teenage sister. A shortage of accommodating relatives forcibly removes the children from their heartland home and into the New York bachelor pad of wealthy Bill Davis (Uncle Bee-yoll to you). There's an undercurrent of insecurity and uncertainty within this uniquely formed family that pervades the first season, appropriate for a series that told its stories with honest emotions rather than showbiz sentiment.

On a lighter note, *Family Affair* should also be remembered for Mr. French, a great TV character, the merchandising phenomenon of Mrs. Beasley, those weird doorknobs in the Davis apartment, and Brian Keith as Uncle Bill, one of the few times a rich guy hasn't been portrayed on television as either a greedy scoundrel (*Dallas*) or a nincompoop (*Silver Spoons*).

GREAT MOMENTS: Buffy arrives on the Davis doorstep in "Buffy" (if you don't get misty when she tells Mrs. Beasley that Uncle Bill doesn't want them, you're not human); Cissy delves into Mr. French's private life in "The Thursday Man."

FAST-FORWARD: Nothing.

EXTRAS: Featurette starring Kathy Garver (Cissy).

Family Guy (1999–)

Volume 1 (28 episodes on 4 discs): ★ ★ ★

Volume 2 (23 episodes on 3 discs): ★ ★ ½

Volume 3 (13 episodes on 3 discs): ★ ★ ½

The Freakin' Sweet Collection (5 episodes on 1 disc): ★ ★

Stewie Griffin: The Untold Story (3 episodes on 1 disc): ★ ★

20th Century-Fox

Video: Full-Frame; Audio: Dolby Digital 2.0

Sometimes crudely animated, always random, *Family Guy* follows the adventures of the Griffin family. Most episodes center around the father, Peter, or Stewie, an evil baby with an eye on world domination and death for his mother. An acquired taste, needless to say. The show is sprinkled with celebrity voices, often heard as the Griffins watch television.

Family Guy bounced around the FOX schedule for three years, collecting a small but loyal following before falling to the network axe. It wasn't until the release of the show on DVD and re-airings on the Cartoon Network that the series captured mainstream attention. In response to the high sales for the DVD volumes, FOX commissioned more episodes, and it is now back on the network's primetime schedule as a possible heir to *The Simpsons.*

A direct-to-DVD release, *Stewie Griffin: The Untold Story,* was unleashed in September 2005, although it is really a collection of three related episodes that will likely air on the FOX schedule by 2006. The *Freakin' Sweet Collection* contains several previously released episodes with censored elements restored and new commentaries.

GREAT MOMENTS: Volume 1: Patrick Duffy and Victoria Principal revisit the famous *Dallas* dream sequence in a rare live-action *Family Guy* scene, in "Da Boom."

FAST-FORWARD: The grating theme song deserves your MUTE button. Also, in very long episodes like the *Stewie Griffin: The Untold Story* "movie," the show's shtick gets old after an hour.

F

EXTRAS: Series volumes include episode commentaries, animatics, and featurettes; Volume 2 includes the original series' pilot pitch.

Fantastic Four (1994–1995)

The Complete Series (26 episodes on 4 discs): ★ ★ ½

Buena Vista Home Video

Video: Full-Frame; Audio: Dolby Digital 2.0

The Marvel Age of Comics began with the Fantastic Four. Created by Stan Lee and Jack Kirby, the FF inaugurated a remarkable new age in superhero comics that led to the birth of the Hulk, Spider-Man, and the X-Men. So why have characters with this kind of pedigree faltered every time they're removed from the printed page? Thus far we've had two live-action misfires and three animated series of varying quality. This is the best of them; the animation's better than the primitive 1960s attempt, and there's no Herbie the Robot from the 1978 series. Still, episodes are hit and miss.

GREAT MOMENTS: A flawed but valiant attempt to adapt the FF's best comic story, the Galactus Trilogy, in "The Silver Surfer and the Coming of Galactus, Parts 1 & 2"; Daredevil appears in "And a Blind Man Shall Lead Them"; Dr. Doom sends the Hulk to destroy the FF in "Nightmare in Green."

FAST-FORWARD: Sue Storm is transformed into the evil Malice in "Worlds Within Worlds," a story that sucked in the comics, too.

EXTRAS: Episode introductions by Stan Lee; "Stan Lee's Soapbox."

Fantasy Island (1978–1984)

The First Season (16 episodes on 4 discs): ★ ★ ★ ½

Sony Pictures Home Entertainment

Video: Full-Frame; Audio: Dolby Digital 2.0

In the 1970s, primetime on Saturday night was dominated by ABC's one-two punch of *The Love Boat* and *Fantasy Island.* Both series offered exotic locations, stories to be enjoyed with one's brain on cruise control, and a diverse assortment of guest stars. The *Pacific Princess* has yet to sail onto DVD, but if we can't get on the boat, at least we have da plane. Da plane!

Sony's first-season set includes the 1977 pilot movie and the 1978 *Return to Fantasy Island* featurette.

GREAT MOMENTS: *Return to Fantasy Island* features appearances from Joseph Cotten, Karen Valentine, Nancy McKeon, George Chakiris, Adrienne Barbeau, and Laraine Day; a conservative husband and wife wish to live in a more wholesome time, so Mr. Roarke sends them back to Salem during the witch trials, in "Superstar/Salem."

FAST-FORWARD: The voodoo story in "Family Reunion/Voodoo."

EXTRAS: Original promo spots; featurette; interviews.

Farscape (1999–2004)

Season 1 (22 episodes on 11 discs): ★ ★ ½

Season 2 (22 episodes on 11 discs): ★ ★ ½

Season 3 (22 episodes on 10 discs): ★ ★ ½

Season 4 (22 episodes on 5 discs): ★ ★

Also available as individual volumes:

Season 1: 11 volumes (2 episodes each on 1 disc): ★ ★

Season 2–4: 5 volumes each (4 episodes on 2 discs): ★ ★

The Starburst Editions, Volumes 1–6 (7 episodes each on 2 discs): ★ ★ ½

Farscape: The Peacekeeper Wars: ★ ★ ½

A.D. Vision; Lions Gate (*The Peacekeeper Wars*)

Video: Full-Frame; Anamorphic Widescreen (*The Peacekeeper Wars*); Audio: Dolby Digital 5.1

Farscape is love-it-or-hate-it sci-fi, and no viewers' opinions will change because of what's written here. While fans will marvel at the aliens invented by Jim Henson's Creatures Shop for this Australian import, detractors will wonder when they'll get the episode where Crichton meets Elmo.

But even the most fervent *Farscape* lovers can't be happy with the mess that was made of the series' DVD release. A.D. Vision unleashed individual volumes and editions before finally gathering the shows into season sets, for which they just wrapped a big box around eleven discs to hold twenty-two shows. If that double-dip wasn't enough, ADV then offered "Starburst Editions" of the same material, with seven episodes each. The only attraction of the new collections is a lower price point, which would be fine if most of the fans didn't already have these shows in some form already.

GREAT MOMENTS: Season 2: Aeryn's loyalties are questioned in "The Way We Weren't"; Season 3: The very strange (but amusingly so) "Scratch 'n' Sniff"; Season 4: Crichton and Chiana are trapped inside a video game in "John Quixote"; the all-female episode "Bringing Home the Beacon."

F

FAST-FORWARD: Season 2: "Taking the Stone" manages to rip off both *Logan's Run* and the Mad Max series; Season 4: The sillier than usual "Coup by Clam."

EXTRAS: Season 1: Cast/crew commentaries; deleted scenes; video profiles of cast and filmmakers; Season 2: Deleted scenes; commentaries; "The *Farscape* Dictionary"; "Main Character Back Stories"; "Alien Encounters," "Weapons and Ships" and "Alien Races" featurettes; Season 3: Deleted scenes; interviews; commentaries; "Cool *Farscape* Facts" by Paul Simpson; set, prop, and costume galleries; Season 4: Cast interviews; deleted scenes; outtakes; "Cool *Farscape* Facts" by Paul Simpson; *The Peacekeeper Wars*; "making of" documentary.

Fat Albert and the Cosby Kids (1972–1982)

Fat Albert and the Cosby Kids (5 episodes on 1 disc): ★ ★ ½

Fat Albert's Greatest Hits: The Ultimate Collection (20 episodes on 4 discs): ★ ★ ½

Volume 1 (12 episodes on 2 discs): ★ ★ ★

Volume 2 (12 episodes on 3 discs): ★ ★ ★

Easter Special: ★ ★

Halloween Special: ★ ★

Ventura Distribution (*Fat Albert* and *Fat Albert's Greatest Hits*); Urban Works (*Volume 1*, *Volume 2*, *Halloween Special*)

Video: Full-Frame; Audio: Dolby Digital 2.0

Between his Emmy-winning stints on *I Spy* and *The Cosby Show*, Bill Cosby spent a decade on Saturday-morning TV, where he narrated the adventures of a gang of cartoon kids inspired by his youth on the streets of Philadelphia. *Fat Albert and the Cosby Kids* combined entertainment and education with the grace of a PBS series, and represents a significant advancement in multiculturalism in children's television, though it rarely addressed the subject directly. Picture and sound quality on all DVD sets are somewhat lacking; the Urban Works collections are the best place to start, as they present the episodes in order from the beginning.

GREAT MOMENTS: Volume 1: Two of Bill Cosby's most famous stand-up routines featuring Fat Albert, "Buck Buck" and "Go Carts," are illustrated in "Moving"; the gang's junkyard band is formed in "Creativity."

FAST-FORWARD: Nothing.

EXTRAS: Volumes 1 and 2: Audio CD of songs from the series.

F

Father Murphy (1981–1983)

Season 1 (21 episodes on 5 discs): ★ ★ ★
Season 2 (13 episodes on 5 discs): ★ ★ ½

Image Entertainment

Video: Full-Frame; Audio: Dolby Digital 2.0

Genial spin-off of *Little House on the Prairie*, starring ex-football bruiser Merlin Olsen as a drifter who poses as a priest to protect a group of orphaned children. In Season 2, when story developments made the man-of-the-cloth guise no longer necessary, Murphy married the local schoolmarm and had a kid of his own. Unfortunately, viewers seemed to prefer him as a priest, as the show was cancelled soon after.

GREAT MOMENTS: Season 1: a pre-Bundy Christina Applegate appears in "A Horse from Heaven."

FAST-FORWARD: Nothing.

EXTRAS: None.

Fawlty Towers (1975–1979)

The Complete Collection (12 episodes on 3 discs): ★ ★ ★ ★ ★

BBC Video

Video: Full-Frame; Audio: Mono

One thing about the British—they're not afraid to build a TV series around a character who is beyond redemption. Such is Basil Fawlty (John Cleese), the manic, short-tempered, social-climbing owner of a seaside inn on the coast of Torquay. Cleese's follow-up to *Monty Python's Flying Circus* will always be on the short list of the funniest situation comedies ever created, and was one of the few BBC series to gain a sizable US following in the days before cable. Fans are still disappointed that only twelve episodes were made, but each one is a thirty-minute masterpiece. The DVD set does right by the show with a delightful assortment of extra features.

GREAT MOMENTS: Basil beats up his car in "Gourmet Night"; Basil responds to a belligerent guest's complaint about the view ("What did you expect to see out of a Torquay hotel bedroom window? Sydney Opera House perhaps? The Hanging Gardens of Babylon? Herds of wildebeest sweeping majestically . . . !") in "Communication Problems"; Basil's goosestep in "The Germans."

FAST-FORWARD: The "Customer Service Tips" clips in the extras. Watching the episodes is much more satisfying.

EXTRAS: Interviews with stars John Cleese, Prunella Scales, and Andrew Sachs; A visit to Torquay, featuring a fascinating look at the real hotelier who inspired the character of Basil Fawlty; outtakes.

Felicity (1998–2002)

The Complete First Season (22 episodes on 6 discs): ★ ★ ★ ★ ★
The Complete Second Season (23 episodes on 6 discs): ★ ★ ★ ½
The Complete Third Season (17 episodes on 5 discs): ★ ★ ★ ½
The Complete Fourth Season (22 episodes on 6 discs): ★ ★ ★ ★

Buena Vista Home Entertainment

Video: Full-Frame; Audio: Dolby Digital Stereo (Season 1); Dolby Digital Surround 5.1 (Seasons 2–4)

The premise was pure genius. Felicity Porter, of the angelic face and cascading ringlets, is about to graduate from a Los Angeles high school, her transition to Stanford's medical program long preordained. But then hunky Ben Covington, whom Felicity has always loved from afar, writes something in her yearbook that suggests he may have noticed her more than she ever believed. So she abandons her carefully prepared life plan, defies her parents, and follows Ben to New York University. And every viewer who was too cautious to explore the Road Not Taken cannot help but be drawn into her plight, especially after she arrives to find Ben has forgotten all about his earlier moment of clarity.

The first season was a phenomenon; female fans debated whether Felicity should continue to pursue Ben or return the affections of the more sympathetic but less studly Noel. And guys tuned in because Keri Russell is gorgeous. By Season 2 the soap-opera excess got to be a bit much; Felicity's feelings toward Ben, Noel's feelings toward Felicity, Ben's feelings toward Julie, Sean's feelings toward Julie—the show had more unrequited love than a comic book convention. The progression from "Who will she choose?" to "Oh, for God's sake, make up your mind" wasn't helped by the shockwaves that resulted from Russell's acquiescence to the most infamous celebrity haircut since Elvis went into the army. But even viewers who lost interest along the way couldn't resist returning to the series for Felicity's senior year, when the Ben-versus-Noel debate was finally resolved.

GREAT MOMENTS: Season 1: Ben's yearbook note and Felicity's response in the pilot episode; the Pink Power Ranger Halloween costume in "Spooked," a reference to the character played by *Felicity* costar Amy Jo Johnson; Jennifer Garner plays Noel's girlfriend in "Thanksgiving"; Season 2: Julie's song about Felicity in "The Depths"; Season 4: The mondo bizarro time-travel arc in "Felicity Interrupted."

FAST-FORWARD: The dysfunctional Meghan-Sean romance (Seasons 2–4).

EXTRAS: Season 1: Commentaries by series creators J.J. Abrams and Matt Reeves; Season 2: Commentaries by stars Keri Russell, Amy Jo Johnson, Scott Foley, Scott Speedman, Amanda Foreman, Greg Grunberg, and Tangi Miller, and creators J.J. Abrams and Matt Reeves; "Finding Felicity" featurette; Emmy Award parody; Season 3: Commentaries, outtakes, and a "making of" featurette; A *MAD TV* parody of *Felicity*; Season 4: Alternate footage from the final episode; cast and crew commentaries; the Museum of Television and Radio's salute to *Felicity*.

Firefly (2002–2003)

Season 1 (15 episodes on 4 discs): ★ ★ ★ ★ ½

20th Century-Fox

Video: Anamorphic Widescreen; Audio: Dolby Digital 5.1

"You can't take the sky from me . . ." Billed as the "anti–*Star Trek*," *Firefly* had no aliens, no warp drive, transporters or tricorders, no sounds in space, and no philosophical quandries easily solved within each episode. The existentialist philosophy of the series was dark and bleak. These were characters who had been through a war, and lost, and now had no purpose in life but to keep moving. As with all of his series, however, creator Joss Whedon established an undercurrent of hope.

After only twelve of its fifteen episodes aired, *Firefly* was cancelled due to poor decision making by the FOX network. Besides weak marketing, FOX decided not to air the two-hour pilot, instead having Whedon create a new first episode, which led to a great deal of confusion. The network aired other episodes out of order, in a time slot in which they were often pre-empted by the baseball season. But cancellation was not the end for *Firefly*; Whedon wrote and directed a motion picture adaptation, *Serenity*, which was released in the fall of 2005.

Firefly has a beautiful video transfer, which captures the dark look of the series. One of its signature visual traits were the Steadicam-in-space effects, in which the camera would seem to zoom in and out, sometimes shakily, outside the ship. These scenes look especially wonderful on DVD.

GREAT MOMENTS: The introductions to all of the characters in the pilot, "Serenity"; the attack by the space-mad Reavers in "Bushwhacked"; ship mechanic Kaylee's excitement at attending a society ball, and Captain Malcolm Reynolds' duel for the honor of Inara, in "Shindig"; the hilarious interactions between Mal and con-artist Saffron in "Our Mrs. Reynolds" and "Trash"; the flashbacks and non-linear narrative of "Out of Gas"; Jayne's almost-betrayal of fugitive siblings Simon and River Tam in "Ariel"; the mentally unbalanced River saving herself and the ship's crew from the villainous bounty hunter, Jubal Early, in "Objects in Space."

FAST-FORWARD: Nothing.

EXTRAS: The episode commentary tracks, from members of the cast and crew, are fantastic, in particular Joss Whedon's for "Objects in Space," the last and arguably best episode of the series. Whedon gives an in-depth discussion not only of the technical aspects of filming, but the existential themes of the episode and the series. The set also includes a gag reel, audition tapes, some excellent deleted scenes, and two behind-the-scenes featurettes.

The Flash (1990–1991)

The Complete Series (22 episodes on 6 discs): ★ ★ ½

Warner Home Video

Video: Full-Frame; Audio: Dolby Digital Mono

The classic DC Comics superhero came with a Batman twist in this heavily hyped hour-long drama. John Wesley Shipp played police scientist Barry

Allen, a character that at the time had been absent from the Flash comics for five years. After a late-night lab session, Barry is altered by a lightning strike and a chemical bath, and discovers he can fight crime by running really fast. The costume and pre-CGI special effects were first-rate. The stories, not so much.

GREAT MOMENTS: An old hero returns in "Deadly Nightshade"; Mark Hamill makes two appearances as the Trickster ("The Trickster," "Trial of the Trickster"), providing the series with its best villain.

FAST-FORWARD: The series' two-hour pilot hasn't aged well, since it takes almost an hour for the action to begin. Sure, the fast-speed effects are cool, but we want to see the foamy red costume!

EXTRAS: None.

The Flintstones (1960–1966)

Season 1 (29 episodes on 4 discs): ★ ★ ★ ½
Season 2 (32 episodes on 4 discs): ★ ★ ★ ½
Season 3 (28 episodes on 4 discs): ★ ★ ★ ★
Season 4 (26 episodes on 4 discs): ★ ★ ★ ★ ½
Season 5 (26 episodes on 4 discs): ★ ★ ★ ★

Warner Home Video
Video: Full-Frame; Audio: Dolby Digital 2.0

While many of us grew up with *The Flintstones* on Saturday mornings, TV historians and senior citizens remember how the series originally broke the cartoon barrier in primetime, paving the way for *Jonny Quest*, *The Simpsons*, and *Family Guy*. A near-constant presence on television for five decades, this Hanna-Barbera classic may be television's most successful animated show. Fred and Wilma Flintstone were clearly modeled after Ralph and Alice Kramden from *The Honeymooners*, and most of the episode plot lines had already been covered by live-action sitcoms; what made *The Flintstones* unique was its "modern Stone Age" setting and the endless array of prehistoric gadgets that turned up in every show.

After releasing Season 1 as a no-frills test balloon, Warner Home Video must have been pleased with the sales figures, as they lavished more attention on the releases beginning with Season 2, which features commentary tracks and a thirty-minute documentary.

GREAT MOMENTS: Season 1: Fred becomes a hipster idol in "Hot Lips Hannigan"; the waitresses' song in "The Drive-In"; Season 2: The *Rear*

Window–inspired "Alfred Brickrock Presents"; Fred finds a secret stash of cash in "Wilma's Vanishing Money"; Season 3: Fred masquerades as "The Kissing Burglar"; the birth of Pebbles in "Dress Rehearsal"; Yogi Bear and Boo Boo make an appearance in "Swedish Visitors"; Season 4: Pebbles gets a celebrity babysitter in "Ann-Margrock Presents"; Bamm-Bamm arrives in "Little Bamm-Bamm"; Season 5: The infamous Madame Yes appears in "Dr. Sinister"; Fred masquerades as Italian racecar driver Goggles Pisano in "Indianrockolis 500"; the Flintstones meet the weird new neighbors in "The Gruesomes."

FAST-FORWARD: Nothing.

EXTRAS: Season 1: A clip from the original series pilot "The Flagstones"; two featurettes; Season 2: "Carved in Stone: The *Flintstones* Phenomenon" documentary; commentaries; "Songs of the Flintstones" music video; Season 3: "Bedrock Collectibles" and "First Families of the Stone Age" featurettes; Season 4: Commentaries; featurette; "The Legendary Music of Hoyt Curtain" documentary; Season 5: Interview with Joe Barbera and William Hanna; original storyboards for the episode "The Gruesomes."

The Flying Nun (1967–1970)

The Complete First Season (30 episodes on 4 discs): ★ ★

Sony Pictures Home Entertainment

Video: Full-Frame; Audio: Dolby Digital Mono

No bonus points for Sally Field's appeal can offset the simple truth that *The Flying Nun* was a dumb show. Watching Sister Bertrille soar over Puerto Rico, one had to wonder what the ABC programmers were ingesting when they tried to capitalize on Field's post-*Gidget* popularity by putting her in a nun's cornette. But they got three seasons out of it, so what do I know?

GREAT MOMENTS: Sister Bertrille fends off a lovesick pelican in "With Love from Irving."

FAST-FORWARD: Every episode is equally sweet and silly.

EXTRAS: "A Look Back at *The Flying Nun*" featurette, featuring an interview with Sally Field.

Footballers' Wive$ (2002–)

Season 1 (8 episodes on 2 discs): ★ ★ ★ ½
Season 2 (8 episodes on 2 discs): ★ ★ ★ ½

Capital Entertainment
Video: Anamorphic Widescreen; Audio: Dolby Digital Stereo

If you're going to go over the top, then a big flying leap is better than a bunny hop. That's the philosophy that fuels *Footballers' Wive$*, a trashy British soap that became the biggest UK phenomenon since the Spice Girls.

GREAT MOMENTS: Season 1: Tanya takes drastic measures to secure her husband's spot on the team in Episode 1; Jason hooks up with Kyle's mother in Episode 6; Season 2: Jason's plunge in the season finale.

FAST-FORWARD: Nothing.

EXTRAS: Seasons 1 and 2: A slang dictionary.

F

Fraggle Rock (1983–1987)

Season 1 (24 episodes on 5 discs): ★ ★ ★ ★
Volume 1: Where It All Began, Special Edition (2 episodes on 1 disc): ★ ½
Volume 2: Dance Your Cares Away (3 episodes on 1 disc): ★ ½
Volume 3: Live by the Rule of the Rock (3 episodes on 1 disc): ★ ½
Volume 4: Doin' Things That Doozers Do (3 episodes on 1 disc): ★ ½
Volume 5: Down in Fraggle Rock (6 episodes on 1 disc): ★ ½

Hit Entertainment
Video: Full-Frame; Audio: Dolby Digital 1.0

Only the rich kids watched *Fraggle Rock* when it debuted. Anyone with parents too cheap to spring for cable, back in the day when it was a luxury, could only imagine the wonders in this Muppet series that was arguably Jim Henson's most ambitious undertaking. The stories tackled moral and ethical issues in a more sophisticated manner than one would expect from characters called Doozers, Gorgs, and Fraggles, but there was enough humor and hummable original songs in each episode that it never felt like school.

Now that season sets are hitting the market, don't bother with the individual volumes that collect anywhere from two to six episodes, sometimes from different seasons.

GREAT MOMENTS: Season 1: Uncle Matt's postcards from "Outer Space"; Gobo is trapped in Doc's workshop in "Don't Cry Over Spilt Milk"; Muppet existentialism in "Gobo's Discovery."

FAST-FORWARD: Nothing.

EXTRAS: Season 1: Cast and crew interviews; the documentary "Down at Fraggle Rock," narrated by Jim Henson.

Frasier (1993–2004)

Season 1 (24 episodes on 3 discs): ★ ★ ★ ★ ½
Season 2 (24 episodes on 4 discs): ★ ★ ★ ★ ½
Season 3 (24 episodes on 4 discs): ★ ★ ★ ★ ★
Season 4 (24 episodes on 4 discs): ★ ★ ★ ★ ★
Season 5 (24 episodes on 4 discs): ★ ★ ★ ★ ★
Season 6 (23 episodes on 4 discs): ★ ★ ★ ½
Season 7 (24 episodes on 4 discs): ★ ★ ★
Season 11 (24 episodes on 4 discs): ★ ★ ★ ½
Season 1–5 & 11 (144 episodes on 24 discs): ★ ★ ★ ★ ★

F

Paramount Home Video
Video: Full-Frame; Audio: Dolby Digital 2.0

If you had taken a poll on which *Cheers* character had the best chance to sustain a spin-off series, Dr. Frasier Crane would have been lucky to finish fourth. But through a change in locale, a new work situation rife with comic possibility, and the masterful casting of David Hyde Pierce as Frasier's even fussier brother, the new series proved the equal of its predecessor.

It takes smart writers to write smart characters, and *Frasier* had a stable unmatched in 1990s television. They rarely stepped wrong in ten years' worth of shows; but in the tradition of nitpickers everywhere, I'd observe that the Maris references were too reminiscent of Norm's unseen wife on *Cheers*, and that the ongoing almost-relationship between Niles and Daphne, a bittersweet triumph through the first few years, could have been resolved earlier than the eighth season. No matter—*Frasier* rocks, and so do the DVD sets, even if they run out of extras between Seasons 4 and 10. (The eleventh (and last) season was released early to capitalize on the series finale.)

GREAT MOMENTS: Season 1: Frasier's ex-wife returns in "The One Where Lilith Comes Back"; Season 2: Niles tests his parenting skills in "Flour Child"; Daphne's blind date has his eye on Frasier in "The Matchmaker"; the Crane brothers open their own restaurant in "The Innkeepers"; Season 3: Niles and Daphne's tango in "Moon Dance"; Shelley Long returns as Diane Chambers in "The One Where Diane Comes Back"; Season 4: Niles poses as Daphne's husband in "The Two Mrs. Cranes"; Season 5: No one believes Frasier's dating a supermodel (Sela Ward) in "Frasier's Imaginary Friend"; "The Ski Lodge" is a classic bedroom farce; Season 7: Niles unwittingly dates a prostitute in "Father of the Bride"; the Cranes wonder if they're descended from Russian royalty in "A Tsar is Born"; Season 11: Patrick Stewart plays yet another man who thinks Frasier is gay in "The Doctor Is Out"; Laura Linney plays a matchmaker in "Match Game."

FAST-FORWARD: Season 4: Frasier's attempt to impress his son on the baseball field in "The Unnatural."

EXTRAS: Season 1: "Behind the Couch: The Making of *Frasier*" featurette; commentary by series creators; Season 2: commentaries; cast and crew interviews; "Celebrity Voices" featurette; Season 3: "The Crane Brothers Remember Season 3"; interviews; featurettes; Season 11: "Frasier Says Farewell" and "Observations, Analyses, and Good-Byes" featurettes.

F

Freaks and Geeks (1999–2000)

The Complete Series (18 episodes on 6 discs): ★ ★ ★ ★ ½

Special Collectors "Yearbook" Edition: Complete Series (18 episodes on 6 discs plus 2 discs of bonus material): ★ ★ ★ ★ ★

Shout! Factory

Video: Full-Frame; Audio: Dolby Digital 5.1

The perfect DVD set? *Freaks and Geeks* may be it.

The show first surfaced in the fall of 1999 on NBC, but the network wasn't sure what they had, and despite critical acclaim and a cult following the ratings never came around. It didn't help that NBC shuffled *Freaks* on the schedule throughout the season before finally giving up, with several episodes still unaired.

For years, *Freaks and Geeks* was one of the most oft-requested series for DVD release. But its time-period authenticity (the show followed the lives of the outcasts of fictional McKinley High circa 1980) meant a lot of music rights to clear, and the cost of doing so seemed prohibitive.

The show's creators insisted on all of the original music's being preserved intact; a special *Collectors Edition* set in the shape of a McKinley High yearbook was offered at freaksandgeeks.com in the hope of raising funds to achieve the goal, and the fans responded. Their efforts were rewarded with a marvelous set that includes two discs packed with extras, including a Museum of Television and Radio sit-down, actor auditions, promos, and an unaired script.

GREAT MOMENTS: Sam tries out for school mascot to impress Cindy in "We've

Got Spirit"; the geeks crank-call the gym coach in "The Diary"; the geeks get an unexpected new D&D partner in Daniel Desario in "Discos and Dragons." Some commentaries are worth listening to for their pure randomness—the actors' parents do commentary on one; the NBC execs who cancelled the show do another; and one commentary has the actors who played teachers talking about the episode in character.

FAST-FORWARD: The NBC promos on one of the *Collectors Edition* discs.

EXTRAS: *Complete Series*: Twenty-nine (!!) audio commentaries on the eighteen episodes, pilot-episode director's cut, booklet with essays by the show's creators, deleted scenes, and outtakes. *Collectors Edition*: Special yearbook, actor auditions, Museum of Television and Radio panel interviews, behind-the-scenes footage, table readings, and much more.

The French Chef (1963–1972)

The French Chef (18 episodes on 3 discs): ★ ★ ★ ½
The French Chef 2 (18 episodes on 3 discs): ★ ★ ★ ½

WGBH Boston
Video: Full-Frame; Audio: Dolby Digital Mono

In her long-running PBS series Julia Child explained the intricacies of haute cuisine to the American housewife. There may never have been a Food Network without the archetype she popularized, and while Giada De Laurentiis and Rachael Ray may be more camera-friendly, Julia could out-sauté both of them, as these forty-year-old shows demonstrate. Child's dry humor and occasional whimsy made her one of TV's most unlikely celebrities. The DVD sets contain complete episodes as originally broadcast, preserving all the unexpected moments that are unavoidable in live television. Watching Julia soldier through her occasional bloopers and kitchen mishaps just made her more beloved.

GREAT MOMENTS: *The French Chef*: Julia misses the pan when she flips her potatoes in "The Potato Show"; the preparation of her "Bœuf Bourguignon" will still impress your friends; *The French Chef 2*: "Gateau in a Cage" is one of Julia's most delightful desserts.

FAST-FORWARD: Nothing.

EXTRAS: The printable recipes on each disc are a nice touch.

The Fresh Prince of Bel-Air (1990–1996)

Season 1 (25 episodes on 4 discs): ★ ★ ★ ★
Season 2 (24 episodes on 4 discs): ★ ★ ★ ½
Season 3 (24 episodes on 4 discs): ★ ★ ★

Warner Home Video
Video: Full-Frame; Audio: Dolby Digital 2.0

As high-concept as sitcoms get, *The Fresh Prince of Bel-Air* riffed on the contrast between Philadelphia's mean streets and cushy Bel-Air, as witnessed by rapper Will Smith, the only hip-hop artist with the Good Housekeeping Seal of Approval. The fish-out-of-water plots were nothing audiences hadn't seen before, but as a showcase for Smith's talent and likability, the premise worked well enough.

Don't be misled by Season 1 packaging that lists two discs—each set contains four discs of material; the confusion is a result of Warner's last-minute decision to upgrade sets from double- to single-sided discs. Tech credits are above average, and it was good to hear the extended version of the series' theme preserved on the first three episodes.

F

GREAT MOMENTS: Season 1: Future Oscar-nominee Don Cheadle hangs with future Oscar-nominee Will Smith in "Homeboy, Sweet Homeboy"; the two-part Halloween episode "Someday Your Prince Will Be in Effect," featuring guest appearances by Tim Russ, Quincy Jones, Bo Jackson, Malcolm-Jamal Warner, and many others; Vivica A. Fox, who played Will Smith's wife in *Independence Day*, appears in "It Had to Be You"; Season 2: Will won't ask full-figured Dee Dee (Queen Latifah) to the dance in "She Ain't Heavy"; Season 3: The Banks family appears on Oprah Winfrey's show in "A Night at the Oprah."

FAST-FORWARD: A typically annoying Kathy Griffin performance in "Not with My Pig, You Don't."

EXTRAS: Season 1: "Back to Bel-Air: A Fresh Look" features interviews with series creators, directors, writers, and stars. No Will Smith, though; Season 3: Gag reel.

Friends (1994–2004)

The Complete First Season (23 episodes on 4 discs): ★ ★ ★ ★ ★
The Complete Second Season (24 episodes on 4 discs): ★ ★ ★ ★ ★
The Complete Third Season (25 episodes on 4 discs): ★ ★ ★ ★ ½
The Complete Fourth Season (24 episodes on 4 discs): ★ ★ ★ ★ ★

The Complete Fifth Season (24 episodes on 4 discs): ★ ★ ★ ★ ★
The Complete Sixth Season (25 episodes on 4 discs): ★ ★ ★ ★
The Complete Seventh Season (23 episodes on 4 discs): ★ ★ ★ ½
The Complete Eighth Season (24 episodes on 4 discs): ★ ★ ★ ★ ★
The Complete Ninth Season (23 episodes on 4 discs): ★ ★ ★ ★
The Complete Tenth Season (18 episodes on 4 discs): ★ ★ ★ ½
The Best of Friends, Volume 1 (10 episodes on 2 discs): ★ ★ ★ ★ ★
The Best of Friends, Volume 2 (10 episodes on 2 discs): ★ ★ ★ ★ ½
The Best of Friends, Volume 3 (10 episodes on 2 discs): ★ ★ ★ ★
The Best of Friends, Volume 4 (10 episodes on 2 discs): ★ ★ ★ ★
The Best of Friends, Season 1 (5 episodes on 1 disc): ★ ★ ★ ★
The Best of Friends, Season 2 (5 episodes on 1 disc): ★ ★ ★ ★
The Best of Friends, Season 3 (5 episodes on 1 disc): ★ ★ ★ ★
The Best of Friends, Season 4 (5 episodes on 1 disc): ★ ★ ★ ★
Friends: The Final Episode: ★ ★ ★

F

Warner Home Video
Video: Full-Frame; Audio: Dolby Digital 5.1

The preeminent sitcom of the 1990s, *Friends* is also the last situation comedy to reach the level of universal acclaim achieved by popular television shows in the pre-cable era. In 1995, if you weren't watching *Friends* there was something wrong with you. After three or four seasons the trendier pop-culture mavens moved on to *Sex and the City* and other passions, but millions stayed with *Friends* and were seldom disappointed. Each time the series lost momentum, as in the wake of Chandler and Monica's marriage, it would bounce back with something new and unexpected, like the budding relationship between Rachel and Joey.

The DVD season sets are mostly wonderful, with one or two caveats; though blooper reels are standard for each complete set beginning with the sixth season, the clip show "The Stuff You've Never Seen," hosted by Conan O'Brien and originally aired during the seventh season, is not included with its corresponding set. Also missing is the Rembrandts' "I'll Be There for You" music video featuring the *Friends* cast, which appears in the *Best of Friends, Volume 1* collection. Those who opted for season sets are entitled to the clip as well. For viewers fearful of a full ten-season commitment, there are "best of" collections grouped both by season and episodes selected by the series' creators.

GREAT MOMENTS: Season 1: Monica's competitiveness first surfaces in "The One with All the Poker"; the performance of the *Odd Couple* theme in "The One with the Dozen Lasagnas"; Season 2: Julia Roberts embarrasses Chandler in

"The One After the Super Bowl"; Monica's "YMCA" dance in "The One with the Bullies"; the emotional rollercoaster of "The One with the Prom Video"; Season 3: The gang's freebie lists, and Isabella Rossellini's appearance in "The One with Frank Jr."; Season 4: "The One with Chandler in a Box"—the series' best Thanksgiving episode; the boys-versus-girls trivia contest in "The One with the Embryos"; Ross marries Emily (almost) in "The One with Ross's Wedding"; Season 5: The one-upmanship in "The One Where Everybody Finds Out"; the shocking season finale in "The One in Vegas, Part 2"; Season 6: Monica and Chandler get engaged in "The One with the Proposal"; Season 7: Susan Sarandon plays a soap-opera diva in "The One with Joey's New Brain"; Season 8: Joey develops a crush on Rachel in "The One Where Joey Dates Rachel"; the brilliant "The One Where Rachel Has the Baby."

FAST-FORWARD: Season 1: The monkey-centric "The One Where Marcel Gets Away"; Season 2: "The One Where Heckles Dies"; David Schwimmer's dual role in "The One with Russ"; Season 5: Phoebe's Fonzie-obsessed doctor in "The One-Hundredth"; Season 6: The clip show "The One with Mac and CHEESE"; Season 8: Alec Baldwin hams it up in "The One in Massapequa."

EXTRAS: Each season set features commentaries on some episodes by *Friends* writers and creators Kevin Bright, Marta Kauffman, and David Crane; outtakes and interviews with *Friends* guest stars begin with Season 6. The final season set also includes a "Friends' Final Thoughts" featurette with new cast/crew interviews, and the "Joey, Joey" music video.

Full House (1987–1995)

Season 1 (22 episodes on 4 discs): ★ ★ ★
Season 2 (22 episodes on 4 discs): ★ ★
Season 3 (24 episodes on 4 discs): ★ ★ ½

Warner Home Video
Video: Full-Frame; Audio: Dolby Digital 1.0

A staple of ABC's family-friendly "TGIF" block for eight seasons, this three-men-and-a-family sitcom starred Bob Saget as a widower raising his kids with help from his brother-in-law and best friend. The Tanner family of San Francisco worked through any conflicts with Brady-like efficiency, though John Stamos and Dave Coulier combined don't add up to one Robert Reed.

The Season 1 set restores the original opening titles, largely unseen since the show's first run; this is where the world first met twins Mary-Kate and Ashley Olsen, who grew up before our eyes from gurgling babies to the young tabloid-fodder millionaires they have become today. *Full House* retains its wholesome charm on DVD, especially with those for whom it was a Friday-night tradition. Sales should spike with the second-season box, 'cause that's when Lori Loughlin shows up.

GREAT MOMENTS: Season 1: The original pilot episode with John Posey in the role of dad Danny Tanner. *Full House* without Bob Saget is much easier to take; Season 2: The Beach Boys perform on "Beach Boy Bingo"; Season 3: Michelle gives birth to a catchphrase with "You got it, dude."

FAST-FORWARD: Get the button ready when the cutesy music starts.

EXTRAS: Season 1: Alternate pilot episode; commentary by creator Jeff Franklin; trivia games; Season 3: A highlight reel of Joey's impersonations.

F

Futurama (1999–2003)

Volume 1 (13 episodes on 3 discs): ★ ★ ★
Volume 2 (19 episodes on 4 discs): ★ ★ ★ ★
Volume 3 (22 episodes on 4 discs): ★ ★ ★ ½
Volume 4 (18 episodes on 4 discs): ★ ★ ★ ★
Monster Robot Maniac Fun Collection (4 episodes on 1 disc): ★ ★ ★

20th Century-Fox
Video: Full-Frame; Audio: Dolby Digital Surround

Pretty simple, really—if you love *The Simpsons* you'll enjoy Matt Groening's sci-fi follow-up, which has the same satiric wit and propensity for the obscure pop-culture reference. If you're amused by the idea of a thirtieth-century game show in which one of the celebrity panelists is the preserved head of Kitty Carlisle, you either already own *Futurama*, or should be leaving for the nearest DVD retailer right away. All four volumes contain commentaries by Groening on every single episode, which he mainly uses to harangue the FOX network for its treatment of the series.

GREAT MOMENTS: Volume 1: Bender encounters Robot Hell in "Hell Is Other Robots"; Volume 2: Flexo is in rare form in "Lesser of Two Evils"; Volume 3: "Amazon Women in the Mood" may be *Futurama*'s funniest episode; Volume 4: The characters regress to infancy in "Teenage Mutant Leela's Hurdles"; the *Star Trek* crossover in "Where No Fan Has Gone Before."

FAST-FORWARD: Nothing.

EXTRAS: All four volumes include commentaries on every episode, deleted scenes, and animatics.

Gidget (1965–1966)

The Complete Series (32 episodes on 4 discs): ★ ★ ★ ★

Sony Pictures Home Entertainment

Video: Full-Frame; Audio: Dolby Digital 2.0

The series that introduced eighteen-year-old Sally Field was a flop the first time around, but found an audience in summer reruns, after being cancelled by ABC. The network scrambled to find a new vehicle for its suddenly in-demand beach bunny, but the best they could do was *The Flying Nun*, which ran three years but wasn't anywhere near as enjoyable. Field was the ideal Gidget—adorable, especially when she spoke directly to the audience during each episode—sassy, spunky, and ever loyal to her understanding dad (Don Porter). Together, they created the best father-daughter sitcom moments since *The Patty Duke Show.*

GREAT MOMENTS: Gidget worries about her father's reaction when she dates a beach legend in "The Great Kahuna"; Gidget joins a folk band in the hilarious "Gidget Gets a Career."

FAST-FORWARD: Any episode that focuses on Gidget's drippy friend Larue.

EXTRAS: Original pilot; "A Look Back at *Gidget*" featurette, featuring an interview with Sally Field.

Gilligan's Island (1964–1967)

Season 1 (37 episodes on 3 discs): ★ ★ ★

Season 2 (32 episodes on 3 discs): ★ ★ ★

Season 3 (30 episodes on 3 discs): ★ ★ ★ ½

Warner Home Video

Video: Full-Frame; Audio: Dolby Digital Mono

Maybe it's not *all* about the theme song, but seriously—would this featherweight series have permeated the pop culture the way it has without that sing-along sea shanty written by series creator Sherwood Schwartz? Perhaps, perhaps not. Certainly critics of the day didn't give it much chance: "Should never have reached the air this season or any other season" (*Los Angeles Times*); "It's impossible that a more inept, moronic or humorless show has ever appeared on the home tube" (UPI). *Variety* predicted that the show had no future; forty years later, the "Ginger or Mary Ann?" debate rages on.

Whatever its faults, however repetitious one finds Gilligan's pratfalls and Mr. Howell's live-action take on Scrooge McDuck, there's no denying the series' indestructible cross-generational appeal. I'll never buy Schwartz's highfalutin claim that he created *Gilligan's Island* as an anti-war parable, but I'll give him all the credit he deserves for creating seven TV characters that millions of people love. That's a much nicer accomplishment, anyway.

GREAT MOMENTS: Season 1: Hans Conreid guest-stars in "Wrongway Feldman"; the Western fantasy sequence in "Sound of Quacking"; Ginger's hula dance in "The Matchmaker"; Season 3: The castaways perform *Hamlet* in "The Producer."

FAST-FORWARD: Season 3: The lame evil-twin story "Gilligan vs. Gilligan."

EXTRAS: Season 1: Commentary by Sherwood Schwartz, "Tropical Tidbits" trivia, "The Gilligan's Island Survival Guide"; "Before the Three-Hour Tour" featurette; the series' original pilot, featuring different actors as Ginger, Mary Ann, and the Professor—a real treat for fans; Season 3: Sherwood Schwartz commentary; "*Gilligan's Island*: A Pop-Culture Phenomenon" featurette.

The Gilmore Girls (2000–)

The Complete First Season (21 episodes on 6 discs): ★★★★★
The Complete Second Season (22 episodes on 6 discs): ★★★★
The Complete Third Season (22 episodes on 6 discs): ★★★★★
The Complete Fourth Season (22 episodes on 6 discs): ★★★★
The Complete Fifth Season (22 episodes on 6 discs): ★★★★★

Warner Home Video
Video: Full-Frame; Audio: Dolby Digital 2.0

Some series reward repeat viewings more than others. *The Gilmore Girls* should rank at or near the top of wonderful shows on the re-watchability scale. The clever dialogue is delivered by stars Lauren Graham and Alexis Bledel at a pace reminiscent of a Howard Hawks screwball comedy, so even third and fourth viewings may reveal previously missed treasures. Graham's failure to not only win an Emmy but even earn a nomination is as scathing an indictment of the Television Academy as has ever been witnessed in the medium. And in an era of television geared toward young adults where dumb means cool and smart is only short for smart-ass, Rory Gilmore is a revelation: a kind and pretty girl who loves to read the classics and yet has a mastery of pop culture that would make Dennis Miller envious.

Sadly, given how much the Gilmore gals love to gab, the otherwise fine DVD sets of the series have not been graced with episode commentaries by Graham, Bledel, or the series' similarly motor-mouthed creator, Amy Sherman-Palladino, until the Season 5 set.

GREAT MOMENTS: Season 1: The perfect first scene of the pilot episode, which sets the tone for the entire series; Rory's golf outing with her grandfather in "Kill Me Now"; Rory's father visits the Girls in "Christopher Returns"; Season 2: Lorelei and Emily strut down the catwalk at a charity fashion show in "Like Mother, Like Daughter"; Season 3: The Gilmores visit Yale in "Let the Games Begin"; Season 4: Rory and Paris go on Spring Break in "Girls in Bikinis, Boys Doin' the Twist"; Luke finally acknowledges his feelings for Lorelei in "Luke Can See Her Face"; Season 5: Luke is dragged to a screening of *Pippi Longstocking* in "We Got Us a Pippi Virgin!"; Rory infiltrates a Yale secret society in "You Jump, I Jump, Jack."

FAST-FORWARD: Occasionally, episodes focus more on the quirky town of Stars Hollow in which the Gilmores reside, resulting in a dangerous drift toward *Northern Exposure* territory. These include Season 3's "Application Anxiety" and "Face-Off," Season 4's "The Festival of Living Art," and Season 5's "Tippecanoe and Taylor, Too." Also, the attempted spin-off of the obnoxious Jess character in Season 3's "Here Comes the Son" can be safely skipped.

EXTRAS: Season 1: "Gilmore Girls Beginnings" featurette; "Gilmore-isms" montage; deleted scenes; pop-up facts during the "Rory's Dance" episode; Season 2: Unaired scenes; pop-up facts; "International Success" featurette; Season 3: Deleted scenes; "All Grown Up," "Our Favorite '80s," and "Who Wants to Fall in Love?" featurettes; Season 4: Pop-up facts; deleted scenes; interactive trivia game; Season 5: Commentaries by creator Amy Sherman-Palladino and writer Daniel Palladino; "*The Gilmore Girls* Turn 100" featurette.

G

Gimme a Break! (1981–1987)

Season 1 (19 episodes on 3 discs): ★ ★

Universal Home Video

Video: Full-Frame; Audio: Dolby Digital 2.0

A large and in-charge sassy African-American woman (Nell Carter) becomes surrogate mother to the three children of a police chief after the passing of his wife. They often butt heads, but this being a saccharine-sweet '80s sitcom, they butt heads with love. Only Season 1 is out thus far, so you'll have to wait a while for Joey Lawrence, Paul Sand, and Rosie O'Donnell.

GREAT MOMENTS: A pre-Blanche Rue McClanahan tries to seduce the Chief in "The Second Time Around"; Sam doesn't quite know how "the birds and the bees" work in "Sam's Affair."

FAST-FORWARD: The show sometimes loses its sense of reality, and crazy situations occur that go beyond the imagination. The Season 2 bonus episode, "Nell Goes to Jail," is one of them. The bonus *Kate and Allie* episode is so bad it makes *Gimme a Break!* look like *Seinfeld* by comparison.

EXTRAS: "The Great '80s Flashback" featurette; bonus Season 2 episode; bonus episodes of *Charles in Charge* and *Kate and Allie.*

The Golden Girls (1985–1992)

Season 1 (25 episodes on 3 discs): ★ ★ ★ ★
Season 2 (26 episodes on 3 discs): ★ ★ ★ ★
Season 3 (25 episodes on 3 discs): ★ ★ ★ ½
Season 4 (26 episodes on 3 discs): ★ ★ ★ ★
Season 5 (26 episodes on 3 discs): ★ ★ ★

Buena Vista Home Entertainment
Video: Full-Frame; Audio: Dolby Digital 2.0

G

A show about four retirees in our youth-obsessed culture? How did *The Golden Girls* ever get on the air? Bea Arthur, Betty White, and Rue McClanahan, veteran scene-stealers all, were joined by stage actress Estelle Getty, who got all of the most memorable punch lines playing Arthur's mother (even though the two actresses were born in the same year). All four stars earned Emmy Awards during the series' six-year run, and there was no shark jumping here until the *Golden Palace* follow-up.

How fun would it be to have the geriatric quartet provide commentaries? Or to have outtakes from a series that must have been as much fun to make as it was to watch? Sadly, season sets thus far have been extras-free, save for clip packages and a waste-of-space look at the Girls' fashion sense by Joan and Melissa Rivers. Thanks, but no thanks.

GREAT MOMENTS: Season 1: Rose feels the world has passed her by in "Job Hunting"; Dorothy and Blanche battle in "The Triangle"; Season 2: Burt Reynolds appears in "Ladies of the Evening"; Season 4: Bob Hope appears in "You Gotta Have Hope"; watch for Quentin Tarantino's appearance as an Elvis impersonator in "Sophia's Wedding."

FAST-FORWARD: Nothing.

EXTRAS: Season 1: Fashion commentary on the series by Joan and Melissa Rivers; Season 3: "Golden Moments" and "*The Golden Girls* Scrapbook" clip collections; Season 4: "Top Ten Guest Stars" clip collection.

Good Times (1974–1979)

The First Season (13 episodes on 2 discs): ★ ★ ★ ½

The Second Season (24 episodes on 3 discs): ★ ★ ★ ★

The Third Season (24 episodes on 3 discs): ★ ★ ★ ★

The Fourth Season (24 episodes on 3 discs): ★ ★ ★ ½

The Fifth Season (24 episodes on 3 discs): ★ ★ ½

Columbia Tristar Home Video

Video: Full-Frame; Audio: Dolby Digital Mono

Next to *Hogan's Heroes*, *Good Times* might take top prize in the "unlikeliest setting for a situation comedy" countdown. There's not much to laugh about in the housing projects of Chicago's south side, but this spin-off from *Maude* focused on a family who balanced punch lines with prejudice, uncertainly over making rent, and the dangers of drugs and gang violence. It was supposed to succeed on its social conscience, like previous entries in the Norman Lear stable, but *Good Times* instead hitched its wagon to the gangly frame of comedian Jimmie Walker, whose "Dy-No-Mite!" catchphrase is all most people still remember about the show.

The first three seasons represent the best of *Times*; the loss of John Amos (his patriarch character is killed in a car accident) resonates throughout Season 4, though it makes for some compelling dramatic shows. The loss of Esther Rolle with Season 5, even though she'd later return, was the beginning of the end for the series, despite the cast addition that season of Janet Jackson as Thelma's adopted daughter.

GREAT MOMENTS: Season 1: Ned the Wino's appearance in "Springtime in the Ghetto"; Season 2: J.J.'s physical examination in "The Enlistment"; the meatloaf that might be made of dog food in "The Dinner Party"; Season 3: James confronts his absentee father in "The Family Tree"; Season 4: The Evans family deals with the loss of James in "The Big Move."

FAST-FORWARD: Season 4's "The Judy Cohen Story."

EXTRAS: None.

Goosebumps (1995–1998)

Chillogy: ★ ★
Cry of the Cat: ★ ★
Deep Trouble: ★ ★ ½
The Haunted Mask II: ★ ★ ★
How I Got My Shrunken Head: ★ ★
Night of the Living Dummy III: ★ ★
Scary House: ★ ★
The Ghost Next Door: ★ ★ ★
Welcome to Dead House: ★ ★
Werewolf of Fever Swamp: ★ ★

20th Century-Fox
Video: Full-Frame; Audio: Dolby Digital 2.0

Three single-disc episode releases a year? Not the most ambitious schedule for these adaptations of the popular R.L. Stine horror novels. With that much time to figure out which titles to bring to DVD, it's hard to explain some of the choices; why release sequels to stories such as "The Haunted Mask" and "Night of the Living Dummy" before the originals? Eh. *Are You Afraid of the Dark?* was better anyway.

G

GREAT MOMENTS: Hannah has trouble with her new neighbors in "The Ghost Next Door"; on a Caribbean adventure, Billy and Sheena ignore the warning to stay away from the coral reef in "Deep Trouble."

FAST-FORWARD: "The Werewolf of Fever Swamp"—too many liberties taken from Stine's original tale.

EXTRAS: None.

The Greatest American Hero (1981–1983)

Season 1 (9 episodes on 3 discs, plus bonus *Greatest American Heroine* episode): ★ ★ ★
Season 2 (22 episodes on 4 discs): ★ ★ ★ ½

Anchor Bay
Video: Full-Frame; Audio: Dolby Digital Stereo

Teacher Ralph Hinkley gets a pair of "super-powered alien jammies" that turn him into the Greatest American Hero. Unfortunately, he's lost the instruction manual, but FBI agent Bill Maxwell and the incredibly hot Connie Sellecca are there to assist. When Ralph is not fighting bad guys or saving the day, he teaches the leftovers from Mr. Kotter's Sweathogs.

The DVD packaging is impressive and gives the series a more modern look than it ever had in the 1980s, but be warned of music substitutions.

GREAT MOMENTS: Season 1: Hinkley gets the suit and meets Bill Maxwell in "The Greatest American Hero"; Season 2: Maxwell falls in love in "Lilacs, Mr. Maxwell."

FAST-FORWARD: Producer Stephen J. Cannell speaks about all of his shows—but very little about *The Greatest American Hero*—in a Season 2 extra.

EXTRAS: Extensive actor interviews on the Season 1 set keep you from noticing that there are only nine episodes, but the highlight is the aborted 1986 pilot for *The Greatest American Heroine*; Season 2: Stephen J. Cannell and Mike Post interviews.

The Greatest '70s Cop Shows (2003)

(5 episodes on 1 disc): ★ ★ ★ ★

Columbia Tristar Home Video

Video: Full-Frame; Audio: Mono

Those who grew up on the disco-era cop and detective shows would prefer season sets, but this collection of the first episodes of *Starsky & Hutch*, *Charlie's Angels*, *The Rookies*, *SWAT*, and *Police Woman* isn't a bad place to start for those who came along later, and for those who were around in the '70s but lost too many brain cells to various controlled substances.

GREAT MOMENTS: The first series appearances of Huggy Bear, Jill Munroe, Nurse Danko, Hondo, Pepper, Sabrina, and Captain Dobey.

FAST-FORWARD: Only the "bonus" trailers.

EXTRAS: Cast bios.

Green Acres (1965–1971)

The Complete First Season (32 episodes on 2 discs): ★ ★ ★ ★ ★

The Complete Second Season (30 episodes on 2 discs): ★ ★ ★ ★ ★

The Complete Third Season (30 episodes on 4 discs): ★ ★ ★ ★ ★

MGM Home Video

Video: Full-Frame; Audio: Dolby Digital 2.0

There are two kinds of people in this world: those who lump *Green Acres* with *The Beverly Hillbillies* and other rural sitcoms of its era, and those who recognize *Green Acres* for what it truly is—one of the most subversive, surreal, and extraordinary television shows ever conceived. "The story of Oliver Douglas in hell," is how *Simpsons* creator Matt Groening described the series, which has more in common with Lewis Carroll and *Monty Python* than *Petticoat Junction*, despite its Hooterville setting. The MGM sets are as no-frills as they come, though encouraging sales of the first two seasons prompted a welcome change to single-sided discs for Season 3. Still no extras, but given how this series' cracked brilliance has yet to be widely acknowledged after four decades, just be glad we're getting season sets at all.

GREAT MOMENTS: Season 1: The Douglases' phone is installed in "Don't Call Us, We'll Call You"; Oliver finds a new use for Lisa's hotcakes in "The Price of Apples"; Season 2: The Army drafts Arnold Ziffel in "I Didn't Raise My Pig to Be a Soldier"; in a community-theater production of *The Beverly Hillbillies*, Oliver plays Jethro opposite Lisa as Granny in the whacked-out masterpiece "The Beverly Hillbillies"; Season 3: Arnold goes Hollywood in the two-parter "A Star Named Arnold is Born."

FAST-FORWARD: Nothing.

EXTRAS: None.

Grey's Anatomy

Season 1 (9 episodes on 2 discs): ★ ★ ★ ★

Buena Vista Home Entertainment

Video: Anamorphic Widescreen; Audio: Dolby Digital 5.1

Shonda Rhime's extremely addictive and compelling medical comedy-drama about a rambunctious group of interns, residents, and attending doctors at the fictional Seattle Grace Hospital became a surprise hit for ABC, eventually outdrawing the ratings of its blockbuster lead-in, *Desperate Housewives*. Credit superior writing, complex characters, and a talented, ethnically diverse cast, led by Golden Globe–winner Sandra Oh. Mastered from HD transfers, the strong, bold colors of *Grey's Anatomy* look beautiful on DVD.

GREAT MOMENTS: The revelation about Meredith's (Ellen Pompeo) mother that closed the pilot, "A Hard Day's Night"; Bailey chewing out the injured bicycle racers in "Winning a Battle, Losing the War"; Izzie, in her underwear, chewing out Alex in "No Man's Land"; George getting syphilis and discovering the source, and the shocking cliffhanger about Dr. McDreamy (Patrick Dempsey) in the season finale, "Who's Zoomin' Who?"

FAST-FORWARD: Nothing.

EXTRAS: The commentary track for the pilot episode, with creator Shonda Rhimes and director Peter Horton, is entertaining and informative. There is also a fun, albeit more flimsy commentary for the episode done by actors Sandra Oh, Katherine Heigl, and T.R. Knight; deleted scenes; behind-the-scenes documentary.

Grounded for Life (2000–2004)

Season 1 (20 episodes on 4 discs): ★ ★ ★ ★
Season 2 (17 episodes on 3 discs): ★ ★ ★ ½

Anchor Bay
Video: Full-Frame; Audio: Dolby Digital 2.0

It was on for four years, and earned a few Emmy nominations and a loyal following, but I'd be willing to bet that most of the people reading this never watched a single episode of *Grounded for Life*. If you did, pat yourself on the back and enjoy the repeat viewings via DVD. If you didn't, remember that TV-on-DVD isn't just about collecting old favorites, but finding new delights you missed the first time around. Anyone who enjoys snarky family sitcoms (think *Roseanne*, *The Simpsons*, even *Married . . . With Children*) should enjoy this take on a young married couple raising three kids when they haven't yet grown up themselves.

GREAT MOMENTS: Season 1: Jimmy's martial arts obsession in "Jimmy Was Kung Fu Fighting," and the Emmy-nominated "Mrs. Finnerty, You've Got a Lovely Daughter."

FAST-FORWARD: Nothing.

EXTRAS: Season 1: Commentaries; interview with creators Mike Schiff and Bill Martin; featurettes "Donal Logue: Meet the Finnertys," "Lynsey Bartilson: Life as Lily," and "Claudia: Not the Sitcom Mom"; blooper reel; Season 2: Interviews with Kevin Corrigan, Jake Burbage, Griffin Frazen, and guest star Ashton Kutcher; blooper reel.

Growing Pains (1985–1991)

The Complete First Season (22 episodes on 4 discs): ★ ★ ½

Warner Home Video

Video: Full-Frame; Audio: Dolby Digital Mono

Dad sets up an office at home so Mom can return to work, and wacky high jinks ensue. *Growing Pains* was a harmless if often bland family comedy that got better with each subsequent season. The early episodes still satisfy as good comfort food, and it's always fun to pop in a DVD and remind your sister about the crush she had on Kirk Cameron.

GREAT MOMENTS: Will Mike lose his virginity to a Madonna look-alike? What do you think? ("Mike's Madonna Story"); Annette Funicello guests as a PTA president who deems the Seavers unfit dance chaperones in "The Seavers vs. the Cleavers."

FAST-FORWARD: If it's an episode about Tracey Gold's Carol character, run far, far away.

EXTRAS: Unaired scenes from the original series pilot, featuring Elizabeth Ward as Carol; "S'mores and More" cast reunion; gag reel.

Gunsmoke (1955–1975)

Fiftieth Anniversary Edition, Volume 1 (17 episodes on 3 discs): ★ ★ ★ ★

Fiftieth Anniversary Edition, Volume 2 (12 episodes on 3 discs): ★ ★ ★ ★ ½

Paramount Home Video

Video: Full-Frame; Audio: Dolby Digital Mono

Television's longest-running and most respected Western was the only dramatic series to span two defining decades in American pop culture. While Marshal Matt Dillon protected Dodge City and wooed Miss Kitty, the nation progressed from Marilyn Monroe to Farrah Fawcett, and from "Rock Around the Clock" to "The Hustle." There are more than six hundred hours of *Gunsmoke*, and we're going to need a bigger bookshelf if they all get to DVD. Until then, enjoy these well-chosen "best of" collections.

GREAT MOMENTS: Volume 1: The first episode, "Matt Gets It," introduced by John Wayne; Burt Reynolds joins the cast in "Quint Asper Comes Home"; Volume 2: "The Jailer," guest-starring Bette Davis, might be *Gunsmoke*'s best episode.

FAST-FORWARD: Nothing.

EXTRAS: Both volumes offer episode introductions by James Arness, and commentaries from Arness, series star Dennis Weaver, and guest stars such as Angie Dickinson, Barbara Eden, Adam West, Bruce Dern, and Ed Asner. You'll also find gag reels, cast appearances on other series such as *The Ed Sullivan Show* and *The Mike Douglas Show*, Emmy Award footage, and (on Volume 1) a Museum of TV and Radio panel with the cast.

Happy Days (1974–1984)

The Complete First Season (16 episodes on 3 discs): ★ ★ ★

Paramount Home Video

Video: Full-Frame; Audio: Dolby Digital 2.0 Mono

If it's been a while since your last visit to Arnold's, keep in mind that the first season of *Happy Days* was quieter and less Fonzie-centric than the many seasons to follow. "Rock Around the Clock" was the opening theme; Richie's older brother, Chuck, was still part of the Cunningham family; and though Henry Winkler was around he had not yet ascended to pop-culture preeminence. With Season 2, the Fonz would trade his beige windbreaker for the iconic black leather jacket, and *Happy Days* moved into the top ten, where it stayed for the next decade. Of course, when Fonzie switches from the white T-shirt to the black, the show begins its downhill slide. No sharks in sight yet, however, so dive in and enjoy.

GREAT MOMENTS: Richie sees his father inside a strip club in "The Skin Game"; Howard schools some arrogant frat boys in poker in "Give the Band a Hand"; Fonzie asks Richie (in drag) to dance in "The Deadly Dares."

FAST-FORWARD: Richie adopts the beatnik lifestyle in "Great Expectations."

EXTRAS: None. Sit on it, Paramount! But one of the upcoming seasons should contain the *Love, American Style* segment "Love and the Happy Days," which features footage from the original pilot and stars Harold Gould as Howard Cunningham.

The Hardy Boys/Nancy Drew Mysteries (1977–1979)

Season 1 (14 episodes on 2 discs): ★ ★ ★ ½

Universal Home Video

Video: Full-Frame; Audio: Dolby Digital 2.0

Every twenty years or so, television introduces a new generation to teen sleuths Frank and Joe Hardy, and Nancy Drew. The 1970s version remains the most popular, propelled by the teen idol status of Parker Stevenson and Shaun Cassidy, and the subsequent success of Pamela Sue Martin in *Dynasty.* Though the whodunits lean more toward Scooby-Doo than Agatha Christie in their simplicity and supernatural overtones, the series still has a charm about it, even for those are aren't stuck in the '70s. The shows in which Nancy and the Hardys join forces do not begin until Season 2.

GREAT MOMENTS: Shaun Cassidy sings "Da-Doo-Ron-Ron" and "That's Rock 'n' Roll," both number-one hits, in "The Mystery of the Flying Courier"; teen idols past and present meet when Rick Nelson appears in "The Flickering Torch Mystery."

FAST-FORWARD: The Hardy Boys shows offer more delights than the Nancy Drew mysteries, but all of them are worth a look.

EXTRAS: Even these spunky detectives couldn't find any.

Hart to Hart (1979–1984)

The Complete First Season (23 episodes on 6 discs): ★ ★ ★ ½

Sony Pictures Home Entertainment

Video: Full-Frame; Audio: Dolby Digital 2.0

Just like *Dynasty*, *Hart to Hart* was a triumph of opulent style over substance. The plots were predictable but the luxury accommodations in which they were set, as well as the sizzling chemistry of stars Robert Wagner and Stefanie Powers, kept viewers coming back for five years. The Harts were never as neurotic as the Carringtons, but after watching friends, business associates, and strangers all drop dead within their midst on a weekly basis, it's hard to imagine there was never some need for therapy.

GREAT MOMENTS: One of Jonathan's employees develops a fatal attraction for her boss in "You Made Me Kill You."

FAST-FORWARD: "Which Way Freeman?"—and most stories that revolve around Max or Freeway.

EXTRAS: Episode commentary; featurette "*Hart to Hart*: The Hart of Season 1."

Harvey Birdman: Attorney at Law (2000–)

Volume 1 (13 episodes on 2 discs): ★ ★ ½

Warner Home Video

Video: Full-Frame; Audio: Dolby Digital Stereo

After putting a new spin on Space Ghost, the Cartoon Network attempted a postmodern revival of another Hanna-Barbera benchwarmer by transforming the superhero Birdman into a lawyer of questionable ability. Season 1 featured nearly all of Hanna-Barbera's most famous creations as plaintiffs in PG-13 situations and was often hilarious, though some may object to the lewd derision of their childhood pals. The show has since descended into the same Dadaist hodgepodge as latter-day *Cartoon Planet* and *The Brak Show*, and is not as much fun.

GREAT MOMENTS: Apache Chief spills hot coffee on his loincloth in "Very Personal Injury"; Scooby and Shaggy are busted for possession in "Shaggy Busted"; Boo Boo Bear is accused of being the terrorist "Unabooboo" in "Death by Chocolate."

FAST-FORWARD: "The Bannon Custody Case"—the gay jokes about Race and Dr. Quest weren't funny the first time around.

EXTRAS: Commentaries; deleted scenes; trailer for "Harvey Birdman—the Movie"; live-action opening sequence.

H

Have Gun Will Travel (1957–1963)

Season 1 (39 episodes on 6 discs): ★ ★ ★ ★
Season 2 (39 episodes on 5 discs): ★ ★ ★ ★
Season 3 (39 episodes on 7 discs): ★ ★ ★ ★

Paramount Home Video

Video: Full-Frame; Audio: Dolby Digital 2.0

Know someone who doesn't like Westerns? Tie them to a chair and insert Disc One from Season 1 of *Have Gun Will Travel.* It won't be long before they realize that all forty-year-old Western shows from the genre's golden age aren't as interchangeable as they thought. As Paladin, Richard Boone played a more complex hero than most of the buckaroos of his day: a hero dressed in black, who preferred fine music and literature to the action at the saloon, and whose sense of chivalry was reflected in the knight on his famed calling card. You never heard Matt Dillon quote Shakespeare, but Paladin had a West Point education as well as a quick draw. *Have Gun Will Travel* turned out sophisticated stories at an alarmingly prodigious rate—check out the episode count of the season sets. A few kinescopes and syndicated cuts turn up in the Seasons 2 and 3 boxes, and we must presume they were all that was available given the otherwise sterling job Paramount did with these collections. In this case it's better to have the shows at all than to complain about the quality.

GREAT MOMENTS: Season 1: Charles Bronson appears in "The Outlaw"; Racism against Asian-Americans is provocatively explored in "Hey Boy's Revenge."

FAST-FORWARD: Nothing.

EXTRAS: Some behind-the-scenes episode descriptions for true fans only.

Hearts Afire (1992–1995)

Season 1 (22 episodes on 4 discs): ★ ★ ★
Season 2 (16 episodes on 3 discs): ★ ★ ½
Season 3 (14 episodes on 3 discs): ★ ★ ½

Image Entertainment
Video: Full-Frame; Audio: Dolby Digital 2.0

The untimely passing of John Ritter was the primary motivation for the DVD debut of *Hearts Afire*, which can claim neither syndicated success nor an enduring fan following. For the majority of readers who've forgotten the show, this was a political sitcom about a senator's legislative assistant (Ritter) and a feisty press secretary (Markie Post). A then-unknown Billy Bob Thornton played a guy named Billy Bob Davis. The Image DVDs seem like a rush job, with occasionally fuzzy transfers and the substitution of instrumental-music tracks for the more expensive originals. But if we're going to release everything of Ritter's, this is better than *Hooperman*.

GREAT MOMENTS: Season 1: Roger Clinton, goofy brother of President Bubba, appears in "The Big Date."

FAST-FORWARD: Nothing.

EXTRAS: Season 1: Gag reel.

Hee Haw (1969–1993)

Collection, Volumes 1–4 (1 disc) Each: ★ ★ ★

Time-Life

Video: Full-Frame; Audio: Dolby Digital 2.0

There were two reasons to watch *Hee Haw*: the gorgeous women and the live performances from country music's top stars from a pre-CMT era when Nashville was not well represented on TV. But if you wanted to enjoy the music of George Jones and Tammy Wynette and Loretta Lynn, and ogle Barbi Benton and Misty Rowe, that meant sitting through some of the most god-awful jokes to ever fertilize a cornfield. That was the trade-off, and the ratio of pleasure to pain is about the same on DVD, so enter at your own risk.

GREAT MOMENTS: Volume 1: Charley Pride performs Hank Williams's "I Can't Help It (If I'm Still in Love with You)" in his first nationally televised appearance; Volume 2: Johnny Cash performs "City of New Orleans"; Volume 3: Tammy Wynette sings "Stand by Your Man"; Volume 4: Waylon Jennings and Jessi Colter duet on "I Ain't the One."

FAST-FORWARD: Just about all of the jokes.

EXTRAS: None.

H

Hercules: The Legendary Journeys (1994–1999)

Season 1 (18 episodes on 7 discs): ★ ★ ★ ★
Season 2 (24 episodes on 7 discs): ★ ★ ★ ½
Season 3 (22 episodes on 9 discs): ★ ★ ★ ★
Season 4 (22 episodes on 8 discs): ★ ★ ★ ★
Season 5 (22 episodes on 9 discs): ★ ★ ★ ★
Season 6 (8 episodes on 5 discs): ★ ★ ★
The Xena Trilogy (3 episodes on 1 disc): ★ ★ ★
Hercules Action Pack (6 episodes on 4 discs): ★ ★ ★
And the Amazon Woman/The Lost Kingdom (2 episodes on 1 disc): ★ ★ ½

Anchor Bay (season sets); Universal Home Video (Xena Trilogy, Action Pack, And the Amazon Woman.)

Video: Full-Frame; Audio: Dolby Digital 5.1 (season sets); Dolby Digital 2.0 (Universal releases)

Though the mix of classic mythology and characters with modern-day sensibilities proved slightly more successful in its *Xena* spin-off, *Hercules: The Legendary Journeys* found a niche with fans of escapist adventure stories with an ever-present wink to the viewers at home. Season 1 includes the five movie-length adventures that preceded the series, which featured Anthony Quinn as Zeus. The stories were more serious than what followed; with Season 2, the series found the mix of action and comedy that would sustain it through four more campaigns. Skip the Universal sets, which are lacking in sound quality and extras compared to Anchor Bay's season releases.

GREAT MOMENTS: Season 1: The debut of Xena in "The Warrior Princess"; Season 2: Hercules joins Jason and the Argonauts to find the Golden Fleece in "Once a Hero"; Season 3: The season finale "Atlantis"; Season 4: *Xena*'s Renee O'Connor visits in "Stranger in a Strange World"; the delightfully tongue-in-cheek "Yes Virginia, There Is a Hercules."

FAST-FORWARD: Season 2: The clip show "Cave of Echoes."

EXTRAS: All the season sets include episode commentaries by Kevin Sorbo, sometimes joined by Michael Hurst (Iolaus); Season 3: Behind-the-scenes interviews with cast and crew; Season 4: Special-effects featurette (in three parts, continues over next two seasons); Season 5: Interviews with Kevin Sorbo and Anthony Quinn; Season 6: Featurette on the final episode.

Here Come the Brides (1968–1970)

The Complete First Season (26 episodes on 6 discs): ★ ★ ★

Sony Pictures Home Entertainment

Video: Full-Frame; Audio: Dolby Digital 2.0

Two years on the air usually isn't enough for the syndication market, so we haven't seen much of *Here Come the Brides* since 1970, even with a cast that includes David Soul, *Star Trek* icon Mark Lenard and *Tiger Beat* cover-boy Bobby Sherman. Its emergence on DVD before dozens of higher-profile series is as delightful as it is unexpected. Set in post–Civil War Seattle, the show revolved around three brothers who import 100 single girls from the East Coast, in the hope of averting a mass exodus of affection-starved male loggers. If all the "brides" don't stay in Seattle for a year, the brothers risk losing their inheritance.

GREAT MOMENTS: The theme song, "Seattle," was a hit for Bobby Sherman; the arrival of the brides in the pilot episode; Bruce Lee appears in "Marriage Chinese Style."

FAST-FORWARD: Nothing.

EXTRAS: None.

Here's Lucy (1968–1974)

Best-Loved Episodes from the Hit Television Series (24 episodes on 4 discs): ★ ★ ★ ★ ½

Shout! Factory

Video: Full-Frame; Audio: Mono

Lucille Ball's third consecutive hit series tends to be overlooked and undervalued, as it never achieved the perennial syndication of *I Love Lucy* or *The Lucy Show*. But *Here's Lucy* produced 144 episodes and was a top-ten hit for four of its six years on the air. Gale Gordon returned as the redhead's vituperative comic foil, this time playing the Mr. Mooney-esque Harrison Carter. Lucy's real-life kids, Lucie Arnaz and Desi Arnaz, Jr., played daughter Kim and son Craig. An added treat was the parade of guest stars, making the show a wonderful time capsule for a show-biz era gone by. Season sets would be preferable, but the *Best-Loved Episodes* compilation benefits from Shout! Factory's typically standout production and the enthusiastic involvement of Lucie and Desi, who offer insightful commentary on most of the twenty-four episodes.

GREAT MOMENTS: Jackie Gleason's unbilled cameo as Ralph Kramden in "Lucy Meets Jack Benny"; Lucy destroys Harry's house while trying to repair a lamp in "Lucy the Fixer"; Ann-Margret raises Craig's blood pressure in "Lucy and Ann-Margret"; guest appearances by Richard Burton and Elizabeth Taylor in "Lucy Meets the Burtons."

FAST-FORWARD: "Lucy and Lawrence Welk" proves that your grandma's favorite bandleader had the comic timing of an avocado.

EXTRAS: Two blooper reels, rehearsal footage, commentaries by Lucie Arnaz and Desi Arnaz, Jr., and guest stars Carol Burnett and Wayne Newton; sketches from *Jack Benny's Carnival Nights* with Lucy and Johnny Carson and *The Ann-Margret Show: From Hollywood with Love*; audience warm-up featuring Lucille Ball's husband Gary Morton; original CBS promos; the *Here's Lucy* syndication sales tape; footage from a benefit dinner, with Lucie and Desi playing their parents in an *I Love Lucy* sketch.

Highlander (1992–1998)

Season 1 (22 episodes on 8 discs): ★ ★ ★ ½

Season 2 (22 episodes on 7 discs): ★ ★ ★ ★

Season 3 (22 episodes on 7 discs): ★ ★ ★ ★

Season 4 (22 episodes on 9 discs): ★ ★ ★

Season 5 (20 episodes on 9 discs): ★ ★ ★
Season 6 (13 episodes on 7 discs): ★ ★
Highlander: Counterfeit: ★ ★ ★
Highlander: The Finale: ★ ★ ★
Highlander: The Raven: ★ ½
Highlander: Unholy Alliance: ★ ★ ½

Anchor Bay
Video: Full-Frame; Audio: Dolby Digital 5.1

The word "hit" is always preceded by the word "surprise" when discussing *Highlander*, because nothing much was expected from its saga of Scottish immortals. The first film earned terrible reviews but did enough business to spawn multiple sequels, and after diminishing returns at the box office the concept was reborn once more on television. So much for "There can be only one."

Highlander still gets no respect, but it should. The first film and the TV show's first four seasons match up well against any more popular fantasy franchise—well cast, well written, packed with exciting action scenes that are the equal of Buffy, Xena, and other current standard-bearers of the genre.

Those new to the show and its surprises should skip watching the "Watchers Chronicles," an extra feature in the DVD sets that reveals future plot developments. The uninitiated should also be aware that the single-disc release "The Finale" contains the last episodes from the show's third season, and not the final episodes of the series. "The Raven" was a failed spin-off attempt that proved even *Highlander* was not immortal.

GREAT MOMENTS: Season 1: Connor McLeod (Christopher Lambert) shatters Duncan's peaceful existence in "The Gathering"; Tessa's jealousy over Vanity in "Revenge Is Sweet"; Duncan faces his greatest challenge in "Band of Brothers"; Season 2: A shocking death in "The Darkness"; the debut of Mako in "Under Color of Authority"; Season 3: "The Samurai" ranks among the series' best episodes; the romantic fadeout in "Finale"; Season 4: The comedic outing "Double Eagle"; Season 5: The Immortals inspire Mary Shelley to write *Frankenstein* in "The Modern Prometheus"; the tragic death that outraged many *Highlander* fans in "Archangel"; Season 6: The final episodes, "To Be" and "Not to Be," inspired by *It's a Wonderful Life*.

FAST-FORWARD: Season 1: Duncan falls prey to a mad scientist in "Deadly Medicine"; Season 2: "The Zone," a show so bad that the producers apologize for it in the commentary track.

EXTRAS: Season 1: On-camera commentary by Executive Producer Bill Panzer; background featurettes; outtakes; Season 2: Commentaries by Bill Panzer,

David Abramowitz, and star Adrian Paul; lost scenes; producer and writer interviews; Seasons 3–5 offer cast interviews; deleted scenes; cast/crew commentaries and outtakes. Season 5 also contains "The Romance of Duncan MacLeod" featurette and footage from the 1998 *Highlander* Convention; Season 6 offers more of the same plus six featurettes.

Highway to Heaven (1984–1989)

Season 1 (24 episodes on 7 discs): ★ ★
Season 2 (24 episodes on 6 discs): ★ ★
Season 3 (25 episodes on 7 discs): ★ ★

A&E Home Video
Video: Full-Frame; Audio: Dolby Digital 2.0

Some actors you just want to watch when they're on television. Michael Landon had that gift, as evidenced by three successful series that ran for a combined total of thirty-one years. *Highway to Heaven* was the last and least of these, but Landon elevated the show's simple premise of angel-helps-people-in-trouble on sheer likability. What fans won't like are the many syndicated cuts of episodes, especially at A&E's inflated prices.

GREAT MOMENTS: Season 1: Helen Hunt plays a cancer patient in the tear-jerking two-parter "Thoroughbreds"; Season 3: Michael Landon spoofs one of his early film appearances in the hilarious "I Was a Middle-Aged Werewolf."

FAST-FORWARD: Nothing.

EXTRAS: Season 1: The feature-length documentary "Michael Landon: Memories with Laughter and Love"; outtakes; Season 2: Commentary on one episode by Cindy Landon and producer Kent McCray; Season 3: Interviews with Cindy Landon, Kent McCray, Susan McCray, and Dennis Korn.

Hill Street Blues (1981–1987)

The Complete First Season (17 episodes on 3 discs): ★ ★ ★ ★ ★
The Complete Second Season (18 episodes on 3 discs): ★ ★ ★ ★ ★

20th Century-Fox
Video: Full-Frame; Audio: Dolby Digital 2.0

The forerunner to every gritty, handheld-camera-shot cop drama, Steven Bochco's *Hill Street Blues* was groundbreaking television in 1981, and its influence can still be glimpsed in nearly every police procedural of the past two decades. Hardly surprising, since many of these shows were created by *Hill Street* alumni David Milch, Dick Wolf, and Scott Brazil.

The show had a harsher edge than we were used to: dialogue that pushed the envelope of acceptability, graphic violence, and a few cops who were as corrupt and screwed up as the perps they chased. The opening credits, played under that wonderful Mike Post theme song, seemed to go on forever, as fifteen characters were introduced and viewers wondered how they'd keep them all straight. Within two or three episodes we knew and cared about them all.

Double-sided discs are always disappointing, particularly for such an important series, but Season 1's cast-reunion featurette is the sort of extra feature that forgives a lot of sins.

GREAT MOMENTS: Season 1: The tense hostage drama and the shooting of Officers Hill and Renko, all in the opening episode "Hill Street Station," left no doubt this was a different kind of cop show; Lieutenant Hunter's "urban tank" in "I Never Promised You a Rose, Marvin"; Season 2: Belker meets self-proclaimed superhero Captain Freedom in "The World According to Freedom."

FAST-FORWARD: Esterhaus's love life, inaugurating the fascination with kinky sex that runs through every Bochco series.

EXTRAS: Season 1: Cast commentaries on two episodes; a terrific featurette that reunites most of the original cast; Season 2: Cast commentaries; featurette "Gregory Hoblit: The *Hill Street Blues* Story"; profiles of Bruce Weitz and Charlie Haid; gag reel.

The Hitchhiker's Guide to the Galaxy (1981)

The Complete Miniseries (on 2 discs): ★ ★ ★ ½

BBC Video

Video: Full-Frame; Audio: Dolby Digital 2.0

It was a radio play first, then a best-selling book, before Douglas Adams's classic sci-fi send-up found its way to television. The 2005 theatrical movie had a bigger budget, but many fans have remained loyal to the 1981 miniseries, despite its modest production values and the bimbo-ization of Trillian. The three-hour running time allows for further exploration of Adams's sardonic take on the destruction of Earth and the insanity of life throughout the galaxy. Plus it's more British, which is as it should be.

GREAT MOMENTS: Simon Jones's note-perfect performance as the ever-befuddled Arthur Dent; the one-liners of Marvin the Paranoid Android.

FAST-FORWARD: Nothing.

EXTRAS: "The Making of *The Hitchhiker's Guide to the Galaxy*" featurette; Douglas Adams tribute from *Omnibus*; audio interview with Douglas Adams; outtakes and deleted scenes.

Hogan's Heroes (1965–1971)

The Complete First Season (32 episodes on 5 discs): ★ ★ ★ ★
The Complete Second Season (30 episodes on 5 discs): ★ ★ ★ ★ ½
The Complete Third Season (30 episodes on 5 discs): ★ ★ ★ ★

Paramount Home Video
Video: Full-Frame; Audio: Dolby Digital Mono

In our more politically correct age, the audacity of *Hogan's Heroes* seems more remarkable than it did when the series debuted in 1965. Nazis as sitcom villains was a tough sell, but the series went to great lengths to defang the Third Reich, not just with the buffoonery of Klink (Emmy-winner Werner Klemperer) and Sergeant Schultz, but in the slyly subversive casting of Jewish actors as German soldiers, among them John Banner (Schultz), Leon Askin (General Burkhalter), and Howard Crane (Major Hochstetter).

But nothing put the Nazis in their place more succinctly than the grin on the face of Bob Crane in the opening-credits sequence. Crane just owned the role of Colonel Hogan, and the series' clever scripts and standout supporting cast produced more than 160 memorable adventures, all of which are worth owning. If all five seasons aren't released, someone deserves a trip to the Russian front.

Season 1 is a typical no-frills Paramount set, but we get the black-and-white pilot with Leonid Kinskey as Vladimir Minsk, and Larry Hovis as a prisoner the Heroes help to escape, though he inexplicably returns as Sergeant Carter, a different character, after Kinskey's discomfort with the series' premise prompted his departure. The video on the set is amazing. *Hogan's Heroes* was never the most visually arresting of shows, with its military greens and browns, but even those drab hues pop on DVD.

GREAT MOMENTS: Season 1: Arlene Martel debuts as French underground agent Tiger in "Hold That Tiger"; Hogan, Newkirk, and LeBeau in drag in "I Look Better in Basic Black"; Season 2: A parachuting Schultz in "Hogan Gives a Birthday Party"; Carter's Hitler impression in "Will the Real Adolf Please

Stand Up?"; Season 3: The Heroes assist in one of World War II's most significant battles in "D-Day at Stalag 13"; "Hogan Go Home," the best of the Colonel Crittendon episodes.

FAST-FORWARD: Season 1: "Anchors Aweigh," a farfetched plot even by *Hogan* standards.

EXTRAS: Season 1 has no-think! NO-THINK! But Season 2 offers commentaries by stars Robert Clary and Sigrid Valdis, home movies, bloopers, and a collection of cast appearances in commercials, other TV shows, and original promos; Season 3: Werner Klemperer on *The Pat Sajak Show*; photo galleries.

Home Improvement (1991–1999)

Season 1 (24 episodes on 3 discs): ★ ★ ★ ½
Season 2 (25 episodes on 3 discs): ★ ★ ★ ½
Season 3 (25 episodes on 3 discs): ★ ★ ★

Buena Vista Home Entertainment
Video: Full-Frame; Audio: Dolby Digital 2.0

Few sitcoms stretched a one-joke premise longer than *Home Improvement*, starring Tim Allen as a grunting, tool-obsessed TV carpenter. But the formulaic stories were expertly rendered by Allen, Patricia Richardson as his smart-cookie wife, comic foil Richard Karn and a set of boys for playing out all the first-date and peer-pressure stories already explored by every other television family. Season 1 also features Pamela Anderson as the original Tool-Time girl.

GREAT MOMENTS: Season 1: Tim hotwires the dishwasher in the pilot episode; the bathroom disasters of "Bubble Bubble Toil and Trouble"; Season 2: Tim's lawnmower race against Bob Vila in "The Great Race."

FAST-FORWARD: Nothing.

EXTRAS: Season 1: Audio commentaries from series creators and executive producers; "Loose Screws: The Show's Most Hilarious Moments" featurette; Season 2: "Loose Screws" featurette, includes outtakes; Season 3: "Tim's Tool Corral" featurette.

Homicide: Life on the Street (1993–2000)

The Complete Seasons 1 & 2 (13 episodes on 4 discs): ★ ★ ★ ★
The Complete Season 3 (20 episodes on 6 discs): ★ ★ ★ ★ ★
The Complete Season 4 (22 episodes on 6 discs): ★ ★ ★ ½
The Complete Season 5 (22 episodes on 6 discs): ★ ★ ★ ★
The Complete Season 6 (23 episodes on 6 discs): ★ ★ ★ ★
The Complete Season 7 (22 episodes on 6 discs): ★ ★ ★
Homicide: The Movie: ★ ★ ★ ★

A&E Home Video
Video: Full-Frame; Audio: Dolby Digital 2.0

Underappreciated, always on the verge of cancellation despite running seven years, *Homicide: Life on the Street* was TV's best cop show since *Hill Street Blues*. Why it never caught fire in the mainstream is a mystery—too much revolving cast turnover, perhaps, or too many two-part stories and season-long arcs that required closer attention. Or maybe the whole thing was just too downbeat, at a time when audiences preferred the escapist pleasures of *Nash Bridges*, which consistently bested *Homicide* in its same time slot for three years. But if the release of classic TV on DVD is about finally owning all the shows you love, it should also be about seeking out the great ones you missed, and here's a series that should be near the top of that list.

GREAT MOMENTS: Seasons 1 & 2: The Emmy-winning "Three Men and Adena"; Season 3: Half the cast is nearly wiped out in "The City That Bleeds"; Season 4: the detectives try to capture a suburban serial killer in "Stakeout"; Lily Tomlin plays a woman who killed her husband in "The Hat"; Season 5: "Prison Riot" was the inspiration for the HBO series *Oz*; "Kaddish" is probably the best of the Munch-centric episodes; Season 6: "Subway" may be *Homicide*'s finest hour; Alfre Woodard reprises her *St. Elsewhere* character of Dr. Roxanne Turner in "Mercy."

FAST-FORWARD: Season 4: The EC Comics–influenced "Heartbeat" is an ambitious but failed experiment.

EXTRAS: Season 1: Commentary with Barry Levinson and Tom Fontana on the pilot episode; interviews with Levinson and Fontana; *Homicide*-themed episode of A&E's *American Justice*; Seasons 3–5 offer cast interviews and commentaries by behind-the-scenes personnel; Season 6: The feature-length documentary "Anatomy of a *Homicide*."

The Honeymooners (1955–1971)

The Classic 39 Episodes (39 episodes on 5 discs): ★ ★ ★ ★ ★

Holiday Classics (4 episodes on 1 disc): ★ ★ ★ ½

The Lost Episodes, Volumes 1–24 (each: 4 episodes on 1 disc): ★ ★ ½

The Lost Episodes, Box Sets 1–6 (each: 4 individual volumes): ★ ★ ½

Paramount Home Video (The Classic 39 Episodes); MPI Home Video (Holiday Classics, The Lost Episodes)

Video: Full-Frame; Audio: Dolby Digital 1.0

Okay, short and sweet: your TV-on-DVD collection sucks unless it contains *The Classic 39 Episodes*. Jackie Gleason as Ralph Kramden was a comedic force of nature, and Audrey Meadows more than holds her own as Ralph's long-suffering but loving wife. Art Carney's Ed Norton set the standard for every wacky neighbor to bolt through the door of a sitcom. The seeds of *Everybody Loves Raymond*, *Seinfeld*, and countless other contemporary comedies can be glimpsed in these thirty-nine shows. They are worthy of study by anyone with a serious interest in pop culture, or can simply be enjoyed as some of the most brilliantly funny moments that television has ever produced.

The "Lost Episodes" volumes consist of *Honeymooners* skits from Gleason's variety show that predate the Classic 39. They're mostly good, occasionally great, but not essential.

GREAT MOMENTS: *The Classic 39 Episodes*: They don't call them classic for nothing—every show is a clinic on television comedy. *Holiday Classics*: In "Christmas Party," the Kramdens meet legendary bandleaders Tommy and Jimmy Dorsey, and Jackie Gleason integrates his other famous characters (the Poor Soul, Al the bartender, Reggie Van Gleason) into the story.

FAST-FORWARD: Nothing.

EXTRAS: *The Classic 39 Episodes*: The Honeymooners Anniversary Special; cast interviews.

House (2004–)

Season 1 (22 episodes on 3 discs): ★ ★ ★

Universal Home Video

Video: Anamorphic Widescreen; Audio: Dolby Digital 5.1

Crotchety old doc Gregory House isn't one to offer gratitude casually, but he ought to say a big "thank you" to Bo Bice and Carrie Underwood, because nobody was watching the doctor unravel his medical mysteries until the series picked up *American Idol* as a lead-in. Since then, *House* has picked up its own following.

GREAT MOMENTS: House tries to figure out how a woman who's never been to Africa could have African sleeping sickness in "Fidelity"; Sela Ward debuts as the doctor's ex-girlfriend in "Three Stories."

FAST-FORWARD: Nothing.

EXTRAS: Featurettes "The Genius of Dr. House," "Real-Life Medical Cases" and "The Concept"; set tour.

H.R. Pufnstuf (1969–1971)

The Complete Series (17 episodes on 3 discs): ★ ★ ★ ★

H.R. Pufnstuf (4 episodes on 1 disc): ★ ★ ★

See also: *The World of Sid & Marty Krofft*

Rhino

Video: Full-Frame; Audio: Mono

I don't care if Sid and Marty Krofft were higher than the Rockies or not when they came up with *H.R. Pufnstuf*—for the record, they deny it in an interview featured in *The Complete Series* box set. It's certainly conceivable that the idea for a dragon named Puff who lives in a psychedelic land of talking flowers and trees could emerge from untainted inspiration. Even in 1969. And all those references to "bad mushrooms" and "crazy smoke" and Orson's "roach-beef sandwich" are just coincidental.

What is indisputable is that the Kroffts brought to Saturday mornings a remarkable series of whacked-out musical adventures that still haven't been surpassed in sheer imagination. Pufnstuf was the first and remains the most popular, though I've always been more of a *Bugaloos* man myself. But if new generations are still tripping out on Living Island, it's not because of Puff or pint-sized song-and-dance moppet Jack Wild, but the inspired villainy of Billie Hayes as Witchiepoo.

GREAT MOMENTS: Witchiepoo rewards her evil trees ("Take two squirrels out of petty cash!") in "The Wheely Bird"; the opening-credits theme ("Once upon a summertime, just a dream from yesterday"); Witchiepoo's dizzy rendition of "Oranges, Poranges" in "Show Biz Witch."

FAST-FORWARD: "Flute, Book, and Candle," not one of the better episodes to begin with, appears to have had its master tape run over by a truck before the DVD conversion.

EXTRAS: New interviews with stars Jack Wild and Billie Hayes, and TV historian Hal Erickson; Sid and Marty Krofft commentary track on "The Magic Path"; 1950s pilot for the Krofft series *Irving.*

Hullabaloo (1965–1966)

A 1960s Music Flashback: Volumes 1–4 (7 episodes on 1 disc): ★ ★ ★ ★ ½
Volumes 5–8 (7 episodes on 1 disc): ★ ★ ★ ★ ½
Volumes 9–12 (7 episodes on 1 disc): ★ ★ ★ ★

MPI Home Video
Video: Full-Frame; Audio: Dolby Digital Stereo

Television was still perceived as disposable entertainment in the 1960s, and rock 'n' roll music even more so, which explains why no one at NBC thought to save the masters from *Hullabaloo*, a show that featured performances both live and lip-synched from the greatest bands from the most creative decade in rock history. At least the MPI compilations, gathered from both surviving color tapes and black-and-white kinescopes, sport digitally restored sound to help compensate for the varying picture quality.

What are fun to watch here are not just the Rock and Roll Hall of Famers—Chuck Berry, Marvin Gaye, the Mamas and the Papas, the Supremes, the Four Seasons, Simon & Garfunkel—but such one-hit wonders and novelty acts as the Cyrkle, Peter and Gordon, Sam the Sham & the Pharaohs, the Nashville Teens, and the Beau Brummels. Another highlight is the mid-show musical medley, featuring singers performing the music of other artists, usually the Beatles or Bob Dylan. Rounding out each episode is the Hullabaloo A-Go-Go, where featured acts like the Yardbirds perform while surrounded by girls in cages.

GREAT MOMENTS: Volumes 1–4: The Byrds' searing cover of Bob Dylan's "The Times They Are A-Changin'"; Smokey Robinson and the Miracles' "Going to a Go-Go"; Volumes 5–8: Frankie Avalon and Annette Funicello sing with Freddie and the Dreamers; Petula Clark's "I Know a Place."

FAST-FORWARD: Sammy Davis, Jr., and the Supremes duetting on "Toot Toot Tootsie" (Volumes 9–12).

EXTRAS: Bonus performances in every volume.

Hunter (1984–1991)

The Complete First Season (20 episodes on 6 discs): ★ ★ ★
The Complete Second Season (23 episodes on 6 discs): ★ ★ ½
The Complete Third Season (22 episodes on 6 discs): ★ ★ ½

Anchor Bay
Video: Full-Frame; Audio: Dolby Digital 2.0

Dispensing ham-fisted Reagan-era justice on the streets of L.A., Fred Dryer was an appealing primetime knockoff of Dirty Harry in this by-the-numbers cop show. The hook of Rick Hunter coming from a Mob family was never sufficiently explored, and the nickname "Brass Cupcake" for Hunter's partner Dee Dee McCall represents the series' most inspired bit of writing in seven seasons.

Syndicated episode cuts, and music substitution in several key scenes (including the opening pilot sequence originally set to CCR's "Bad Moon Rising") is bound to disappoint fans. Every time this happens, the reputation of DVD as an archival format for television's past takes another hit.

GREAT MOMENTS: Season 1: Dennis Farina and a pre-Sipowicz Dennis Franz guest-star in "The Snow Queen"; former Miss USA Shawn Weatherly distracts Hunter in "The Shooter"; Season 2: Dee Dee is sexually assaulted and Hunter's out for vengeance in the powerful two-parter "Rape and Revenge"; Season 3: The story arc following the breakup of Hunter and McCall's partnership; Trekkies will enjoy the guest appearances of Brent Spiner in "The Contract" and Marina Sirtis in "Down and Under."

FAST-FORWARD: Nothing.

EXTRAS: Season 1: Interviews with creator Stephen J. Cannell and star Stepfanie Kramer.

I Dream of Jeannie (1965–1970)

The Complete First Season [black-and-white] (30 episodes on 4 discs): ★ ★ ★ ½
The Complete First Season [color] (30 episodes on 4 discs): ★ ★ ★ ½

Sony Pictures Home Entertainment
Video: Full-Frame; Audio: Dolby Digital 2.0

Often paired with *Bewitched* in the baby-boomer memory, *I Dream of Jeannie* wasn't nearly as sophisticated or clever as its magical forerunner, though Barbara Eden sparkles in the role that made her a classic TV icon, and Larry Hagman never received enough credit for his virtuosity in pratfalls and double-takes. As with its *Bewitched* DVD collections, Sony released *Jeannie*'s black-and-white first season in both original and colorized versions. Purists will prefer the black-and-white, but this was a series made for color, and fans can be forgiven for wanting to see that famous harem outfit in its full pink glory before the release of Season 2.

GREAT MOMENTS: Major Nelson meets Jeannie in "The Lady in the Bottle"; Major Healey finds out about Jeannie and tricks her into changing masters in "The Richest Astronaut in the Whole Wide World."

FAST-FORWARD: Nothing.

EXTRAS: Commentary on the pilot by Barbara Eden, Larry Hagman, and Bill Daily; cast interviews.

I Love Lucy (1951–1961)

The Complete First Season (36 episodes on 9 discs): ★ ★ ★ ★
The Complete First Season [re-release] (36 episodes on 7 discs): ★ ★ ★ ★ ★
Season 1, Volumes 1–9 (4 episodes each on 1 disc): ★ ★ ★ ½
The Complete Second Season (31 episodes on 5 discs): ★ ★ ★ ★ ★
The Complete Third Season (31 episodes on 5 discs): ★ ★ ★ ★ ★
The Complete Fourth Season (30 episodes on 5 discs): ★ ★ ★ ★ ★
The Complete Fifth Season (26 episodes on 4 discs): ★ ★ ★ ★ ★
The Complete Sixth Season (27 episodes on 4 discs): ★ ★ ★ ★ ½
Fiftieth Anniversary Special: ★ ★ ★

I

Paramount Home Video
Video: Full-Frame; Audio: Dolby Digital 1.0

This is where all discussions of situation comedy must begin; though *I Love Lucy* may not be the first example of the form, it's the show that set the standard, and established the language of the thirty-minute comedy series. But this is no antiquated museum piece; fifty years after some of these shows first aired, the series is still funnier than most of the network sitcom output of the past decade. If you pay attention to television at all beyond its function as a night light, you know this already, so let's proceed to discussing the DVDs.

Paramount stumbled out of the gate with its first *I Love Lucy* releases—nine individual volumes containing four episodes each. After season sets emerged as the collectors' preference, the studio not only followed suit with subsequent sets, but re-released the first season in a more suitable package.

Picture and sound quality is nothing short of astonishing. The show always had a technical advantage over other '50s product, having been shot on film rather than tape, and the results have been restored for the DVD to absolute pristine condition. Original animated credits and bumpers, many not seen in half a century, once again grace television's most legendary episodes.

GREAT MOMENTS: Let's bypass the obvious—the Vitameatavegamin commercial (Season 1's "Lucy Does a TV Commercial"), Lucy in the chocolate factory (Season 2's "Job Switching"), the grape stomping in Italy (Season 5's "Lucy's Italian Movie")—all of which figure into the core curriculum of Classic TV 101, to make room for a few more: Season 1: Lucy lip-synchs to a sped-up recording of Carmen Miranda singing "Mama Yo Quiero" in "Be a Pal"; Lucy and Ricky perform "Cuban Pete," a staple of their nightclub act, in "The Diet"; Season 2: The birth of Little Ricky, a seminal moment in TV history, in "Lucy Goes to the Hospital"; Season 3: Lucy bets that she can be completely honest for twenty-four hours in "Lucy Tells the Truth"; Lucy and Ethel's second TV commercial in "The Million-Dollar Idea"; Season 4: Lucy meets William Holden at the Brown Derby, and lights her nose on fire, in "L.A. at Last"; the classic mirror routine between Lucy and Harpo Marx in "Harpo Marx"; Season 5: Lucy tries to make Ricky jealous in "Lucy Meets Charles Boyer"; Season 6: The tobacco-shop scene in "The Ricardos Visit Cuba"; George Reeves reprises his most famous role in "Lucy Meets Superman"; the egg-breaking dance in "Lucy Does the Tango," which generated the longest laugh in the series' history.

FAST-FORWARD: The Mertzes do not appear in "Lucy Plays Cupid" (Season 1) which pulls the show's focus off its regular cast and onto guest stars Bea Benaderet and Edward Everett Horton.

EXTRAS: Every season set contains a wealth of remarkable rarities, including deleted footage, lost scenes, outtakes, the identification of flubs that can still be seen in the episodes, behind-the-scenes featurettes, episodes of Lucy's radio show that inspired the series, and other special features. Season 6 also includes commentaries from Keith Thibodeaux ("Little Ricky"), writers Bob Schiller and Madelyn Pugh Davis, and guest stars Doris Singleton and Barbara Eden.

I Spy (1965–1968)

Volumes 1–19 (each: 4 episodes on 1 disc): ★ ★ ★

Box Sets 1–3 (each: 7 previously released volumes on 3 discs): ★ ★ ★ ½

The Robert Culp Collection 1 & 2 (each: 3 episodes on 1 disc): ★ ★ ★

Image Entertainment

Video: Full-Frame; Audio: Dolby Digital 2.0

Bill Cosby received most of the headlines, not to mention an Emmy Award, for his groundbreaking work on the lighthearted action/espionage series *I Spy*. As the first African-American performer to have a starring role in a dramatic television series, he deserved such accolades. But this has reduced Robert Culp's contributions to an afterthought among all but the most knowledgeable fans, and that's a shame. Though Image's work here is a far cry from its stellar production on *The Dick Van Dyke Show* DVDs, the company should be applauded for collecting two volumes of episodes written by Culp, which rank among the series' finest shows. Now if Image would just go back and put some proper season sets out, the series would be properly preserved.

GREAT MOMENTS: All of the *Robert Culp Collection* episodes.

FAST-FORWARD: Nothing.

EXTRAS: Robert Culp provides commentary for the *Robert Culp Collection* releases.

I

In Living Color (1990–1994)

Season 1 (12 episodes on 3 discs): ★ ★ ★ ★

Season 2 (26 episodes on 4 discs): ★ ★ ★

Season 3 (30 episodes on 3 discs): ★ ★ ★

Season 4 (33 episodes on 3 discs): ★ ★ ½

Season 5 (26 episodes on 3 discs): ★ ★ ½

20th Century-Fox

Video: Full-Frame; Audio: Dolby Digital 2.0

While this groundbreaking sketch-comedy series deserves higher praise than "the black *Saturday Night Live*," especially given the state of *SNL* in recent years, the series' DVD releases haven't done *In Living Color* any favors. Musical performances were cut for the first-season release, and Seasons 2 and 3 are missing entire sketches. Sure, what's left still justifies the purchase, but we can't give it two snaps up in a circle.

GREAT MOMENTS: Any appearance by Homey the Clown, Fire-Marshall Bill, or the Men on Film; Season 3: "Home Alone 3," with Michael Jackson.

FAST-FORWARD: The Head Detective sketches.

EXTRAS: Season 1: Episode commentaries; "Back in Step with the Fly Girls" and "Looking Back in Living Color" featurettes; Season 2: Episode commentaries; "Appreciating *In Living Color*" and "Notorious *In Living Color* Characters" featurettes.

The Incredible Hulk (1978–1982)

The Television Series Ultimate Collection (18 episodes on 6 discs): ★ ★ ★
The Original Television Premiere: ★ ★ ★ ½
The Incredible Hulk Returns/The Trial of the Incredible Hulk: ★ ★
The Death of the Incredible Hulk: ★ ★

Premiere and *Ultimate Collection*: Universal Home Video; *Returns/Trial*: Anchor Bay; *Death of*: 20th Century-Fox

Video: Full-Frame; Audio: Dolby Digital Mono

We know whose name is in the title, but David Banner emerged as a much more interesting character than the Hulk, thanks to Bill Bixby's nuanced performance as the tortured scientist with a dark and destructive secret. The series had neither the budget nor the inclination to follow the comic book's lead, and pit the Hulk in battle against super-villains like the Leader and the Abomination, so instead we followed Banner as he moved from town to town, trying to avoid the authorities and the intrepid reporter determined to expose the doctor's double life. We liked this show a lot better the first time, when it was called *The Fugitive*. Still, Marvel-ites might get a perverse kick out of the "Returns" and "Trial" TV movies that followed the series, for their hilariously awful takes on Daredevil and the Mighty Thor.

GREAT MOMENTS: Ultimate Collection: Banner is trapped halfway between human and Hulk form in "Prometheus."

FAST-FORWARD: Banner tries to cure himself by shooting up Native American horse tranquilizers in "Rainbow's End."

EXTRAS: *Television Premiere*: introduction by Lou Ferrigno.

Jeeves and Wooster (1990–1993)

The Complete First Season (5 episodes on 2 discs): ★ ★ ★ ★ ★
The Complete Second Season (6 episodes on 2 discs): ★ ★ ★ ★ ★
The Complete Third Season (6 episodes on 2 discs): ★ ★ ★ ★ ½
The Complete Fourth Season (6 episodes on 2 discs): ★ ★ ★
The Complete Jeeves and Wooster Megaset
(23 episodes on 8 discs): ★ ★ ★ ★ ★

A&E Home Video
Video: Full-Frame; Audio: Dolby Digital Mono

The books of P.G. Wodehouse are such celebrations of the written word that it's inevitable something will be lost in the translation to television of his most enduring creations, Bertie Wooster and faithful butler Jeeves. But these irresistible episodes are nearly as delightful as their magnificent source material. As with every A&E release that's available both by season and in a complete series set, the latter offers the best bargain.

GREAT MOMENTS: Just about everything in the first three seasons.

FAST-FORWARD: Nothing.

EXTRAS: None.

The Jeffersons (1975–1985)

The Complete First Season (13 episodes on 2 discs): ★ ★ ★ ½
The Complete Second Season (24 episodes on 3 discs): ★ ★ ★ ½
The Complete Third Season (24 episodes on 3 discs): ★ ★ ★
The Complete Fourth Season (26 episodes on 3 discs): ★ ★ ★

J

Sony Pictures Home Entertainment
Video: Full-Frame; Audio: Dolby Digital 2.0

The first and most successful of the many *All in the Family* spin-offs, *The Jeffersons* followed George and Weezie from Queens to a deluxe apartment in the sky. George's bluster and racial commentary fueled most episodes, or provided many of the punch lines when the plots fell back on such sitcom staples as being locked in a room and mistaken identity. What's missing is the pilot episode, "The Jeffersons Move On Up," which originally aired as an episode of *All in the Family.*

GREAT MOMENTS: Season 1: In the provocative "Jenny's Low," Tom and Helen's children discuss how they're treated as different-looking offspring of an interracial marriage; Season 2: Louis Gossett, Jr., hits on Weezie in "George's Best Friend"; Season 3: George Jefferson portrays founding father Thomas Jefferson in "George and the President."

FAST-FORWARD: Nothing.

EXTRAS: None.

Jem! (1985–1988)

The Complete First and Second Seasons (26 episodes on 4 discs): ★ ★ ★ ½
Season 3, Part 1 (19 episodes on 3 discs): ★ ★ ★ ½

Rhino

Video: Full-Frame; Audio: Dolby Digital 5.1

Ah, Jem, Jem, you glam-rock vixen. You taught us life lessons just as you kept those bratty Starlight Girls in line; you romanced Rio, even if he didn't always see that your secret identity, Jerrica Benton, was the real catch; and even though you eventually went Hollywood, you never lost sight of what got you there. We are better citizens today because of what we learned from the Holograms. And don't you believe all those website postings that say they admire you and Kimber and your friends, but secretly prefer the songs of the Misfits and their Euro-trash funk. Those people probably listen to Courtney Love now. At least Rhino recognizes your legacy—how many cartoons from the '80s get a Dolby Digital 5.1 mix for their DVDs? "Glitter and Gold" and "Like a Dream" never sounded better.

GREAT MOMENTS: *The Complete First and Second Seasons*: The Starbright Trilogy; the gondola chase from "In Stitches."

FAST-FORWARD: Kimber's whining.

EXTRAS: First and Second Season: Interviews with series creator Christy Marx and Samantha Newark, the speaking voice of Jem; commentaries by Marx; a "Music only" setting; excerpts from the *Jem!* production bible; Season 3, Part 1: Interview with Britta Phillips, the singing voice of Jem, and writer Roger Slifer; commentaries; "Music only" setting.

The Jetsons (1962–1963)

Season 1 (24 episodes on 4 discs): ★ ★ ★ ★

Warner Home Video

Video: Full-Frame; Audio: Mono

If you smile at the memory of the immortal words, "Jane! Stop this crazy thing!", here's your show. As with other releases from the first batch of Hanna-Barbera animated classics, *The Jetsons* arrives looking and sounding better than it has in years, though the colorful package contains only a modicum of extras. As with *Jonny Quest*, the Season 1 label is misleading as there wasn't a second season; this is the original *Jetsons* series in its entirety. It just seems as if there must be more because these twenty-four episodes ran nearly nonstop on Saturday mornings for fourteen years. Worth a look today for the jazzy score, the futuristic household devices that have since become reality, and the never-ending battle for corporate supremacy between Spacely Sprockets and Cogswell Cogs.

GREAT MOMENTS: The performance of "Eep Opp Ork Ah-Ah" in "A Date with Jet Screamer"; Astro joins the family in "The Coming of Astro"; Jane enters a beauty pageant for which George winds up a judge in "Miss Solar System."

FAST-FORWARD: The recycled *Flintstones* plot of "Test Pilot."

EXTRAS: Featurettes "The Jetsons: Family of the Future" and "Space-Age Gadgets"; commentaries by Janet Waldo, the voice of Judy Jetson.

Joan of Arcadia (2003–2005)

The First Season (23 episodes on 6 discs): ★ ★ ★ ½

Paramount Home Video

Video: Anamorphic Widescreen; Audio: Dolby Digital 2.0

Sometimes God can be a real pain in the butt. That's not the main message of *Joan of Arcadia*, but it's certainly what young Joan Girardi thinks every time the Almighty asks her to carry out a seemingly innocuous task. The personification of God is always tricky, but the series deftly walks a fine line, that allows Joan (wonderfully played by Emmy nominee Amber Tamblyn) to accuse her creator of being "snippy," while not offending open-minded believers and non-believers alike. Though there is humor in God's requests of Joan, the series also illustrates that while living a life of faith is not always easy, the results are worth any discomfort one might experience along the journey. Fans were justifiably miffed when *Joan of Arcadia* was cancelled after two seasons—now, we may never know if Kevin will dance at his wedding.

The DVD sets could be a little better in their tech credits; there's an orange glow to many of the scenes set in the Girardi home. Music substitution is also a disappointment, most notably in the series' opening-credits sequence, which plays intact only once on each disc.

GREAT MOMENTS: "Saint Joan," a fine series' finest hour; the colorful climax of "Anonymous"; God asks Joan to build a boat in "The Boat."

FAST-FORWARD: Adam's moping and Grace's antisocial rants could try the patience of saints; "Night Without Stars" renders the Girardi family characters unrecognizable from previous episodes.

EXTRAS: Deleted scenes; cast/crew commentaries; featurettes "The Creation of *Joan of Arcadia*" and "*Joan of Arcadia*—A Look at Season 1."

Joey (2004–2006)

The Complete First Season (24 episodes on 4 discs): ★ ★ ½

Warner Bros. Home Video

Video: Full-Frame; Audio: Dolby Digital 5.1

Matt LeBlanc's *Friends* spin-off wasn't the next *Frasier* as NBC had hoped, but it wasn't *AfterMASH* either, as mixed reviews and poor ratings might suggest. Despite the genuine goomba chemistry LeBlanc's Joey Tribbiani shared with abrasive sister Gina (*The Sopranos*' Drea de Matteo), Mr. "How you doin'?" was too often set adrift amidst bland supporting characters and the same struggling-actor storylines we watched for ten years on *Friends*.

GREAT MOMENTS: Joey mixes his roles when he's cast in three different plays in "Joey and the Perfect Storm"; Lucy Liu plays a neurotic producer in "Joey and the Plot Twist."

FAST-FORWARD: A dumber-than-usual Joey in "Joey and the Nemesis."

EXTRAS: None.

The Joey Bishop Show (1961–1965)

The Complete Second Season (34 episodes on 6 discs): ★ ½

Questar

Video: Full-Frame; Audio: Mono

Even if you overlook Questar's beginning its collections with Season 2—a case can be made for this, as *The Joey Bishop Show* underwent a complete format change in its second season, with Bishop's Joey Barnes character being promoted from a press agent's assistant to the host of his own talk show—this is still a pretty sorry excuse for a DVD set. The quality of both picture and sound is extremely lacking, and each episode runs without the opening-credits sequence. This show deserves to be seen by a wider audience, but the availability of this substandard release may discourage another distributor from doing the job properly.

GREAT MOMENTS: None.

FAST-FORWARD: You'd have to buy it first.

EXTRAS: None.

The Judy Garland Show (1963–1964)

Collection (14 episodes on 4 discs): ★ ★ ★ ★

Legends: ★ ★ ★ ★

Songs for America: ★ ★ ★ ½

Volumes 1–8: Each: ★ ★ ★ ★

Pioneer Entertainment

Video: Full-Frame; Audio: Dolby Digital 5.1

Behind-the-scenes confusion doomed *The Judy Garland Show* as much as time-slot competition from the Western hit *Bonanza.* While a revolving door of producers experimented with comedy and interview segments, all viewers wanted was to hear Judy sing. Still, the series produced more magical musical moments in two years than some variety shows manage in a decade. Of the individual volumes released on DVD, the third is the Christmas show, and Volume 6 also includes a rare outtake from the videotaping of the series' first episode, featuring guest star Mickey Rooney. *Legends* is an outstanding sampler.

GREAT MOMENTS: Volume 1: Judy duets with daughter Liza Minnelli; Volume 5: a now-legendary performance with Barbra Streisand; Volume 7: Judy sings the biggest hits from her movies, including "The Man That Got Away."

FAST-FORWARD: Nothing.

EXTRAS: Commentaries with producer George Schlatter and director Norman Jewison; production outtakes.

Just Shoot Me (1997–2003)

Seasons 1 & 2 (31 episodes on 4 discs): ★ ★ ★ ½

Sony Pictures Home Entertainment

Video: Full-Frame; Audio: Dolby Digital 2.0

Just Shoot Me was the *Wings* of the millennium era—a show that a lot of people watched, but that never generated *Entertainment Weekly* covers and mega-hit status. Perhaps that's why it seems like a fresh, pleasant surprise on DVD. George Segal, Laura San Giacomo, Wendie Malick, and David Spade were a unique comic ensemble, and though the series could bite with the best of them, something one would expect given its fashion-world premise, *Just Shoot Me* also had sincerity and heart, two words rarely associated with anything involving Spade.

GREAT MOMENTS: Maya is too honest with her fashion critiques in "The Emperor," guest-starring Dana Carvey.

FAST-FORWARD: Nothing.

EXTRAS: Commentaries by series writers and creators; "Always in Fashion" featurette.

Justice League (2001–)

Season 1 (26 episodes on 4 discs): ★ ★ ★ ★ ★

Justice League (Volumes 1–3): ★ ★ ★ ★

Volume 1: Secret Origins (3 episodes on 1 disc): ★ ★ ★ ★

Volume 2: Justice on Trial (4 episodes on 1 disc): ★ ★ ★ ★

Volume 3: Paradise Lost (4 episodes on 1 disc): ★ ★ ★ ½

Volume 4: Star Crossed (3 episodes on 1 disc): ★ ★ ★ ★ ½

Volume 5: The Brave and the Bold (4 episodes on 1 disc): ★ ★ ★ ★

Unlimited—Season 1, Volume 1: Saving the World (3 episodes on 1 disc): ★ ★ ★ ★

Unlimited—Season 1, Volume 2: Joining Forces (3 episodes on 1 disc): ★ ★ ★ ★

Warner Home Video

Video: Full-Frame; *Star Crossed*: Anamorphic Widescreen; Audio: Dolby Digital 2.0

A superb revival of the famed DC superhero team, more sophisticated than *Super Friends*, stylish in its character designs and action sequences, with the anime influence kept mercifully to a minimum. Warner Bros. initially incurred the wrath of fans by releasing episodes in single-disc collections. We all knew the season sets were coming eventually, but chumps that we are, we still bought the individual volumes before they were properly collected.

GREAT MOMENTS: Volume 2: Aquaman is finally cool in "The Enemy Below"; Volume 4: The three-part, movie-length "Star Crossed" bids goodbye to Hawkgirl, and teases a Batman–Wonder Woman romance; Volume 5: Lex Luthor gathers a team of super-villains against the League in "Injustice for All"; *Unlimited*, Season 1, Volume 1: Fred Savage and Jason Hervey, the bickering *Wonder Years* siblings, voice the title characters in "Hawk and Dove."

FAST-FORWARD: Nothing.

EXTRAS: Volume 2: Director Bruce Timm offers episode introductions; "The Look of the League" featurette; Volume 3: Bruce Timm episode introductions; "Draw the Dark Side" featurette; Volume 4: "Hawkman: From Comics to Cartoon" featurette; *Unlimited*, Volume 2: "Voices of Justice" featurette; Volume 5: Behind-the-scenes featurette. Note: The Season 1 set contains all the extras released with the individual volumes.

Keeping Up Appearances (1990–1995)

The Full Bouquet (44 episodes on 8 discs): ★ ★ ★ ★
Series 1 (6 episodes on 1 disc): ★ ★ ★
Series 3 (7 episodes on 1 disc): ★ ★ ★
Series 4 (6 episodes on 1 disc): ★ ★ ★
Series 1 & 2 (20 episodes on 4 discs): ★ ★ ★ ½
Series 3–5 (24 episodes on 4 discs): ★ ★ ★
Deck the Halls With Hyacinth (4 episodes on 1 disc): ★ ★ ★
Hats Off to Hyacinth (5 episodes on 1 disc): ★ ★ ½
Hints from Hyacinth (5 episodes on 1 disc): ★ ★ ½
Home Is Where the Hyacinth Is (5 episodes on 1 disc): ★ ★ ★
Living the Hyacinth Life (6 episodes on 1 disc): ★ ★ ½

BBC Video

Video: Full-Frame; Audio: Dolby Digital 2.0

Class division, and the envy and insecurity it inspires, probably fueled more Britcom plots than any other subject. No series captured the fine art of class-climbing better than *Keeping Up Appearances*, starring Patricia Routledge as the redoubtable Hyacinth Bucket (pronounced "Bouquet"). The DVD releases by BBC Video constitute the kind of hodgepodge mess of which Hyacinth would not approve. The offerings include half-series sets, full series sets, and several combinations thereof. The easiest way to cut through the confusion is to buy *The Full Bouquet*, which contains all the episodes and all the extras in one tastefully designed package.

GREAT MOMENTS: Series 1: Hyacinth entertains the clergy in "The New Vicar"; Series 2: Hyacinth sings in "The Candlelight Supper"; Series 3: The "Outdoors/Indoors Luxury Barbecue and Finger Buffet" in "A Celebrity for the Barbecue."

FAST-FORWARD: The travails of Onslow and Daisy are best taken in smaller doses.

EXTRAS: Series 1: Outtakes; Series 1 and 2: Profile of Patricia Routledge, plus Routledge appearances in five bonus comedy sketches and "The Kitty Monologues"; outtakes; Series 3: Outtakes; Series 4: "Second Chance Shorts" commercial with Hyacinth and Elizabeth; outtakes; Series 3–5: cast interviews; BBC special "The Memoirs of Hyacinth Bucket."

The King of Queens (1998–)

The First Season (25 episodes on 3 discs): ★ ★ ★ ★
The Second Season (25 episodes on 3 discs): ★ ★ ★ ★ ½
The Third Season (25 episodes on 3 discs): ★ ★ ★ ★
The Fourth Season (25 episodes on 3 discs): ★ ★ ★ ½

Sony Pictures Home Entertainment
Video: Full-Frame; Audio: Dolby Digital Surround

The series that launched the hot-girl-with-fat-guy sitcom genre became, with surprisingly little fanfare, television's best blue-collar comedy since *Roseanne*. The season box sets are remarkably consistent in both the quality of episodes and the tech quality of the DVDs. Unlike some series that burned brighter and ended faster, *The King of Queens* has all the elements of a perennial; one day your grandchildren will be laughing at this stuff.

GREAT MOMENTS: Season 1: Doug and Carrie's silent argument at "The Cello Concert"; the first *Everybody Loves Raymond* crossover, "Road Rayge"; Carrie's last-minute birthday party in "Crappy Birthday"; Season 2: The battle over godparent status in "Parent Trapped"; Carrie grows jealous of a Cooper's waitress in "I, Candy"; the flashback episode "Meet-By-Product"; Season 3:

Doug is embarrassed over Carrie's shopping for him at the "Big and Tall" shop in "Fatty McButterpants."

FAST-FORWARD: Season 3: Doug's Ralph Kramden dream sequence in "Inner Tube."

EXTRAS: Season 1: Commentary on the pilot episode with creator Michael Weithorn and star Kevin James; "Just Having Fun" behind-the-scenes featurette; Season 2: Commentaries; "Kevin James: A Day in the Life of an International Superstar" featurette.

King of the Hill (1996–)

The Complete First Season (13 episodes on 3 discs): ★ ★ ★ ½
The Complete Second Season (23 episodes on 4 discs): ★ ★ ★ ★
The Complete Third Season (25 episodes on 3 discs): ★ ★ ★ ★ ½
The Complete Fourth Season (24 episodes on 3 discs): ★ ★ ★ ★
The Complete Fifth Season (20 episodes on 3 discs): ★ ★ ★ ½
The Complete Sixth Season (21 episodes on 3 discs): ★ ★ ★

20th Century-Fox
Video: Full-Frame; Audio: Dolby 2.0 Surround

After forcing parents into action committees with his exploration of brain-dead youth, *Beavis and Butthead*, Mike Judge exposed the red-stater that lurked beneath his MTV facade with *King of the Hill*, the story of a propane-gas salesman and his family set in the wilds of Arlen, Texas. Like *The Simpsons*, the series has attracted an amazing who's who of guest voice talent, including Meryl Streep, Reese Witherspoon, Sally Field, Kathleen Turner, Mary Tyler Moore, and Heather Locklear.

GREAT MOMENTS: Season 2: Bobby becomes a plus-size model in "Husky Bobby"; Season 3: Peggy supports corporal punishment in "To Spank with Love"; Season 4: Hank has female troubles in "Aisle 8A."

FAST-FORWARD: Nothing. Even the lesser episodes boast a few memorable throwaway lines.

EXTRAS: Commentaries, deleted scenes, and behind-the-scenes featurettes are included with the first two season sets.

Knight Rider (1982–1986)

Season 1 (22 episodes on 4 discs): ★ ★ ★
Season 2 (21 episodes on 3 discs): ★ ★ ★ ½
Season 3 (21 episodes on 3 discs): ★ ★ ★ ½
Season 4 (22 episodes on 3 discs): ★ ★

Universal Home Video
Video: Full-Frame; Audio: Dolby Digital 2.0

In the 1980s, two cars vied for the title of TV's coolest ride: the General Lee on *The Dukes of Hazzard* and KITT on *Knight Rider*. It's debatable how much either show had to offer beyond its signature vehicle, though that didn't stop fans from arguing their finer points. The consensus was that David Hasselhoff had better hair than either John Schneider or Tom Wopat, but none of Michael Knight's female associates were hotter than Daisy Duke.

There's not much else to say about *Knight Rider*—it's a guy and his talking car solving crimes, battling their respective evil twins, and sharing playful banter that sometimes made Hasselhoff sound more robotic than the car, which was voiced by *St. Elsewhere* star William Daniels. Those who were fans at age twelve will probably love getting reacquainted with the series, but your mileage may vary.

GREAT MOMENTS: Season 1: The "origin" story, "Knight of the Phoenix"; the debut of KITT's evil twin KARR in "Trust Doesn't Rust"; Season 2: David Hasselhoff sings, sending millions of German hearts a-flutter, in "Let It Be Me"; Geena Davis guest-stars in "KITT the Cat"; Season 3: The rematch fans demanded in "KITT vs. KARR"; Season 4: KITT faces its greatest challenge yet in the two-part season-opener "Knight of the Juggernaut."

FAST-FORWARD: Season 2: The obligatory amnesia episode "Knightmares"; Season 4: Michael is bamboozled in the awful "Voodoo Knight."

EXTRAS: Season 1: Commentary with David Hasselhoff and writer-creator Glen Larson; two featurettes; the TV movie *Knight Rider 2000*; Season 4: "The Great '80s TV Flashback" featurette; KITT blueprints.

Knots Landing (1979–1993)

The Complete First Season (13 episodes on 5 discs): ★ ★ ★

Warner Home Video
Video: Full-Frame; Audio: Dolby Digital Mono

The spin-off from *Dallas* that brought Gary and Valene Ewing to southern

California proved enormously popular, and one could make the case for Joan Van Ark, Donna Mills, and Michele Lee as TV's original desperate housewives. Nicollette Sheridan got her start here, and she's just one among dozens of familiar faces that passed through this quiet cul-de-sac in *Knots'* fourteen-year run. The roll call of steamy temptresses and the men who loved them includes Lisa Hartman, William Devane, Alec Baldwin, Ava Gardner, Michelle Phillips, Kristy Swanson, and Halle Berry.

GREAT MOMENTS: Julie Harris debuts as Liliame Clements in "Will the Circle Be Unbroken"; Gary must choose between booze and Val in "Bottom of the Bottle, Part 2."

FAST-FORWARD: Nothing.

EXTRAS: Cast interviews and commentaries.

Kojak (1973–1978)

Season 1 (22 episodes on 3 discs): ★ ★ ★ ½

Universal Home Video

Video: Full-Frame; Audio: Dolby Digital 2.0

After guest-starring as the heavy in more TV shows than even he could count, Telly Savales finally achieved stardom with a character that seemed like a natural extension of his hard-boiled but charismatic personality. The first season of *Kojak* won Savales the Emmy, and earned praise from real law enforcement for its no-nonsense portrayal of crime and punishment. Parodies aside, it wasn't all lollipops and "Who loves ya, baby?" on Theo Kojak's rough South Manhattan beat. The stories felt real, as did the detective's willingness to rough up an occasional street hood if it brought him closer to cracking a case. The one mystery left unsolved is the Season 1 set's omission of *The Marcus-Nelson Murders*, the series' two-hour pilot movie. It's a disappointing oversight that may be corrected in a subsequent release.

GREAT MOMENTS: "Die Before They Wake" guest-stars Tina Louise and features Kojak's first "Who loves ya?"; Jackie Cooper plays a jewel thief who masquerades as a man of the cloth in "Last Rites for a Dead Priest."

FAST-FORWARD: Nothing.

EXTRAS: None.

Kolchak: The Night Stalker (1971–1972)

The Night Stalker/The Night Strangler: ★ ★ ★ ★

MGM Home Video

Video: Full-Frame; Audio: Dolby Digital 2.0

Just as *Dark Shadows* was winding down, creator-director Dan Curtis teamed with writer Richard Matheson (*The Twilight Zone*) for another unique spin on the vampire genre, and scored one of the biggest ratings for a made-for-TV movie in the history of the medium. *The Night Stalker*, with its rumpled hero, Carl Kolchak (Darren McGavin), may be television's first X-File. Chris Carter, who created Mulder and Scully, acknowledged his debt to the movie by casting McGavin as a veteran FBI agent who walked the wild side before Mulder earned his "Spooky" nickname. *The Night Strangler* is a worthy follow-up, and is almost certainly the only movie to feature both legendary actor John Carradine and Grandpa Munster Al Lewis.

GREAT MOMENTS: Every frame of *The Night Stalker*; the appearance of Margaret Hamilton and the underground city in *The Night Strangler.*

FAST-FORWARD: Nothing.

EXTRAS: Interview with director Dan Curtis.

Kung Fu (1972–1975)

Season 1 (16 episodes on 3 discs): ★ ★ ★ ★

Season 2 (23 episodes on 4 discs): ★ ★ ★

Season 3 (24 episodes on 4 discs): ★ ★ ★

Warner Home Video

Video: Anamorphic Widescreen (Season 1); Full-Frame (Seasons 2 & 3); Audio: Dolby Digital 2.0

Following the first wave of martial arts films to spin-kick their way into theaters in the 1970s, *Kung Fu* became something of a phenomenon, though its appeal was more cerebral than visceral. As Kwai Chang Caine, the quiet man who walked the Earth, dispensing Eastern philosophy in the American West, David Carradine created a new heroic archetype. It's a role that defined his career, and it wasn't even supposed to be his—the series was originally intended as a vehicle for Bruce Lee. Though Carradine had some martial arts experience, he wasn't in Lee's class, so most of the series' fight scenes were put together in editing. They had novelty value at the time, but thirty years later these rudimentary skirmishes won't measure up for viewers raised on Buffy and Xena.

The first-season DVD set presents the episodes remastered in widescreen. It's an odd choice that apparently didn't go over too well, hence the return to full-frame for Seasons 2 and 3. Certainly most viewers prefer to watch the shows as originally broadcast, but even the widescreen shows boast a stunning picture quality.

GREAT MOMENTS: Season 1: The *Defiant Ones*–inspired adventure "Chains"; Season 2: Harrison Ford appears in "Crossties."

FAST-FORWARD: Season 2: Caine meets a male witch in "El Brujo."

EXTRAS: Season 1: Featurettes "From Grasshopper to Caine" and "The Tao of Kwai Chang Caine"; Season 2: David Carradine commentaries on two episodes; "A Dinner with David Carradine and Friends" featurette; Season 3: "David Carradine's Shaolin Diary: Back to the Beginning."

The L Word (2004–)

Season 1 (14 episodes on 5 discs): ★ ★ ½
Season 2 (13 episodes on 4 discs): ★ ★ ★

Showtime Home Video
Video: Anamorphic Widescreen; Audio: Dolby Digital 5.1

Call it the flipside to *Queer as Folk*, another Showtime series focusing on gay characters. But where that show tends toward soap opera, *The L Word* revels in the satiric, mixing its frank love scenes and revolving relationships with healthy doses of humor. And hey, look! It's Jennifer Beals!

GREAT MOMENTS: Season 1: Tim catches Jenny and Marina in an unexpected position in "Lawfully"; Season 2: The lesbian cruise in "Land Ahoy."

FAST-FORWARD: Nothing.

EXTRAS: Season 1: Several featurettes, as well as deleted scenes, a blooper reel, and an original puppet show performed by the cast; Season 2: Cast and fan commentaries and a cast photo shoot.

La Femme Nikita (1997–2001)

The Complete First Season (22 episodes on 6 discs): ★ ★ ★ ★
The Complete Second Season (22 episodes on 6 discs): ★ ★ ★ ★
The Complete Third Season (22 episodes on 6 discs): ★ ★ ★ ½

Warner Home Video
Video: Full-Frame; Audio: Dolby Digital Surround

Apparently, the appeal of hot chicks who kick ass transcends all cultures and borders; the 1990 French film *La Femme Nikita* spawned adaptations in America and Japan, as well as this series that earned a cult following to rival any sci-fi franchise of the past twenty years. From the prodigious ranks of TV's warrior women, only Peta Wilson looks like she could probably still take you if the cameras weren't rolling.

A music-rights mix-up delayed the release of Season 2 for two years, but the sets are now back on track and fans remain confident they'll get the remainder of the series in due course.

GREAT MOMENTS: Season 1: The evocative pilot, "Nikita"; the action-packed "Gambit"; Season 2: Nikita tries to bring down Section One in "End Game."

FAST-FORWARD: It's all good.

EXTRAS: Season 1: Deleted scenes and episode commentaries; Season 2: Commentaries and gag reel; Season 3: Deleted scenes, commentaries, gag reel, and the featurette "Designing Nikita."

Lancelot Link, Secret Chimp (1970–1972)

The Original TV Series (22 episodes on 2 discs): ★ ★ ★

Image Entertainment
Video: Full-Frame; Audio: Dolby Digital 1.0

A Saturday morning classic, *Lancelot Link* was a live-action send-up of Maxwell Smart and other super-spies, performed by an all-chimpanzee cast. Lance, agent of APE (Agency to Prevent Evil), battled the bad guys from CHUMP (Criminal Headquarters for Underworld Master Plan). Hey, makes as much sense as UNCLE. Our stalwart simian was assisted by femme fatale Mata Hairi, and reported to Commander Darwin (the best line in any episode was Lance to the Commander: "What's your theory, Darwin?"). Fans still remember the monkey rock band the Evolution Revolution, Lance's swank bachelor pad with the secret coffee-table entrance, and the rogues' gallery, especially Wang Fu and Dr. Strangemind.

GREAT MOMENTS: Lance goes undercover as a beach bum in "The Surfin' Spy"; any appearance by Ali Assa Seen.

FAST-FORWARD: Nothing.

EXTRAS: None.

Land of the Lost (1974–1977)

The Complete First Season (17 episodes on 3 discs): ★ ★ ★ ½
The Complete Second Season (13 episodes on 3 discs): ★ ★ ★ ½
The Complete Third Season (13 episodes on 2 discs): ★ ★ ½
Land of the Lost (4 episodes on 1 disc): ★ ★
See also: *The World of Sid & Marty Krofft*

Rhino
Video: Full-Frame; Audio: Dolby Digital 2.0

Sophistication is not a quality associated with the Sid and Marty Krofft canon, but *Land of the Lost* comes close. With scripts by such *Star Trek* vets as David Gerrold and Dorothy Fontana, and stop-motion special effects that—for their time—surpassed anything on the Saturday-morning tube, this adventure saga of the Marshall family's struggles in a strange prehistoric universe built a following among kids, teenagers and their parents. As Chaka would say, this is one *wesasa* show (that's Pakuni for "very good").

GREAT MOMENTS: Season 1: The Marshalls first encounter the Sleestaks in "The Sleestak God"; Will passes up a chance to leave the Land of the Lost to help his injured father in "The Search"; Holly meets her future self, who helps her overcome a deadly trap in "Elsewhen"; Season 3: Uncle Jack arrives in "After Shock."

FAST-FORWARD: Season 2: The Dopey-centric "Tarpit."

EXTRAS: All season sets include cast interviews and episode commentaries; Season 1 also offers a Pakuni language dictionary; the *Land of the Lost* disc features new interviews with Sid and Marty Krofft, and series stars Kathy Coleman and Phillip Paley.

L

The Larry Sanders Show (1992–1998)

The Complete First Season (13 episodes on 3 discs): ★ ★ ★ ★ ½

Columbia Tristar Home Video

Video: Full-Frame; Audio: Dolby Digital 2.0

"What lurks behind the curtain?" is a question that has intrigued audiences since *The Wizard of Oz*; with *The Larry Sanders Show*, Garry Shandling pulled back the curtain on a late-night talk show to expose the petty personalities, rampant insecurities, and barely restrained tolerance of annoying guests that viewers at home never see. There's probably a real-life event behind every *Sanders* storyline, gathered first-hand during Shandling's years as a *Tonight Show* guest host. The mix of an outstanding ensemble cast and A-list guest stars (Robin Williams, Peter Falk, Carol Burnett, Billy Crystal) lampooning their public personas makes for classic comedy, but the show hasn't made the same buzz-worthy splash on DVD that it did in its original run; four years have passed since the release of Season 1. Perhaps HBO's habit of using maximum compression for its DVD releases (ironic since its shows have shorter seasons that its broadcast-network counterparts) has finally come back to haunt the network. But even if one overlooks the less-than-satisfying picture quality, $39.95 for thirteen shows and almost no extras? In the words of Hank Kingsley, "Hey now!"

GREAT MOMENTS: Larry wonders why the Garden Weasel wasn't called "The Amazing Rat Stick" during a live commercial in "What Have You Done for Me Lately?"; sparks fly between Garry and Mimi Rogers in "The Flirt"; Dana Carvey's guest-host success makes Larry nervous in "The Guest Host"; Larry's rudeness in a supermarket comes back to haunt him in "A Brush with the Elbow of Greatness."

FAST-FORWARD: Nothing.

EXTRAS: "Garry Shandling Talks" featurette; interview with Garry Shandling by Tom Shales.

Las Vegas (2003–)

Season 1: Uncut and Uncensored (23 episodes on 3 discs): ★ ★ ★

Season 2: Uncut and Uncensored (24 episodes on 3 discs): ★ ★ ½

Universal Home Video

Video: Anamorphic Widescreen; Audio: Dolby Digital 5.1

Las Vegas was among the first network series to promote "uncensored" episode cuts for its DVD release. Fans who raced to the store with visions of

Vanessa Marcil sunbathing topless were disappointed by what amounted to a couple of seconds added to a few episodes such as "New Orleans." The "Uncut" claim seems even more disingenuous since the show's opening theme, "A Little Less Conversation" by Elvis Presley, has been excised from every episode except the pilot.

Those caveats aside, the series has a modern-day *Love Boat* appeal, with its new batch of guest stars checking into the Montecito every week, and by just showing up, James Caan adds some much-needed weight to the feather-light plots. In Josh Duhamel, Molly Sims, Vanessa Marcil, and Nikki Cox, *Las Vegas* has assembled the best-looking cast for a one-hour series since *Charlie's Angels* left the air, and offers the added appeal of former *Angel* Cheryl Ladd as Caan's estranged wife.

GREAT MOMENTS: Season 1: Danny's attempts to avoid Big Ed's wrath in the pilot episode; Jean-Claude Van Damme, playing himself and dying after a movie stunt gone awry in "Die Fast, Die Furious"; Wayne Newton appears in "Pros and Cons"; Nikki Cox's wardrobe; Season 2: Ed is reunited with his former partner (played by Alec Baldwin) in "Degas Away with It"; Sylvester Stallone appears in "To Protect and Serve Manicotti."

FAST-FORWARD: Season 1: The voodoo-chile nonsense in "New Orleans," despite a guest appearance from Little Richard; Paris Hilton's appearance in "Things That Go Jump in the Night."

EXTRAS: Season 1: Commentaries by the cast and creator Gary Scott Thompson; featurettes "Las Vegas: The Big Gamble," "Inside the Montecito," and "Rumble in the Montecito," which is more a promotion of the Arena Football League than the TV series; Season 2: An un-bleeped outtake reel from the first two seasons, featuring more F-bombs in twelve minutes than the Osbournes utter in a week; "VIP Access Only" featurette.

Laverne & Shirley (1976–1983)

The Complete First Season (15 episodes on 3 discs): ★ ★ ★ ★

Paramount Home Video

Video: Full-Frame; Audio: Dolby Digital 2.0

L

Spun off so successfully from *Happy Days* that it replaced that show at the top of the Nielsen ratings, *Laverne & Shirley* blended the nostalgic appeal of its predecessor with elaborate physical comedy stunts not seen in primetime since the glory days of Lucy and Ethel. Which is not to say *L&S* should ever be mentioned alongside *I Love Lucy* in its comic innovation (the antics of

Lenny and Squiggy have certainly not aged well), but the series worked on its own terms.

GREAT MOMENTS: The Fonz visits his favorite girls in "Society Party" and "The Bachelor Party"; Laverne tries to win a bowling tournament while loopy on cold medication in "Bowling for Razzberries."

FAST-FORWARD: Too much Lenny and Squiggy in "Hi Neighbor."

EXTRAS: Not even a Boo-Boo Kitty featurette.

Law & Order (1990–)

The First Year (22 episodes on 6 discs): ★ ★ ★

The Second Year (22 episodes on 3 discs): ★ ★ ★

The Third Year (22 episodes on 3 discs): ★ ★ ★ ★

The Fourth Year (22 episodes on 3 discs): ★ ★ ★ ★

The Fourteenth Year (24 episodes on 3 discs): ★ ★

Universal Home Video

Video: Full-Frame; Audio: Dolby Digital 2.0

When all is said and done, there could be enough *Law & Order* episodes to start their own cable network.

In an industry where nearly every new pitch is described as a crossover of established winners ("It's *Leave It to Beaver* meets *The Sopranos*!") the *Law & Order* premise seemed so obvious ("It's a cop show and a lawyer show!") it's amazing it took this long for someone to make it work. And it's worked for fifteen years, through frequent cast turnover and a constant supply of "ripped from the headlines" cases. It's now to the point where any time a celebrity or politician has a brush with the law, you can start counting the days until the *L&O* dramatization.

There were high hopes for the DVD releases after *The First Year*, but Universal switched from single-sided to double-sided discs for subsequent sets, and further disappointed fans when *The Fourteenth Year* episodes had scenes missing from several shows.

GREAT MOMENTS: Season 1: Samuel L. Jackson and Philip Seymour Hoffman guest in "The Violence of Summer"; the Mayflower Madam–inspired "By Hooker by Crook"; Season 2: Logan deals with the death of his partner in "Confession"; Jerry Orbach guest-stars as a lawyer, prior to his Brisco days, in "The Wages of Love"; Season 3: Jerry Orbach joins the series in "Skin Deep"; the quest to apprehend a drug lord nearly claims Ceretta in "Prince of Darkness"; Season 14: A carjacked SUV contains a deadly surprise in "Patient Zero."

FAST-FORWARD: Nothing.

EXTRAS: Season 1: "The Creation of *Law & Order*" featurette; Season 2: Cast interviews; featurette; Season 3: A tribute to Jerry Orbach; deleted scenes; Season 4: Deleted scenes; Season 14: Set tour with Jerry Orbach.

Law & Order: Criminal Intent (2001–)

The First Year (22 episodes on 6 discs): ★ ★ ★ ½
The Second Year (22 episodes on 3 discs): ★ ★
Premiere Episode (2 episodes on 1 disc): ★ ★ ★

Universal Home Video
Video: Full-Frame; Audio: Dolby Digital 2.0

Rather than follow the detectives as they crack a case, *L&O: Criminal Intent* also documents how the crime is committed, a technique that hasn't been employed very often since *Columbo.* Bobby Goren (Vincent D'Onofrio) and Alex Eames (Kathryn Erbe) generate a modern-day Holmes and Watson vibe as they track down whatever criminals are left over from the other two *Law & Order* series. Arguably the weakest link in the *L&O* franchise, *Criminal Intent* still has its moments.

GREAT MOMENTS: Season 1: *L&O* detectives Green and Brisco lend a hand in "Poison"; Griffin Dunne plays a lecherous lawyer in "Jones"; Season 3: The Enron-inspired "Mis-Labeled."

FAST-FORWARD: Nothing.

EXTRAS: Season 1: "Criminal Intent: The Beginning" featurette; character profiles; Season 3: "Criminal Intent: The Private Eye?" and "Who Is Robert Goren?" featurettes; set tour; Premiere Episode: The first episode of the original *Law & Order* series; "Criminal Intent: The Beginning" featurette.

Law & Order: Special Victims Unit (1999–)

The First Year (22 episodes on 6 discs): ★ ★ ★ ½
The Second Year (21 episodes on 3 discs): ★ ★ ★ ★
The Fifth Year (25 episodes on 4 discs): ★ ★ ★ ½
Premiere Episode (2 episodes on 1 disc): ★ ★ ★

Universal Home Video
Video: Full-Frame; Audio: Dolby Digital 2.0

The title's somewhat misleading in *Special Victims Unit,* for it's not the victims that are special but the perps—grade-A sleazebags whose vile acts test the restrictions of network primetime portrayals of crime and punishment. The quality writing and overall professionalism one expects from a *Law & Order* franchise are still evident, and that's been reason enough for otherwise well-adjusted viewers to follow detectives Stabler and Benson down some very twisted paths. Universal has opted for a haphazard release schedule on all its *L&O* sets, a frustrating practice for those who prefer to watch the seasons in order.

GREAT MOMENTS: Season 1: A taxi driver is murdered in a particularly ghoulish fashion in "Payback"; Season 5: Richard Belzer's dramatic turn in "Legacy"; Stabler and Benson play Mulder and Scully in "Unusual Suspects."

FAST-FORWARD: The front-loaded promos on the first disc of each set. Season 3: "Mad Hops" is a misfire.

EXTRAS: Season 1: "Special Victims Unit: The Beginning" featurette; Dann Florek squad-room walk-through; Season 5: "Police Sketch" actor profiles; *Premiere Episode*: The first episode of the original *Law & Order* series; "*Special Victims Unit*: The Beginning" featurette; Dann Florek squad-room walk-through.

Leave It to Beaver (1957–1963)

The Complete First Season (39 episodes on 3 discs): ★ ★ ★
The Complete Second Season (39 episodes on 3 discs): ★ ★ ★ ★

Universal Home Video
Video: Full-Frame; Audio: Dolby Digital 1.0

One of the original classic family sitcoms, *Leave It to Beaver* has left its mark on the culture, giving us catchphrases and characters still familiar to generations born decades after its final episode. Not many people in corporate America haven't had the displeasure of knowing or losing a job to a disciple of Eddie Haskell. The first season is also available in a limited-edition "lunchbox" package; like the school bus for the *After School Specials* and the Homer's Head case for *The Simpsons*, it will delight some, and frustrate others who like their DVD sets to line up neatly on a video-storage shelf. Fortunately, the standard edition is traditionally packaged.

GREAT MOMENTS: Season 1: Beaver and Wally buy an alligator in "Captain Jack"; Beaver loses the money he needs for a haircut, so he decides to give himself one in "The Haircut"; Season 2: Wally's fashion sense in "Wally's New Suit"; Beaver tries to find a teacher's infamous spanking machine in

"Price of Fame."

FAST-FORWARD: Gosh, Wally, why would you want to do that?

EXTRAS: Season 1 (both editions): The original pilot, "It's a Small World"; *Lunchbox Edition*: A Cleaver family photo album.

Lexx (1997–2002)

Series 1, Volumes 1–4 (each: 1 episode on 1 disc): ★ ★ ★
Series 2 (20 episodes on 5 discs): ★ ★ ★
Series 3 (13 episodes on 4 discs): ★ ★ ★
Series 2, Volumes 1–5 (each: 4 episodes on 1 disc): ★ ★ ½
Series 3, Volumes 1–4 (each: 3 episodes on 1 disc): ★ ★ ½
Series 4, Part 1 (12 episodes on 3 discs): ★ ★ ★
Series 4, Part 2 (12 episodes on 3 discs): ★ ★ ★
Series 4, Volumes 1–6 (each: 4 episodes on 1 disc): ★ ★ ½

Acorn Media
Video: Full-Frame; Audio: Dolby Digital 2.0

The appeal of a sci-fi series built around an attractive female lead who occasionally takes her clothes off should be obvious. But *Lexx* had more on its mind than giving fan-boys scenes they'd never see on *Star Trek* or *Doctor Who*. Creator Paul Donovan hatched a kinky comic tale of three misfits on the run aboard the most powerful ship in the galaxy. A short synopsis is impossible; start with the original four-episode miniseries, and if that satisfies then follow up with Series 2, when the show's top pinup girl, Xenia Seeberg, replaces Eva Haberman as the sex-slave Xev.

GREAT MOMENTS: Series 1, Volume 2: Tim Curry appears in "Super Nova"; Series 2: The debut of Xenia Seeberg in "Lyekka"; the delightful musical episode "Brigadoon"; Series 3: Stan and Xev finally seal the deal in "Love Grows."

FAST-FORWARD: Nothing.

EXTRAS: The Series 2 and 3 sets offer "making of" featurettes and cast and crew interviews; Series 4 contains a farewell message from creator Paul Donovan.

Lidsville (1971–1973)

The Complete Series (17 episodes on 3 discs): ★ ★

Rhino

Video: Full-Frame; Audio: Mono

Arguably the dumbest of the shows from the Krofft Saturday-morning canon, *Lidsville* begins with a typically loopy premise, a land of talking hats, but dour Butch Patrick is no Jack Wild, and Billie Hayes's performance as Weenie the Genie doesn't have the manic appeal of her Witchiepoo from *H.R. Pufnstuf.* Even Charles Nelson Reilly's scenery-devouring turn as evil magician Horatio J. Hoo-Doo can't push this one into the win column.

GREAT MOMENTS: Witchiepoo meets Hoo-Doo in "Have I Got a Girl for Hoo-Doo."

FAST-FORWARD: "Is There a Mayor in the House?" and "The Old Hat Home" borrow old *Pufnstuf* plots.

EXTRAS: New interviews with stars Butch Patrick, Billie Hayes, and Charles Nelson Reilly; commentaries by cast and producers Sid and Marty Krofft.

The Life and Legend of Wyatt Earp (1955–1961)

From Ellsworth to Tombstone (25 episodes on 4 discs): ★ ★ ★

Rhino

Video: Full-Frame; Audio: Dolby Digital 2.0

What separated *The Life and Legend of Wyatt Earp* from the crowded trail of TV Westerns in the 1950s was its attention to historic detail, and the decision to follow the lawman's life as it happened, from Ellsworth to Dodge City to Tombstone. That journey of 226 episodes over six seasons would obviously be better served with season sets on DVD, rather than Rhino's highlights collection.

GREAT MOMENTS: The six-part O.K. Corral story.

FAST-FORWARD: Nothing.

EXTRAS: Interviews with stars Hugh O'Brian and Mason Dinehart III; biography of producer Louis F. Edelman; featurette on Hugh O'Brian Youth Leadership.

Little House on the Prairie (1974–1983)

Season 1 (24 episodes on 6 discs): ★ ★ ★ ★
Season 2 (22 episodes on 6 discs): ★ ★ ★ ★ ★
Season 3 (21 episodes on 6 discs): ★ ★ ★ ★ ★
Season 4 (22 episodes on 6 discs): ★ ★ ★ ★ ★
Season 5 (21 episodes on 6 discs): ★ ★ ★ ★ ½
Season 6 (26 episodes on 6 discs): ★ ★ ★ ½
Season 7 (22 episodes on 6 discs): ★ ★ ½
Season 8 (22 episodes on 6 discs): ★ ★ ½
A Little House on the Prairie Christmas (2 episodes on 1 disc): ★ ★ ½
As Long as We Are Together (2 episodes on 1 disc): ★ ★ ½
Christmas 1 (2 episodes on 1 disc): ★ ★ ★
Christmas 2 (2 episodes on 1 disc): ★ ★ ★
The Collection (1 episode on 1 disc): ★ ★ ½
I'll Be Waving as You Drive Away (2 episodes on 1 disc): ★ ★ ★ ★
Journey into Spring (1 episode on 1 disc): ★ ★ ½
Laura Ingalls Wilder (2 episodes on 1 disc): ★ ★ ★
Little House on the Prairie 4-Pack (7 episodes on 4 discs): ★ ★ ½
The Lord Is My Shepherd (2 episodes on 1 disc): ★ ★
The Premiere Movie: ★ ★ ★
The Premiere: ★ ★ ★
Remember Me (2 episodes on 1 disc): ★ ★ ½
There's No Place Like Home (2 episodes on 1 disc): ★ ★

Goldhil Media; GoodTimes Entertainment (*Christmas 1*, *Christmas 2*, *The Collection*, *Laura Ingalls Wilder*, *The Lord Is My Shepherd*, *The Premiere*, *Remember Me*)

Video: Full-Frame; Audio: Dolby Digital 2.0

Wonderful books, adapted into wonderful television. Throughout his career Michael Landon became synonymous with quality family entertainment, and though *Bonanza* may rank higher with old-school classic TV fans, it is *Little House on the Prairie* that will stand as Landon's crowning achievement, not just as an actor but as writer, producer, and director. This was his show as much as any series can be attributed to the creative vision of one man, and beyond its status as a godsend for those who believe TV is going to hell in a handbasket, *Little House* was even able to appeal to viewers who would rather jam an ice pick in their forehead than sit through anything described as "heartwarming."

The Goldhil season sets, despite the drawback of inconsistent video quality and the occasional syndicated episode cut, still rate the edge over the individual volumes released by both Goldhil and GoodTimes. The good extras don't kick in until the later seasons.

GREAT MOMENTS: Season 1: The pilot; Season 2: A sensitive look at the unlikely problem of drug abuse on the prairie in "Soldier's Return"; Season 3: The Ingalls try their hand at prospecting in "Gold Country, Parts 1 & 2"; Season 4: The outlaw James brothers hide out in Walnut Grove in "The Aftermath"; the heartbreaking "I'll Be Waving as You Drive Away"; Season 5: The return to Walnut Grove in "There's No Place Like Home"; Season 6: Nellie proves she has a heart in "Annabelle"; Season 7: Half-Pint gets married in "Laura Ingalls Wilder"; Season 8: The holiday episode "A Christmas They Never Forgot."

FAST-FORWARD: Nothing.

EXTRAS: Seasons 1 and 2: Photo album; episode quiz; Seasons 3 and 4: Behind-the-scenes featurette; Seasons 5 and 6: Cast interviews; commentary by Alison Arngrim; Season 7: Cast interviews and commentary by Alison Arngrim; Season 8: Cast interviews; "Laura's Long Winters" documentary.

Live Aid (1985)

Highlights (4 discs): ★ ★

Warner Home Video

Video: Full-Frame; Audio: Dolby Digital 2.0

Everybody who was anybody in the music business was at London's Wembley Stadium or Veteran's Stadium in Philadelphia on July 13, 1985, for Live Aid, a two-day concert to alleviate famine in Ethiopia. And if the good intentions of the event outstripped the execution, and if just as many Africans were starving after the concert as before, it doesn't take away from the nobility of the effort, or the exhilaration of the performances.

Twenty years later, the release of a four-disc Live Aid retrospective would be cause for celebration, were it not a severely flawed record of this once-in-a-lifetime event. The list of omitted performances—eighty-five of them, including songs by Sade, Sting, the Beach Boys, the Pretenders, Madonna, Elton John, the Cars, Santana, Neil Young, and Crosby, Stills & Nash—is as long as the moments that made the cut. The booklet accompanying the set blames technical glitches and lost tape reels, which doesn't say much for the event organizers. The conspiracy theorists among us await the release of an "Ultimate Collection" after the rest of the performances are "discovered," thus inciting a new round of fund-raising.

GREAT MOMENTS: U2 on "Sunday Bloody Sunday"; Queen's amazing six-song set; Mick Jagger and Tina Turner duet on "State of Shock"; Eric Clapton performs "Layla."

FAST-FORWARD: Patti Labelle's cover of "Imagine."

EXTRAS: The Mick Jagger–David Bowie "Dancing in the Streets" video.

Lizzie McGuire (2001–2003)

Box Set, Volume 1 (22 episodes on 2 discs): ★ ★ ★
Fashionably Lizzie (4 episodes on 1 disc): ★ ★ ½
Growing Up Lizzie (4 episodes on 1 disc): ★ ★ ★ ½
Star Struck (4 episodes on 1 disc): ★ ★ ½
Totally Crushed (4 episodes on 1 disc): ★ ★ ½

Buena Vista Home Entertainment
Video: Full-Frame; Audio: Dolby Digital 2.0 (Box Set); Dolby Digital 5.1 (individual releases)

Here's the safe, sweet high-school sitcom that transformed Hilary Duff into a teen queen and made the Disney Channel cool again for those who had outgrown cartoons. *Lizzie McGuire* was never particularly ambitious, but the cast was at least as photogenic as the *Saved by the Bell* gang, and the jokes were actually funnier. No one older than voting age will get much out of it, or believe for a moment that a girl who looked like Hilary Duff could be unpopular in high school; but for its target audience, the show's little life lessons are deftly delivered with more than a spoonful of sugar.

GREAT MOMENTS: Box Set: The innovative pilot "Pool Party"; *Totally Crushed*: Lizzie falls for her substitute English teacher in "The Greatest Crush of All"; Lizzie meets Aaron Carter in "Here Comes Aaron Carter."

FAST-FORWARD: Nothing.

EXTRAS: Box Set: Cast commentaries (no Duff, though); "The Cast Dishes the Dirt" and "Get the Lizzie Look" featurette; *Growing Up Lizzie*: "I Can't Wait" music video.

Lois & Clark: The New Adventures of Superman (1993–1997)

The Complete First Season (21 episodes on 6 discs): ★ ★ ★ ★ ½
The Complete Second Season (22 episodes on 6 discs): ★ ★ ★ ½
The Complete Third Season (22 episodes on 6 discs): ★ ★ ★

Warner Home Video
Video: Full-Frame; Audio: Dolby Digital 2.0

Where *Smallville* gave us Superman by way of *Dawson's Creek*, *Lois &*

Clark: The New Adventures of Superman took its inspiration from *Moonlighting.* Dean Cain played the skinniest Man of Steel since Kirk Alyn, opposite a not-yet-Desperate Teri Hatcher as Lois Lane. While previous versions of the Superman story focused on costumed action, *Lois & Clark* spotlighted the "love triangle for two" between Lois, Clark, and Clark's heroic alter ego.

Warner Home Video's Season 1 collection gives the series an equally heroic treatment, with documentaries and bonus features that would make you think *L&C* is still as popular now as it was ten years earlier.

Watch for some fantastic performances among Lois & Clark's coworkers at the *Daily Planet*: there's Lane Smith as an Elvis-loving Perry White, and Tracy Scoggins as the seductive Cat Grant, plus Michael Landes as Jimmy Olsen. Unfortunately, many of these supporting players are gone by Season 2, when the new team of show producers cleaned house.

GREAT MOMENTS: Season 1: Morgan Fairchild comes to the *Daily Planet* with a pheromone that takes away inhibitions in "Pheromone, My Lovely"; the *Daily Planet* gang is held hostage in "Fly Hard"; a spectacular two-part season finale ("Barbarians at the Planet"/"House of Luthor") features cameo appearances by James Earl Jones and 1950s "Lois Lane" Phyllis Coates; Season 2: Most *L&C* fans agree that "Tempus Fugitive" was the series' best episode; George and Weezie Jefferson (Sherman Hemsley and Isabel Sanford) are reunited in "Season's Greedings," written by Dean Cain; Season 3: Lois reacts to learning Clark's secret in "We Have a Lot to Talk About."

FAST-FORWARD: Season 3: The amnesia/clone arc; the filler episode "Never on Sunday."

EXTRAS: Season 1: Original pilot presentation; "From Rivals to Romance" documentary featuring interviews with most of the series cast; special-effects featurette; pilot-episode commentary with actor Dean Cain, creator Deborah Joy LeVine, and director Robert Butler; Season 2: Commentary by Dean Cain; featurettes "Secrets of Season 2" and "Marveling Metropolis: The Fans of *Lois & Clark.*"

The Lone Gunmen (2001)

The Complete Series (14 episodes on 3 discs): ★ ★ ★

20th Century-Fox

Video: Anamorphic Widescreen; Audio: Dolby Digital 2.0

Creatively it was the more successful of the *X-Files* spin-offs, despite being cancelled after thirteen episodes while *Millennium* somehow plodded along for three seasons. The further adventures of Langly, Frohike, and Byers were assisted by two new and more camera-friendly characters, probably at the insistence of a network worried about the extent of geek appeal. Fortunately, Stephen Snedden as moneyman Jimmy Bond and Zuleikha Robinson as mystery-woman Yves Adele Harlow proved worthy additions to the cast. Stories alternated supernatural phenomena with government conspiracy, rarely wandering far from the sort of cases tackled by Mulder and Scully. It's difficult to watch the pilot episode now, as it focused on the hijacking of a commercial airline with the intent of crashing it into the World Trade Center. The episode aired six months before the tragic events of September 11, 2001.

GREAT MOMENTS: Frohike demonstrates his martial arts skills in "Bond, Jimmy Bond"; Jimmy's Elvis impression in "Maximum Byers"; the Gunmen dance—badly—in "Tango de los Pistoleros."

FAST-FORWARD: The seen-it-before plot of "Three Men and a Smoking Diaper" isn't helped by Christopher Rich's performance as a Bill Clinton-esque senator.

EXTRAS: The final appearance of the Gunmen in the *X-Files* episode "Jump the Shark"; episode commentaries; a "making of" featurette.

Lonesome Dove (1989–1992)

Lonesome Dove: ★ ★ ★ ★ ½

Streets of Laredo: ★ ★ ★

Dead Man's Walk: ★ ★ ½

Lonesome Dove Collection (3 episodes on 3 discs): ★ ★ ★ ★ ½

The Outlaw Years (22 episodes on 5 discs): ★ ★ ½

The Complete Series (21 episodes on 5 discs): ★ ★ ½

Trimark (*Lonesome Dove*) Artisan (*Collection*) Platinum Disc Corporation (*The Outlaw Years*, *The Complete Series*)

Video: Full-Frame; Audio: Dolby Digital 2.0

For those who just want the original miniseries, Trimark has it priced to move, with a few bonus features thrown in as well. But for those who can't get enough of Gus and Woodrow, Artisan's Collection also includes the sequel, *Streets of Laredo*, and the prequel, *Dead Man's Walk*. Each subsequent return to the material has resulted in diminishing returns, though *The Complete Series* will satisfy anyone curious about the acting prowess of WWE superstar Bret "The Hit Man" Hart.

GREAT MOMENTS: All of *Lonesome Dove*, arguably television's last great mini-series.

FAST-FORWARD: Western fans starved for new material may enjoy all the related *Dove* product, but nothing beyond the original series qualifies as must-see.

EXTRAS: *Lonesome Dove*: Interviews with writer Larry McMurtry and producer Suzanne De Passe.

The Loretta Young Show (1953–1961)

Season 1 (30 episodes on 3 discs): ★ ★

Timeless Media Group

Video: Full-Frame; Audio: Dolby Digital 5.1

Despite several Emmy statues and an impressive eight-year run, *The Loretta Young Show* was a dramatic anthology series more famous for its story introductions than the stories themselves. Each episode opened with Loretta Young sweeping into an elegant living room wearing a gorgeous designer gown, which she'd twirl in like Wonder Woman before welcoming viewers to the show. Young also appeared in several episodes, becoming one of the first movie stars to embrace television. All of which makes for an interesting curio now, though I'm not sure how many DVDs they're going to move. Perhaps aware of the limited sales potential, Timeless Media didn't spend much on restoration for the thirty episodes included in the Season 1 set, some of which appear without the celebrated introductions.

GREAT MOMENTS: Loretta's entrances, sporting the height of haute couture circa 1953. A pre-*Bewitched* Elizabeth Montgomery stars in "Marriage Crisis."

FAST-FORWARD: Depends on one's tolerance for vintage melodrama.

EXTRAS: Loretta Young biography, home movies, film trailers, and bonus clips.

Lost (2004–)

The Complete First Season (24 episodes on 7 discs): ★ ★ ★ ★

Buena Vista Home Entertainment

Video: Anamorphic Widescreen; Audio: Dolby Digital 5.1

Thirty minutes into its pilot, *Lost* was already appointment television. As the first season progressed, producers promised more than they delivered whenever it came time to reveal the secrets of the survivors and the island. And with strange creatures, mysterious numbers, and other unknown quantities on the fringes of the castaways' makeshift society, there's a risk of

Lost falling into the same convoluted mythos that sank *Twin Peaks* and *The X-Files*. But as of this writing we're still along for the ride.

GREAT MOMENTS: The harrowing plane crash sequence in the pilot episode; the first Locke flashback in "Walkabout"; Hurley builds a golf course in "Solitary."

FAST-FORWARD: Shannon's whining.

EXTRAS: Tons of them. Cast and creative team commentaries, in which the episode is sometimes stopped so points can be explained in detail; cast audition tapes, deleted scenes, and outtakes; two "making of" featurettes, footage of *Lost* at ComiCon, and the salute to *Lost* at the Museum of Television and Radio.

Lost in Space (1965–1968)

Season 1 (30 episodes on 8 discs): ★ ★ ★ ½
Season 2, Volume 1 (16 episodes on 4 discs): ★ ★ ★
Season 2, Volume 2 (14 episodes on 4 discs): ★ ★ ★
Season 3, Volume 1 (15 episodes on 4 discs): ★ ★ ★
Season 3, Volume 2 (9 episodes on 3 discs): ★ ★ ★

20th Century-Fox
Video: Full-Frame; Audio: Dolby Digital 2.0

For those who prefer their Robinsons straight up, there's Season 1, which offers earnest black-and-white sci-fi adventures featuring the family, their excitable robot, and sinister stowaway Dr. Zachary Smith. For Robinsons with a wacky twist, start with the color episodes in Season 2. Smith's cowardly antics became the focal point of nearly every show, as stories descended into camp and limited budgets made every alien planet look like it was made of Styrofoam. There's a certain goofy charm to it all now, especially for those who were too young for the comparative sophistication of *Star Trek*, but have fond memories of the robot shouting, "Danger, Will Robinson!"

The decision to release split-season boxes for the show's final two years was made to lower the price point per set, but it was a smoke-and-mirrors move on Fox's part, as fans are going to want them both anyway, and the total cost of the separate volumes for Seasons 2 and 3 was about the same as the price for the Season 1 box.

GREAT MOMENTS: Season 1: The Robinsons' mission begins in "The Reluctant Stowaway"; a guest appearance by *Forbidden Planet*'s Robby the Robot in

L

"War of the Robots"; Season 2, Volume 1: "The Golden Man," perhaps the best of the color episodes; Season 2, Volume 2: The *Fantastic Voyage*–inspired "Trip Through the Robot"; Season 3, Volume 2: The Robinsons are attacked by a giant carrot in the series' most infamous episode, "The Great Vegetable Rebellion."

FAST-FORWARD: Season 1: "His Majesty Smith" foreshadows the sillier stores of the series' final two seasons.

EXTRAS: Season 1: Unaired pilot "No Place to Hide"; Season 2, Volume 2: 1966 *Lost in Space* interviews; Season 3, Volume 1: *Lost in Space* memories featurette with cast interviews; Season 3, Volume 2: 1995 interview clips; original episode promos.

The Lucy Show (1962–1968)

Collectors Edition (8 episodes on 1 disc): ★

The Lost Episodes Marathon (5 episodes on 1 disc): ½

The Lucy Show (30 episodes on 3 discs): ★ ★

The Lucy Show Marathon (30 episodes on 3 discs): ½

St. Clair Vision (*The Lucy Show*); Vintage Home Entertainment (*Collectors Edition*); Delta (*The Lost Episodes Marathon* and *The Lucy Show Marathon*)

Video: Full-Frame; Audio: Dolby Mono

It's only available in public-domain collections, but since *I Love Lucy* and *Here's Lucy* have already received the deluxe treatment on DVD, it's only a matter of time before *The Lucy Show* gets a release worthy of its leading lady. Until then, the St. Clair set is the best; while the picture and sound quality are nowhere near what should be acceptable on DVD, you get thirty shows for less than ten bucks.

GREAT MOMENTS: *The Lucy Show*: The classic slapstick bit in "Lucy and Viv Put in a Shower"; Lucy's get-rich-quick scheme backfires in "Lucy, the Bean Queen"; Milton Berle milks a laugh after Lucy dumps a salad on his head in "Lucy Meets the Berles."

FAST-FORWARD: Nothing.

EXTRAS: *The Lucy Show*: Highlights of Lucy's radio show *My Favorite Husband.*

M*A*S*H (1972–1983)

Season 1 (24 episodes on 3 discs): ★ ★ ★ ½
Season 2 (24 episodes on 3 discs): ★ ★ ★ ★
Season 3 (24 episodes on 3 discs): ★ ★ ★ ★ ½
Season 4 (24 episodes on 3 discs): ★ ★ ★ ★ ½
Season 5 (24 episodes on 3 discs): ★ ★ ★ ★ ½
Season 6 (25 episodes on 3 discs): ★ ★ ★ ★
Season 7 (26 episodes on 3 discs): ★ ★ ★ ★ ★
Season 8 (26 episodes on 3 discs): ★ ★ ★ ★ ★
Season 9 (20 episodes on 3 discs): ★ ★ ★ ★ ★
Season 10 (21 episodes on 3 discs): ★ ★ ★ ★ ½

20th Century-Fox
Video: Full-Frame; Audio: Dolby Digital 1.0

A series that was better than the movie from which it was adapted, *M*A*S*H* ranks among TV's crown jewels. No other series survived such significant cast turnover without any drop in quality or viewer loyalty, or could effortlessly shift between laugh-out-loud comedy, heartfelt drama, and heartbreaking tragedy, often in the space of a single twenty-four-minute episode. The laughs were more prevalent in the early years, but it was fascinating to watch the show mature with each passing season, as one-joke characters Klinger and Hot Lips developed into intelligent, sympathetic human beings; sadly, that never happened to Frank Burns, whose obnoxious super-patriot act hasn't aged as well.

The option of eliminating the laugh track on episodes in the DVD sets is a good one, as some find the canned guffaws distracting. However, that's the only "extra" available for one of television's most influential series. Cast and writer commentaries and behind-the-scenes features are sorely missed.

GREAT MOMENTS: Season 1: The camp makes a film about military life in "Yankee Doodle Doctor"; Ron Howard plays a wounded soldier in "Sometimes You Hear the Bullet"; Season 2: Henry's fitness to command is challenged in "The Trial of Henry Blake"; Season 3: Hawkeye and Margaret discover newfound respect for one another in "Aid Station"; the shocking climax of "Abyssinia, Henry"; Season 4: B.J. Hunnicutt arrives in "Welcome to Korea"; a wounded soldier claims to be Jesus in "Quo Vadis, Captain Chandler?"; "The Interview," a documentary-like episode filmed in black-and-white; Season 5: Sidney Freedman writes a letter to Freud about the 4077 denizens, and a practical joker is on the loose, in "Dear Sigmund"; Season 6: Charles Emerson Winchester debuts in "Fade Out, Fade In"; Season 7: Hawkeye makes an impromptu visit to the peace talks in "Peace on Us"; the 4077's family members gather for a dinner dance in New York City in "The Party"; Season 8: Radar's departure in "Goodbye Radar, Parts 1 & 2"; the medical emergency, played out in real time (complete with onscreen clock) in "Life Time"; Winchester consoles a concert pianist after his arm is amputated in "Morale Victory"; Susan Saint James plays a journalist who falls for B.J. in "War Correspondent"; Season 9: Hawkeye builds a monument to military stupidity in "Depressing News"; B.J. receives a surprise anniversary party in "Oh, How We Danced"; Season 10: The extraordinary finale "Goodbye, Farewell, and Amen."

FAST-FORWARD: *M*A*S*H* didn't misfire often, but a couple shows can be skipped, including "Cowboy" (Season 1), "Iron Guts Kelly" (Season 3), "Soldier of the Month" (Season 4), and "Hawkeye's Nightmare" (Season 5).

EXTRAS: None. Attention, all personnel at 20th Century-Fox: Thanks for nothing.

MacGyver (1985–1992)

Season 1 (22 episodes on 6 discs): ★ ★ ½
Season 2 (22 episodes on 6 discs): ★ ★ ★ ★
Season 3 (20 episodes on 5 discs): ★ ★ ★ ★
Season 4 (18 episodes on 6 discs): ★ ★ ★ ★ ½
Season 5 (21 episodes on 6 discs): ★ ★ ★ ★

Paramount Home Video
Video: Full-Frame; Audio: Dolby Digital 2.0

First, the bad news: these are no-frills season sets that aren't worthy of a show as popular as *MacGyver*. A featurette about how the writers came up with the "MacGyverisms" that made the series famous should have been an obvious inclusion, had Paramount desired to give consumers a little more for their money than just the episodes. However, those episodes are enough to justify the purchases. Though the series took some time in finding its way, *MacGyver* soon embraced the formula that would keep it on the air for seven years; a family-friendly adventurer (an ideally cast Richard Dean Anderson) gets in and out of scrapes by using his wits instead of a machine gun.

GREAT MOMENTS: Season 1: Teri Hatcher debuts as Penny Parker in "Every Time She Smiles"; Season 2: During a mission in Southeast Asia to rescue a group of orphans, MacGyver runs into an old girlfriend in "The Road Not Taken"; Season 3: Murdoc returns again in "The Widowmaker"; Season 4: Murdoc and Penny Packer both appear in "Cleo Rocks"; the feel-good final scene in "The Outsiders"; Season 5: The Christmas story "The Madonna."

FAST-FORWARD: Season 1: The series was still searching for its strengths in the poorly written and performed "The Golden Triangle"; Season 4: The clip show "Unfinished Business"; Season 5: The dreaded evil-twin cliché surfaces in "Two Times Trouble."

EXTRAS: None.

Mad About You (1992–1999)

The First Season (22 episodes on 2 discs): ★ ★ ★ ★

The Second Season (25 episodes on 3 discs): ★ ★ ★ ★

The Mad About You Collection (21 episodes on 4 discs): ★ ★ ★ ★ ½

Columbia Tristar Home Video

Video: Full-Frame; Audio: Dolby Surround

Isolated incident, or dangerous future precedent? That's what TV-on-DVD fans wonder after Columbia bailed out on season sets of *Mad About You* after two releases, following up instead with a "best of" collection. As such collections go the episodes are well selected, and with the introductions by Paul Reiser and Helen Hunt, commentaries, and other extras, it's as good as these sorts of things get. Somebody took the time to do right by the series, quite a contrast to the Season 1 set, which packed twenty-two episodes on two discs with no additional material. Still, a show nominated for forty-five Emmys that clearly still has a following deserves to have its entire run available for home-video collection, especially considering all the crap that's already out. But the "best of" set puts the likelihood of Seasons 3–7 in jeopardy.

GREAT MOMENTS: Season 1: Jamie meets Paul's ex-girlfriend in "Out of the Past"; Barbara Feldon appears in "The Spy-Girl Who Loved Me"; Season 2: Jamie complains about her job at an inopportune moment in "Married to the Job"; *Collection*: The Thanksgiving episode "Giblets for Murray"; Andre Agassi and Christie Brinkley appear in the Buchmans' virtual-reality fantasies in "Virtual Reality."

FAST-FORWARD: Season 1: Jerry Lewis hams it up in "The Billionaire."

EXTRAS: *Collection*: Introductions to each episode by Paul Reiser and Helen Hunt; commentaries on the pilot and final episodes; blooper reel; featurettes "Mad About the Theme" and "Mad About Guest Stars."

Magnum, P.I. (1980–1988)

The Complete First Season (18 episodes on 4 discs): ★ ★ ★ ★
The Complete Second Season (22 episodes on 3 discs): ★ ★ ★ ★
The Complete Third Season (22 episodes on 3 discs): ★ ★ ★ ★
The Complete Fourth Season (22 episodes on 3 discs): ★ ★ ★ ★

Universal Home Video
Video: Full-Frame; Audio: Dolby Digital 2.0

The inspiration behind *Magnum, P.I.* that helped the series survive for eight seasons, rather than burning out after three or four, was in playing against Tom Selleck's manly man image while not undercutting his character's bravery, intelligence, and inherent decency. Selleck played a private eye in Hawaii, which is high-concept to the core, but he had already proven his comedic talents in several memorable *Rockford Files* appearances as the suave but incompetent detective Lance White, so producers knew they could make more of Thomas Magnum than a Dirk Squarejaw hero in flowered shirts. A trio of like-minded costars, beautiful scenery, clever stories, and a wink to the camera when necessary all helped make the series a worthy successor to *Hawaii Five-O*, which had previously held *Magnum*'s time slot for twelve years. Tech credits are fine but extras are limited in the series sets released thus far.

GREAT MOMENTS: Season 1: Magnum's attempt to elude two charging Dobermans in the pilot, "Don't Eat the Snow in Hawaii"; Season 2: An exploration of Magnum's exploits as a Naval Intelligence officer in Vietnam in the two-part "Memories Are Forever"; Magnum faces one of his most unique adversaries in "The Jororo Kill"; Season 3: "Did You See the Sunrise?" features an Emmy-worthy performance from Selleck; Magnum goes time-travelin' in "Flashback"; Season 4: "Home from the Sea" is Magnum's finest hour; Carol Burnett costars in "Rembrandt's Girl."

FAST-FORWARD: Season 2: Viewers' affections for Higgins might be stretched thin when John Hillerman takes on a dual role in "The Elmo Ziller Story."

EXTRAS: Season 1: Four bonus episodes from subsequent seasons, including the crossover with *Simon & Simon*; Season 4: Bonus fifth-season episode.

Malcolm in the Middle (2000–)

Season 1 (16 episodes on 3 discs): ★ ★

20th Century-Fox

Video: Full-Frame; Audio: Dolby Digital 4.0

What is it about the neuroses prevalent in middle children that makes for such interesting TV? *Malcolm in the Middle* is a single-camera comedy centering around middle kid Malcolm (Frankie Muniz), who is wise beyond his years, and much wiser than his siblings. Most stories focused on Malcolm's reactions to the craziness brought on by the rest of his extremely dysfunctional family.

Aside from the good performances from Muniz, keep an eye on Jane Kaczmarek and Bryan Cranston as Malcolm's parents, Lois and Hal. The portrayal of Lois might be the most scarily realistic manifestation of a TV mom yet.

GREAT MOMENTS: The series' pilot is a perfect example of why this show caught on and inspired many imitators soon after its premiere; "Home Alone 4," where the boys and Francis have the place to themselves when the parents are out of town, is another fun show.

FAST-FORWARD: The first season is about as good as it gets. If later seasons ever hit DVD, proceed with caution.

EXTRAS: Extended pilot episode; commentaries by the show's creator, stars, directors, and writers; gag reel; deleted scenes; promotional TV spots; featurettes.

The Man Show (1999–2003)

Season 1, Volume 1 (10 episodes on 3 discs): ★ ★ ½
Season 1, Volume 2 (12 episodes on 3 discs): ★ ★ ½
Season 2 (26 episodes on 6 discs): ★ ★
Season 3 (26 episodes on 4 discs): ★ ★
Season 4 (19 episodes on 3 discs): ★ ★

Red (Season 1 sets); Eagle Rock Entertainment (Seasons 2–4)

Video: Full-Frame; Audio: Dolby Digital Stereo

In the era of political correctness, where a guy could be sued for sexual harassment after requesting extra breasts in his KFC bucket, *The Man Show* was billed as a safe haven for guys to indulge in their baser instincts. A frequent segment featured hot girls jumping on trampolines, for no other purpose than it was fun to watch. There's something admirable about exploitation in its purest form, but sadly the DVDs dashed any hopes of seeing the body parts that were blurred on Comedy Central. A pretty gutless decision for a show that wallowed so proudly in its immaturity.

GREAT MOMENTS: Season 1, Volume 1: Scott Baio is inducted into the Man Show Hall of Fame; the Wheel of Destiny.

FAST-FORWARD: The Man Show Boy segments.

EXTRAS: None.

Married . . . With Children (1987–1997)

The Complete First Season (13 episodes on 2 discs): ★ ★ ½

The Complete Second Season (22 episodes on 3 discs): ★ ★ ★ ½

The Complete Third Season (23 episodes on 3 discs): ★ ★ ★

The Complete Fourth Season (23 episodes on 3 discs): ★ ★ ★

The Most Outrageous Episodes! Volume 1 (5 episodes on 1 disc): ★ ★

The Most Outrageous Episodes! Volume 2 (5 episodes on 1 disc): ★ ★

Sony Pictures Home Entertainment

Video: Full-Frame; Audio: Dolby Digital 2.0

Twenty years later it's hard to imagine how shocking *Married . . . With Children* once seemed. The series was a blatant attempt to attract controversy to the struggling new FOX network by presenting a rude, crude, sex-obsessed brood that was the antithesis of the Huxtables on *The Cosby Show*, TV's top sitcom at the time. The network eventually got its wish when a protest movement against the series during its third season gained national attention and spiked the ratings.

Married . . . doesn't deserve derision for it's low-aiming humor, but it can be held accountable for spawning an entire generation of family sitcoms about feuding parents and kids. Most of the imitators couldn't raise the familial battles to the satiric level that *Married . . . With Children* explored so well.

The Frank Sinatra–crooned theme song is missing from Season 3 on, a victim of budgeting, and Sony also pulled a Beastie Boys song out of a Season 1 show. These alterations and a few syndicated episode cuts make the sets less than perfect, but essential for Bundy lovers nonetheless.

GREAT MOMENTS: Season 2: The family moves into Al's shoe store while their home is fumigated in "The Great Escape"; the Bundys and the Rhoades switch identities on a TV game show in "Just Married . . . With Children";

Season 3: Al builds himself a private bathroom in "A Dump of My Own"; Season 4: Traci Lords plays a dental assistant, and Al drools more than usual during his appointment, in "Tooth or Consequences"; the two-part holiday show "It's a Bundyful Life," guest-starring Sam Kinison.

FAST-FORWARD: Nothing until the later seasons.

EXTRAS: Season 1: *The Reunion Special*; Season 2: Cast interviews (found in Easter eggs); Season 3: *Reunion Special* clips.

The Mary Tyler Moore Show (1970–1977)

The Complete First Season (24 episodes on 4 discs): ★ ★ ★ ★ ★
The Complete Second Season (24 episodes on 3 discs): ★ ★ ★ ★ ★
The Complete Third Season (24 episodes on 3 discs): ★ ★ ★ ★ ★
Starter Set: The Best of Season 1 (4 episodes on 1 disc): ★ ★
Mary and Rhoda: ★ ★ ½

Series: 20th Century-Fox; *Mary and Rhoda*: Ventura Distribution
Video: Full-Frame; Audio: Dolby Digital 2.0

We all got one when we bought it—a promotional card inside our Season 1 sets promising "More Laughs from Season 2!" and a release date of March 2003. In March 2005 we were still waiting, as *The Mary Tyler Moore Show* became the first classic series to be in jeopardy of not being granted a full DVD release after disappointing sales of its first season. This had happened already with bad shows and good shows and even a few borderline-great shows; but this? This was like having access to all the Shakespeare plays but *Hamlet.* If TV is to be released on DVD, then *The Mary Tyler Moore Show* had better damn well be included, or no one's classic-television collection is complete.

Season 1 sales figures were not released, leaving fans to wonder if the show really sold worse than *The Dick Van Dyke Show, All in the Family,* or other classics from the '60s and '70s, or if 20th Century-Fox had inflated expectations, and then pulled the plug when they were not met. Finally, in the summer of 2005, the series became a beacon of hope for other shows suffering *seasonus interruptus* on home video, as Season 2 was finally unveiled. Fox simultaneously re-released Season 1 for $29.98, barely half its 2003 debut price. As frustrating as that may have been for those who already owned it, it's refreshing to see a company realize that the market has changed, and act accordingly.

In 2000, ABC aired a made-for-TV reunion movie with Moore reprising the role of Mary Richards opposite Valerie Harper as Rhoda. It didn't come off quite as memorably as anyone had hoped, but it was still a joy to see these old friends back together.

GREAT MOMENTS: Season 1: The first appearance of Ida Morgenstern in "Support Your Local Mother"; the holiday episode "Christmas and the Hard-Luck Kid"; Season 2: Lou anchors the WJM News in "Thoroughly Unmilitant Mary"; Lou baby-sits Bess in "Baby Sit-Com"; Season 3: Rhoda wins a beauty contest in "Rhoda the Beautiful"; Georgia Engel debuts as Georgette in "Rhoda Morgenstern: Minneapolis to New York."

FAST-FORWARD: Nothing.

EXTRAS: Season 1: Feature-length, behind-the-scenes documentary featuring new interviews with cast and creative personnel; Emmy Award clips; original CBS promos; Season 2: Episode commentaries by Ed Asner, Gavin MacLeod, Jay Sandrich, Allan Burns, and Treva Silverman; Emmy clips; "Eight Characters in Search of a Sitcom" featurette.

McCloud (1970–1977)

Seasons 1 & 2 (11 episodes on 3 discs): ★ ★

Universal Home Video

Video: Full-Frame; Audio: Dolby Digital 2.0

Who didn't love when Sam McCloud, a New Mexico deputy marshal, would walk into a New York police station and draw snickers from the hard-boiled, Big Apple cops for his sheepskin coat and cowboy hat—and then beat them to the bad guys every time? *McCloud* ranked just under *Columbo* in popularity among the recurring anthologies from the *NBC Mystery Movie* series, and while it's great to have these episodes on DVD, it's disappointing that the six first-season shows have been edited together into three ninety-minute stories.

GREAT MOMENTS: The iconic image of McCloud riding a horse down a Manhattan street in "Portrait of a Dead Girl"; McCloud ropes a suspect out of a taxicab in "Fifth Man in a String Quartet."

FAST-FORWARD: Nothing.

EXTRAS: The bonus episode of *McMillan and Wife* was a nice cross-promotional idea for *NBC Mystery Movie* fans, though one of the later *McCloud* TV movies might have been a more appropriate choice.

McMillan and Wife (1971–1977)

Season 1 (8 episodes on 2 discs): ★ ★ ★ ½

Universal Home Video

Video: Full-Frame; Audio: Dolby Digital 2.0

Columbo offered more satisfying intellectual puzzles, but *McMillan and Wife* was the classiest of the *NBC Mystery Movie* features, from its jazzy Jerry Fielding theme to the upscale San Francisco setting, to the sophisticated repartee between Police Commissioner McMillan (Rock Hudson) and his sassy wife, Sally (Susan Saint James). She was a pistol, as people used to say, and could even pull off the fashion excesses of the '70s, while Hudson was saddled with neckties wide enough to land planes on.

GREAT MOMENTS: The bicycle chase through the hilly streets of San Francisco in "Once Upon a Dead Man"; Mac's masquerade ball costume in "Husbands, Wives, and Killers"; the Irish wake in "The Face of Murder."

FAST-FORWARD: Nothing.

EXTRAS: None.

Medium (2005–)

The Complete First Season (16 episodes on 5 discs): ★ ★ ★ ½

Paramount Home Video

Video: Anamorphic Widescreen; Audio: Dolby Digital 2.0

It's rare to find a show about a psychic as well done as *Medium* (medium, rare, well-done—why do I feel like going to Outback now?). Patricia Arquette took home an Emmy for her Season 1 performance as Allison Dubois, a district attorney's assistant who uses her second sight in the cause of justice. And feel free to insert the joke here about how she already knows if you're going to buy the Season 1 set.

GREAT MOMENTS: Allison becomes obsessed with a 1960s sitcom in "I Married a Mind Reader."

FAST-FORWARD: Nothing.

EXTRAS: Cast and crew commentaries; featurettes "The Making of *Medium*" and "The Real Allison Dubois."

MI-5 (2002–2004)

Volume 1 (6 episodes on 3 discs): ★ ★ ★
Volume 2 (10 episodes on 5 discs): ★ ★ ★ ½

BBC Video
Video: Anamorphic Widescreen; Audio: Dolby Digital 5.1

For those who prefer their British spies sans tuxedo and quip free, there is *MI-5*, a British series named after the UK's national intelligence agency (the original title, *Spooks*, was altered for US release). Its team of counter-terrorism agents, led by the ever-somber Tom Quinn (Matthew MacFadyen), fights a battle that cannot be won, and that sobering reality is never far removed from each densely plotted episode. It's all expertly crafted, but sometimes you just want to scream at the TV, "Lighten up!" And if the episodes don't provoke that reaction, you'll definitely scream at the annoying MENU screens, on which each option is represented only by an object in the MI-5 office.

GREAT MOMENTS: Volume 1: The explosive ending of "Looking After Our Own"; Volume 2: MI-5 must handle security for a US presidential visit in "Without Incident."

FAST-FORWARD: Nothing.

EXTRAS: Both volumes offer commentaries on every episode, behind-the-scenes featurettes and cast and crew interviews.

Miami Vice (1984–1989)

Season 1 (22 episodes on 3 discs): ★ ★ ★ ★
Season 2 (22 episodes on 3 discs): ★ ★ ★ ★

Universal Home Video
Video: Full-Frame; Audio: Dolby Digital 5.1

"MTV Cops" was the two-word pitch that sold NBC on *Miami Vice*. The pastel colors, techno soundtrack, and Day-Glo fashions may date the series now, but in the 1980s this was as cool as TV got. Creator Michael Mann brought a filmmaker's eye to episodic television, with superbly edited action sequences set to the most popular hits of the day. *Miami Vice* earned a more deluxe treatment from Universal than their other vintage series releases; the studio even popped for a Dolby 5.1 soundtrack, probably to showcase all the original music they paid dearly to acquire (more than $2.5 million according to some sources). Now, if only they'd hurry up and release the Sheena Easton shows.

GREAT MOMENTS: Season 1: "Heart of Darkness," a delightfully seedy tale that plays to the sounds of John Waite, ZZ Top, Devo, and George Benson; the Eagles' Glenn Frey guest-stars and sings the hit theme song to "Smuggler's Blues"; A pre-*Moonlighting* Bruce Willis appears in "No Exit"; Season 2: Crockett and Tubbs hit New York City in "The Prodigal Son."

FAST-FORWARD: Nothing.

EXTRAS: Season 1: Five behind-the-scenes featurettes; Season 2: "Ride with Vice" featurette.

The Mickey Mouse Club (1955–1959; 1991–1994)

Walt Disney Treasures Presents the Mickey Mouse Club (5 episodes on 2 discs): ★ ★ ★ ★

The Best of the Mickey Mouse Club (5 episodes on 1 disc): ★ ★ ½

The Mickey Mouse Club: The Best of Britney, Justin, and Christina: ★ ★

Walt Disney Home Entertainment

Video: Full-Frame; Audio: Dolby Digital 2.0

What do you call a release of the first five episodes of *The Mickey Mouse Club*? A good start. Fans who pop open the silly tin can packaging will certainly relish this visit to the early days of the series that introduced the world to Annette Funicello, and those familiar with the show only from the thirty-minute segments that ran on the Disney Channel will be glad to see episodes restored to their full sixty-minute length. But this collection barely scratches the surface of the delights provided by a show that once held down nine of the top ten spots in a year-end ratings survey of daytime television. So we need more. And *The Best of the Mickey Mouse Club* follow-up release still does not suffice, as it's a collection of just five more shows culled from a previous series of VHS releases. It's not likely that Disney will release every show, since the series played five days a week for nearly four years, but that wouldn't be necessary.

The cartoons in every episode are already available elsewhere, and the serials merit separate releases of their own. So how about one more volume for the best of the Mouseketeers, a collection of all the series' best-loved moments? This should include songs like Darlene Gillespie's "Blind Date," Jimmie Dodd and Bobby Burgess performing "Father and Son," and Karen Pendleton's "Gee, But It's Hard to Be Eight." Corny? Perhaps. But as Lorraine Santoli writes in her book about the Club, "It was a great time—innocent and full of the notion that it was a beautiful and uncomplicated world."

In 1991, the Club was revived for a new Disney Channel series. It paled next to the original, but you can't deny the Disney genius for casting: the second batch of Mouseketeers included Britney Spears, Christina Aguilera, boy-band stars Justin Timberlake and J.C. Chasez, *Felicity* star Keri Russell, and actor Ryan Gosling.

GREAT MOMENTS: Jimmie Dodd's simple but eloquent lessons on good citizenship; the opening of the Mouse Cartoon vault with the familiar chant "Meeska, Mooska, Mousketeer"; the famous musical signoff ("M-I-C . . . see you real soon . . . K-E-Y . . . why? Because we like you!").

FAST-FORWARD: *Walt Disney Treasures*: Wally Boag's balloon animals segment on Guest Star Day.

EXTRAS: *Treasures*: Color footage of the animated opening sequence, and of the Mouseketeers at the opening of Disneyland, both unseen in nearly fifty years; Leonard Maltin shares memories of the series with six original cast members, including Cubby O'Brien, Sharon Baird, and Doreen Tracy.

Mighty Morphin Power Rangers (1993–2005)

Ultimate Rangers: The Best of the Power Rangers (8 episodes on 1 disc): ★ ★

Buena Vista Home Entertainment

Video: Full-Frame; Audio: Dolby Digital 2.0

During its five-hundred-plus episode run, the Power Rangers went through more incarnations and cast changes than *Doctor Who* did in two decades. The eight episodes in *Ultimate Rangers*, selected by fans, represent a cross-section of milestones in the series. Non-converts will be hard-pressed to tell any difference.

GREAT MOMENTS: The Rangers are pushed to their limit to save Earth from alien invasion in "Countdown to Destruction"; *Felicity* costar Amy Jo Johnson plays the Pink Ranger, and the White Ranger makes his debut in "White Light"; three different Red Rangers join forces in "Forever Red."

FAST-FORWARD: Nothing.

EXTRAS: None.

Millennium (1996–1999)

Season 1 (22 episodes on 6 discs): ★ ★ ★

Season 2 (23 episodes on 6 discs): ★ ★ ★ ½

Season 3 (22 episodes on 6 discs): ★ ★ ½

Warner Home Video

Video: Full-Frame; Audio: Dolby Digital Surround

Chris Carter tried unsuccessfully to duplicate his *X-Files* success with another Friday creep-fest. Lance Henriksen played Frank Black, a former FBI profiler with the ability to "see" the tragedies of victims. Black moves with his family to Seattle to start a new life as the series opens, though he continues to work freelance cases for a mysterious organization called the Millennium Group.

Everything seemed to change with each new season of the show, dividing fan opinion. As *Millennium* completed its second season under the direction of *X-Files* alums Glen Morgan and James Wong, the show had become a much different, mythology-driven vehicle. The third season hit the reset button yet again, and introduced Klea Scott as FBI agent Emma Hollis. The changes, however, weren't enough to bring back casual viewers who were put off by the violence and darkness in the show's early episodes.

Look for a pre-*Lost* Terry O'Quinn in the role of Peter Watts in all three seasons. His performance and presence is one of the series' stronger elements.

GREAT MOMENTS: Season 1: Sarah-Jane Redmond's Lucy Butler plagues Frank Black throughout the series, but perhaps never so chillingly as in the series' first real "shocker" episode, "Lamentation"; Season 2: Two factions of the Millennium Group go to war in "Owls" and "Roosters"; the producers take a wicked stab at network censors in "Somehow Satan Got Behind Me"; Frank confronts a deadly outbreak in "The Fourth Horseman" and "The Time Is Now."

FAST-FORWARD: "The Wild and the Innocent" (Season 1) is not worth your time. And though the *X-Files* episode "Millennium," included with Season 3 as an added bonus, makes an attempt to wrap up Frank's story, you're better off stopping at the series' final episode, which offers a more satisfying conclusion.

EXTRAS: "Making of" featurettes for all three seasons; commentary on selected episodes by creator Chris Carter, members of the crew, and actors Lance Henriksen and Klea Scott; Season 3: A bonus *X-Files* "Millennium" episode.

Mr. Ed (1961–1965)

Best of Mr. Ed, Volume 1 (21 episodes on 2 discs): ★ ★ ★ ★

Best of Mr. Ed, Volume 2 (20 episodes on 2 discs): ★ ★ ★ ½

MGM Home Video

Video: Full-Frame; Audio: Mono

You wonder what goes on at the meetings; MGM released *Green Acres* and *Mr. Ed* simultaneously on DVD, both in no-frills packages of two double-sided discs and zero extras. But where *Green Acres* received season sets, *Mr. Ed* was relegated to "best of" collections, featuring selected shows from the series' four-season run. Was there some secret formula that prescribed the variance, or are there simply more pig lovers than horse lovers at MGM?

Whatever the reason, fans of Wilbur and his talking palomino will have to content themselves with highlights, but at least the shows look great and for the most part have been chosen by someone well versed in the legacy of Ed. However, two gems remain unreleased—Ed's brief stint with the Los Angeles Dodgers in "Leo Durocher Meets Mr. Ed," featuring guest appearances by Vin Scully and Sandy Koufax, and "Love and the Single Horse," a *Beverly Hillbillies* crossover with Irene Ryan as Granny and Raymond Bailey as Mr. Drysdale. Volume 3, anyone?

GREAT MOMENTS: Ed's brushes with fame linger longest in the memory. Volume 1 features Zsa Zsa Gabor ("Zsa Zsa"), George Burns ("George Burns Meets Mr. Ed"), and Clint Eastwood ("Clint Eastwood Meets Mr. Ed"). "Mae West Meets Mr. Ed" is included in Volume 2.

FAST-FORWARD: Nothing.

EXTRAS: None.

Mr. Rogers' Neighborhood (1968–2001)

A Day at the Circus (2 episodes on 1 disc): ★ ★ ★ ★ ★

Adventures in Friendship (2 episodes on 1 disc): ★ ★ ★ ★ ★

Anchor Bay

Video: Full-Frame; Audio: Mono

Fred Rogers's name will not appear on top-ten lists of the most important figures in American television. That's because no statistics exist on how many children found in his friendship a moment of solace from an otherwise unhappy life, or the numbers of kids who grew up to be better parents by remembering the lessons he taught. Tell me who was doing more important work in the medium

over a thirty-year time span, then tell me why we don't celebrate Mr. Rogers with the same reverence as Murrow, Lear, and Lucy. Fred Rogers made television a better place to visit, and no one before or since has established a more enduring bond with his audience from opposite sides of the screen.

Anchor Bay made a fuss over packaging on these too-brief collections; the *Friendship* box comes wrapped in a sweater, and the *Circus* set contains either a wooden trolley or a toy mail truck like Mr. McFeely's. But the real gifts are the programs. For those who love children, or who just miss their neighbor, enough of these can't be put out, or gotten to market with speedy enough delivery.

GREAT MOMENTS: Fred's performances of It's You I Like" and "Won't You Be My Neighbor?"

FAST-FORWARD: Nothing.

EXTRAS: Both releases include a storybook, a parenting booklet, and "Sing-along Song" features.

Monk (2002–)

Season 1 (13 episodes on 4 discs): ★ ★ ★ ½
Season 2 (16 episodes on 4 discs): ★ ★ ★ ½
Season 3 (16 episodes on 4 discs): ★ ★ ½
Also available: The Premiere Episode: ★ ★ ★

Universal Home Video
Video: Anamorphic Widescreen; Audio: Dolby Digital 2.0 Surround

Viewers with a high tolerance for neurotics should enjoy this offbeat mix of comedy, drama, and mystery, where the whodunit solutions aren't nearly as critical as which phobias Monk (a twitchy Tony Shalhoub, who won something like fifty Emmy Awards for this role) must overcome to close the case. The first two seasons benefit from the chemistry between Shalhoub and Bitty Schram as Sharona, the detective's long-suffering assistant. Schram's departure midway through Season 3 prompted an outbreak of *Monk*-phobia, i.e., fear of watching the show without her. Universal should expect slipping sales for the Season 4 box.

GREAT MOMENTS: Season 1: The pilot—"Mr. Monk and the Candidate"; Kevin Nealon guest-stars in "Mr. Monk Goes to the Asylum"; Season 2: Monk tries to keep topless photos of Sharona out of a skin mag in "Mr. Monk Meets the Playboy"; Monk's home is invaded, prompting one of the detective's biggest meltdowns, in "Mr. Monk and the Paperboy."

FAST-FORWARD: The replacement theme song used for the DVDs.

EXTRAS: Season 1: Five featurettes; Season 2: Character profiles; "The Minds Behind *Monk*" featurette.

The Monkees (1966–1968)

Season 1 (32 episodes on 6 discs): ★ ★ ★ ★ ★
Season 2 (26 episodes on 6 discs): ★ ★ ★ ★ ½
The Monkees Volumes 1 & 2 (4 episodes each on 1 disc): ★ ★ ★
The Monkees: Our Favorite Episodes (4 episodes on 1 disc): ★ ★ ★

Rhino
Video: Full-Frame; Audio: Dolby Digital 5.1

The passage of time has been kind to the Monkees. For a few months their music outsold the Beatles', while being reviled by critics as corporate-driven pap. But the songs—"I'm a Believer," "Last Train to Clarksville," "Daydream Believer"—sound even better now, and objections over their derivation have dissipated now that manufactured music is the rule rather than the exception. At least Micky Dolenz, Davy Jones, Peter Tork, and Mike Nesmith could actually sing and (once given the chance) play their own instruments. These days, the Monkees would be exemplars of authenticity compared to "artists" like Ashlee Simpson, who are so manufactured they should have a bar code stamped on their butts.

The series remains fresh and funny, buoyed by likable leads, inventive filming technique, and pioneering efforts in music video. *The Monkees'* Emmy acknowledgment as Best Comedy Series in 1966 represents a rare moment of forward thinking by the stodgy Television Academy. Both seasons are worth having, and it's fascinating to watch the starring quartet's evolution from guys who were grateful to have a job to arrogant rock stars who ignored the scripts and turned the show into thirty minutes of freeform excess.

The season set packaging is clever, albeit at the sacrifice of convenience: square boxes designed like a vintage phonograph, in which the discs lay flat, are awkward to store on one's DVD shelf. Inside, the flimsy cardboard sleeves may sport colorful vintage graphics, but one tilt the wrong way could result in damage. One other warning: the series' theme plays over the MENU screen at a much louder decibel level than in the episodes, so those switching back and forth between shows run the risk of being blasted off the couch.

GREAT MOMENTS: Season 1: The wink to *I Dream of Jeannie* in "The Spy Who Came in from the Cool"; the cinema verité of "Monkees on Tour," capturing

Monkeemania at its height; Season 2: Davy Jones revives the days of the English dance hall on "Cuddly Toy" in "Everywhere a Sheik, Sheik."

FAST-FORWARD: Season 2: "The Monkees in Paris" is the series at its most self-indulgent.

EXTRAS: Commentary by series creator Bob Rafelson, director James Frawley, songwriter Bobby Hart, and all four Monkees; vintage commercials and a memorabilia gallery (Seasons 1 and 2); Season 2: the bizarre special *33⅓ Revolutions per Monkee*, featuring '60s counterculture icons Brian Auger and Julie Driscoll.

Monty Python's Flying Circus (1969–1974)

Collection [the complete series] (45 episodes on 14 discs): ★ ★ ★ ★ ★
Individual volumes (3 episodes on 1 disc): Volumes 1–15: ★ ★ ★ ★
Volumes 16 & 17: ★ ★ ★ ½
Life of Python (documentary): ★ ★ ★ ★

A&E Home Video
Video: Full-Frame; Audio: Mono

When watching Monty Python, viewers can be so immersed in laughing at the unbridled genius on display that they might never notice how the show's original audience was hardly laughing at all. On the early episodes in particular, large chunks of show go by with nary a chuckle from a confused British populace. Which is understandable in retrospect, as Python was revolutionary stuff. This was comedy that said you don't need a beginning, middle, and end to a sketch; you can randomly insert unrelated material into a scene, forget about transitions, mix cartoons with live action, or even run the closing credits at the beginning of the show. For Americans the idea of this insanity's being concocted by six proper-looking English gentleman (and one eccentric Yankee animator) just made the results more entertaining.

The complete series *Collection* is essential to any library of classic television. Yes, it's another A&E shelf-gobbler, released before the invention of reasonable packaging for TV series—but in this case there's no debate on whether it's worth the space or the price. The *Life of Python* documentary, mainly of interest to completists, collects a variety of rare material, including two *Flying Circus* episodes filmed in German.

GREAT MOMENTS: Volume 2: John Cleese demonstrates self-defense techniques against fresh fruit; Volume 3: "The Lumberjack Song," and the classic Dead

Parrot sketch; Volume 5: The Ministry of Silly Walks; Volume 8: The Spam-loving Vikings; Volume 9: The Argument Clinic.

FAST-FORWARD: The departure of John Cleese is felt in later volumes, especially in the "Golden Age of Ballooning" episode (Volume 13).

EXTRAS: Career highlights, including clips from Python's Hollywood Bowl performances.

Moonlighting (1985–1989)

Seasons 1 & 2 (25 episodes on 6 discs): ★ ★ ★ ★ ★
Season 3 (15 episodes on 4 discs): ★ ★ ★ ★ ★
The Pilot: ★ ★ ★ ★

Lions Gate (season sets); Anchor Bay (The Pilot)
Video: Full-Frame; Audio: Dolby Digital 2.0 (season sets); Dolby Digital 1.0 (The Pilot)

The magic didn't last long, but in its first three seasons *Moonlighting* was a program for the ages. The series dazzled jaded TV fans and confused Emmy voters, who in 1985 couldn't wrap their minds around the concept of a sixty-minute comedy, hence Bruce Willis's win for Best Actor in a Drama Series. The series arrives on DVD beautifully packaged with deluxe features, and with episodes sporting almost all their original music (only the "William Tell Overture" in the chase scene of *The Lady in the Iron Mask* seems to be missing). The Seasons 1 & 2 set also includes the pilot episode, which makes the earlier Anchor Bay release superfluous, but if you buy it you'll get a great commentary track from Bruce Willis and series creator Glenn Gordon Caron.

GREAT MOMENTS: Seasons 1 & 2: The film noir–style, black-and-white "The Dream Sequence Always Rings Twice," introduced by Orson Welles in his final TV appearance; Maddie bets Dave he can't act like a mature adult for one week in "My Fair David"; Season 3: The Stanley Donen–choreographed musical number in "Big Man on Mulberry Street"; *The Taming of the Shrew*, *Moonlighting*-style, in "Atomic Shakespeare."

FAST-FORWARD: Nothing.

EXTRAS: Seasons 1 & 2: Episode commentaries by Bruce Willis, Cybill Shepherd, and series creator Glenn Gordon Caron; "Not Just a Day Job—The Story of *Moonlighting*" and "The *Moonlighting* Phenomenon" featurettes; *The Pilot*: Commentary by Willis and Caron; Bruce Willis's original screen test; Season 3: New interviews with Willis and Shepherd in the "Memories of *Moonlighting*" featurette.

Mork & Mindy (1978–1982)

The Complete First Season (25 episodes on 4 discs): ★ ★ ★

Paramount Home Video

Video: Full-Frame; Audio

It's just as well that Robin Williams was given free rein to turn *Mork & Mindy* into his personal primetime improv exercise, as there wasn't much of a show there otherwise. No disrespect to Pam Dawber, who set up and reacted to Mork's stream-of-consciousness routines with charming aplomb, but the series never settled on a satisfying supporting cast, and by the time Jonathan Winters debuted as Mork's baby, all pretense of scripted stories had vanished. Season 1 offers the best batch of episodes, and on DVD Mork's rainbow-colored suspenders never looked brighter.

GREAT MOMENTS: Mork survives a blind date with Laverne DeFazio (Penny Marshall) in the pilot episode; Mindy vies with Morgan Fairchild for Mork's affections in "Mork's Seduction"; Robin Williams at his most inspired in "Mork's Mixed Emotions."

FAST-FORWARD: A very uncomfortable David Letterman plays a self-help guru in "Mork Goes Eck"; any appearance by Robert Donner as Exidor.

EXTRAS: None-nu, None-nu.

The Munsters (1964–1966)

Season 1 (39 episodes on 3 discs): ★ ★ ★
Season 2 (32 episodes on 3 discs): ★ ★ ½

Universal Home Video

Video: Full-Frame; Audio: Mono

If you came of age in the 1960s, you were either an *Addams Family* fan or a *Munsters* fan. Most kids watched one or the other, but nobody liked them both. I confess that my loyalties were in the *Addams* camp, because while the idea of a traditional family sitcom played out with refugees from old Universal horror films was certainly unique, once the premise was established I never thought *The Munsters* did anything all that memorable with it. But here's a chance to get reacquainted with both Marilyns—Beverley Owen in the first thirteen shows, Pat Priest from there on—and that groovy surf-rock theme song.

GREAT MOMENTS: Season 1: The first appearance of the Munster Koach in

"Rock-a-Bye, Munster"; Don Rickles guest-stars and Herman performs "Singin' in the Rain" in "Dance with Me, Herman"; Herman joins the Los Angeles Dodgers in "Herman the Rookie"; Season 2: Herman records a hit record in "Will Success Spoil Herman Munster?"

FAST-FORWARD: Season 1: The evil twin story "Knock Wood, Here Comes Charlie."

EXTRAS: Season 1: The original *Munsters* pilot; Season 2: "America's First Family of Fright," "Fred Gwynne: More Than a Munster," "Yvonne De Carlo: Gilded Lady" and "Al Lewis: Forever Grandpa" featurettes.

The Muppet Show (1976–1981)

Season 1 (24 episodes on 4 discs): ★ ★ ★ ★ ½
Best of the Muppet Show, Volumes 1–8 [Sony]
(each: 3 episodes on 1 disc): ★ ★ ★ ½
Best of the Muppet Show, Volumes 1–15 [Time-Life] (each: 3 episodes on 1 disc): ★ ★ ★ ½

Buena Vista Home Entertainment (Season 1); Sony Pictures Home Entertainment (*Best of, Volumes 1–8*); Time-Life (*Best of, Volumes 1–15*)

Video: Full-Frame; Audio: Dolby Digital 2.0 (Season 1); Dolby Digital 1.0 (*Best of*)

Sorry to break it to those who haven't watched *The Muppet Show* in decades, but not all of the sketches hold up. Sure, "Pigs in Space" is still funny and the Swedish Chef may be the most hilarious Muppet ever created (though these days he'd no doubt be censored by an offended Swedish protest group), but a lot of the jokes in between fall flat.

And it doesn't matter, because the real appeal of these classic episodes comes from the A-list guest stars, including golden-age movie greats (Gene Kelly, Bob Hope, Julie Andrews) then-current hit-makers (Linda Ronstadt, Debbie Harry, Elton John), and a few delightfully leftfield choices (Alice Cooper? Rudolf Nureyev?).

The "best of" collections released by Sony and Time-Life are identical through the first eight volumes; Time-Life then released seven more single-disc sets, prior to the first-season release from Buena Vista, the start of what should be the definitive *Muppet Show* collection.

GREAT MOMENTS: Season 1: The episode hosted by Vincent Price; Juliet Prowse's dance with Muppet gazelles to Scott Joplin's "Solace"; Ethel Merman and Miss Piggy duet on "Anything You Can Do"; *Best of, Volume 1*: Elton John performs "Crocodile Rock" with Muppet crocodiles; Kermit receives a dancing lesson from Gene Kelly; *Best of, Volume 2*: A "Pigs in Space" episode with guest stars Mark Hamill, C3P0, and R2D2; and, of course, the inspired heckling of Statler and Waldorf.

FAST-FORWARD: If you try it, expect a karate chop from Miss Piggy.

EXTRAS: Season 1: The UK segments, and the original series pitch to the CBS network, which barely resembles the show as we know it; "Muppet Morsel"–subtitled trivia tracks; "best of" volumes; "Did you know?" trivia Easter eggs.

Murder One (1995–1997)

Season 1 (23 episodes on 6 discs): ★ ★ ★ ★ ★
Season 2 (18 episodes on 5 discs): ★ ½

20th Century-Fox
Video: Full-Frame; Audio: Dolby Digital 2.0

Referring to the episodes as "chapters" was not just a literary conceit by creator Steven Bochco; the complex story arc that unfolded over *Murder One*'s bravura first season merits comparison to a classic mystery novel, packed with riveting characters, shocking twists, and a clever solution that doesn't cheat. Brilliant attorney Ted Hoffman (Daniel Benzali) defends corrupt entrepreneur Richard Cross and spoiled actor Neil Avedon, both accused of the murder of Jessica Costello. Stanley Tucci's performance as the charismatic scumbag Cross should have been a lock for the Emmy; in fact, *Murder One* deserved the same awards recognition of previous Bochco triumphs *Hill Street Blues* and *L.A. Law*. Instead, the network panicked after ratings stiffed (the show was scheduled opposite *ER*), and changed both cast and format for Season 2.

GREAT MOMENTS: Season 1: Every scene with Daniel Benzali, Stanley Tucci, and/or Bobbie Phillips.

FAST-FORWARD: Season 1: Some of the domestic difficulties of Ted and his wife can be safely skipped, as can all of Season 2.

EXTRAS: Season 1: "Making the Case" featurette; commentaries by director Randall Zisk and actor Jason Gedrick.

Murder, She Wrote (1984–1996)

Season 1 (22 episodes on 3 discs): ★ ★ ★ ½

Season 2 (22 episodes on 3 discs): ★ ★ ★ ½

Season 3 (22 episodes on 3 discs): ★ ★ ★

Universal Home Video

Video: Full-Frame; Audio: Mono

Where Jessica Fletcher goes, death is sure to follow. But since Jessica looks like Angela Lansbury, she's always the last person the cops suspect. Didn't anybody see *The Manchurian Candidate*? *Murder, She Wrote* kept viewers guessing whodunit for twelve seasons. The formula rarely changed, but the parade of guest suspects from golden-age Hollywood and '70s-and-'80s-era TV always made the show more fun—sort of like *The Love Boat* with a body count. The series also turned Lansbury into the Susan Lucci of the primetime Emmys; with her several nominations for playing Jessica, she now stands at zero for eighteen. No extras on these good-looking sets, but the book-jacket packaging was a nice touch.

GREAT MOMENTS: Season 1: Jessica's reluctant transformation from author to super-sleuth in "The Murder of Sherlock Holmes"; Jessica is trapped inside a remote-controlled station wagon in "Hit, Run, and Homicide"; Season 2: Jessica goes to London to help a cousin in peril in "Sing a Song of Murder," guest-starring Patrick Macnee, Glynis Johns, and Olivia Hussey.

FAST-FORWARD: Season 1: The downbeat "Funeral at Fifty-Mile."

EXTRAS: Even Ms. Fletcher couldn't find any except for a bonus episode of *Magnum, P.I.* in the Season 3 set.

Murphy Brown (1988–1998)

Season 1 (22 episodes on 4 discs): ★ ★ ★ ★ ½

Warner Home Video

Video: Full-Frame; Audio: Dolby Stereo

Acclaimed on its arrival as the heir apparent to *The Mary Tyler Moore Show*, *Murphy Brown* was a hit with critics, audiences, and Emmy voters, but the *FYI* news team couldn't penetrate the pop culture as profoundly as the staff of WJM News. Granted, Vice President Dan Quayle's tiff with Murphy over the merits of single-parenting generated front-page news, but Corky Sherwood never personified blond Twinkie news babes as Ted Baxter did vain, blowhard anchors. The show was also more topical (and has thus

become more dated a decade later) than *MTM*, which was set in a newsroom but rarely delved into the issues of its day.

Murphy ran a couple of seasons too long, which soured the aftertaste, but it's ripe for rediscovery, and Season 1, which achieved a consistency in quality beyond the scope of most sitcoms, belongs in any TV collection. The series was shot on film rather than tape, which always helps the video quality. But the picture sharpness is surpassed by the sharpness of creator Diane English's writing, the talent of a marvelous ensemble cast, and the career-defining performance of Candice Bergen, who received her first good reviews since hosting *Saturday Night Live* a decade earlier. Why it took so long to realize that comedy was her calling, I'll never know.

GREAT MOMENTS: Season 1: The challenge dance in "Murphy's Pony"; Murphy's recitation of a gunman's statement, while the *FYI* news team is held hostage in "Set Me Free"; Linda Ellerbee steals Murphy's catchphrase in "The Summer of '77"; Connie Chung chastises Murphy for appearing on a sitcom in "TV or Not TV."

FAST-FORWARD: Nothing.

EXTRAS: Documentary; commentaries from creator Diane English and Candice Bergen.

My Favorite Martian (1963–1966)

Season 1 (37 episodes on 3 discs): ★ ★ ★
Season 2 (38 episodes on 3 discs): ★ ★
Volumes 1–3 (each: 4 episodes on 1 disc): ★ ★

Rhino
Video: Full-Frame; Audio: Dolby Digital Mono

While *My Favorite Martian* doesn't hold up as well as other '60s sitcoms with various supernatural characters (*Bewitched*, *Jeannie*, *Munsters*, etc.), it still deserved a better treatment on DVD. Cheap packaging is the first clue that Rhino put little to no effort into the release, which doesn't even offer a SELECT EPISODE option on the MENU screen—you get PLAY ALL or SCENE SELECTIONS, and have to find the start of each show for yourself. The second-season release is even worse, with poor-quality video and five episodes cut for syndication. For non-discriminating fans only.

GREAT MOMENTS: Season 1: Martin tries to make Tim a hero to impress a pretty neighbor in "How to Be a Hero Without Even Trying"; Martin absorbs an electrical charge and short-circuits the town in "Danger! High Voltage."

FAST-FORWARD: Nothing.

EXTRAS: None.

My Little Margie (1952–1955)

Volume 1 (12 episodes on 2 discs): ★ ★ ★
Volume 2 (12 episodes on 2 discs): ★ ★ ★

VCI Entertainment
Video: Full-Frame; Audio: Mono

Fans of golden-age TV will be glad that *My Little Margie* is on DVD, even without any deluxe presentation. Though the series enjoyed a successful four-year run beginning in 1952 and was popular in reruns for the next decade, it's now just a fading memory for the AARP generation, too obscure even for a TV Land revival. Gale Storm played twenty-one-year-old Margie Albright, though she was thirty at the time and no more convincing as a young adult than the senior class of *Beverly Hills, 90210.* But Storm had one of those personalities that seemed to burst through the TV screen, and was a joy to watch even if she spent most episodes caught up in predictable *Lucy*-esque high jinks, much to the consternation of her father, played by silent-screen star Charles Farrell. That the series is available at all for discovery by the grandchildren of its original audience might be a hopeful sign that we won't have to wait much longer for other classic programs of the era.

GREAT MOMENTS: Volume 1: Margie adopts a horse in "A Horse for Vern"; Margie becomes a fashion model in "Miss Whoozis."

FAST-FORWARD: Some dated ethnic stereotyping in "Papa and Mambo."

EXTRAS: An episode of *The Lucy Show.* No, I don't know why, either.

My So-Called Life (1994–1995)

The Complete Series (19 episodes on 6 discs): ★ ★ ★ ★
The Complete Series (Lunchbox): ★ ★ ★ ½
Volume 1 (3 episodes on 1 disc): ★ ★ ★

BMG (*The Complete Series* and *Volume 1*); Another Universe (*Lunchbox*)
Video: Full-Frame; Audio: Dolby Digital 5.1

As proven more recently by *Arrested Development*, it doesn't matter how many critics fall all over themselves to praise a series if the audience refuses

to show up. The most recent previous series to receive such unheeded accolades was *My So-Called Life*, hailed in 1994 as "the first TV show to get adolescence right." More than ten years later, the nineteen-episode run remains an object of near-worship among fans, driving prices on out-of-print DVD box sets to double the original retail value on eBay. Claire Danes as Angela Chase became the poster girl for teen angst, and the series tackled several serious and controversial issues at a time when doing so risked sponsor support. Still, those too old to identify with Angela's high school hell may not get what the fuss is about, and those who grew up on the WB's torrent of pretty teens in turmoil might find her too whiny for words.

GREAT MOMENTS: Someone brings a gun to Liberty High in "Guns and Gossip"; Angela and Jordan hold hands in "Self-Esteem"; Rayanne's overdose in "Other People's Mothers"; Angela is devastated by Rayanne and Jordan in "Betrayal."

FAST-FORWARD: Some of Angela's neurotic introspection could be too much for non-converts.

EXTRAS: *Lunchbox*: Producer interviews.

Mystery Science Theater 3000 (1988–1999)

Collection—Volume 1 (4 episodes on 4 discs): ★ ★ ★ ★ ½
Collection—Volume 2 (3 episodes on 4 discs): ★ ★ ★
Collection—Volume 3 (3 episodes on 4 discs): ★ ★ ★ ½
Collection—Volume 4 (4 episodes on 4 discs): ★ ★ ★ ½
Collection—Volume 5 (4 episodes on 4 discs): ★ ★ ★
Collection—Volume 6 (4 episodes on 4 discs): ★ ★ ★ ½
Collection—Volume 7 (4 episodes on 4 discs): ★ ★ ★
Collection—Volume 8 (4 episodes on 4 discs): ★ ★ ★
The Essentials (2 episodes on 1 disc): ★ ★ ★
Individual Episodes: *The Crawling Hand*; *Eegah!*; *I Accuse My Parents*; *Manos: The Hands of Fate*; *Mitchell*; *Red Zone Cuba*; *The Beginning of the End*; *The Brain That Wouldn't Die*; *The Hellcats*; *The Wild World of Batwoman*; Each: ★ ★ ★

Rhino
Video: Full-Frame; Audio: Dolby Digital 2.0

What can you say about a series hatched in the wilds of Minnesota, with a budget of about eight bucks, that featured a guy in a jumpsuit and a pair of converted can openers making fun of the worst movies ever made? How about, it won a Peabody Award? *Mystery Science Theater 3000* was an early hit for two once-struggling cable networks (Comedy Central first, then the Sci-Fi Channel), and was one of the first series to unite fans via the Internet. Some of those fans worried when Mike Nelson took over for original ringleader Joel Hodgson in the screening room, but *MST 3000* remained as delightfully snarky as ever, and the movies were just as horrible. Fans will want every volume, but one or two may be enough for non-Misties.

GREAT MOMENTS: Volume 1: The classic bad horror film *The Creeping Terror*; Volume 3: *The Atomic Brain*; Volume 6: *Teenagers from Outer Space*; *The Essentials*: Pia Zadora makes her cinema debut in *Santa Claus Conquers the Martians.*

FAST-FORWARD: The skits aboard the Satellite of Love aren't as funny as the movie heckling.

EXTRAS: Some sets have 'em, some don't. Among the highlights: Volume 1: Original trailers and non-robot-invaded versions of the films; Volume 5: An interview with Mike Nelson and writer Kevin Murphy.

The Naked City (1958–1963)

Set 1 (12 episodes on 3 discs): ★ ★ ★ ★
Set 2 (12 episodes on 3 discs): ★ ★ ★ ★
Button in the Haystack (4 episodes on 1 disc): ★ ★ ★
Death of Princes (4 episodes on 1 disc): ★ ★ ★ ★
New York to L.A. (4 episodes on 1 disc): ★ ★ ★ ½
Portrait of a Painter (4 episodes on 1 disc): ★ ★ ★
Prime of Life (4 episodes on 1 disc): ★ ★ ★ ★
Spectre of the Roses Street Gang (4 episodes on 1 disc): ★ ★ ★ ½

Image Entertainment
Video: Full-Frame; Audio: Dolby Digital Mono

One of the delights of watching *The Naked City* now is the street-level look at New York City in the late 1950s and early '60s. The series was shot on location throughout the Big Apple, and the gritty black-and-white cityscapes, set to the mournful trumpet of Billy May's theme, lend a menacing noir backdrop to these seamy police procedurals. There are eight million stories in the Naked City, according to the famous closing narration, but the DVD sets focus only on the series' final three years, which feature Paul Burke as Detective Adam Flint.

GREAT MOMENTS: *Death of Princes*: A family man (Theodore Bikel) moonlights

N

as a paid assassin in "Murder Is a Face I Know"; *Prime of Life*: Gene Hackman plays a young reporter covering an execution in "Prime of Life."

FAST-FORWARD: *Button in the Haystack*: Dennis Hopper's scenery-chewing in "Shoes for Vinnie Winford."

EXTRAS: Set 2: Original commercials.

The Nanny (1993–1999)

The Complete First Season (22 episodes on 3 discs): ★ ★

Sony Pictures Home Entertainment

Video: Full-Frame; Audio: Dolby Digital 2.0

Fran Fine, like Fran Drescher, is an acquired taste, and while *The Nanny* is as ideal a showcase as one could imagine for her gal-from-Queens persona, that voice could peel the paint off a school bus. It's a one-note show, but enough viewers liked that note to keep *The Nanny* around for six seasons. If you were one of them, enjoy.

GREAT MOMENTS: The role-switching antics in "The Butler, the Husband, the Wife, and Her Mother"; "Imaginary Friend" is an impressive physical-comedy showcase for Fran Drescher.

FAST-FORWARD: "The Christmas Episode"—in which the most Jewish woman on television lectures Maxwell about the true meaning of Christmas.

EXTRAS: Audio commentaries by star Fran Drescher; "The Making of *The Nanny*" featurette.

Navy NCIS (2003–)

Season 1 (23 episodes on 6 discs): ★ ★ ½

Paramount Home Video

Video: Anamorphic Widescreen; Audio: Dolby Digital 5.1

Mark Harmon is the current holder of the title once held by Robert Conrad and Michael Landon: that of an actor who is always on television, but usually worth watching. *Navy NCIS* (it stands for Naval Criminal Investigative Service) is yet another scientific/investigative whodunit, a military *CSI* buoyed by a cast of quirky professionals and Harmon's man on a mission. Debuting to little fanfare, *NCIS* proved a suitable replacement for *JAG* (somebody call the acronym police!), the series from which it emerged,

which had finally been canceled after something like thirty-seven seasons. What's missing from the Season 1 DVD set is the pilot episode "*Navy NCIS*: The Beginning," a combination of footage from the two *JAG* episodes ("Ice Queen" and "Meltdown") that introduced the *NCIS* characters.

GREAT MOMENTS: A Navy Commander dies on Air Force One in "Yankee White"; the team matches wits with a terrorist mole in "Bete Noir."

FAST-FORWARD: A Wizards & Warriors game gets out of hand in "The Immortals."

EXTRAS: Featurettes "Creating Season 1," "Building the Team," and "Defining the Look"; commentary by co-creator Don Bellisario.

Ned and Stacey (1995–1997)

The Complete First Season (24 episodes on 3 discs): ★ ½

Sony Pictures Home Entertainment

Video: Full-Frame; Audio: Dolby Digital 2.0

Begging the question, "Does *every* show really have to be released on DVD?" there is *Ned and Stacey*. Thomas Haden Church and Debra Messing have both gone on to much better things, which is the only reason why this strained sitcom about a marriage of convenience, that both stars hated every moment of doing, is available for purchase. The most shocking aspect of this release is not how bad the show is, as most people already knew that, but that they actually got Emmy-winner Messing and Oscar-nominee Church to film new interviews reflecting on this undistinguished interlude in their careers.

GREAT MOMENTS: Look elsewhere.

FAST-FORWARD: Once you start, you might not stop.

EXTRAS: Interviews with Thomas Haden Church and Debra Messing; commentary with creator Michael Weithorn.

The New Avengers (1976–1977)

Season 1 (13 episodes on 4 discs): ★ ★ ★ ½

Season 2 (13 episodes on 4 discs): ★ ★ ★

A&E Home Video

Video: Full-Frame; Audio: Dolby Digital 2.0

A welcome, if not always successful revival of the 1960s classic, with Patrick Macnee, still dapper as John Steed, now joined by two younger agents in the

N

quest to protect queen and country. *The New Avengers* made a star of Joanna Lumley long before her sweetie-darling days on *Ab Fab*, while Gareth Hunt as Gambit handled most of the rough stuff, which hardly seemed necessary as Steed rarely broke a sweat in the original series, either.

GREAT MOMENTS: Season 1: The Avengers whistle the Colonel Bogey march as they beat up on leftover Nazis in "The Eagle's Nest"; sleeping gas takes out the entire city of London in "Sleeper"; Season 2: Steed's past comes back to haunt him in "Dead Men Are Dangerous"; Mrs. Peel returns—sort of—in "K Is for Kill, Part 1."

FAST-FORWARD: Season 1: The boring espionage tale "To Catch a Rat"; Season 2: The vaguely racist "Trap," with British actors playing Chinese villains.

EXTRAS: None.

The New Scooby-Doo Movies (1972–1973)

The Best of the New Scooby-Doo Movies (15 episodes on 4 discs): ★

Warner Home Video

Video: Full-Frame; Audio: Dolby Digital 2.0

Bad enough that Warner Bros. didn't put all twenty-five episodes in one "Complete Series" collection; the "best of" selections must have been picked by Scooby-Dumb. Why choose three episodes with the Harlem Globetrotters and two with Don Knotts, while the shows with Josie and the Pussycats, Davy Jones, and Sandy Duncan are left out? Legal rights, schmegal rights—do it right or don't do it at all.

GREAT MOMENTS: The Mystery, Inc. gang helps Batman and Robin round up the Joker and the Penguin in "The Dynamic Scooby-Doo Affair"; the Mystery Machine meets Speed Buggy in "The Weird Winds of Winona."

FAST-FORWARD: The two Three Stooges crossovers. Curly Joe is almost as annoying as Scrappy.

EXTRAS: Three featurettes: "The Hanna-Barbera Kennel Club Roasts Scooby-Doo," "Uptown with Scooby-Doo and the Harlem Globetrotters," and "Girls Rock: Spotlight on Daphne and Velma."

Newlyweds: Nick and Jessica (2003–2005)

The Complete First Season (10 episodes on 2 discs): ★ ★

The Complete Second and Third Seasons (20 episodes on 3 discs): ★ ★

The Complete Fourth Season (10 episodes on 2 discs): ★ ½

The Nick and Jessica Variety Hour: ★ ★

Paramount Home Video

Video: Full-Frame; Audio: Dolby Digital 2.0

In its never-ending search to find something to air other than music videos, MTV sent a cadre of camera-people to record every waking moment in the lives of Nick Lachey and Jessica Simpson, because Jessica's dumb and pretty and Nick is . . . married to her. A little of their brain-numbing bliss goes a long way. As for the *Nick and Jessica Variety Hour*: while I give the newlyweds kudos for reviving the *Sonny & Cher*–style music-and-comedy special, it would have worked better if either was adept at music or comedy.

GREAT MOMENTS: Season 1: Jessica's now-famous confusion over the ingredients in Chicken of the Sea and Buffalo wings; Jessica's first golf lesson.

FAST-FORWARD: The references to Jessica's bathroom activities have only become more nauseating.

EXTRAS: Season 1: Highlight reel; bonus interviews; music videos; Seasons 2 & 3: Highlight reels; deleted scenes; *Happy Birthday Jessica, from Nick* special; Season 4: Deleted scenes.

NewsRadio (1995–1999)

Seasons 1 & 2 (28 episodes on 3 discs): ★ ★ ★

Season 3 (25 episodes on 3 discs): ★ ★ ★ ★

Sony Pictures Home Entertainment

Video: Full-Frame; Audio: Dolby Digital 2.0

The "Where's Waldo?" of 1990s sitcoms, *NewsRadio* assembled a stellar ensemble cast (Phil Hartman, Maura Tierney, Dave Foley, Khandi Alexander, Andy Dick, Joe Rogan), only to be set adrift in the NBC primetime schedule, changing days and time slots more than a dozen times over five years. Fans who needed a map and compass to find the show in its original run should be delighted to have all the episodes in one place at last. A generous stock of commentary tracks adds to the appeal of the first two DVD releases.

GREAT MOMENTS: Seasons 1 & 2: Bill and Dave try to wean themselves from their addictions in "Smoking"; the first "Super Karate Monkey Death Car" reference in "Negotiation"; Season 3: Jerry Seinfeld appears in "The Real Deal"; Dave and Bill are stranded in "Airport."

FAST-FORWARD: Nothing.

EXTRAS: Seasons 1 & 2: Twenty episode commentaries from cast and creators; gag reel; behind-the-scenes featurette; Season 3: Commentaries, a gag reel, and featurettes.

Night Court (1984–1992)

The Complete First Season (13 episodes on 2 discs): ★ ★ ★ ★

Warner Home Video

Video: Full-Frame; Audio: Dolby Digital Mono

After his frequent guest appearances as a flimflam man on *Cheers* and several memorable *Tonight Show* appearances, it was only a matter of time before NBC found a series to showcase the talents of Harry Anderson. *Night Court*, with Anderson as a Doogie Howser of the judicial set with better taste in music (his passion for Mel Tormé fueled several episodes) was an immediate hit, though Season 1 may be unrecognizable now to viewers who came in late. Liz Williams? Lana Wagner? Who are these people, and how long do we have to wait before the Markie Post episodes kick in? Fortunately, the colorful and ever-changing collection of misfits that trudge through Judge Stone's court always keeps things interesting.

GREAT MOMENTS: Michael J. Fox appears in the holiday episode "Santa Goes Downtown"; a hooker falls for the judge in "Once in Love with Harry."

FAST-FORWARD: Nothing.

EXTRAS: "Comedy's Swing Shift" featurette with creator Reinhold Weege and star Harry Anderson; commentary on the pilot by Weege.

Night Gallery (1970–1973)

The Complete First Season (14 episodes on 3 discs): ★ ★ ★

Universal Home Video

Video: Full-Frame; Audio: Mono

Jim Benson, coauthor of the companion guide to *Night Gallery*, posted on amazon.com that he couldn't figure out why this series, given its association with such entertainment giants as Rod Serling and Steven Spielberg, would receive a lackluster DVD treatment from Universal, while shows like *The Dukes of Hazzard* and *Wonder Woman* merit a more deluxe package. Well, Jim, it's because those shows were watched by millions more people and have been prominent in syndication for more than two decades, while *Night Gallery* never successfully shook off its reputation as a *Twilight Zone* retread.

Which is not to say there weren't a few memorable episodes in this 1970s horror anthology, or that the series didn't benefit from first-class talent both behind the camera (Spielberg, in his directorial debut, writer Richard Matheson) and in front (Diane Keaton, Joan Crawford, Agnes Moorehead, Patty Duke, and many more). But the finished product never consistently measured up to the sum of its parts.

GREAT MOMENTS: The spine-chilling climax of "The Dead Man"; "They're Tearing Down Riley's Bar," Serling's best script for the series.

FAST-FORWARD: "Make Me Laugh"; "Lone Survivor."

EXTRAS: None.

Nip/Tuck (2003–)

The Complete First Season (12 episodes on 5 discs): ★ ★ ★ ½

The Complete Second Season (16 episodes on 6 discs): ★ ★ ★ ★

Warner Home Video

Video: Anamorphic Widescreen; Audio: Dolby Digital 2.0

Hot plastic surgeons plying their trade in Miami, where there's always a surplus of blondes looking to increase the wattage on their headlights. That was probably the pitch to the network, but *Nip/Tuck* moved beyond such surface delights and into the hearts and minds of its provocative characters, resulting in unexpectedly poignant and powerful melodrama. Dylan Walsh and Julian McMahon are superbly cast as the docs.

GREAT MOMENTS: Season 1: Secrets are revealed in "Sophia Lopez II"; Season 2: Sean confronts his fortieth birthday in "Erica Noughton"; Jill Clayburgh plays a disgruntled patient, and Matt discovers that Ava has a son in "Bobbi Broderick"; Sean learns he's not Matt's father in "Agatha Ripp."

FAST-FORWARD: Nothing.

EXTRAS: Season 1: The featurettes "Giving Melodrama a Facelift," "Realistic Expectations: The Practice of Plastic Surgery," and "Are Those Real or Fake?"; gag reel, deleted scenes, and "A Perfect Lie" music video; Season 2: Featurette "Recurring Pain"; unaired scenes.

N

Northern Exposure (1990–1995)

The Complete First Season (8 episodes on 2 discs): ★ ★ ★
The Complete Second Season (7 episodes on 2 discs): ★ ★ ★
The Complete Third Season (23 episodes on 3 discs): ★ ★ ★
The Complete Fourth Season (25 episodes on 3 discs): ★ ★ ½

Universal Home Video
Video: Full-Frame; Audio: Dolby Digital 2.0

Once *St. Elsewhere* creators Joshua Brand and John Falsey embraced surrealism in that show's infamous final episode, there was apparently no going back. Their next series, *Northern Exposure*, started out weird and just got worse. It's ostensibly about a New York doctor who must spend four years in tiny Cicely, Alaska, to pay back his medical-education expenses, but that's just the first brushstroke on a complex canvas of odd characters and Fellini-esque adventures. You'll know after two or three episodes if it's right for you. I tend to think they did some of this stuff better on *Green Acres.*

The first two seasons consist of fewer than ten shows each, though that's not reflected in the price. You're paying extra for the parka packaging and Universal's costs in obtaining music rights. *Northern Exposure* finally got a full-season order in its third year, by which time the series had already earned an Emmy and a legion of supporters. So you get more episodes in that set, but this time they didn't pay for all the original music, and the DVDs no longer have their own winter coat.

GREAT MOMENTS: Season 1: The "Legend of Adam" in "Aurora Borealis"; Season 2: The Russian invasion in "War and Peace"; Season 3: The flashback episode "Cicely"; Season 4: The Bubble Man cometh in "Blowing Bubbles."

FAST-FORWARD: Nothing.

EXTRAS: All season sets feature deleted scenes, alternate takes, and bloopers.

NYPD Blue (1993–2005)

The Complete First Season (22 episodes on 6 discs): ★ ★ ★ ★ ★
The Complete Second Season (22 episodes on 6 discs): ★ ★ ★ ★ ½
The Complete Third Season (22 episodes on 4 discs): ★ ★ ★ ★

20th Century-Fox
Video: Full-Frame; Audio: Dolby Digital 4.0; Season 3: Dolby Digital 2.0

When will the self-appointed arbiters of good taste realize that the more people are told not to watch something, the faster they'll tune in? Steven

Bochco's *NYPD Blue* earned full marks in condemnation from the usual suspects, and lasted twelve years and 261 episodes. Of course, if all the series had were a few dirty words and flashes of nudity, it wouldn't have endured. Anchored by Dennis Franz's multi-Emmy-winning lead, *NYPD Blue* deserves serious consideration as the best cop show in TV history, especially given its ability to survive multiple cast changes as well as any series since *M*A*S*H.* The first two DVD season sets offer copious extras, including behind-the-scenes docs that are longer than the episodes. But those deluxe sets must not have reached sales expectations, as Fox switched to double-sided discs, shorter featurettes, and Dolby 2.0 sound for the Season 3 release.

GREAT MOMENTS: Season 1: Sipowicz makes certain the new series earns its parental-guidance warning with the line "Ipso this, you pissy little bitch!" in the pilot episode; Donna Abandando drops her robe and thousands cheer in "Medavoy's Eyeful"; Season 2: Jimmy Smits's arrival in "Andy Meets Bobby"; Season 3: Sipowicz crashes and burns in "A Death in the Family."

FAST-FORWARD: Any brief (but not brief enough) glimpses of Dennis Franz's backside.

EXTRAS: Season 1: Writer/director commentaries; featurettes "The Making of Season 1," "Love on *NYPD Blue*," and "Cast Blotter"; Season 2: Writer/director commentaries; featurettes "Season of Change," "Wedding Bell Blues," and "The Music of Mike Post"; Season 3: Commentaries; featurettes "Life in the Fifteenth Precinct," "Father and Son," and "The Women of *NYPD Blue*."

The O.C. (2003–)

Season 1 (27 episodes on 7 discs): ★ ★ ½
Season 2 (24 episodes on 7 discs): ★ ★ ½

Warner Home Video

Video: Full-Frame; Audio: Dolby Digital Surround 2.0

The glitz and glamour of Orange County provides the backdrop for *The O.C.*, a twenty-first-century *90210* from creator Josh Schwartz and music-video director McG.

Premiering in the summer of 2003, *The O.C.* quickly became the FOX net's latest "it" show, with its cast and music plastered all over the entertainment media. Residents of Orange County will remind you the region never had a "The" preceding its name until this show made it trendy. The series follows the Cohen family, led by patriarch Peter Gallagher, as they

O

take in troubled-teen Ryan Atwood from the wrong side of the tracks (actually, Chino). Joining them next door in their upscale Newport Beach community are the Coopers: troubled Jimmy; self-absorbed and always-shacking-up Julie; and nails-on-chalkboard-annoying Marissa.

Be warned that although these episodes aired on HDTV widescreen on FOX during the 2003–2004 season, Warner Home Video decided to release the episodes in the full-screen format. Seth's loving glances at Ryan won't have the same cinematic luster.

GREAT MOMENTS: Season 1: Summer has a Wonder-ful surprise for Seth in the mixed-religion "Best Chrismukkah Ever"; Seth, Summer, Marissa, and Ryan meet their televised counterparts on the fictional series *The Valley* in "The L.A."; Linda Lavin shows up as Sandy's overbearing mother in "The Nana."

FAST-FORWARD: Season 1: A midseason arc featuring Taylor Handley as Oliver Trask is definitely worth skipping. And don't hold your breath waiting for Mischa Barton's acting to improve; it doesn't.

EXTRAS: Season 1: Deleted scenes with commentary by creator Josh Schwartz; creator commentary on the series pilot; "Casting *The O.C.*" and "The Real O.C." featurettes containing behind-the-scenes footage and cast/crew interviews; "The Music of *The O.C.*" looks at some of the music heard in the show's first season; Season 2: Extended cut and outtakes from "Rainy Day Women" episode; cast/crew commentaries; "Beachy Couture" featurette; "The *O.C.* Obsessed Completely Retrospective TV Special"; gag reel.

The Office (2001–2003)

The Complete First Season (6 episodes on 2 discs): ★ ★ ★ ★ ½

The Complete Second Season (6 episodes on 1 disc): ★ ★ ★ ★ ½

The Collection: ★ ★ ★ ★ ½

The Office Special: ★ ★ ★ ★ ½

BBC Video

Video: Anamorphic Widescreen; Audio: Dolby Digital 2.0

The first question is why anybody would want to shoot a documentary about Wernham-Hogg, paper merchants in the sleepy town of Slough. But as episode 1 of *The Office* opens there's Regional Manager David Brent, explaining to the BBC cameras how he's "a friend first, a boss second, probably an entertainer third . . ." as another day of corporate tedium begins.

Brent, as played by series writer and co-creator Ricky Gervais, is the smarmy, supercilious idiot that everyone survived in a past job, a guy with a horrible sense of humor who thinks he's the funniest, greatest boss in the world. Other familiar types include Gareth ("I am team leader") Keenan, the corporate suck-up, and Tim, a regular guy who recognizes the dead-end world in which he's trapped, but who lacks the resolve to do anything about it. *The Office* is as much tragedy as comedy, as the mix of characters and situations isn't all that exaggerated from the typical office environment. The show wisely aired without a laugh track, which would have undercut the awkward silences built into every episode.

O

This is an ideal series to experience for the first time on DVD, as each episode builds upon events in the previous story, and taken collectively they paint a devastating portrait of the corporate culture—so much so that you can't help but care for these characters, however little they may have done to earn your affection. Even Brent, who during the first season you'd gladly strangle if given the opportunity, becomes a more pitiful figure in the second year, as he finally begins to see himself through the eyes of his staff.

The Collection gathers the full series in one package. Three years after the final episode, *The Office Special* reunites the cast for a two-part Christmas episode that brings the story of Wernham-Hogg to a satisfying conclusion.

GREAT MOMENTS: Season 1: Gareth's views on gays in the military in Episode 2; David performs songs from his rocker days in Episode 4; Season 2: David shows off his dance moves in Episode 5; *The Office Special*: Dawn opens Tim's Secret Santa gift.

FAST-FORWARD: Like many great British shows, *The Office* quit before giving viewers a reason to skip an episode.

EXTRAS: Season 1: Behind-the-scenes documentary, which includes some very funny outtakes; deleted scenes; Season 2: "Making of" documentary; deleted scenes; outtakes; *Special*: Director's Commentary; documentary; Golden Globes featurette; the making of the "Freelove Freeway" single; "Freelove Freeway" music video; "If You Don't Love Me by Now" music video.

The Office (2004–)

Season 1 (6 episodes on 1 disc): ★ ★ ½

Universal Home Video

Video: Anamorphic Widescreen; Audio: Dolby Digital 2.0

Yes, it's better than NBC's attempt to replicate *Coupling*, but this Americanization of another popular Britcom can't quite overcome the inevitable comparisons to its untouchable predecessor. Still, Steve Carell should be lauded for trying to put an original spin on unctuous office-manager Michael Scott, rather than replicating the performance of Ricky Gervais.

O

GREAT MOMENTS: "Diversity Day" offers the most cringe-inducing lines, which is how excellence is measured by *Office* standards.

FAST-FORWARD: Nothing.

EXTRAS: Deleted scenes; cast and crew commentaries on five of the six episodes.

Once and Again (1999–2002)

The Complete First Season (22 episodes on 6 discs): ★ ★ ★
The Complete Second Season (22 episodes on 6 discs): ★ ★ ★

Buena Vista Home Entertainment
Video: Full-Frame; Audio: Dolby Digital 2.0

Romance among fortysomethings, a topic rarely explored on television, found its way into primetime courtesy of *Thirtysomething* creators Edward Zwick and Marshall Herskovitz. Granted, stars Billy Campbell and Sela Ward didn't look forty, so that was kinda cheating, but their characters were given kids old enough for teen angst so we bought the premise. The first season of *Once and Again* traced the reluctant relationship of divorced singles Rick and Lily, from first meeting to awkward in-law gatherings to concerns about losing at love a second time. Possibly too sensitive and soap-ish for some viewers, but as long as genuine romance remains an endangered species on the idiot box, shows like this are always welcome. The first-season box was a no-frills valentine for fans, who had to wait three years before the release of Season 2.

GREAT MOMENTS: Season 1: Rick and Lily's first date in the pilot episode; an awkward holiday dinner in "Thanksgiving"; the ambiguous ending of "A Door, About to Open"; Season 2: Lily confronts Carla's family in "Thieves Like Us"; "Booklovers" may be the series' finest hour.

FAST-FORWARD: Season 1: The stunt-casting of David Clennon as *Thirtysomething* boss Miles Drentell in "Mediation."

EXTRAS: None.

One Tree Hill (2003–)

The Complete First Season (22 episodes on 6 discs): ★ ★ ★
The Complete Second Season (22 episodes on 6 discs): ★ ★ ½

Warner Home Video

Video: Full-Frame (Season 1); Anamorphic Widescreen (Season 2); Audio: Dolby Digital 2.0

O

It's been a struggle for *One Tree Hill* to avoid the "just another teen drama" tag at a time when the airwaves were flooded with similar material. The soap suds pile up quickly with all the usual goings-on—sibling rivalry, divorce, infidelity, peer pressure, drugs, teenage pregnancy, and that old stand-by, the life-threatening coma—and seeing Moira Kelly play the mom of a high school student is going to make those who remember her in *The Cutting Edge* feel very old. On the plus side, the DVD sets are more generous with the extras than are many other WB series.

GREAT MOMENTS: Season 1: The battling brothers must join forces after being tossed off the team bus in "Every Night Is Another Story"; the "Boy Toy" auction in "To Wish Impossible Things"; Season 2: The time-capsule confessions in "Unopened Letters to the World."

FAST-FORWARD: You're either all in or all out.

EXTRAS: Season 1: Deleted scenes; cast/crew commentaries; "Oh, Chariot" musical performance from Gavin DeGraw; "Building a Winning Team" featurette; "Diaries from the Set" feature; Season 2: Commentaries; deleted scenes; "The Music of One Tree Hill" featurette; "Diaries from the Set" and "Change Is Good" features.

Only Fools and Horses (1981–2002)

The Complete Series 1–3 (23 episodes on 4 discs): ★ ★ ★ ★ ★
The Complete Series 4 & 5 Plus Specials
(17 episodes on 4 discs): ★ ★ ★ ★ ★

BBC Video

Video: Full-Frame; Audio: Dolby Digital 2.0

Given all the British situation comedies that have made their way to US shores over the past three decades, it's surprising that the show often cited as the best of them all has never connected with the American audience that treasures *Fawlty Towers* and *Are You Being Served?* Perhaps *Only Fools and Horses* comes off as too British, with its talk of wideboys and council flats and "Lovely jubbly!" But anyone willing to meet the cultural divide halfway will discover a series that more than lives up to its celebrated reputation. *Horses* debuted in 1981, and so enduring was its popularity that the 2002 Christmas special was watched by two out of every three households in England. Buy it now and thank me later.

GREAT MOMENTS: Series 1–3: "Friday the Fourteenth"; "A Touch of Glass"; "Who's a Pretty Boy?"; Series 4 & 5: "Royal Flush."

FAST-FORWARD: Nothing.

EXTRAS: Series 1–3: The one-hour-plus documentary "The Story of *Only Fools and Horses*, and a clever Cockney-to-American translation tool dubbed the "Peckham Concise Trotter Dictionary."

The Oprah Winfrey Show (1985–)

The 20th Anniversary Collection (6 discs): ★ ★ ★ ★ ½

Paramount Home Video
Video: Full-Frame; Audio: Dolby Digital 2.0

In which Oprah Winfrey reflects on her two-decade journey from local talk-show host to the most powerful woman in the world. Superbly chosen clips cover every aspect of *The Oprah Winfrey Show* in chronological order—the celebrity guests, the controversies, the Book Club, the giveaways, the weight fluctuations, the philanthropic enterprises (which includes the DVD set, since Oprah's giving her cut to charity) and too many hairstyles to count.

GREAT MOMENTS: Oprah's tribute to *The Mary Tyler Moore Show*, followed by a surprise visit from Mary; Oprah sings backup for Tina Turner; the makeover shows (oh, admit it, you watched them); the red wagon full of fat; the day everybody in the audience got a car.

FAST-FORWARD: The Matthew McConaughey interview makes the cut? Really?

EXTRAS: Oprah's fiftieth birthday bash; Oprah's visit to Africa; featurette "Behind the Scenes: A Day in the Life of *The Oprah Winfrey Show*."

The Original Television Christmas Classics

(5 shows on 3 discs): ★ ★ ★ ★

Sony Pictures Home Entertainment
Video: Full-Frame; Audio: Dolby Digital 2.0

The title says it all—four outstanding holiday specials, unfortunately packaged with one misfire. *Rudolph the Red-Nosed Reindeer*, *Santa Claus Is Comin' to Town*, and *Frosty the Snowman* deserve a place in every Christmas-DVD library. The pleasant surprise here is *The Little Drummer Boy*, which hasn't received the volume of annual airings of its Rankin-Bass–produced contemporaries, perhaps because the story revolves around Jesus, not Santa. It's a beautifully written (and narrated, by Greer Garson) hour of television. Sadly, *Frosty Returns* is a loser, whose spot in this set should have gone to another Rankin-Bass classic, *The Year Without a Santa Claus*.

GREAT MOMENTS: The Island of Misfit Toys and Burl Ives's performance of "Holly Jolly Christmas" in *Rudolph*; Fred Astaire's narration of "Santa Claus Is Comin' to Town"; the African King's speech about baby Jesus in "The Little Drummer Boy."

FAST-FORWARD: *Frosty Returns*.

EXTRAS: A twelve-song bonus music CD.

The Osbournes (2003–2004)

The First Season (10 episodes on 2 discs): ★ ★ ½

The Second Season (10 episodes on 2 discs): ★ ★

Season 2.5 (10 episodes on 2 discs): ★ ★

Miramax

Video: Full-Frame; Audio: Dolby Digital 2.0

For the briefest of pop-culture moments, America was obsessed with the antics of doddering Prince of Darkness Ozzy Osbourne and his weird but loving family. It was all good fun until Sharon's second-season cancer diagnosis, and in hindsight we realize we're watching two kids en route to rehab. But the real problem is the rewatchability issue of all reality TV. Sure, it's amusing to watch Ozzy struggle with the cable remote and clean up after the dogs, but are those moments you'll want to revisit, like a great episode of a sitcom? No f**king way.

GREAT MOMENTS: Season 1: The Beverly Hills Police Department appear as unbilled guest stars in "Won't You Be My Neighbor?"; Ozzy in drag in "Tour of Duty"; Season 2: Ozzy at a White House press dinner in "What Goes Up"; Season 2.5: Ozzy and Jack go fishing in "Angler Management."

FAST-FORWARD: Season 2: Kelly's embarrassing drunken antics in "Smells Like Teen Spirits."

EXTRAS: Tons of 'em in Season 1: commentaries; bonus footage; "Conversations with the Osbournes" featurette; an "Ozzy Translator"; a season-highlights clip reel; Season 2: Commentaries on all episodes by Sharon, Kelly, Jack, and the missing Osbourne daughter, Aimee; Season 2.5: Bonus footage; commentaries on all episodes.

The Outer Limits (1963–1965; 1995)

The Original Series, Season 1 (32 episodes on 4 discs): ★ ★ ★ ★ ½
The Original Series, Season 2 (17 episodes on 3 discs): ★ ★ ★ ★

MGM/UA Home Video
Video: Full-Frame; Audio: Dolby Digital Mono

The Outer Limits: The New Series (1995–2002)

Aliens Among Us Collection (6 episodes on 1 disc): ★ ★
Death & Beyond Collection (6 episodes on 1 disc): ★ ★
Fantastic Androids & Robots Collection (6 episodes on 1 disc): ★ ★
Mutation & Transformation Collection (6 episodes on 1 disc): ★ ★ ½
Sex & Science-Fiction Collection (6 episodes on 1 disc): ★ ★
Time, Travel, & Infinity (6 episodes on 1 disc): ★ ★ ½
DVD Collection (36 episodes on 6 discs): ★ ★

MGM/UA Home Video
Video: Full-Frame; Audio: Dolby Digital Stereo

What began as an attempt to emulate the success of *The Twilight Zone* quickly evolved into TV's first great pure science-fiction series. "There is nothing wrong with your television set. Do not attempt to adjust the picture," cautioned narrator Vic Perrin, as *The Outer Limits* transported viewers on a sixty-minute journey to strange new worlds. It didn't matter than the various rubber-suited aliens could look silly, because to *The Outer Limits* the monsters were metaphors to comment on social injustice, the military-industrial complex, and other cogent issues. The anthology format attracted top-flight writers, including Harlan Ellison and Joseph Stefano, and such stars as Cliff Robertson, Leonard Nimoy, Martin Landau, Bruce Dern, Martin Sheen, and William Shatner.

Concerns over the packaging of thirty-two hour-long shows on four double-sided dual-layered DVDs in Season 1 evaporate after viewing a few episodes. You can't turn back time on 1963 production values, but both video and sound surpass expectations. The "Do not adjust your DVD player" voiceover on the MENU screens was a nice touch.

Both *Original Series* volumes are cornerstones of any TV sci-fi collection. The 1995 revival series, like the various *Twilight Zone* revivals, managed some nice moments but nothing as indelible as the originals.

GREAT MOMENTS: Only in the *Original Series*. Season 1: "The Bellero Shield," a sci-fi take on Shakespeare's *Macbeth*; Earth soldiers fight for their lives in an alien POW camp in "Nightmare"; Robert Culp plays a scientist who schemes to unite Earth's nations against a manufactured alien enemy in "The Architects of Fear."

FAST-FORWARD: *Original Series*: "Behold Eck!" and "The Invisible Enemy," both from Season 2.

EXTRAS: *The Original Series*: None; *The New Series*: Seven featurettes, including cast and crew interviews; "The Story of the *Outer Limits*" documentary.

Oz (1997–2003)

Season 1 (8 episodes on 3 discs): ★ ★ ★ ½
Season 2 (8 episodes on 3 discs): ★ ★ ★ ½
Season 3 (8 episodes on 3 discs): ★ ★ ★ ★
Season 4 (16 episodes on 3 discs): ★ ★ ★ ½
Season 5 (8 episodes on 3 discs): ★ ★ ★

HBO Home Video
Video: Full-Frame; Audio: Dolby Digital 2.0 (Season 1); Dolby Digital 5.1 (Seasons 2–5)

An uncompromising look at life behind bars that puts every R-rated prison flick to shame, *Oz* is certainly a breakthrough for television, though how welcome that breakthrough is will depend on one's tolerance for extreme violence, profanity, homosexual rape, and some of the most lurid storylines ever written for the small screen. This is hardcore TV that disturbs as it fascinates, and is most definitely not for every taste. Good as these seasons are, however, HBO should do some hard time for pricing eight-episode sets north of fifty bucks, the going rate for seasons of other shows with three times as much material.

GREAT MOMENTS: Season 2: O'Reilly is diagnosed with breast cancer in "Great Men"; the shockingly violent "Escape from Oz"; Season 3: Schillinger's son arrives at Oz in "Unnatural Disasters"; Season 5: The bizarre but effective musical episode "Variety."

FAST-FORWARD: If you're squeamish, you'll be leaning on the FF button.

EXTRAS: Season 1: Commentaries by series creator Tom Fontana and actor Lee

Tergesen; deleted scenes; "Behind the Walls" music video; Season 2: "The Museum of Television and Radio Seminar" featurette; cast and crew featurette; Season 3: Deleted scenes; commentaries by Tom Fontana and director Chazz Palminteri; Season 4: Commentaries by Fontana and actors Lee Tergesen and Rita Moreno; deleted scenes; Season 5: Deleted scenes; commentaries by Fontana and actor Dean Winters.

Partners in Crime (1980–1982)

Set 1 (5 episodes on 1 disc): ★ ★ ★ ★
Set 2 (6 episodes on 2 discs): ★ ★ ★ ★

Acorn Media
Video: Full-Frame; Audio: Dolby Digital 2.0

Agatha Christie's least-heralded and most lighthearted crime-solvers were Tommy and Tuppence Beresford, who debuted in one of the author's earliest works but were rarely heard from again after she achieved greater success with Hercule Poirot and Miss Marple. But these two volumes of *Partners in Crime* stories, set in the Roaring '20s among the British jet set, will appeal to anyone who enjoys sparkling dialogue, gorgeous period costumes, clever stories, and the charming romantic chemistry that made *Hart to Hart* a hit in the 1980s.

GREAT MOMENTS: Set 1: Tommy and Tuppence begin their sleuthing career in "The Secret Adversary"; the Partners' masquerade ball costumes in "Finessing the King"; Set 2: The solution to "The Crackler."

FAST-FORWARD: Set 2: "The Case of the Missing Lady."

EXTRAS: None.

The Partridge Family (1970–1974)

The Complete First Season (25 episodes on 3 discs): ★ ★ ★ ★ ½
The Complete Second Season (24 episodes on 3 discs): ★ ★ ★ ★ ½

Columbia Tristar Home Video
Video: Full-Frame; Audio: Dolby Digital 2.0

When you're a teen idol a certain level of derision comes with the territory, but watching *The Partridge Family* on DVD suggests that David Cassidy deserved a better legacy. As a vocalist he is light years ahead of the current teenybopper faves, especially if you unplugged their studio enhancement, and as Keith Partridge he displayed a self-deprecating charm that played well off the dry wit of Susan Dey's Laurie, and the derisive barrages from kid brother Danny (Danny Bonaduce). Add Shirley Jones as a musical MILF, that famous multicolored bus and some of the most infectious bubblegum pop tunes of the 1970s, and the result is one of the era's most delightful situation comedies.

Eight episodes to a disc is pushing it, but picture and sound are wonderful, and at least they're single-sided. It's doubtful a 5.1 mix would do much to sweeten the soundtrack; as it is the crystal-clear 2.0 picks up every shake of Tracy's tambourine. Fans will appreciate the extras in the *First Season* set, a rarity for vintage Columbia releases. The studio dug into its vaults for two episodes from the *Partridge Family 2200 A.D.*, cartoon, and filmed two new documentaries tracing the history of the show and its music. The "skip-to-the-music" feature for each episode was a good idea poorly executed; several songs were omitted from said function, including the group's biggest hit, "I Think I Love You."

GREAT MOMENTS: Season 1: The Partridge bus gets a skunk for a stowaway in "But the Memory Lingers On"; to save a Detroit nightclub owned by Richard Pryor and Lou Gossett, Jr., Keith writes a song that is "kind of an afro thing" in "Soul Club"; two Angelic visits—Farrah Fawcett in "The Sound of Money" and Jaclyn Smith in "When Mother Gets Married"; the Partridge Family performs its number-one hit "I Think I Love You" in "My Son, the Feminist"; Season 2: Danny starts stealing and selling Keith's personal effects in "I Can Get It for You Retail"; the Christmas episode "Don't Bring Your Guns to Town, Santa."

FAST-FORWARD: Season 1: Grandpa Partridge's midlife crisis in "Whatever Happened to the Old Songs."

EXTRAS: Season 1: "Boarding the Bus" and "The Sound of the Partridge" featurettes; commentaries by Shirley Jones and Danny Bonaduce; two episodes of the animated series *Partridge Family 2200 A.D.*; a four-song Partridge Family CD sampler.

Party of Five (1994–2000)

The Complete First Season (22 episodes on 5 discs): ★ ★ ★ ★

Columbia Tristar Home Video

Video: Full-Frame; Audio: Dolby Surround

Long before the Beaudelaire children met Count Olaf in the Lemony Snicket books, the family most susceptible to a series of unfortunate events was the Salingers from *Party of Five*. Through seven years, siblings Charlie, Bailey, Julia, Claudia, and Owen braved the worst life could throw at them—death, illness, poverty, drug addiction—and somehow survived to tell the tale. At its best this was compelling, uplifting drama, worthy of the enthusiastic fan support that rallied after low ratings threatened to cancel the series after its first season.

P

Those fans may need to reenter the fold for *Party of Five* to finish its run on DVD; Season 1 appeared back in 2002, but not even the renewed popularity of Matthew Fox from *Lost* or Jennifer Love Hewitt's regular appearances in *Maxim* and *Stuff* hastened the arrival of Season 2, finally released in 2005. As if the Salingers needed one more problem.

GREAT MOMENTS: The Salinger siblings confront the drunk driver who killed their parents in "Thanksgiving"; Megan Ward's performance as Bailey's drug-addicted girlfriend in "Aftershocks" and "The Ides of March"; Julia writes Bailey's term paper, despite the fragile state of her own academic career, in "Homework."

FAST-FORWARD: "Fathers and Sons"—one problem too many as Julia's ex-boyfriend moves in to escape his abusive father.

EXTRAS: Commentary by stars Scott Wolf, Lacey Chabert, and Matthew Fox, and series creators Chris Keyser and Amy Lippman; featurettes "A Look Back" and "A Family Album."

Pee-Wee's Playhouse (1986–1991)

Set 1 (23 episodes on 5 discs): ★ ★ ★ ★
Set 2 (22 episodes on 5 discs): ★ ★ ★ ★
Christmas Special: ★ ★ ★

Image Entertainment
Video: Full-Frame; Audio: Dolby Digital 2.0

Parents and discerning children should always be grateful to those Saturday-morning programs that aspired to more than selling merchandise, especially in the 1980s when it seemed every cartoon was based on a toy line. Picking up where Sid and Marty Krofft left off, *Pee-Wee's Playhouse* introduced a surreal world of wonder with colorful characters, laughs, music, and gently taught lessons. The two Image sets contain the entire series, which might have run longer had it not been for Pee-Wee portrayer Paul Reubens's embarrassing brush with the law.

GREAT MOMENTS: The appearances of Phil Hartman as Captain Carl and Laurence Fishburne as Cowboy Curtis; the Penny cartoons.

FAST-FORWARD: The final five episodes, which suffered from an abundance of stock footage and a reliance on film clips. However, don't miss Pee-Wee's emotional signoff in the final show, filmed after Paul Reubens's arrest for public indecency.

EXTRAS: Set 1: Two "lost" shows never released; Set 2: Six "lost" shows.

The Perils of Penelope Pitstop (1969–1970)

The Complete Series (17 episodes on 3 discs): ★ ★

Warner Home Video

Video: Full-Frame; Audio: Dolby Digital 2.0

A pleasing timewaster from the Hanna-Barbera stable, though Penelope is too often reduced to supporting-player status in her own cartoon to accommodate the antics of the Ant Hill Mob, who like Ms. Pitstop were a lot more fun in *Wacky Races.* Classic kid-vid fans will enjoy Gary Owens's narration; Paul Lynde's snickering villain, the Hooded Claw; and seeing a prototype for Speed Buggy in the Ant Hill Mob's car, Chugga-Boom.

GREAT MOMENTS: Just about all of Paul Lynde's lines, especially the Claw's maniacal laughter.

FAST-FORWARD: Yak-Yak, the most annoying member of the Mob.

EXTRAS: Featurette "Penelope Pitstop's Spinouts" ("The Players in Perils" is listed as a featurette but it's just a collection of clips); two episode commentaries by Janet Waldo (voice of Penelope), Gary Owens, and H-B designer Iwao Takamoto; a collectible litho cel.

Perry Mason (1957–1966)

Season 1, Volume 1 (19 episodes on 5 discs): ★ ★ ★ ★

Paramount Home Video

Video: Full-Frame; Audio: Dolby Digital Mono

All the clichés of the courtroom drama were either created or perfected on *Perry Mason.* Mason, attorney at law, defined his profession for television as Marcus Welby had for doctors and Joe Friday for cops. As played by Raymond

Burr, he personified everything that was honorable and noble about lawyers, though it helped that all of his clients were innocent, and this was before someone could win millions in court for spilling coffee in her lap.

The character first appeared in a 1934 book by Erle Stanley Gardner. More than seventy Mason novels followed, as well as radio and film adaptations, but it's on TV that Perry became a household name. You'll need these in the collection for historic significance, but they're still entertaining as well. Watching D.A. Hamilton Burger go down in flames never gets old.

P

GREAT MOMENTS: Perry gets his first win in "The Case of the Restless Redhead"; a bride-to-be is charged with murder in "The Case of the Crimson Kiss"; and, of course, the confessions from the witness stand that bring many of Mason's trials to a close.

FAST-FORWARD: Nothing.

EXTRAS: None. Objection, Your Honor!

Peter Gunn (1958–1961)

Set 1 (16 episodes on 2 discs): ★ ½

Set 2 (16 episodes on 2 discs): ★ ½

A&E Home Video

Video: Full-Frame; Audio: Mono

A stylish and classy early entry in the TV detective genre, that sadly wound up on the wrong end of a sucker-punch by A&E. Poor picture and sound quality combined with syndicated cuts of the episodes result in two very disappointing collections.

GREAT MOMENTS: None, given the condition of the episodes.

FAST-FORWARD: Good idea.

EXTRAS: None.

Petticoat Junction (1963–1970)

The Ultimate Collection (20 episodes on 3 discs): ★ ★ ★ ½

The Ultimate Christmas Collection (3 episodes on 1 disc): ★ ★

MPI Home Video

Video: Full-Frame; Audio: Dolby Digital 2.0

While it's wonderful to have twenty episodes from *Petticoat Junction*'s rarely syndicated first season on DVD in *The Ultimate Collection*, it's also frustrating not to have the entire first season, which consisted of thirty-eight shows, in one set. As if to make up for this disappointment, MPI presents the shows in a lovingly crafted package, featuring episode introductions by Linda Kaye ("Betty Jo") Henning. *The Christmas Collection*, however, seems superfluous. Why not just pack those three shows into the first set?

GREAT MOMENTS: Betty Jo enters the annual horseshoe tournament in "The Ringer"; Dennis Hopper plays a hippie poet who romances Bobbie Jo in "Bobbie Jo and the Beatnik."

FAST-FORWARD: Nothing.

EXTRAS: Episode Introductions with Linda Kaye Henning; "The History of Hooterville" documentary; original sponsor commercials with cast; cast interviews.

Pink Lady and Jeff (1980)

The Complete Series (6 episodes on 3 discs): ★ ★

Rhino

Video: Full-Frame; Audio: Mono

It's rightly remembered as one of TV's true disasters, but there's no kitsch like '70s kitsch and the passage of time now makes *Pink Lady and Jeff* seem more charming in its cluelessness than it probably deserves. The mix of third-rate comic Jeff Altman with a singing duo of pretty Japanese women who couldn't speak English never had a chance, but what other show offers Greg Evigan singing "Don't Go Breakin' My Heart" and the vocal stylings of Hugh Hefner on "Chicago (My Kind of Town)"? Throw in Donny Osmond, Larry Hagman, Jerry Lewis, Robby the Robot, and Alice Cooper, and the result is . . . well, still pretty bad. Better than *The Brady Bunch Hour*, though.

GREAT MOMENTS: Episode 2: Teddy Pendergrass sings "On Broadway"; Episode 5: Pink Lady performs one of its Japanese disco hits, proving the girls can actually sing when they know how to pronounce the words; a bikini-clad Mie and Kei end each show in a hot tub.

FAST-FORWARD: Pink Lady sings Motown (Episode 6); all the comedy sketches, except for Altman's occasionally amusing Art Nuvo character.

EXTRAS: New introductions of each show by Jeff Altman, who also shares his memories of the Pink Lady era; clips from Pink Lady in the media, including all the show's bad reviews.

Planet of the Apes (1974)

The Complete TV Series (14 episodes on 4 discs): ★ ★ ½

20th Century-Fox

Video: Full-Frame; Audio: Dolby Digital 2.0

After five motion pictures, audiences still hadn't tired of those damn, dirty apes, so CBS figured they had a surefire hit in this prequel of sorts to the original film, in which astronauts Burke and Virdon (Ron Harper and James Naughton) take a wrong turn and crash-land in a future controlled by gorillas with rifles. Roddy McDowall, who played both Cornelius and Caesar in the film series, once again endured three-hour makeup sessions to be transformed into the kindly Galen, his third simian alter ego. Episodes alternated between straightforward adventure and social commentary, but negative reviews and a time slot opposite *The Six Million Dollar Man* resulted in rapidly dwindling returns and a quick cancellation.

GREAT MOMENTS: The fugitive astronauts bond with a family of ape farmers in "The Good Seeds"; Galen's ex-fiancée discovers the truth about Earth's prehistory in "The Surgeon"; Burke and Virdon try to cure a malaria-infected village before Dr. Zaius orders its destruction in "The Cure."

FAST-FORWARD: The cliché-heavy racial-intolerance story "The Deception."

EXTRAS: None.

Police Woman (1974–1978)

The Complete First Season (23 episodes on 5 discs): ★ ★ ★ ½

Sony Pictures Home Entertainment

Video: Full-Frame; Audio: Dolby Digital

Angie Dickinson was TV's first female crime-fighter of the 1970s, though she'd soon have plenty of help from the Bionic Woman, Wonder Woman, and Charlie's Angels. Otherwise, *Police Woman* was fairly standard cop fare, but the first DVD set earns an extra half-star for the inclusion of the pilot, which should be a no-brainer but has been missed more than once in similar sets (I'm lookin' at you, Rockford); and Angie's episode commentaries, which add a new dimension to the viewing of old shows.

GREAT MOMENTS: The rarely seen pilot, with Bert Convy in the Earl Holliman role of Angie's commanding officer; Pepper goes undercover as a stewardess, and Larry Hagman guest-stars in "Seven-Eleven."

FAST-FORWARD: Nothing.

EXTRAS: Commentaries with Angie Dickinson; outtakes.

P

Popular (1999–2001)

Season 1 (22 episodes on 6 discs): ★ ★ ★ ½

Season 2 (21 episodes on 6 discs): ★ ★

Buena Vista Home Entertainment

Video: Full-Frame; Audio: Dolby Digital 2.0

The high-concept-to-the-hilt premise had teenage dream-girl Brooke and misfit Sam forced to coexist as stepsisters when their parents marry. But *Popular* was at its best in the scenes set inside Kennedy High, where a delightful supporting cast played with all the stereotypes and mixed in a few inspired flights of fancy. Beware of multiple music substitutions, though a few original cuts made it onto the DVDs. And shame on the creators for knowing the axe was coming yet refusing to wrap up their stories. Season 1 is recommended for the curious; proceed to Season 2 only if still in need of a Mary Cherry fix.

GREAT MOMENTS: Season 1: Bridges are built in a locked bathroom in "Caged"; Season 2: the controversial "Fag."

FAST-FORWARD: Season 2: "The Brain Game," a surprising choice for one of the few cast commentaries of the season.

EXTRAS: Both seasons feature audio commentaries from the cast and crew.

The Powerpuff Girls (1998–2005)

Down 'n' Dirty (10 episodes on 1 disc): ★ ★ ★ ★

Meet the Beat-Alls (7 episodes on 1 disc): ★ ★ ★ ★ ½

Power Pack: Down 'n' Dirty/Powerpuff Bluff/The Mane Event (26 episodes on 3 discs): ★ ★ ★ ★

Powerpuff Bluff (10 episodes on 1 disc): ★ ★ ★ ★

The Mane Event (6 episodes on 1 disc): ★ ★ ★

Warner Home Video

Video: Full-Frame; Audio: Dolby Digital 2.0

Some people win gold stars for their school projects. Craig McCracken, who attended the California Arts Institute in 1992, created the Powerpuff Girls for his project, and three years later launched a series on the Cartoon Network that brought him millions in merchandising. Hopefully, he also got a passing grade.

The adventures of kindergarten super-chicks Bubbles, Blossom, and Buttercup will tickle adults almost as much as their pint-sized target audience, especially in such clever stories as "Meet the Beat-Alls."

P

GREAT MOMENTS: The brilliant "Meet the Beat-Alls," with more Fab Four references than you can shake a Yellow Submarine at; the Emmy-nominated "Bare Facts" in *Powerpuff Bluff.*

FAST-FORWARD: Nothing.

EXTRAS: All releases offer interactive games, and some feature bonus episodes from other Cartoon Network series. Episodes such as "Meet the Beat-Alls" and "Bought and Sold" (on *Down* 'n' *Dirty*) have commentaries by series characters.

Prime Suspect (1991–2003)

Prime Suspect: ★ ★ ★ ★ ½
Prime Suspect 2: ★ ★ ★ ★
Prime Suspect 3: ★ ★ ★ ★ ★
Prime Suspect 4: ★ ★ ★ ½
Prime Suspect 5: ★ ★ ★ ★
Prime Suspect 6: ★ ★ ★ ★

HBO Home Video
Video: Full-Frame; Audio: Dolby Digital 2.0

Does Jane Tennison ever get a nice, simple shoplifting to investigate? The *Prime Suspect* cases are engrossing stories, but the crimes are so grisly, and the suspects so seedy, that you need a shower after watching them. The DVD releases may be the first opportunity for some American audiences to see the stories uncut (*Prime Suspect* made its US debut on *Masterpiece Theatre*, where it was subject to the editing whims of individual PBS affiliates). Usually, anything with Helen Mirren has to be trimmed for nudity, but here the objectionable material is of a less-pleasing variety.

GREAT MOMENTS: Tennison's ongoing battles with Detective Otley in the original *Prime Suspect*; Tennison investigates the murder of a teenage "rent boy" in *Prime Suspect 3.*

FAST-FORWARD: Nothing.

EXTRAS: *Prime Suspect 6*: Cast and crew interview.

The Prisoner (1968–1969)

The Complete Series (17 episodes on 10 discs): ★ ★ ★ ★ ½
Volumes 1–5 (3 or 4 episodes each on 2 discs): ★ ★ ★ ★

A&E Home Video
Video: Full-Frame; Audio: Dolby Digital 2.0

P

We never got the answers we wanted from *The Prisoner*, but that was the plan all along. Creator/writer/star Patrick McGoohan was out to challenge the audience with his Kafkaesque story of a spy held prisoner in a surreal "Village," whose futile quest for answers echoed that of the viewer's. Was Number 6, as the spy was designated, really John Drake, McGoohan's *Secret Agent* character? And who was the elusive Number 1, the man in charge? His identity was revealed in the bizarre final episode, but the face beneath the mask was likely meant to be symbolic, and reinforced the powerful and frightening message behind this remarkable series—we are all prisoners. The *Complete Series* set offers all seventeen episodes, but those seeking more information won't get it—by hook or by crook.

GREAT MOMENTS: Number 6 finally escapes—or does he? in "The Chimes of Big Ben"; the "degree absolute" interrogation showdown between Number 6 and Number 2 in "Once Upon a Time"; the mind-blowing series finale, "Fall Out," certain to fascinate some viewers and outrage others.

FAST-FORWARD: Nothing.

EXTRAS: Interview with series production-manager Bernie Williams, who also narrates rare location footage shot in 1966; "The Prisoner Video Companion" program; alternate footage from "The Chimes of Big Ben" episode; interactive map of the Village.

Prisoner: Cell Block H (1979–1986)

Twenty-Fifth Anniversary Collector's Edition (10 episodes on 3 discs): ★ ★ ★

A&E Home Video
Video: Full-Frame; Audio: Dolby Digital 2.0

There's no adequate way to assemble a "best of" collection for a soap opera that ran eight years and nearly 700 episodes. Fans will be disappointed at the limited quantity of material, and newcomers are likely to be confused at being dropped into the middle of storylines that developed over months prior to the episodes selected. Still, those who followed *Prisoner: Cell Block H* in its early-'80s heyday, when the Australian soap became a surprise cult hit in America, might enjoy getting reacquainted with the ladies of Wentworth Detention Centre. It won't be a very long reunion, with just ten episodes in this twenty-fifth-anniversary collection, but brief visiting hours are what you'd expect from a show about a prison.

P

GREAT MOMENTS: The tunnel escape; the first appearance of sadistic guard Joan "The Freak" Ferguson; the Lou Kelly Riot.

FAST-FORWARD: Nothing.

EXTRAS: Interviews with stars Val Lehman and Anne Phelan, and casting-director Jan Russ.

Profiler (1996–2000)

Season 1 (21 episodes on 6 discs): ★
Season 2 (19 episodes on 6 discs): ★ ★ ★
Season 3 (21 episodes on 6 discs): ★ ★ ★ ½
Season 4 (20 episodes on 5 discs): ★ ★

A&E Home Video
Video: Full-Frame; Audio: Dolby Digital Stereo

While no one can prove *CSI* lifted many of its visual tricks from *Profiler*, the stylistic similarities are undeniable. But while *CSI* became the number-one show in America, the adventures of Ally Walker as forensic psychologist Dr. Sam Waters drew a smaller crowd by Nielsen standards, perhaps because *Profiler* rarely offered any humor as counterpoint to its grim tales. For Sam it was one grisly crime scene after another, while dodging the attacks of Jack of All Trades, a brutal serial killer. No wonder the girl rarely dates.

One episode, "I'll Be Watching You," is missing from the Season 1 set, due to its extensive use of the Police song "Every Breath You Take." Music substitution on DVD is regrettable enough, but when these legal issues actually result in the removal of a full episode, that's inexcusable, especially at A&E's premium prices.

While Jamie Luner proved surprisingly adept as a replacement for the departed Ally Walker in Season 4, she couldn't save the show. By then, everyone was watching *CSI*.

GREAT MOMENTS: Season 1: Lori Petty plays a chilling serial killer in "Venom"; Season 2: The introduction of "Jill" (Traci Lords) in "Primal Scream"; Season 3: Sam causes a gang of jewel thieves to self-destruct in "Three-Carat Crisis"; Season 4: Sam departs in "Reunion."

FAST-FORWARD: Season 4: "Clean Sweep," is the second half of a crossover with the series *Pretender*, that's pretty useless without the first part.

EXTRAS: Season 1: Commentary on the pilot by stars Ally Walker and Robert Davi; "Profiles of Evil: Inside the Criminal Mind" episode of the A&E series *American Justice*; Season 2: Commentary with investigative criminal-profiler Pat Brown; Season 3: Commentary by Roma Maffia; Season 4: Interview with series consultant Howard Teten, former FBI unit chief and criminal profiler; commentary by Executive Producer Clifton Campbell.

P

Profit (1996)

The Complete Series (8 episodes on 3 discs): ★ ★ ★ ½

Anchor Bay

Video: Full-Frame; Audio: Dolby Digital 2.0

Giving new meaning to the term "short-lived series," *Profit* was axed after just four episodes by the trigger-happy FOX network, despite critical raves and a premise that FOX should have realized would take time to sink in. Corporate shark Jim Profit (Adrian Pasdar) made J.R. Ewing look like Mr. Rogers, as he lied, cheated, and murdered his way up the ladder, before heading home each night to sleep naked on the floor in a cardboard box, a habit that originated in his abused childhood. A protagonist without conscience is a tough sell, but there's an allure to pure evil that has always been part of classic fiction, and *Profit* taps into that territory with a bravery rarely exhibited by network television.

GREAT MOMENTS: Jim's unique greeting for his stepmother in "Sykes"; Profit terrorizes an innocent woman to close a business deal in "Cupid."

FAST-FORWARD: Nothing.

EXTRAS: The "Greed Kills" documentary, more than one hour in length, features interviews with star Adrian Pasdar and co-creators David Greenwalt and John MacNamara, who also provide commentary tracks on four episodes.

Providence (1999–2002)

The Providence Collection (12 episodes on 4 discs): ★ ★ ★

Artisan Entertainment

Video: Full-Frame; Audio: Dolby Digital 2.0

Highlight reels are most entertaining to those who watched the lowlights as well, which makes *The Providence Collection* highlight set a nice pickup for fans of the series, although they'll be ticked off by the change of theme song. It's all weddings, births, holiday dinners, and christenings in this twelve-episode set, but removing these special moments out of the context of the weekly stories defuses their momentousness, especially for new viewers. Sales of the box will most likely determine whether *Providence* will ever get the season-set treatment.

GREAT MOMENTS: Lynda makes her first ghostly appearance in "Home Again"; Robbie and Tina get married in "Best Man."

FAST-FORWARD: Nothing.

EXTRAS: Commentaries by Melina Kanakaredes, Paula Cale, Mike Farrell, Michael Fresco, Seth Peterson, Concetta Tomei, Monica Wyatt, and creator John Masius; gag reel; cast interviews.

Punk'd (2002–)

The Complete First Season (8 episodes on 2 discs): ★ ★ ★

The Complete Second Season (10 episodes on 2 discs): ★ ★ ★

Paramount Home Video

Video: Full-Frame; Audio: Dolby Digital 2.0

It shouldn't be funny watching Justin Timberlake on the verge of tears, but the guy is rich and good-looking and he got to see Britney naked, which is more than any of us can say, so why not take some pleasure in his financial downfall—even if it's being staged by another teen heartthrob who's just as cocky? The concept of *Punk'd* is pure *Candid Camera*, though the pranks pulled by Allen Funt were never as vicious as those orchestrated by Ashton Kutcher. But media-savvy celebrities are tougher targets than the man on the street, so it takes more sophisticated means to make them squirm.

The meticulously choreographed scams in *Punk'd* are humorous once, but are they worthy of repeat viewings? Fans probably know the answer already given MTV's endless reruns of the series. The DVD season sets sweeten the pot with uncut versions, commentaries, and a couple of extra segments that never made the actual show. You don't have to be a sadist to want these in your collection, but it probably helps.

GREAT MOMENTS: Season 1: The IRS makes Justin Timberlake cry; Pink's reaction after Ashton reveals her boyfriend's arrest is a joke; Season 2: Halle Berry being denied entrance to her movie premiere; Hilary Duff's encounter with a psychotic driving instructor.

FAST-FORWARD: Season 1: Stephen Dorff getting stiffed with a phony $8,000 bar tab.

EXTRAS: Season 1: Deleted scenes; two never-aired segments; "Punk Your Friends" option; Season 2: Deleted scenes; commentaries; two new segments.

Punky Brewster (1984–1986)

Season 1 (20 episodes on 4 discs): ★ ★ ★ ½
Season 2 (22 episodes on 4 discs): ★ ★ ★ ½

Shout! Factory
Video: Full-Frame; Audio: Dolby Digital 2.0

Shout! Factory's *Punky Brewster* sets take children of the 1980s back to this Sunday-night mainstay that has been virtually unseen in syndication. Soleil Moon Frye stars opposite George Gaynes as the pint-sized Punky, a young girl out on her own after being abandoned by her mother. In the days of "Just Say No" and the era of "Very Special Episodes," this was primo childhood fun. Original varying opening titles for the early episodes are restored for the DVD release. Shout! Factory does its usual bang-up job in providing a high-quality set that should leave fans waiting for the final two seasons.

GREAT MOMENTS: Season 1: Punky wants Santa to bring her mother back for Christmas in "Yes, Punky, There Is a Santa Claus"; the producers attempt—and fail—to launch a Punky spin-off with "Fenster Hall"; Season 2: The five-part story "The Perils of Punky," in which Punky and Henry face separation.

FAST-FORWARD: If you were over fifteen years old when this show debuted in 1984, you might not get it.

EXTRAS: The sets include interviews with actors Cherie Johnson, Ami Foster, and George Gaynes, as well as writer-creator David W. Duclon; bonus "It's Punky Brewster" cartoon episodes are included on every disc.

A Pup Named Scooby-Doo (1988–1991)

Volume 1 (4 episodes on 1 disc): ★ ★

Volume 2 (4 episodes on 1 disc): ★ ★

Warner Home Video

Video: Full-Frame; Audio: Dolby Digital 2.0

Scooby completists will want them, and little kids may love them, but the adventures of these pint-sized versions of the Mystery Inc. characters don't measure up to the originals.

Q

GREAT MOMENTS: Volume 1: The Shirley McLoon character, inspired by Shirley MacLaine, in "A Bicycle Built for Boo."

FAST-FORWARD: All of it, if you need more than two hands to count your birthdays.

EXTRAS: None.

Quantum Leap (1989–1993)

The Complete First Season (8 episodes on 3 discs): ★ ★ ★

The Complete Second Season (22 episodes on 3 discs): ★ ★ ★ ★ ½

The Complete Third Season (22 episodes on 3 discs): ★ ★ ★ ★

The Complete Fourth Season (22 episodes on 3 discs): ★ ★ ★

The Pilot Episode: ★ ★ ★

Universal Home Video (season sets); Image Entertainment (Pilot Episode)

Video: Full-Frame; Audio: Dolby Digital 2.0

After a botched time-travel experiment, Dr. Sam Beckett is unable to return to his regularly scheduled life. Guided by Al, a holographic observer, Beckett must "leap" into other people's bodies to help them solve their personal crises, while hoping that each leap brings him closer to his old self. The ingenious premise of *Quantum Leap* opened the show to limitless possibilities that were admirably explored with a mix of humor and social commentary. The DVD sets are certainly worth a look, though the budget-induced music substitutions are disappointing, as every episode is a period piece that uses music to evoke its time and place. While newcomers to the *QL* cult won't mind, Leapers know their show and will surely object to the alterations.

GREAT MOMENTS: Season 1: The *Casablanca* pastiche "Play It Again, Seymour"; Sam leaps into an African American at the dawn of the civil rights movement in "The Color of Truth"; Season 2: Sam must stop a Navy nurse from remarrying while her husband is missing in Vietnam in "M.I.A."; Season 3: Sam has a chance to save his family in "The Leap Home, Parts 1 & 2"; Scott Bakula sings in "Glitter Rock"; Season 4: Project Quantum Leap is threatened in "A Leap for Lisa."

FAST-FORWARD: Nothing.

EXTRAS: Season 1: Interviews with stars Scott Bakula and Dean Stockwell and series creator Donald P. Bellisario; "A Kiss with History" "making of" featurette; Season 4: Bonus episode "Liberation."

Q

Queer as Folk (1999–2000)

Series 1 (8 episodes on 2 discs): ★ ★ ★ ½
Series 2 (2 episodes on 1 disc): ★ ★

CITV

Video: Anamorphic Widescreen; Audio: Dolby Digital 2.0

The original UK miniseries that not only inspired the Showtime series, but supplied most of the plotlines of its first three seasons, will be of interest mainly to those who wish to compare and contrast the two. As with the American version, the leads are charismatic and the sex is graphic, but the original music has been altered for the DVD sets, and the Manchester accents are sometimes tough to decipher without subtitles.

GREAT MOMENTS: Series 1: The pilot episode ("Episode One") wastes no time in shattering taboos; Phil's funeral in Episode 4.

FAST-FORWARD: Nothing.

EXTRAS: None.

Queer as Folk (2000–)

Season 1 (22 episodes on 6 discs): ★ ★ ★
Season 2 (20 episodes on 6 discs): ★ ★ ★
Season 3 (14 episodes on 5 discs): ★ ★ ★ ½
Season 4 (14 episodes on 4 discs): ★ ★ ★ ½

Showtime Home Video

Video: Anamorphic Widescreen; Audio: Dolby Digital Surround

There's an "It's about time!" sentiment attached to *Queer as Folk* among viewers who share the persuasion of its homosexual characters. But there's something of a mixed message being sent in this otherwise laudable drama. At a time when society tells us we shouldn't define people by their sexuality, here's a show about gay men (and a few gay women) that could have made this point with dramatic eloquence. Some say it has, and yet the first line in the first episode of the first season is, "The thing you need to know is, it's all about sex." And that sentiment is enthusiastically explored in scenes that, had they been part of a motion picture, would stretch an "R" rating into NC-17 territory. The characters frequently define themselves by sex, and that portrayal may have those outside the tribe wondering if *Queer as Folk* is any more enlightened in its presentation of alternative lifestyles than the stereotypical portrayals of a more closeted era. Draw your own conclusions from the well-endowed DVD collections.

Q

GREAT MOMENTS: Season 1: The characters are introduced in "Episode 101"; the King of Babylon contest in "Episode 120"; Season 2: The boys all conclude that it's time for a change in their lives in "Episode 202"; Season 3: The Brian-Justin drama in "Episode 301"; Ben panics over his health in "Episode 303"; Season 4: The custody trial in "Episode 401."

FAST-FORWARD: Nothing.

EXTRAS: Season 1: Commentaries; gag reel; deleted scenes introduced by Hal Sparks; "Meet the Folk" featurette; Season 2: Three featurettes; wrap-party outtakes; Season 3: Three featurettes; commentary; music video; Season 4: Four featurettes.

Quincy, M.E. (1976–1983)

Seasons 1 & 2 (16 episodes on 3 discs): ★ ★

Universal Home Video

Video: Full-Frame; Audio: Dolby Digital 2.0

Give Universal credit for clever marketing; its *Quincy* boxed set hails the title character, played by Jack Klugman, as "The Original Crime Scene Investigator." Perhaps, though Quincy's medical exams on the deceased aren't nearly as graphic as the *CSI* variety. Klugman does rate the edge in crankiness, however. He's the misunderstood genius of the coroner's office, always fighting for justice only to be hampered by both the police and his superiors. The show often mistakes shouting for good dramatic acting, and Quincy's Asian slurs against assistant Sam Fujiyama, delivered in good-natured jest as they are, haven't aged well.

GREAT MOMENTS: Donna Mills and June Lockhart appear in "A Star Is Dead"; Quincy questions his methods in "The Two Sides of Truth."

FAST-FORWARD: "Has Anybody Here Seen Quincy?", a Klugman-less pilot for a new series about the Japanese physician–amateur detective Dr. Hiro.

EXTRAS: None.

Reba (2001–)

Season 1 (22 episodes on 3 discs): ★ ★
Season 2 (24 episodes on 3 discs): ★ ★
Season 3 (22 episodes on 3 discs): ★ ★

20th Century-Fox
Video: Full-Frame; Audio: Dolby Digital 2.0

As sitcoms starring country-music singers go, *Reba* is better than anything Jeff Foxworthy has come up with yet, but that's not saying much. The singer's fans have split into two camps on the show: those who enjoy her easygoing way with a quip as a mom with a complicated family, and those who wonder what a God-and-apple-pie country star is doing in a show that mines laughter from infidelity and teenage pregnancy. It's not aggressively awful, like the medley of one-season-and-out NBC sitcoms that *Friends* couldn't save as the lead-in, but this is still just a show to watch only if there's nothing else on and it's raining outside.

GREAT MOMENTS: Season 1: The pilot efficiently sets up all the central conflicts and relationships; *Newhart* costars Peter Scolari and Julia Duffy appear in "The Story of a Divorce."

FAST-FORWARD: Nothing.

EXTRAS: Season 1: Cast/crew commentaries; interview with Reba McEntire and Melissa Peterman; deleted scenes; bloopers/outtakes; featurettes "On the Scene with Barbra Jean" and "Creating *Reba*."

R

Red Dwarf (1988–1999)

Series 1 (6 episodes on 2 discs): ★ ★
Series 2 (6 episodes on 2 discs): ★ ★
Series 3 (6 episodes on 2 discs): ★ ★ ½
Series 4 (6 episodes on 2 discs): ★ ★ ★
Series 5 (6 episodes on 2 discs): ★ ★ ★
Series 6 (6 episodes on 2 discs): ★ ★ ★

BBC Video
Video: Full-Frame; Audio: Dolby Digital 2.0

Science-fiction and comedy are two genres that have not meshed well on television, the odd *Star Trek* episode notwithstanding. The British series *Red Dwarf* is the closest thing we've had to a successful hybrid, though that success has been more widely acknowledged in its homeland. In America, the *Red*

Dwarf following is devoted but small even by cult show standards. One reason might be that this is a very difficult series to jump into at any point except Episode one of Series 1. And even that won't help when cast and story changes between Series 2 and 3 confused even regular viewers. The good news for fans is that the DVD sets are as tricked out as any ever released by the BBC.

GREAT MOMENTS: Series 1: Lister gets acquainted with his new shipmates in "The End"; Series 3: Kryten's warranty expires in "The Last Day"; Series 4: The season finale, "Meltdown"; Series 6: "Gunmen of the Apocalypse," winner of an International Emmy Award.

FAST-FORWARD: Nothing.

EXTRAS: Each series set boasts more than one hour of various extras, including commentaries, deleted scenes, interviews, outtakes, and featurettes.

Remington Steele (1982–1987)

Season 1 (22 episodes on 4 discs): ★ ★ ★ ★
Season 2 (21 episodes on 4 discs): ★ ★ ★
Season 3 (24 episodes on 4 discs): ★ ★ ★

20th Century-Fox
Video: Full-Frame; Audio: Dolby Digital Mono

"Before he was Bond . . . he was Remington Steele." 20th Century-Fox happily plays the 007 card in its promotion of the *Steele* DVDs—which is ironic as it was *Steele* that prevented Pierce Brosnan from accepting the James Bond role when it was first offered. As a result, we got three movies with Timothy Dalton while Brosnan, tied to his TV contract, limped through *Steele's* final season and some halfhearted TV movies while waiting for another opening at the British Secret Service.

Which is not to say that *Remington Steele* isn't worth a look. Actually the show is quite wonderful, particularly in its first season as Steele and his private-eye partner Laura Holt (Stephanie Zimbalist) first dance the dance of we-both-want-to-but-won't-admit-it, and before the arrival of Doris Roberts, whose Mildred Krebs never meshed with the slick, sophisticated stories on which the series thrived.

GREAT MOMENTS: Season 1: The Agatha Christie–inspired "In the Steele of the Night"; Remington meets the Abbot of Costello in "Vintage Steele"; Season 2: The agency tries to help a client with amnesia and five ex-wives in "Altared Steele"; Season 3: Someone's hunting old Hollywood stars in "Cast in Steele," guest-starring Dorothy Lamour, Virginia Mayo, and Lloyd Nolan.

FAST-FORWARD: Season 2: Too much Mildred in "High-Flying Steele."

EXTRAS: Season 1: Commentaries by series creators Michael Gleason and Robert Butler, and writer Susan Baskin; a "making of" featurette with no participation from the series' stars; Season 2: More commentaries by writers and directors; three featurettes; Season 3: Commentary on "The Baking of Steele in the Chips"; three episode commentaries.

The Ren & Stimpy Show (1991–1996)

The First and Second Seasons (18 episodes on 3 discs): ★ ★ ★
Season 3 and a Half-ish (17 episodes on 3 discs): ★ ½
Season 5 and Some More of 4 (17 episodes on 3 discs): ★ ½

Paramount Home Video
Video: Full-Frame; Audio: Dolby Digital 2.0

R

When you promise "Uncut" episodes, you'd better deliver. *Ren & Stimpy* fans were happy-happy to see their show on DVD, but their joy-joy was not unconfined after discovering a few minutes of footage missing from some episodes. John K. (that's how most sites acknowledge series creator John Kricfalusi, so they don't have to keep looking up "Kricfalusi") has defended the releases while acknowledging that cuts were made, explaining that the footage may be lost or was simply forgotten.

The first season benefits from John K.'s direct input. He was then fired from his own show by Nickelodeon for pushing the envelope too far. Subsequent seasons couldn't maintain the right mix of gross-out humor and surreal satire, though Kricfalusi did return to oversee a few later episodes when the series was picked up by Spike TV.

GREAT MOMENTS: *The First and Second Seasons*: George Liquor, one of the characters that got John K. in hot water, debuts in "Man's Best Friend"; Breakfast gets its own superhero in "Powdered Toastman."

FAST-FORWARD: *Season 3 and a Half-ish*: "To Salve or Not to Salve" recycles animation from the superior first-season show "Stimpy's Invention."

EXTRAS: *The First and Second Seasons*: "In the Beginning" featurette; audio commentary by series creator John K. and writer Eddie Fitzgerald; bonus "banned" episode. *Season 3 and a Half-ish*: John K. commentaries; "Ren & Stimpy on Ren & Stimpy" featurette; *Season 5 and Some More of 4*: Episode commentaries.

Rescue Me (2004–)

The Complete First Season (13 episodes on 3 discs): ★ ★ ★ ½
The Complete Second Season (13 episodes on 4 discs): ★ ★ ★

Sony Pictures Home Entertainment
Video: Anamorphic Widescreen; Audio: Dolby Digital 5.1

Rescue Me isn't what you'd expect from a post–9/11 series about New York City firefighters. While the bravery of Truck Company 62 is never in doubt, these heroes are less admirable in their off-duty hours. Co-creator and star Denis Leary had never found a character to complement his magnetic screen presence, so he wrote one himself in Tommy Gavin, a philanderer of questionable morals dealing with a collapsed marriage and the ghostly image of his cousin, a fellow firefighter who perished in the World Trade Center. This testosterone-heavy series can be harsh and homophobic, and the video quality isn't what it should be on DVD, but at its best *Rescue Me* is riveting stuff.

GREAT MOMENTS: Season 1: Tommy's first conversation with his departed cousin in "Guts"; a female firefighter joins the squad in "Immortal"; the climactic firefighting scenes in "Sanctuary"; Season 2: Tommy's confrontation with a street vendor selling 9/11 memorabilia in "Voicemail."

FAST-FORWARD: Season 2: The awkward birthday party in "Believe."

EXTRAS: Season 1: Commentary by series creators Denis Leary and Peter Tolan; blooper reel, deleted scenes, and five behind-the-scenes featurettes; Season 2: Blooper reel, deleted scenes, and behind-the-scenes featurettes.

The Rifleman (1958–1963)

Set 1 (20 episodes on 4 discs): ★ ★ ½
Set 2 (20 episodes on 4 discs): ★ ★ ½
Set 3 (20 episodes on 4 discs): ★ ★ ½
Set 4 (20 episodes on 4 discs): ★ ★ ½
Volumes 1–5 (each: 5 episodes on 1 disc): ★ ★

MPI Home Video
Video: Full-Frame; Audio: Dolby Digital 1.0

The good news for fans of golden-age Westerns, the most under-represented genre of TV on DVD: about half of *The Rifleman*'s 164 episodes are now available. The bad news: they're all mixed up. Each set contains twenty shows plucked out of order from the series' five seasons. Episodes in the first two sets seem to have been selected for their higher-profile guest stars, and since they sold well MPI has since dived back into the vault to fill in the gaps. Not a very good system, but as it's unlikely that anyone will now bring season sets to market as well, it's the best all you buckaroos can expect.

GREAT MOMENTS: Set 1: Lucas and Mark are attacked by Mexican bandits in "The Vaqueros," guest-starring Martin Landau.

FAST-FORWARD: Nothing.

EXTRAS: None.

The Rockford Files (1974–1980)

Season 1 (21 episodes on 3 discs): ★ ★ ★ ★
Season 2 (22 episodes on 3 discs): ★ ★ ★ ★ ½

Universal Home Video
Video: Full-Frame; Audio: Dolby Digital 2.0

In *Maverick*, James Garner played the antithesis of a rough-and-tumble cowboy hero. In *The Rockford Files*, Garner tapped into that same cowardly con-man persona as a private detective who lives in a trailer and keeps his gun in a coffee can. Few shows have been so successfully fueled by the charisma of one lead actor. Cannon and Barnaby Jones solved more cases in the 1970s, but Rockford was cooler, even if he usually got stiffed by his clients.

GREAT MOMENTS: Season 1: Rockford doesn't mix well with the upper class in "The Countess"; Jim's con-artist skills are expertly employed in "Tall Woman in Red Wagon"; an ex-con hires Rockford to solve a twenty-year-old crime in "The Hammer of C Block."

FAST-FORWARD: Nothing.

EXTRAS: Season 1: Interview with James Garner; Season 2: The series pilot, "Backlash of the Hunter," which should have been included with the Season 1 set.

Rocky & Bullwinkle & Friends (1959–1962)

The Complete Season 1 (26 episodes on 4 discs): ★ ★ ★ ★ ★
The Complete Season 2 (52 episodes on 4 discs): ★ ★ ★ ★ ★
The Complete Season 3 (33 episodes on 4 discs): ★ ★ ★ ★ ★

The Best of Dudley Do-Right: Volume 1: ★ ★
The Best of Fractured Fairy Tales: Volume 1: ★ ★
The Best of Mr. Peabody & Sherman: Volume 1: ★ ★
The Best of Rocky & Bullwinkle: Volume 1: ★ ★ ★ ½

SonyWonder
Video: Full-Frame; Audio: Dolby Digital 2.0

If you're under forty, you probably believe *The Simpsons* is the most sophisticated and hilarious animated series ever created. If you're over forty, that accolade belongs to *Rocky & Bullwinkle.* Though the adventures of moose and squirrel debuted in 1959, it's astonishing how contemporary the material remains, the odd reference to Ramon Navarro aside. Satire and silliness have rarely coexisted so brilliantly. The DVD sets preserve episodes as originally run, with two Bullwinkle shorts in each half-hour, along with other Jay Ward creations, including Dudley Do-Right, Fractured Fairy Tales, Mr. Peabody and Sherman, and Aesop and Son. An option that would play just the Bullwinkle segments would have been nice, but SonyWonder's worst mistake was plastering an unnecessary R&B logo in the bottom corner of the screen. They should get docked at least half a star for that, but the episodes are so good that I don't have the heart.

R

GREAT MOMENTS: Season 1: The world's economy is revealed to hinge on cereal-box tops in "The Box-Top Robbery"; Fractured Fairy Tales' satire on Disneyland in "Sleeping Beauty"; Season 2: In "Metal-Munching Mice," Boris unleashes mechanical mice to eat America's television antennas.

FAST-FORWARD: The "Aesop and Son" shorts are the weakest link in the Ward canon.

EXTRAS: Season 1: Never-before-seen Bullwinkle puppet segments, and the rarely seen "U.S. Saving Stamp Club" episode; vintage TV spots; Season 2: June Foray interview; "Moosecalls: The Best of Bullwinkle Sings"; vintage TV commercials; Season 3: Live Bullwinkle puppet clips; "The Best of Bullwinkle Follies."

Roger Ramjet (1965–1968)

Hero of Our Nation (15 episodes on 1 disc): ★ ★ ★
Man of Adventure (15 episodes on 1 disc): ★ ★ ★
Hero of Our Nation—Deluxe Edition (120 episodes on 3 discs): ★ ★ ★ ★

Image Entertainment (Hero of Our Nation and Man of Adventure); SonyWonder (Deluxe Edition)
Video: Full-Frame; Audio: Dolby Digital Mono

Though it's often lumped with the Jay Ward stable for its ability to entertain children with silly adventures and adults with witty dialogue and bad puns, Ken Snyder's *Roger Ramjet* never achieved the acclaim it deserved. Put the blame on Roger's secret weapon in his war on crime, a Proton Energy Pill. Parents' concern over the effect a pill-popping superhero might have on young viewers kept the show out of syndication for decades. Surprisingly, there's been no research on whether the name of Roger's arch-enemy, Noodles Romanoff, helped kids say no to Hungarian food.

The *Deluxe Edition* is the way to go, though its inclusion of 120 of the 156 five-minute episodes seems odd, as with one more disc they could have released the complete series. Picture and sound are just average, but they always were.

GREAT MOMENTS: *Deluxe Edition*: The first appearance of the Solenoid Robots in "TV Crisis"; Noodles Romanoff and his No-Goods disguise themselves as a rock band in "The Cockroaches"; Roger's exploits are immortalized in the movie *Ramjet of Lompoc* in "Hollywood."

FAST-FORWARD: The theme song, which repeats an awful lot between five-minute episodes.

EXTRAS: *Hero of Our Nation*: Commentary by Gary Owens, voice of Roger Ramjet.

R

Roots (1977–1978)

Twenty-Fifth Anniversary Edition (8 episodes on 3 discs): ★★★★★

Warner Home Video

Video: Full-Frame; Audio: Dolby Digital 2.0

Sometimes the viewing public will surprise you. How else to explain the enormous ratings garnered by *Roots*, TV's first miniseries, which explored one of the darkest chapters from America's past? At a time when television served as the ultimate escapist ride, this sobering history lesson shattered all viewership numbers and deservedly swept the Emmys. More than a quarter-century later, *Roots* has lost none of its impact. An essential addition to any TV-on-DVD collection.

GREAT MOMENTS: Kunta Kinte refuses to accept his slave name; Kunta marries Bell; the birth of Kizzy.

FAST-FORWARD: Nothing.

EXTRAS: Commentaries by Executive Producer David L. Wolper and stars Ed

Asner, LeVar Burton, Cicely Tyson, John Amos, Sandy Duncan, and Leslie Uggams; the documentary "Remembering *Roots*."

Roosanne (1988–1997)

The Complete First Season (23 episodes on 4 discs): ★ ½

The Complete Second Season (21 episodes on 4 discs): ★ ★ ★ ★ ½

The Complete Third Season (25 episodes on 4 discs): ★ ★ ★ ★ ½

Anchor Bay

Video: Full-Frame; Audio: Dolby Digital 2.0

R

The strangest thing about the first *Roseanne* DVD set is how Anchor Bay thought enough of the series to arrange new interviews with Roseanne and John Goodman, to track down a blooper reel and include a "Wisdom from the Domestic Goddess" feature, while releasing versions of the shows that had been cut for syndication. This was the second Carsey-Werner series to receive such substandard treatment, after *The Cosby Show* had also debuted on DVD with two to three minutes excised from each show. If Barr doesn't care that much about her work, why should we? The episodes are uncut from Season 2 on.

GREAT MOMENTS: Season 1: Roseanne's bowling-night escapades and George Clooney's mullet in "Lovers' Lanes"; a tornado rips through Lanford in "Toto, We're Not in Kansas Anymore"; Season 2: Halloween high jinks in "Boo!"; Darlene's poem in the Joss Whedon–penned "Brain-Dead Poet's Society"; Season 3: Roseanne teaches Darlene's home economics class about how to budget in the real world in "Home-Ec" (look for Leonardo DiCaprio as one of Darlene's classmates).

FAST-FORWARD: The strange fantasy sequences in "Sweet Dreams" (Season 2).

EXTRAS: Season 1: "Roseanne on *Roseanne*: A New Candid Interview"; "John Goodman Takes a Look Back"; "Wisdom from the Domestic Goddess"; blooper reel; Season 2: John Goodman interview and audition footage; blooper reel; footage from the first-season launch party; "Wacky Jacky" featurette; Season 3: Interviews with Laurie Metcalf and Lecy Goranson.

Roswell (1999–2002)

Season 1 (22 episodes on 6 discs): ★ ★ ½

Season 2 (21 episodes on 6 discs): ★ ★ ½

Season 3 (18 episodes on 5 discs): ★ ★

20th Century-Fox

Video: Anamorphic Widescreen; Audio: Dolby Digital 5.1

Once upon a time there were three human teenagers and three alien teenagers, and this being a WB show you just knew they were all going to be dreamy. Read any of *Roswell*'s hundreds of online message-board submissions for the behind-the-scenes stories of cast romances and breakups that actually affected one character's story arc, and the battles between the show's creators and the WB over ramping up the action (a network demand) that probably shortened its lifespan. Of course, the fact that all these message boards exist, plus the impressive DVD sales numbers, indicate that plenty of fans are still out there for a show that in its first run seemed to get lost in a crowd of teen shows on the WB and elsewhere. Those fans will certainly appreciate the wonderful assortment of extras with each set, and be disappointed by the original-music substitutions.

R

GREAT MOMENTS: Season 1: The pilot; Season 2: The time-travel adventure "The Summer of '47"; Maria's episode introductions; Season 3: The *Bewitched*-inspired "I Married an Alien."

FAST-FORWARD: Nothing.

EXTRAS: Season 1: Commentaries; deleted scenes with commentary; three featurettes; gag reel; "Save Yourself" music video; Season 2: Multiple commentary track and three featurettes; Season 3: Commentaries; "Class of 2002" featurette; "Shiri Appleby's *Roswell* DVD Tour to Japan."

Rowan & Martin's Laugh-In (1968–1973)

The Best of—Volume 1 (6 episodes on 3 discs): ★ ★ ★ ½

The Best of—Volume 2 (6 episodes on 3 discs): ★ ★ ★

Rhino

Video: Full-Frame; Audio: Mono

So much to love here and, sadly, also much to gripe about. I'll grant that *Laugh-In* may not be best-served by season sets, with its now-dated topical humor and the percentage of jokes per show that fell flat the first time around. But Rhino is doing fans a disservice with these poorly chosen "best of" sets, that only hint at the impact of this once-revolutionary comic revue.

All the famous characters and cast members and catchphrases are here, from Judy Carne's "Sock it to me!" and Arte Johnson's German soldier ("Verrrrrry Interesting!") to Lily Tomlin as Ernestine and Ruth Buzzi's purse-bashing Gladys Ormphby. And the array of guest stars (Jack Benny, Greer Garson, Sammy Davis, Jr., John Wayne, Richard Nixon, Johnny Carson, Bob Hope, Jack Lemmon) verify *Laugh-In*'s status as the "in" show of its time. Tech credits on the DVDs are also impressive—the colors seem ready to burst off the screen—and the packaging cleverly replicates the series' joke-wall finale (just try to resist opening the windows). But watch out for the MENU-screen music that blasts out at a much higher volume than the audio on the episodes, a problem peculiar to some Rhino sets.

The downside? Packaging six episodes on three discs per set is not a good return on one's investment, and fans could name you a dozen better shows than the selections included here. How, on Volume 2, do you bypass the series' 1960s glory days and include an episode from the 1971 season, by which time Goldie Hawn and Judy Carne had been replaced by the likes of Johnny Brown and Barbara Sharma? Whoever made that call at Rhino deserves the Flying Fickle Finger of Fate.

GREAT MOMENTS: The Farkel Family sketches (Volumes 1 and 2); Judy Carne, wearing a skullcap and slipping one by the censors with the line "Gee, I never thought I'd be bald (balled) on live television!"; every single appearance of Goldie Hawn.

FAST-FORWARD: The Gladys and Tyrone engagement/wedding skits on Volume 2.

EXTRAS: Volume 1: Interviews with Gary Owens, Ruth Buzzi, and Arte Johnson; Volume 2: Interviews with Alan Sues, Dick Martin, and TV historian Hal Erickson.

The Saint (1962–1969)

The Saint Megaset (48 episodes on 14 discs): ★ ★ ★ ★
1966 Volumes 1 & 2 (6 episodes on 2 discs): ★ ★ ★
1966 Volumes 3 & 4 (6 episodes on 2 discs): ★ ★ ★
1966 Volumes 5 & 6 (7 episodes on 2 discs): ★ ★ ★
1966 Volumes 7 & 8 (7 episodes on 2 discs): ★ ★ ★ ½
1968 Volumes 9 & 10 (7 episodes on 2 discs): ★ ★ ★
1968 Volumes 11 & 12 (7 episodes on 2 discs): ★ ★ ★ ★
1968 Volumes 13 & 14 (7 episodes on 2 discs): ★ ★ ★ ★

The Early Episodes, Set 1 (12 episodes on 3 discs): ★ ★ ★ ½
The Early Episodes, Set 2 (12 episodes on 4 discs): ★ ★ ★ ½

A&E Home Video
Video: Full-Frame; Audio: Mono

Here's the show that landed Roger Moore the role of James Bond after Sean Connery's departure, and how much one enjoyed Moore's era as 007 will determine one's interest in this stylish series. As Simon Templar, a classy criminal who travels to exotic locations to help the rich and the beautiful, Moore is clearly in his element. Some men are born to wear white dinner jackets, and he's one of them. All most viewers recall of *The Saint* is the cartoon halo that hovered over Templar's head in the prologue scenes, but if the stories tend toward the interchangeable, they don't want for sumptuous distraction.

The main drawback to the A&E sets is the price; six or seven one-hour episodes and no extras for $39.95? I went for that early on when A&E released *The Avengers*, but the market has changed since then. The Megaset lowers the cost per episode, but still requires a $200 investment. Those looking to cherry pick should start with the latter two volumes of the color series, and the two "Early Episodes" collections, featuring more stories based on the novels of *Saint* creator Leslie Charteris.

GREAT MOMENTS: *Megaset*: Julie Christie guest-stars in "Judith"; "The Fiction Makers" and "Vendetta for the Saint," both of which boasted theatrical production values (and were released worldwide as motion pictures).

FAST-FORWARD: Nothing.

EXTRAS: None.

Sanford and Son (1972–1977)

The First Season (14 episodes on 2 discs): ★ ★ ½
The Second Season (24 episodes on 3 discs): ★ ★ ★
The Third Season (24 episodes on 3 discs): ★ ★ ★ ★
The Fourth Season (24 episodes on 3 discs): ★ ★ ★ ★ ½
The Fifth Season (24 episodes on 3 discs): ★ ★ ★ ★
The Sixth Season (24 episodes on 3 discs): ★ ★ ★

Sony Pictures Home Entertainment
Video: Full-Frame; Audio Dolby Digital 1.0

As with *All in the Family*, Norman Lear adapted *Sanford and Son* from a British series, *Steptoe and Son*. Don't look for any episodes of that show in the *Sanford* DVD sets, however, which like too many other TV classics have been released bereft of extras. As was typical of many sitcoms from the 1970s, the series earned enough laughs and viewers in its first season to stay on the schedule, peaked in its middle years, then stuck around one or two seasons too many. There's footage missing from a couple of episodes in almost every season set; thankfully, none of it includes moments in which Redd Foxx clutches his chest and yells "Elizabeth! This is the big one!"

GREAT MOMENTS: Season 1: Fred and Lamont are hired by a rich socialite in "The Piano Movers"; Season 2: Fred tries to get rich off a fender-bender in "Whiplash"; the Sanfords are cast in a porno movie in "Rated X"; Season 3: Grady's cousin Emma drives everyone crazy in "Hello Cousin Emma, Goodbye Cousin Emma."

FAST-FORWARD: Redd Foxx always delivers enough laughs to make even the lesser episodes worth a look.

EXTRAS: None.

S

Sapphire and Steel (1979–1982)

Boxed set: The Complete Series (34 episodes on 6 discs): ★ ★ ★ ★ ½

A&E Home Video

Video: Full-Frame; Audio: Stereo

How can I hate A&E for its price points and packaging on shows like *The Saint*, yet love them for bringing *Sapphire and Steel* to DVD? The American cult for this British time-travel adventure could probably fit in a phone booth (if we still had phone booths), but those who take a chance based on the casting of familiar faces David McCallum (*The Man from U.N.C.L.E.*) and Joanna Lumley (*The New Avengers, Absolutely Fabulous*) will be richly rewarded with its dark, paranormal tales of mysterious characters tackling strange assignments to safeguard the structure of Time (as in clocks and calendars, not the magazine). You'll have to overlook the substandard special effects, but the stories are so engrossing that this shouldn't be difficult.

GREAT MOMENTS: Steel matches wits with a parapsychologist in "Assignment II"; Sapphire and Steel meet Silver in "Assignment III"; the use of photographs as weapons in "Assignment IV."

FAST-FORWARD: Nothing.

EXTRAS: None.

Saturday Night Live (1975–)

Twenty-Five Years of Music (5 discs): ★ ★ ★ ★
Twenty-Fifth Anniversary: ★ ★ ★
The Best of Dan Aykroyd: ★ ★ ★
The Best of Alec Baldwin: ★ ★ ½
The Best of John Belushi: ★ ★ ★ ½
The Best of the Blues Brothers: ★ ★
The Best of Dana Carvey: ★ ★ ★ ½
The Best of Jimmy Fallon: ★ ★ ★
The Best of Chris Farley: ★ ★ ½
The Best of Will Ferrell: ★ ★ ★
The Best of Will Ferrell, Volume 2: ★ ½
The Best of Tom Hanks: ★ ★ ½
The Best of Phil Hartman: ★ ★ ★
The Best of Chris Kattan: ★ ½
The Best of Jon Lovitz: ★ ★ ★
The Best of Steve Martin: ★ ★ ★
The Best of Tracy Morgan: ★
The Best of Eddie Murphy: ★ ★ ★ ½
The Best of Mike Myers: ★ ★ ★ ½
The Best of Gilda Radner: ★ ★ ★
The Best of Chris Rock: ★ ½
The Best of Adam Sandler: ★ ★
The Best of Molly Shannon: ★ ★
The Best of David Spade: ★ ★
The Best of Christopher Walken: ★ ★ ★
Christmas: ★ ★ ★ ½
The First Five Years: ★ ★ ½
Halloween: ★ ★
Mr. Bill's Disasterpiece Theater (3 discs): ★

Lions Gate

Video: Full-Frame; Audio: Dolby Digital 2.0; Dolby Digital 5.1 (*Twenty-Five Years of Music*)

It's a rite of passage now on its fourth generation. Kids discover *Saturday Night Live*, quote the sketches at school on Monday morning, then start dissing the show when the cast changes because they're certain that any new *SNL* can never be as good as the one they first embraced. No other series has been written off so often, only to bounce back with another collection of young, innovative comic talent to keep the franchise going.

S

The strategy of releasing compilation DVDs focusing on one performer has its merits and its drawbacks. While season sets might have been preferable, even *SNL* loyalists would admit that every show serves up a few sketches that don't belong on anyone's home-video shelf. Unfortunately, the so-called "best of" collections frequently suffer from the same problem: classic moments are presented alongside bits that should never have made the cut.

The Twenty-Fifth Anniversary, originally broadcast as a primetime special, has a nostalgic class-reunion appeal, especially for those who grew up with the original cast. *Christmas* is probably the most consistently amusing collection of skits, while the Mr. Bill release actually fills three discs with a guy squashing Play-Doh.

GREAT MOMENTS: *Best of Christopher Walken*: The Blue Oyster Cult "Behind the Music" sketch (more cowbell!); *Christmas*: Alec Baldwin plays a memorable NPR guest; *Best of Chris Farley*: The Chippendales sketch with Patrick Swayze; *Best of Gilda Radner*: Baba Wawa and Roseanne Roseannadanna; *Best of Dan Aykroyd*: The Bass-o-Matic.

S

FAST-FORWARD: There are usually at least one or two sketches on every disc worth skipping—you'll find them.

EXTRAS: *Twenty-Fifth Anniversary*: Lorne Michaels interview; press coverage of *SNL*'s twenty-fifth anniversary; *Mr. Bill's Disasterpiece Theater*: creator interviews, rare footage.

Saved by the Bell (1989–1993)

Seasons 1 & 2 (33 episodes on 5 discs): ★ ★ ★
Seasons 3 & 4 (29 episodes on 4 discs): ★ ★
Season 5 (24 episodes on 3 discs): ★ ½

Lions Gate
Video: Full-Frame; Audio: Dolby Digital 1.0

Young troublemaker Zack Morris (Mark-Paul Gosselaar) is the charismatic center of a group of friends at Bayside High in this popular live-action Saturday-morning series. *Saved by the Bell* also introduced fans to bumbling principal Mr. Belding, bodacious Kelly, dweeb-ish goofball Screech, and a pre-*Showgirls* Elizabeth Berkeley as Jessie Spano (whose "you sexist pig" rants lose a lot of their punch once you've seen her hump a pole). Although the series occasionally grappled with serious issues (Jessie gets addicted to caffeine pills!), most of the content is about as risqué as an *Archie* comic book.

The Lions Gate DVD sets are surprisingly shoddy. Episodes are listed in airdate order rather than continuity; as a result, *SBTB*'s actual first episode, where several characters are introduced, appears on the third disc of Season 1. Opening titles alternate between the original version and the generic syndicated variant used on TBS and other local stations. Fans have reported missing scenes from the Seasons 3 & 4 sets, and the flimsy DVD packaging is easily bent or torn. The video quality on the Season 5 documentary is very poor.

Saved by the Bell started on the Disney Channel as *Good Morning Miss Bliss* in 1988. That series is still MIA on DVD, and was not included in any of the home-video-rights packages, even though the shows later aired as "Junior High" episodes in syndication. The Lions Gate *SBTB* sets comprise the original series' Saturday-morning run, but don't include the original cast's "Hawaiian-style" TV movie.

GREAT MOMENTS: Season 2: Zack hires an actor to impersonate his father in "Rent-A-Pop."

FAST-FORWARD: You might need to fast-forward through entire episodes if you'd like to see some of the show's two-parters in sequence. DVD commentary with creator Peter Engel sounds like he's reading from cue cards.

EXTRAS: Seasons 3 & 4: Commentary tracks by creator Peter Engel and stars Lark Voorhies and Dustin Diamond; Season 5: Behind-the-scenes documentary.

S

Saved by the Bell: The College Years (1993–1994)

Season 1 (19 episodes on 3 discs): ★ ★ ½

Image Entertainment

Video: Full-Frame (1:33:1); Audio: Dolby Digital 1.0

And you thought the kids from Bayside would never graduate from high school. A primetime sequel to the original *Saved by the Bell* brought Zack, Kelly, Slater, and Screech to the fictional California University, but their Saturday-morning following didn't follow them to Tuesdays at 8 PM, and the series was cancelled after nineteen episodes. *The College Years* ended with longtime couple Zack and Kelly deciding to run off to Las Vegas (and into a TV movie not yet on DVD) to marry.

While there are no extras on this set, it is produced at a much higher quality than the Lions Gate releases of the original series.

GREAT MOMENTS: Celebrity guests (they were celebrities at the time, anyway) Marsha Warfield, Jenna von Oÿ, Brian Austin Green, Marv Albert, Dennis Haskins, and Jonathan Brandis save Thanksgiving in "A Thanksgiving Story";

Lark Voorhies returns as Lisa Turtle for the show's final episode.

FAST-FORWARD: Kelly's flirtation with Professor Lasky implies the series was after a more mature audience.

EXTRAS: None.

Saved by the Bell: The New Class (1993–2000)

Season 1 (13 episodes on 2 discs): ★ ½
Season 2 (26 episodes on 3 discs): ★ ★
Season 3 (26 episodes on 3 discs): ★
Season 4 (26 episodes on 3 discs): ★ ★
Season 5 (26 episodes on 4 discs): ★ ½
Seasons 6 & 7 (26 episodes on 4 discs): ★

Image Entertainment
Video: Full-Frame; Audio: Dolby Digital 1.0

S

While Zack and Kelly moved to primetime (see above), Principal Belding was faced with a new class of students at Bayside High. While the original *Saved by the Bell* was never Shakespeare, or even *Welcome Back, Kotter*, the *New Class* initially fielded such a weak batch of character clones that viewers felt nostalgic for the old gang. Hence the Season 2 reappearance of Dustin Diamond's Screech, now a principal's assistant, and a mix of new and returning characters turning up with almost every subsequent season. Thankfully, unlike Lions Gate's handling of the original series, Image Entertainment put the stories in their proper order, so two-part episodes are not improperly split.

GREAT MOMENTS: Season 2: Zack, Lisa, and Slater return to help save the school in "Goodbye Bayside."

FAST-FORWARD: Any stories focusing on Lindsay or Tommy D. are worth skipping.

EXTRAS: None.

Schoolhouse Rock (1973–1996)

Schoolhouse Rock: Special Thirtieth Anniversary Edition (complete series on 2 discs): ★ ★ ★ ★ ★

Buena Vista Home Entertainment
Video: Full-Frame; Audio: Dolby Digital 2.0

Quick—recite the preamble to the Constitution. The kids of the '70s or '80s probably still remember the words thanks to *Schoolhouse Rock*. Genius is an overused accolade, particularly in television, but for this groundbreaking series of animated shorts no other description will suffice. The idea originated with advertising gurus who observed how children knew all the words to pop songs but couldn't remember their multiplication tables. They set math class to music, and the first effort, "Three is a Magic Number," launched a Saturday-morning phenomenon that ran between cartoons on ABC for more than a decade, and later expanded into equally appealing series covering grammar, American history, and science.

The set includes all forty-six *Schoolhouse Rock* shorts, from the classics everybody remembers to lesser-known but equally enchanting efforts, and an all-new short about the presidential voting process ("I'm Gonna Send Your Vote to College") which unfortunately was written before the hanging-chad election of 2000. What's amazing about these Emmy-winning features is how nefariously catchy the songs remain, and how they communicate an extraordinary amount of material in just three minutes. Though childhood nostalgia will fuel sales, *Schoolhouse Rock* remains a potent teaching tool and would be a great purchase for parents of young kids.

GREAT MOMENTS: "Conjunction Junction," "I'm Just a Bill," "Figure Eight," "Interjections," "Three Is a Magic Number," "No More Kings," etc., etc.

FAST-FORWARD: With the exception of "Dollars and Sense," the Money Rock episodes haven't aged well.

EXTRAS: The making of "I'm Gonna Send Your Vote to College" actually covers the entire history of the series, including interviews with the two most prominent *Schoolhouse Rock* performers, Jack Sheldon and Bob Dorough; creator commentaries for ten episodes; clips from Daytime Emmy ceremonies; the Nike commercial set to "Three Is a Magic Number." "Scooter Computer and Mr. Chips," a follow-up effort about computers by the same creators; the "long-lost" short "The Weather Show"; covers of *Schoolhouse* songs by Better Than Ezra ("Conjunction Junction") and the Lemonheads ("My Hero, Zero").

The Scooby-Doo/Dynomutt Hour (1976–1977)

The Complete Series (16 episodes on 4 discs): ★ ★ ★

Warner Bros. Home Video

Video: Full-Frame; Audio: Dolby Digital Mono

Over the course of four decades the Scooby gang has been repackaged more often than a stale fruitcake at Christmas, but fans kept coming back, even as the Mystery, Inc. detectives were repeatedly saddled with unnecessary supporting characters. Scooby-Dum, who debuts in *The Scooby-Doo/Dynomutt Hour*, was the first misstep on the road to hell that led to Scrappy. Blue Falcon and Dynomutt rank among Hanna-Barbera's more enjoyable benchwarmers, but despite the "Complete Series" claim, episodes are missing from the set.

GREAT MOMENTS: A rock singer accidentally awakens an ancient evil in "Mamba Wamba and the Voodoo Hoodoo"; a rare appearance by femme fatale Scooby-Dee in "The Chiller Diller Movie Thriller"; the vanilla, chocolate, and strawberry ghosts in "The Ghosts of the Bad Humor Man."

FAST-FORWARD: The Scooby-Dum scenes.

EXTRAS: Featurette "Eerie Mystery of Scooby-Doo and Dynomutt's History"; the "In Their Own Words" feature contains interviews with the original voice actors.

S

Scooby-Doo, Where Are You? (1969–1970)

The Complete First and Second Seasons (25 episodes on 4 discs): ★ ★ ★ ★
Scooby-Doo's Original Mysteries (5 episodes on 1 disc): ★ ★ ★

Warner Home Video

Video: Full-Frame; Audio: Dolby Digital 2.0

This, the original Scooby-Doo series, remains the gold standard among Mystery Inc. fans. There were no guest stars, no crossovers, and most importantly, no Scrappy. Just a groovy van, four meddling kids, and one cowardly canine, unmasking evildoers between trips to the malt shop. The above two seasons laid the groundwork for several subsequent Scooby incarnations of varying quality. The *Original Mysteries* disc offers the series' first five episodes.

GREAT MOMENTS: "Foul Play in Funland" adds a new twist to the familiar whodunit pattern; "Jeepers! It's the Creeper" features one of the series' most memorable villains.

FAST-FORWARD: Nothing.

EXTRAS: Featurette on Scooby fans and collectors; "America Loves Scooby-Doo" music video.

Scrubs (2004–)

Season 1 (24 episodes on 3 discs): ★ ★ ★ ½

Season 2 (22 episodes on 3 discs): ★ ★ ★ ★

Season 3 (22 episodes on 3 discs): ★ ★ ★ ★ ½

Buena Vista Home Entertainment

Video: Full-Frame; Audio: Dolby Digital 2.0

In an era when good situation comedies are an endangered species, *Scrubs* is a revelation. It's not perfect, and it's hard not to wonder how many hospital stories are left to tell after fifty-some years of TV doctor shows, but a likable cast led by Zach Braff and Sarah Chalke infuses the usual interns-learning-the-ropes material with fresh spirit, and the fantasy sequences add a cheeky dose of surrealism. Much of *Scrubs* is delightfully silly, but this is also a show that can switch from comedy to serious moments with the grace of *M*A*S*H*, and that's saying something.

The Season 1 DVD set contains some music alteration, which is only more egregious because it happened on a 2004 series, and by this time networks should be anticipating the DVD release, and negotiate music rights and other issues accordingly. Everything's original in Season 2.

S

GREAT MOMENTS: Season 1: *St. Elsewhere* stars William Daniels, Ed Begley, Jr., Stephen Furst, and Eric Laneuville appear in "My Sacrificial Clam"; the interns lose their first patient in "My Old Lady"; Season 2: Colin Hay's musical stylings in "My Overkill"; Dr. Cox's narration in "His Story"; Season 3: Michael J. Fox plays a doctor with obsessive-compulsive disorder in "My Catalyst"; Turk and Carla are married by Mr. Sulu (George Takei) in "My Best Friend's Wedding."

FAST-FORWARD: Nothing.

EXTRAS: Season 1: Outtakes; commentaries; deleted scenes; featurettes "Alternate Lines" and "Not Just Another Medical Show"; interview with Zach Braff; "Superman" music video; Season 2: Cast/crew commentaries; deleted scenes; outtakes; interview with John C. McGinley; five featurettes; Season 3: Seven featurettes; commentaries; deleted scenes; outtakes.

SCTV Network 90 (1981–1983)

Volume 1 (9 episodes on 5 discs): ★ ★ ★ ★ ★
Volume 2 (9 episodes on 5 discs): ★ ★ ★ ★ ★
Volume 3 (9 episodes on 5 discs): ★ ★ ★ ★ ★
Volume 4 (12 episodes on 6 discs): ★ ★ ★

Shout! Factory
Video: Full-Frame; Audio: Dolby Digital 2.0

When it first aired in the wee hours, following *Saturday Night Live*, *SCTV* seemed to pale in comparison to its more pop culture–friendly lead-in. The Canadian import presented its TV parodies as the programming schedule of a small-town station owned by a bizarre cast of characters. But where *SNL* poked at the ribs of its targets, *SCTV* drew blood, and now you can start an argument over which show really holds up better. The superb cast (John Candy, Joe Flaherty, Eugene Levy, Andrea Martin, Dave Thomas, Catherine O'Hara, Rick Moranis, Martin Short) created ingenious send-ups of the medium, as well as such unforgettable characters as the McKenzie brothers, Count Floyd, Lola Heatherton, Ed Grimley, and Johnny LaRue.

S

The Shout! Factory sets cost a lot, especially at just nine episodes each, but the company spent quite a bit to get all the rights straightened out, and packed each collection with wonderful extras. They're not perfect—you won't get all the original music (no Schmenge Brothers doing "Stairway to Heaven"), but you'll get most of it, including performances from the Talking Heads, Al Jarreau, and the Plasmatics. Though Volume 4 has a higher episode count, it contains shows from the era following the departure of Thomas, Moranis, and O'Hara.

GREAT MOMENTS: Volume 1: The "Great White North" segments; Rick Moranis plays Woody Allen opposite Dave Thomas as Bob Hope in "Play It Again, Bob"; the *Leave It to Beaver* parody; "Indira: The Musical": Volume 2: The Farm Film Reports; Dr. Tongue's Evil House of Pancakes; Volume 3: The Battle of the PBS Stars; Martin Short's tour de force performance in "Jerry Lewis on the Champs Elysées"; Volume 4: The debut of Ed Grimley.

FAST-FORWARD: Volume 3: "The Days of the Week" soap-opera parody.

EXTRAS: Too many to list; each volume contains multiple commentaries, tributes to original cast members, documentary featurettes, and new cast interviews. Volume 1 also offers the 1999 Aspen Comedy Festival SCTV Tribute Reunion. In Volume 2, there's footage of *SCTV* at the 1982 Emmy Awards, the Norman Seeff photo sessions for *Life* magazine, and an in-depth look at the Juul Haalmeyer Dancers. Volume 3 is packaged with a bonus audio CD featuring classic moments from the Second City Stage, and "*SCTV* at the Museum of Television and Radio" featurette; with Volume 4, you'll get a set of collectible trading cards.

Seinfeld (1989–1998)

Seasons 1 & 2 (17 episodes on 4 discs): ★ ★ ★ ★ ½
Season 3 (22 episodes on 4 discs): ★ ★ ★ ★ ★
Season 4 (24 episodes on 4 discs): ★ ★ ★ ★ ★
Season 5 (22 episodes on 4 discs): ★ ★ ★ ★ ★
Season 6 (24 episodes on 4 discs): ★ ★ ★ ★ ★

Columbia Tristar Home Video
Video: Full-Frame; Audio: Dolby Digital 2.0

Seinfeld was to the 1990s what *I Love Lucy* was to the 1950s, *The Dick Van Dyke Show* was to the 1960s, and *The Mary Tyler Moore Show* was to the 1970s: a classic sitcom that is both definitive of its time and timeless. A notable achievement, and even more impressive for being accomplished in a television era that offered viewers between fifty and five hundred channels from which to choose.

"It's about nothing" has become an overused catch-all description that's never been accurate. What *Seinfeld* is "about" is life, which cannot be summarized in a two-sentence plot description. Specifically, it's about the minutiae of life, an extension of the observational humor in Jerry Seinfeld's stand-up routines. The series has given names to people and phenomena we all know but have never formally categorized—low-talkers, re-gifters, "shrinkage," the kiss hello. From such inconsequential incidents as finding a car in a parking garage or waiting for a table in a restaurant, *Seinfeld* weaved densely plotted stories that transform some of life's most mundane and frustrating moments into brilliant comedy.

Fans waited a long time for DVDs, gritting their teeth while lesser series debuted in the home-video market. But the delay was time well spent, for when the first three seasons arrived they did so with a sumptuous menu of extras.

GREAT MOMENTS: Seasons 1 & 2: George's "Costanza, Lord of the Idiots" speech in "The Apartment"; the series' first groundbreaking episode, "The Chinese Restaurant"; Season 3: "The Library," with George's atomic-wedgie flashbacks and Jerry's run-in with library-cop Lieutenant Bookman; Jerry's encounter with a rental-car agent in "The Alternate Side"; the first "Hello, Newman" in "The Suicide"; the *JFK* parody with Kramer, Newman, and

Keith Hernandez in "The Boyfriend"; Season 4: The Trivial Pursuit game in "The Bubble Boy"; "The Contest"—'nuff said; Teri Hatcher and Megan Mullally guest in "The Implant," featuring the immortal line, "They're real, and they're spectacular"; Season 5: Jerry's *Today Show* appearance in "The Puffy Shirt"; George's monologue ("The sea was angry that day, my friends") at the end of "The Marine Biologist"; Season 6: Kramer's first name is revealed in "The Switch"; Mel Tormé serenading Kramer in "The Jimmy."

FAST-FORWARD: Seasons 1 & 2: The annoying Rava and Ray in "The Statue"; Season 4: "The Movie"—a thinly disguised retread of "The Chinese Restaurant"; Season 5: "The Raincoats" seems padded to fill a one-hour running time.

EXTRAS: Every season set offers interviews and episode commentaries with the cast and creators, deleted scenes, outtakes and bloopers, trailers, and extended cuts of the Jerry Seinfeld stand-up comedy footage aired over the opening and closing credits of most episodes; Season 3 also introduces fans to the "real" Kramer.

7th Heaven (1996–)

Boxed Sets: Season 1 (22 episodes on 6 discs): ★ ★ ★
Season 2 (22 episodes on 6 discs): ★ ★ ★

Paramount Home Video
Video: Full-Frame; Audio: Dolby Digital 2.0

A valiant, if not always successful attempt to revive the "Show for the Whole Family," a genre that's been on life support since *The Waltons* left the air. Though this series about a minister's brood may ultimately be best remembered as the launching pad for Jessica Biel, the real key to the Camdens' success was the casting of Catherine Hicks, one of those special actors who improves every project, whether she's dodging killer dolls in *Child's Play* or helping Captain Kirk kidnap a whale in *Star Trek IV*. At times the *7th Heaven* Sap-o-Meter almost reaches Brady level, but there are worse things to get stuck in on television. Those with a cynical mindset need not apply. Paramount should seek forgiveness, however, for the front-loaded promos at the start of the Season 2 set that cannot be skipped or fast-forwarded on most DVD players.

GREAT MOMENTS: Season 1: Matt discovers that no crime is too small when you're a minister's son in "America's Most Wanted"; "Who Knew?" the first and best of the series' "drugs are bad" shows.

FAST-FORWARD: Season 1: A heavy-handed "very special" episode on racism, "The Color of God."

EXTRAS: None.

Sex and the City (1998–2004)

The Complete First Season (12 episodes on 2 discs): ★ ★ ★ ★ ★
The Complete Second Season (18 episodes on 3 discs): ★ ★ ★ ★ ★
The Complete Third Season (18 episodes on 3 discs): ★ ★ ★ ★ ★
The Complete Fourth Season (18 episodes on 3 discs): ★ ★ ★ ★ ½
The Complete Fifth Season (8 episodes on 2 discs): ★ ★ ★ ★
The Complete Sixth Season, Part 1 (12 episodes on 3 discs): ★ ★ ★ ★
The Complete Sixth Season, Part 2 (8 episodes and bonus on 3 discs): ★ ★ ★ ★
The Complete Series (94 episodes on 20 discs): ★ ★ ★ ★ ★

HBO Home Video

Video: Full-Frame; Audio: Dolby Digital 2.0 (Seasons 1–4); Dolby Digital 5.1 (Seasons 5 and 6)

S

In the early days of television comedy, women over thirty had a prominent place in the sitcom world—as the dutiful wife ready to kiss her husband after a long day at work, have dinner on the table, and look no less than perfect while raising precocious children. As the years passed, there were single mothers, raising families on their own, but single women over thirty remained a rarity, even after Mary Richards turned the world on with her smile.

Fast-forward to the new millennium, and a fresh new look at the single life after thirty on *Sex and the City.* Sarah Jessica Parker stars as Carrie Bradshaw, a writer who chronicles the New York singles scene with a little help and insight from her confidantes, Miranda, Charlotte, and Samantha. True friends, sharing love, laughter, and life, and a special relationship with the fifth lady, New York City.

GREAT MOMENTS: Season 1: Miranda is mistaken for a lesbian in "Bay of Married Pigs"; Charlotte's aversion to a particular sex act in "Valley of the Twentysomething Guys"; Season 2: Carrie's humiliating cover story for *New York* magazine in "They Shoot Single People, Don't They?"; Miranda meets Steve Brady in "The Man, the Myth, the Viagra"; the Tantric sex workshop in "Was It Good for You?"; Season 3: Miranda and Carrie have a fight over their relationships with men in "Cock A Doodle Doo!"; Season 4: Carrie's "fashion road-kill" moment in "The Real Me"; the death of Miranda's mother in "My Motherboard, Myself"; Big and Carrie say goodbye to the strains of "Moon River" in "I Heart NY"; Season 5: The Atlantic City road trip in "Luck Be an Old Lady"; Season 6: Samantha's breast-cancer diagnosis begins a poignant story arc that plays out through the remainder of the series.

FAST-FORWARD: Season 4: Samantha's lesbian tryst with Maria (Sonia Braga) lacks humor or chemistry, as does Carrie's Season 5 romance with intense artist Alexander Petrovsky (Mikhail Baryshnikov).

EXTRAS: Season 1: "Inside *Sex and the City*" featurette; writer–executive producer Michael Patrick King provides commentary on Seasons 3 to 6 episodes; Season 5: "Behind the Seams" featurette focuses on the series' fashion sense; Season 6, Part 1: A Museum of Television and Radio seminar featuring all four series stars; Season 6, Part 2: Three alternate endings to the series finale; two farewell featurettes; deleted scenes; an Aspen Comedy Arts Festival Seminar featuring Sarah Jessica Parker and Michael Patrick King.

S

Sherlock Holmes (1984–1994)

The Adventures of Sherlock Holmes (13 episodes on 5 discs): ★ ★ ★ ★ ★

The Return of Sherlock Holmes (11 episodes on 5 discs): ★ ★ ★ ★ ★

The Casebook of Sherlock Holmes (6 episodes on 3 discs): ★ ★ ★ ★

The Memoirs of Sherlock Holmes (6 episodes on 3 discs): ★ ★ ★

The Eligible Bachelor: ★ ★ ★

The Hound of the Baskervilles: ★ ★ ★ ★

The Sign of Four: ★ ★ ★ ★

The Last Vampyre: ★ ★ ½

MPI Home Video

Video: Full-Frame; Audio: Dolby Digital Mono

Prior to this acclaimed BBC series, it was believed that the role of Sherlock Holmes was like that of Hamlet or Tarzan—open for interpretation by any number of actors, and capable of sustaining performances both introspective and over-the-top. But from the moment Jeremy Brett set up residence at 221B Baker Street, his portrayal of Holmes was heralded as definitive. This was the great detective as imagined by his creator, Arthur Conan Doyle, with the less-appealing aspects of his personality intact, and without the standard-issue costume and "Elementary, my Dear Watson!" clichés, delightfully embodied as they were a generation earlier by Basil Rathbone. Brett was joined by two Watsons, David Burke and Edward Hardwicke, both ideally cast as well. There were diminishing returns as the series continued, largely unavoidable due to Jeremy Brett's declining health, which is most noticeable in the *Memoirs* collection. But how marvelous to have so many accurate and respectful television adaptations of the classic cases.

GREAT MOMENTS: *Adventures*: The dueling deductions game between Sherlock and his brother Mycroft in "The Greek Interpreter"; Holmes meets his match in Irene Adler, a.k.a. the Woman, in "A Scandal in Bohemia"; *Return*: Marina Sirtis (*Star Trek: The Next Generation*) meets Holmes in "The Six Napoleons."

FAST-FORWARD: The poorly paced and too freely adapted *The Last Vampyre.*

EXTRAS: *Casebook*: Interview with Jeremy Brett and Edward Hardwicke; *Memoirs*: an interview with Arthur Conan Doyle's son, Adrian.

The Shield (2002–)

The Complete First Season (13 episodes on 4 discs): ★ ★ ★ ½
The Complete Second Season (13 episodes on 4 discs): ★ ★ ★
The Complete Third Season (15 episodes on 4 discs): ★ ★ ★
The Complete Fourth Season (13 episodes on 4 discs): ★ ★ ★ ★

20th Century-Fox
Video: Full-Frame; Audio: Dolby Digital 2.0

"He's not a cop. He's Al Capone with a badge." So says Police Captain Aceveda of Vic Mackey, the head of a corrupt strike team that uses extreme methods to lower violent crime in one of Los Angeles's toughest neighborhoods. *The Shield*'s question of whether the ends justify the means takes on added resonance in a post–9/11 world, where a lot of people are glad that a guy like Mackey is patrolling the streets. A fine ensemble cast led by Emmy-winner Michael Chiklis helps *The Shield* stand out from a crowded TV field of urban police stories, as does the FX series' delight in pushing the limits of what basic cable will tolerate in violence, sex, and profanity.

GREAT MOMENTS: Season 1: Vic keeps a basketball player under house arrest so he can win a bet on the game in "The Spread"; Rival department factions join forces when someone starts killing cops in "Circles"; Season 2: The origins of the Barn are explained in "Co-Pilot"; Season 3: "Strays," directed by David Mamet; Season 4: Glenn Close becomes Mackey's new boss in "The Cure."

FAST-FORWARD: Nothing.

EXTRAS: Each season set offers cast/crew commentaries; deleted scenes (more than thirty on some sets) and featurettes. The Season 4 set includes an eighty-minute documentary on the series.

Sigmund and the Sea Monsters (1973–1975)

Season 1 (17 episodes on 3 discs): ★ ★ ½

Sigmund and the Sea Monsters (4 episodes on 1 disc): ★ ★

See also: The World of Sid & Marty Krofft

Rhino

Video: Full-Frame; Audio: Dolby Digital 1.0

Who ever heard of a friendly sea monster? The same guys that thought up talking trees and singing bugs and hats with legs, that's who. By episode count, *Sigmund and the Sea Monsters* was a more successful series that *H.R. Pufnstuf*, *Lidsville*, and *The Bugaloos*. It's everything you'd expect from a Saturday-morning Krofft show, including the memorable theme song.

GREAT MOMENTS: Season 1: Sigmund moves into the clubhouse in "The Monster Who Came to Dinner"; Jack Wild (*H.R. Pufnstuf*) appears in "Wild Weekend."

FAST-FORWARD: Nothing.

EXTRAS: *Sigmund*: Interviews with stars Johnny Whitaker and Scott Kolden.

S

Silk Stalkings (1991–1999)

Season 1 (20 episodes on 6 discs): ★ ★ ★

Season 2 (23 episodes on 6 discs): ★ ★

Season 3 (20 episodes on 6 discs): ★ ★ ★

Season 4 (22 episodes on 3 discs): ★ ★ ★

Best of Season 1 (4 episodes on 1 disc): ★ ★ ★

Anchor Bay

Video: Full-Frame; Audio: Dolby Digital 2.0

In its early days, the programmers at the USA Network were experts at teasing viewers with too-racy-for-TV content, only to bait-and-switch them with shows that could run on any broadcast network. The worst offender was *Silk Stalkings*, which aired simultaneously in a late-night time slot on CBS. But with that title, and a lead actress with a porn-star name like Mitzi Kapture, who could blame fans for expecting this seedy crime-drama to stretch the FCC guidelines?

Surprisingly, this is a case where you may come for the sex but you'll stay for the stories. Given the prodigious number of bikini- and lingerie-clad women in nearly every episode, *Silk Stalkings* didn't have to be nearly as well written and performed as it was. And now on DVD you can freeze-frame those moments where you could swear a nipple got by the censors. But buyer beware: in the Season 2 box, the episode "Dead Weight" is missing the last ten minutes. Thus far, Anchor Bay has not corrected the error. Also note the switch from single-sided to double-sided discs with Season 4.

GREAT MOMENTS: Season 1: Rita tries to trap a serial sex offender killed in "Men Seeking Women"; Season 2: "Soul Kiss"; Season 3: The two-part season-opener "Natural Selection" offers more suspense than innuendo; "Champagne on Ice" may be the series' most risqué episode.

FAST-FORWARD: Just about everything after Chris and Rita leave Palm Beach.

EXTRAS: Season 1: New interviews with the cast and creator Stephen J. Cannell.

The Simple Life (2003–2005)

The Simple Life (7 episodes on 1 disc): ★ ★ ★
Road Trip (10 episodes on 1 disc): ★ ★
Interns (16 episodes on 2 discs): ★ ★ ½

20th Century-Fox
Video: Full-Frame; Audio: Dolby Digital Surround

In which Paris Hilton and Nicole Richie, two underfed blondes sharing the road and seemingly often sharing a brain, discover what people born without trust funds do all day. The first go-round has them in rural America, stripped of both credit cards and common sense. In Seasons 2 and 3, Paris and Nicole sulk and loaf through a new variety of occupations, laughing at their inability to do what working folk must every day to survive. Many of the situations would be offensive if they weren't so obviously scripted—would a funeral home really allow a ditzy hotel heiress to vacuum up the ashes of someone's departed relative?

GREAT MOMENTS: *The Simple Life*: Paris thinks you go to Wal-Mart to buy walls; *Road Trip*: Nicole cooks a dog-food sausage; *Interns*: A rare glimpse into the girls' humanity during their stint at a nursing home.

FAST-FORWARD: The 3,000 times Paris shows off her extensive vocabulary by summing up a person/place/thing with "That's hot."

EXTRAS: *The Simple Life*: Outtakes; *Road Trip*: Deleted scenes.

The Simpsons (1990–)

The Complete First Season (13 episodes on 3 discs): ★ ★ ½
The Complete Second Season (22 episodes on 4 discs): ★ ★ ★
The Complete Third Season (23 episodes on 4 discs): ★ ★ ★ ★
The Complete Fourth Season (22 episodes on 4 discs): ★ ★ ★ ★ ★
The Complete Fifth Season (22 episodes on 4 discs): ★ ★ ★ ★ ★
The Complete Sixth Season (25 episodes on 4 discs): ★ ★ ★ ★
The Complete Seventh Season (25 episodes on 4 discs): ★ ★ ★ ★ ★
Bart Wars (4 episodes on 1 disc): ★
Christmas with the Simpsons (4 episodes on 1 disc): ★ ★ ½
Simpsons Christmas 2 (4 episodes on 1 disc): ★
The Simpsons Gone Wild (4 episodes on 1 disc): ★
The Simpsons Treehouse of Horror (4 episodes on 1 disc): ★ ★ ★

20th Century-Fox
Video: Full-Frame; Audio: Dolby Digital 5.1

S

What began as filler segments on *The Tracy Ullman Show* made the unlikely evolution into primetime's longest-running animated series. Other accolades have followed, including a claim to the best situation comedy on television. Ever. Fans are convinced such high praise is deserved, but there is a segment of the population that, no matter how long the series runs or how many raves it invokes, just doesn't get it.

While that debate rages on, *The Simpsons* DVD sets bring all the magic back, from the early days of rougher animation when Bart was more of a focus than his bumbling dad Homer through its ascension to one of TV's most sharply observant and well-oiled humor machines.

Fox issued the first five seasons with similar packaging; with Seasons 6 and 7, they packed the DVDs inside Homer- and Marge-shaped heads. D'oh! Reacting to fan complaints, Fox offered to send "replacement boxes" to completists who wanted the sets to sit properly on their shelves.

GREAT MOMENTS: Season 3: Homer invents a drink that turns Moe's into a national phenomenon in "Flaming Moe's"; Season 4: Marge appears in community theater in "A Streetcar Named Marge"; "Krusty Gets Kancelled" is a longtime fan favorite; Season 5: Bart is stalked by Sideshow Bob in "Cape Feare"; the musical number in "Homer and Apu"; Season 6: "Who Shot Mr. Burns? Part 1" is a play on a classic *Dallas* cliffhanger; Season 7: "The Simpsons' 138th Episode Spectacular" is a fun retrospective; the Smashing Pumpkins play "Homerpalooza." And of course, the annual "Treehouse of Horror" episodes are always a lot of fun (Season 2–on).

FAST-FORWARD: Individual-episode releases aren't really worth your time, as you might as well get the shows in season sets. Likewise, those looking for *Star Wars* tie-ins with *Bart Wars* will be disappointed.

EXTRAS: Almost every episode from every set has commentary by cast and crew members and the full array of extras. Among the highlights: Season 1: Bonus *Tracy Ullman Show* shorts ; an unfinished episode; Season 2: "Do the Bartman" and "Deep Deep Trouble" music videos; Emmy Awards clip; Season 5: "A Look Back" with producer James L. Brooks; Season 6: "Springfield's Most Wanted" TV special.

The Singing Detective (1986)

The Complete Series (6 episodes on 3 discs): ★ ★ ★ ★

BBC Video

Video: Full-Frame; Audio: Dolby Digital Stereo

S

Sometimes crime stories are combined with full-blown musical numbers, and the result is a near-masterpiece like *The Singing Detective.* And other times you get *Cop Rock.* Funny how that works out. Here's a stylish gumshoe noir set in post–World War II Britain, played out in the imagination of a disfigured, hospital-bound mystery writer named Philip Marlow. Not the famous one, but as Marlow confesses, "What else could I do but write detective stories?" Michael Gambon superbly plays both the teller of the tale and its main character, and Dennis Potter's ambitious script creates two separate but equally compelling worlds that cross over in unique and delightfully unexpected ways. The familiar music, a medley of 1930s and '40s standards, provides a poignant counterpoint to Marlow's grim reality, and the desperate acts of his characters. One caveat—besides being just a bit too long, the series is definitely not for younger viewers.

GREAT MOMENTS: The first hospital fantasy sequence, delightfully staged to "Dem Bones" in "Skin"; Marlow's verbal sparring with his psychiatrist in "Lovely Days"; the evangelicals' bedside performance of "Accentuate the Positive" in "Clues."

FAST-FORWARD: Philip's childhood flashbacks cause the narrative to drag in spots, particularly in the latter episodes.

EXTRAS: The documentary *Dennis Potter: Under My Skin*; commentaries by Michael Gambon and director Jon Amiel; featurettes.

Six Feet Under (2001–2005)

Season 1 (13 episodes on 4 discs): ★ ★ ★ ★ ★
Season 2 (13 episodes on 5 discs): ★ ★ ★ ★ ½
Season 3 (13 episodes on 5 discs): ★ ★ ★ ★
Season 4 (12 episodes on 5 discs): ★ ★ ★ ★
Season 5 (12 episodes on 5 discs): ★ ★ ★ ★

HBO Home Video

Video: Full-Frame (Seasons 1 & 2); Anamorphic Widescreen (Seasons 3–5); Audio: Dolby Digital 5.1

Oscar-winning screenwriter Alan Ball (*American Beauty*) created a memorably dysfunctional family of funeral-home proprietors in this critically acclaimed HBO series which blended black comedy, biting satire, and domestic drama in its exploration of life in the face of death.

When Nathaniel Fisher is killed in a hearse accident on Christmas Eve, the four surviving Fishers' lives change drastically. The series follows Nate's return to the family business after years of avoidance, the younger, gay brother David's gradual process of coming out, youngest sister Claire's artistic exploration, and mother Ruth's evolution from repressed housewife to free spirit. An impressive supporting cast is led by Rachel Griffiths, Michael St. Patrick, Lili Taylor, Jeremy Sisto, and Joanna Cassidy.

S

Picture quality is good but unexceptional. A disturbing amount of grain and edge enhancement is evident in many scenes, especially in those that are darkly lit (and since this is a show about a funeral home, there are a lot). The later seasons, shot in HD, had more impressive transfers.

GREAT MOMENTS: Season 1: Nate's meltdown at his father's funeral in the pilot episode; Claire's musical dream sequence in "The Foot"; Claire and Ruth being stuck with a sappy mother and daughter from hell, and David coming out to Nate and Brenda, in "An Open Book"; Season 2: Ruth joins a self-actualization cult in "The Plan"; the Christmas flashbacks in "It's the Most Wonderful Time of the Year"; David and Claire get high together in "The Last Time"; Season 3: Nate's postmortem trip into alternate universes in "Perfect Circles"; Ruth's wedding to George in "I'm Sorry, I'm Lost"; Season 4: The death by floating blowup dolls in "A Case of Rapture"; David's horrifying abduction in "That's My Dog"; Season 5: The final ten minutes of "Everybody's Waiting."

FAST-FORWARD: This series hasn't turned out a single bad episode.

EXTRAS: As with most HBO sets, there aren't too many goodies, besides a small number of worthwhile commentaries by Alan Ball and a number of the series' other writers and directors, and some excellent deleted scenes from the pilot. The first set contains an excellent documentary on the filming and scoring of the show's unique opening-credits sequence, and the Season 2 box has a morbidly fascinating featurette on the construction of the series' corpses.

Sledge Hammer! (1986–1988)

Season 1 (23 episodes on 4 discs): ★ ★ ★ ★
Season 2 (19 episodes on 4 discs): ★ ★ ★ ½

Anchor Bay
Video: Full-Frame; Audio: Unknown

A delayed-reaction hit, *Sledge Hammer!* found an audience while on the brink of cancellation, which made creator Alan Spencer's decision to kill the entire cast in a nuclear explosion all the more inconvenient when the show was picked up for a second year. This prompted the infamous "Hammer—the Early Years" credit at the start of Season 2, which tickled some fans and had others irate over continuity errors. On some shows I'd sympathize, but in the whacked-out world of Hammer, a nihilistic cop whose relationship with his .44 Magnum can only be described as "complex," such inconsistencies barely register.

Spencer first conceived the character when he was sixteen years old, but his spoof on Clint Eastwood's *Dirty Harry* took eight years to get produced, a result of near-unanimous industry revulsion. The show earned surprisingly strong reviews, but ABC scheduled it opposite every ratings monolith of the late 1980s, from *Dallas* to *The Cosby Show*. An enduring cult of Hammerheads has been spreading the word for nearly two decades, and their efforts have been rewarded with the release of both seasons on DVD.

David Rasche was perfectly cast as Sledge, a lovable lunkhead who flips pancakes with his gun and discourages suicidal high-rise jumpers by shooting at them. With his trademark line "Trust me, I know what I'm doing," Rasche shared the gift for deadpan lunacy associated with Leslie Nielsen in *Police Squad* and the *Naked Gun* films. Anne-Marie Martin was the perfect foil as partner Dori Doreau.

GREAT MOMENTS: Season 1: Hammer goes undercover in the Famous School for Elvis Impersonators in "All Shook Up"; amnesia renders Dori as gun-crazy as Sledge in "Desperately Seeking Dori"; Season 2: Hammer's imaginary conversation with his gun in "They Call Me Mr. Trunk."

FAST-FORWARD: Season 2: The *Robocop* parody "Hammeroid."

EXTRAS: Season 1: The documentary *Go Ahead, Make Me Laugh* features new interviews with Alan Spencer, David Rasche, Anne-Marie Martin, and Harrison Page; unaired pilot episode; original commercials; commentary by Alan Spencer; Season 2: commentaries by Alan Spencer and Anne-Marie Martin; documentary saluting frequent series director Bill Bixby; "Gun Crazy: Memorable Moments with the Cast of *Sledge Hammer!*," featuring interviews with the cast.

Smallville (2001–)

Season 1 (21 episodes on 6 discs): ★ ★ ★
Season 2 (23 episodes on 6 discs): ★ ★ ★ ★ ½
Season 3 (22 episodes on 6 discs): ★ ★ ★ ½
Season 4 (22 episodes on 6 discs): ★ ★ ★
Other Releases: Smallville pilot movie (Canadian): ★ ★ ★

S

Warner Home Video
Video: Anamorphic Widescreen; Audio: Dolby Digital 2.0

Superman received a *Dawson's Creek* makeover courtesy of the WB, with this story of young Clark Kent battling adolescent angst in a small Kansas town. Tom Welling was ideally cast as the superhero-in-training coming to terms with his powers, but the show has maintained a "no flights, no tights" policy since day one, so female fans will have settle for imagining young Kent in red and blue spandex.

While the series often resorted to repetitive storylines featuring "Freak of the Week" guest villains and characters undergoing personality changes from Kryptonite exposure (only to snap back none the wiser by the closing credits), *Smallville* also excelled in forging the paths of Clark Kent and arch-rival Lex Luthor toward their divergent destinies. Back-to-back viewings on DVD also underscore the lack of chemistry between Clark and dream-girl Lana Lang, whose constant haranguing about "secrets and lies" will have some diving for the MUTE button. Actually, Clark and Lex often seem like a more suitable love connection, which adds a kinky vibe to their already complex relationship.

All the DVD sets are in anamorphic widescreen, which gives the series a cinematic feel. Prior to the Season 1 set a DVD of the series' first and second episodes in movie form was released in Canada. The extras from this DVD were later used in the Season 1 set.

GREAT MOMENTS: *Smallville*'s season-finale cliffhangers never disappoint, from the tornado in Season 1 to half the cast's being apparently wiped out at the end of the third season. Season 2's "Rosetta" and "Insurgence" rank with the series' best efforts, and Season 3's "Shattered" is a fantastic Lex Luthor showcase. "Rosetta" (Season 2) and "Legacy" (Season 3) feature two of the last television acting appearances of the late Christopher Reeve. Season 3: Michael McKean plays Clark's future boss, Perry White, in "Perry"; Season 4: Erica Durance debuts as Lois Lane in "Crusade"; Clark meets the Flash in "Run"; Chloe discovers Clark's super powers in "Pariah."

FAST-FORWARD: "Reaper" (Season 1), "Redux" (Season 2), "Magnetic" (Season 3), and "Ageless" (Season 4) can be safely skipped.

EXTRAS: Deleted scenes, gag reels, and commentaries on selected episodes in all four seasons; Season 2: "Christopher Reeve: The Man of Steel" featurette; Season 4: The "Being Lois Lane" featurette includes interviews with Noel Neill, Margot Kidder, Dana Delany, and Erica Durance; "Inside the Writers' Room" documentary.

Soap (1977–1981)

The Complete First Season (25 episodes on 3 discs): ★ ★ ★

The Complete Second Season (23 episodes on 3 discs): ★ ★ ★ ★ ★

The Complete Third Season (22 episodes on 3 discs): ★ ★ ★ ★

The Complete Fourth Season (16 episodes on 3 discs): ★ ★ ★

Columbia Tristar Home Video

Video: Full-Frame; Audio: Mono

If you thought Ellen DeGeneres caught hell for coming out on a situation comedy, you should have been around in the dark ages of 1977, when *Soap* cast Billy Crystal as homosexual Jodie Dallas. Before the first episode aired more than 30,000 letters poured into ABC, only nine of which were favorable. Sponsors pulled their support and some network affiliates refused to air the show. Though *Soap* dealt with other hot-button issues as well, most of the stories were too silly to be taken seriously, which is hardly criticism as it was conceived as a parody of daytime dramas.

The dysfunctional families of sisters Jessica Tate (the delightful Katherine Helmond) and Mary Campbell (Cathryn Damon) introduced a slew of memorable characters, particularly ventriloquist Jay Johnson as Chuck (and Bob), sex-crazed Corrine (Diana Canova), and Robert Guillaume's Emmy-winning portrayal of the Tate's butler, Benson, whose departure for a spin-off series after Season 2 was the first sign of diminishing returns.

Columbia Tristar's season sets are a mixed bag. Season 1 offers no extras, syndicated cuts on two shows, plus sequences cut from other episodes over music-rights issues (hence the lower rating for an otherwise classic season); for Season 2, every episode is uncut and the creator interviews are a nice treat for fans. The superior technical quality of the third-season shows proves what can be done to twenty-five-year-old material when a studio spends some money.

GREAT MOMENTS: Season 1: The "Who killed Peter Campbell?" cliffhanger; Season 2: the reluctant romance of Danny and Elaine, and Carol leaving Jodie at the altar.

FAST-FORWARD: Nothing until Season 4.

EXTRAS: Season 2: "Making of" featurette and original series pilot.

The Sonny & Cher Show (1971–1977)

The Ultimate Collection (9 episodes on 3 discs): ★ ★ ★ ★
The Christmas Collection: ★ ★ ★ ★

Respond 2
Video: Full-Frame; Audio: Mono

This will do until the season sets come along, and they'd better for those of us who can't get enough polyester-clad entertainment. *The Sonny & Cher Show* had mass crossover appeal in both its original incarnation and with the follow-up series that debuted after the couple had divorced. The nine episodes here were wisely selected more for their musical offerings than for the comedy skits between.

David Letterman fans who await Paul Schaffer's annual holiday tribute to Cher, with his impersonation of the diva's uniquely nasal cover of "Oh, Holy Night," won't be able to resist buying the actual footage in *The Christmas Collection*, featuring highlights from the duo's three Christmas variety shows.

GREAT MOMENTS: *Ultimate Collection*: The performances of hits "The Way of Love," "A Cowboy's Work Is Never Done," "The Beat Goes On," "Gypsies, Tramps, and Thieves," and "I Got You Babe"; Cher duets with Tina Turner; *Christmas Collection*: "Oh, Holy Night"; '70s icons Shields and Yarnell.

FAST-FORWARD: *Ultimate Collection*: Several comedy spots haven't dated well. *Christmas Collection*: the third rendition of "Jingle Bells," which opens every holiday special.

EXTRAS: *Ultimate Collection*: Commentary from Cher on select segments; interview with producers Allan Blye and Chris Bearde; the 1969 TV pilot episode; original network promos; Sonny & Cher karaoke; a fifteen-track *Greatest Hits* CD; *Christmas Collection*: a video jukebox.

The Sopranos (1999–)

The Complete First Season (13 episodes on 4 discs): ★ ★ ★ ★ ★
The Complete Second Season (13 episodes on 4 discs): ★ ★ ★ ★ ★
The Complete Third Season (13 episodes on 4 discs): ★ ★ ★ ★
The Complete Fourth Season (13 episodes on 4 discs): ★ ★ ★ ½
The Complete Fifth Season (13 episodes on 4 discs): ★ ★ ★ ★ ★

HBO Home Video
Video: Anamorphic Widescreen; Audio: Dolby Digital 5.1

Not much left to be said about *The Sopranos*—since its debut in 1999 the series has been the recipient of every accolade television has to offer, and with good reason. Its dominance of such Emmy categories as Best Writing for a Drama Series (one year, four out of the five nominees were *Sopranos* episodes) has prompted some to wonder if pay cable series can fairly be judged alongside network shows that must conform to FCC content restrictions. But as with some of HBO's other celebrated original series, some may find the quality buried too deeply beneath objectionable levels of profanity, sex, and violence.

GREAT MOMENTS: Tony begins seeing Dr. Melfi in "The Sopranos"; Tony joins Meadow for a university tour—and to kill a guy—in "College"; Season 2: Big Pussy wears a wire to Anthony Jr.'s confirmation party in "D-Girl"; secrets are revealed in "Funhouse"; Season 3: "Army of One" is another strong season climax; Season 4: Ralph faces a crisis in "Whoever Did This"; Tony and Carmela's marriage dissolves in "Whitecaps"; Season 5: Tony meets some ghosts of business deals past in "The Test Dream"; Adriana's betrayal and fate in "Long-Term Parking" and "All Due Respect."

FAST-FORWARD: Season 3: Ralphie's vicious beating of a Bing dancer in "University" is hard to watch.

EXTRAS: Season 1: Peter Bogdanovich interviews series creator David Chase; commentary on Episode 1 by Bogdanovich and Chase; featurettes; Season 2: four director commentaries; two featurettes; documentary "The Real Deal"; Season 3: commentaries by David Chase and actors Steve Buscemi and Michael Imperioli; behind-the-scenes featurette; Season 4: commentaries by cast and writers; Season 5: commentaries by series directors.

South Park (1997–)

The Complete First Season (13 episodes on 3 discs): ★ ★ ★ ★ ½
The Complete Second Season (18 episodes on 3 discs): ★ ★ ★ ½
The Complete Third Season (17 episodes on 3 discs): ★ ★ ★ ★
The Complete Fourth Season (14 episodes on 3 discs): ★ ★ ★ ★ ½
The Complete Fifth Season (14 episodes on 3 discs): ★ ★ ★ ★
The Complete Sixth Season (17 episodes on 3 discs): ★ ★ ★
The Complete Seventh Season (15 episodes on 3 discs): ★ ★ ★
Volumes 1–6 (each: 4 episodes from the first
two seasons on 1 disc): ★ ★ ★ ½
The Chef Experience (3 episodes on 1 disc): ★ ★ ★ ½
Christmas in South Park (3 episodes on 1 disc): ★ ★ ★
Ghouls, Ghosts, and Underpants Gnomes (4 episodes on 1 disc): ★ ★ ★
Insults to Injuries (4 episodes on 1 disc): ★ ★ ★ ★ ½
The Passion of the Jew (3 episodes on 1 disc): ★ ★ ½
Timmy! (4 episodes on 1 disc): ★ ★ ½
Winter Wonderland (4 episodes on 1 disc): ★ ★

S

Warner Home Video (Seasons 1 & 2, Volumes 1–6); Paramount Home Video (Seasons 3–6)

Video: Full-Frame; Audio: Dolby Digital 2.0

South Park revels in everything that's not supposed to be funny in our enlightened society, and thank heaven somebody is still brave enough to do that. This is brilliant television, not just in its use of ingenious original music, and its skewering of hypocrisy and celebrities and ripped-from-the-headlines issues, but also because amidst the profanity, the poop jokes, and the racial, ethnic, and religious humor is a message of "can't we all just get along?" tolerance. Some viewers will never see past the dirty words and cheap animation, but they're not even reading this anymore, so the heck with 'em. Go with the season sets if you haven't already; picture and sound are fine given what they had to work with, and creators Trey Parker and Matt Stone offer insightful commentaries on most episodes.

GREAT MOMENTS: Season 1: "Cartman Gets an Anal Probe"; Cartman meets Sally Struthers in Ethiopia in "Starvin' Marvin"; Season 2: Chef's performance of the title song in "Chef's Chocolate Salty Balls"; Season 4: The astonishing "Cartman Joins NAMBLA"; Season 5: The S-word episode "It Hits the Fan"; Timmy throws down in "Cripple Fight"; the Emmy-nominated (yes, you read that right) "Osama Bin Laden Has Farty Pants"; "Scott Tenorman Must Die" is as twisted as episodic television gets; Season 6: The Tolkien send-up "The Return of the Lord of the Rings to the Two Towers"; Season 7: Jennifer Lopez is savaged in "Fat Butt and Pancake Head."

FAST-FORWARD: Season 2: The Terence and Philip cartoon that ran instead of the cliffhanger resolution about Cartman's father, and the resolution that finally aired in the next episode, "Cartman's Mom Is Still a Dirty Slut"—a rare one-two misfire; Season 6: "Freak Strike" is one of many sixth-season shows that suggest Trey and Matt are running out of steam.

EXTRAS: Episode introductions by Trey Parker and Matt Stone are a part of every *South Park* collection; Season 1: Jay Leno's *South Park* appearance; two Christmas music videos; Season 2: "Chef's Chocolate Salty Balls" music video; "Going Down to South Park" documentary; Seasons 3 to 7: Parker and Stone offer five-to-seven-minute commentaries on each episode.

Space Ghost Coast to Coast (1994–2004)

Volume 1 (16 episodes on 2 discs): ★ ★ ★ ★

Volume 2 (14 episodes on 2 discs): ★ ★ ★ ★

Volume 3 (24 episodes on 2 discs): ★ ★ ½

Warner Home Video

Video: Full-Frame; Audio: Mono

S

Back when the absurdist theater of *Space Ghost Coast to Coast* debuted on the Cartoon Network, the cable channel was as cutting edge as the Faith and Values Network. But with this one surreal oddity, the place where old Hanna-Barbera shows went to die evolved into a haven for late-night programming apparently hatched by people who forgot to take their meds. The genesis of the Adult Swim programming block is apparent in this talk-show parody, in which '60s-era superhero Space Ghost interviews a diverse assortment of celebrities, while being heckled and harassed by his old nemeses Zorak and Moltar. It makes no sense but it holds your interest, especially when people who should have better things to do, like Charlton Heston, astronaut Buzz Aldrin, and the Bee Gees show up in the Ghost Planet monitor. Buyer beware: series "episodes" run just twelve minutes each, so there's not as much program here as you might expect.

GREAT MOMENTS: Volume 1: *Batman* stars Adam West, Lee Meriwether, and Eartha Kitt meet Space Ghost in "Batmantis"; Volume 2: the eclectic lineup of David Byrne and Donny Osmond in "Fire Drill"; Randy Savage voices Space Ghost's rasslin' grandfather in "Piledriver."

FAST-FORWARD: Volume 1: The Bobcat Goldthwait interview.

EXTRAS: Volume 1: Commentaries from creative team; Volume 2: Commentaries on all episodes; additional interview footage with Matt

Groening; the original pitch pilot; Volume 3: Commentaries, "Space Ghost's Mysterious NASA Experience" featurette, interviews with Bob Odenkirk and David Cross.

Space: 1999 (1974–1976)

The Megaset (48 episodes on 16 discs): ★ ★ ★ ½

Individual volumes 1–16 (each: 6 episodes on 2 discs): ★ ★ ★

A&E Home Video

Video: Full-Frame; Audio: Dolby Digital 2.0

S

Action, excitement, intergalactic thrills—*Space: 1999* didn't have any of these. But there was certainly a surplus of *gravitas* on Moonbase Alpha, the ill-fated research colony that was launched into space while still attached to Earth's wayward moon. The crew, led by Commander John Koenig and Dr. Helene Russell (Martin Landau and Barbara Bain), all went about their tasks with deadly earnestness, always serious, often tetchy, steeped in scientific dispassion.

Visually, *Space: 1999* was state-of-the-art sci-fi, but lavish production values and special effects failed to impress America's three networks, which passed on the British import in 1975. Its two seasons aired in syndication, drawing a small but fiercely loyal audience. The DVD *Megaset* restores each episode to its original broadcast length, including footage never aired in the United States.

GREAT MOMENTS: A mysterious omnipotent being offers guidance in "Black Sun"; the outer-space horror story "Dragon's Domain," the laughable monsters in the otherwise terrific "The Bringers of Wonder, Parts 1 & 2."

FAST-FORWARD: "Alpha Child," a rapidly-aging-baby story that every sci-fi fan has seen before; Koenig and Russell regress into primitive cave people in "The Full Circle."

EXTRAS: *Megaset*: Vintage cast and crew interviews, behind-the-scenes featurettes, theatrical trailers for two reworked *Space: 1999* films: *Destination Moonbase Alpha* and *Alien Attack*.

Speed Racer (1966–1968)

DVD Collection Signature Edition (52 episodes on 5 discs): ★ ★ ★ ★

Collector's Edition (11 episodes on 1 disc): ★ ★ ★ ½

Collector's Edition, Volume 2 (12 episodes on 1 disc): ★ ★ ★ ½

Collector's Edition, Volume 3 (13 episodes on 1 disc): ★ ★ ½
Collector's Edition, Volume 4 (8 episodes on 1 disc): ★ ★

Signature Edition: Speed Racer Enterprises; *Collector's Editions*: Artisan Entertainment/Lions Gate

Video: Full-Frame; Audio: Dolby Digital 2.0

In the 1970s, long before anyone knew what "anime" was, a lot of us were watching it courtesy of *Speed Racer*, a Japanese import that had a different feel than other animated shows of the day. So enduring is its cross-generational appeal that MTV was still airing original episodes in the wee hours of the 1990s.

Fans of Speed, Trixie, Pops, and that annoying monkey are advised to splurge on the *DVD Collection Signature Edition*, which features the entire series plus a variety of wonderful extras. Only 1,000 were made, however, so the only place to pick one up now may be eBay. The *Collector's Edition* sets have been criticized for the use of altered and time-compressed opening and closing credits.

GREAT MOMENTS: *Collector's Edition*: The Masked Racer, later known as Racer X, is revealed to be Speed's brother, Rex, in "Challenge of the Masked Racer"; *Collector's Edition, Volume 2*: The debut of Twinkle Banks in "Girl Daredevil."

FAST-FORWARD: *Collector's Edition*: "The Secret Engine" is the only story in the series without an auto race.

EXTRAS: *Signature Edition*: A Volkswagen TV commercial with Speed Racer and friends; a music video of Sponge's cover of the series' memorable theme song; the Mach-5 video; the 1997 *Speed Racer* pilot "The Silver Phantom," which first aired in the USA in 2001.

Spider-Man (1967–1968)

The '67 Collection (52 episodes on 6 discs): ★ ★

Buena Vista Home Entertainment

Video: Full-Frame; Audio: Dolby Digital Mono

If you grew up on this one, brace yourself. Sure, it was cool when you were six years old, but good heavens is it dull now. The shorter episodes on the first two discs still have their moments, as they feature many of the most popular villains from the comic-book series. But the half-hour shows, supervised by Ralph Bakshi, seem to consist almost entirely of endlessly repeated sequences of Spidey web-swinging through New York City, which were used to fill out thirty-minute stories that weren't that great in the first place.

GREAT MOMENTS: "The Menace of Mysterio"; "The Golden Rhino"; "The Origin of Spider-Man."

FAST-FORWARD: "Swing City," "Phantom from the Depths of Time," "The Devious Dr. Dumpty," and too many others to mention.

EXTRAS: None.

Spider-Man: The New Animated Series (2003–)

Season 1 (13 episodes on 2 discs): ★ ★ ★
Volume 1: The Mutant Menace (3 episodes on 1 disc): ★ ★ ½
Volume 2: High-Voltage Villains (3 episodes on 1 disc): ★ ★ ½
Volume 3: The Ultimate Face-Off (3 episodes on 1 disc): ★ ★ ½
Volume 4: Extreme Threat (3 episodes on 1 disc): ★ ★ ½

Sony Pictures Home Entertainment
Video: Anamorphic Widescreen; Audio: Dolby Digital 5.1

S

Loosely based on the popular *Ultimate Spider-Man* comic-book series, *The New Animated Series* finds Peter Parker back in high school, battling new versions of his familiar foes. Continuity buffs will find much to grumble about, but taken on its own merits this umpteenth Spidey cartoon is a fun addition to the canon. Neil Patrick Harris voices the web-slinger.

GREAT MOMENTS: The new Electro debuts in "The Party"; Silver Sable attacks in "Spider-Man Dis-Abled."

FAST-FORWARD: Nothing.

EXTRAS: Season 1: Commentaries, outtake reel, test footage, and five behind-the-scenes featurettes.

Spin City (1996–2002)

Michael J. Fox—His All-Time Favorites, Volume 1
(11 episodes on 2 discs): ★ ★
Michael J. Fox—His All-Time Favorites, Volume 2
(11 episodes on 2 discs): ★ ★

Universal Home Video
Video: Full-Frame; Audio: Dolby Digital 2.0

It ran for six successful seasons and starred two TV MVPs in Michael J. Fox and Heather Locklear, so why hasn't *Spin City* been released in season sets, rather than "best of" collections that, even if purchased together, don't add up to one season's worth of shows? Odds are that Universal will get it right eventually, so fans would be advised to wait. Besides, with all due respect to Michael J. Fox, any collection that leaves out such classic episodes as "Porn in the USA" and "Dick Clark's Rockin' Make-Out Party '99" doesn't reflect the series at its best.

GREAT MOMENTS: Volume 1: Stuart's air hockey exploits in "Dog Day Afternoon"; Fox's *Family Ties* mom, Meredith Baxter-Birney, guests in the two-part "Family Affair." Volume 2: Supermodel Heidi Klum asks Mike out in "There's Something About Heidi."

FAST-FORWARD: Nothing.

EXTRAS: Episode introductions by Michael J. Fox.

Sports Night (1998–2000)

The Complete Series (45 episodes on 6 discs): ★ ★ ★ ★ ½

S

Buena Vista Home Entertainment

Video: Full-Frame; Audio: Dolby Digital 2.0

Aaron Sorkin is one of the few television writers whose voice is discernible no matter which of his characters is speaking. All the signposts of the erudite style that came to prominence in *The West Wing* were already apparent in *Sports Night*. The series, a behind-the-scenes look at an ESPN-type network, served up issues-oriented plotlines, long snappy conversations delivered during brisk walks down hallways, and the ability of any character to produce at will an obscure historical or literary reference, the kind that any normal human being would have to look up, to illustrate whatever point Sorkin's trying to make.

The rhythms of a standard sitcom don't apply in these forty-five half-hour episodes. There are no punch lines delivered every third beat, which may be why ABC felt the need to slap on a laugh track in the early episodes. Smart viewers didn't need it, but they were scarce during *Sports Night*'s all-too-brief existence. For those who missed the series the first time, here's Felicity Huffman before *Desperate Housewives* and Peter Krause before *Six Feet Under*, in a series that is arguably better than their buzz-generating follow-ups. Kudos to Buena Vista for releasing the full two-season run in one set. In the face of such generosity it may be wrong to complain about the absence of commentaries and other extra features, but they are missed nonetheless.

GREAT MOMENTS: Jeremy is reluctant to cover a hunting story in "The Hungry and the Hunted"; the spirit of Thespis, the Greek god of Theater, haunts *Sports Night* in "Thespis"; *West Wing* star Janel Moloney delivers her first Aaron Sorkin dialogue in "The Six Southern Gentlemen of Tennessee"; costar Robert Guillaume's stroke is written into the series in "Eli's Coming"; Casey accurately predicts the teams that compete in the 2000 World Series in "La Forza Del Destino."

FAST-FORWARD: Nothing.

EXTRAS: None.

Stargate: Atlantis (2004–)

Season 1 (20 episodes on 5 discs): ★ ★ ½
Rising (Pilot Episode): ★ ★ ½

S

MGM Home Video
Video: Anamorphic Widescreen; Audio: Dolby Digital 5.1

A new Stargate crew investigates a secret Antarctica base and strange new aliens from the Pegasus galaxy in this spin-off from *Stargate SG-1.* The idea was to draw new viewers into the *Stargate* universe by giving them a fresh starting point, but this Sci-Fi Channel series wound up preaching only to the converted.

GREAT MOMENTS: The comic outing "Letters from Pegasus."

FAST-FORWARD: The *Logan's Run*–inspired "Childhood's End."

EXTRAS: *Rising*: Commentary by director Martin Wood and actor Joe Flanigan; "Preview to Atlantis" featurette.

Stargate SG-1 (1997–)

Season 1 (21 episodes on 5 discs): ★ ★ ★
Season 2 (22 episodes on 5 discs): ★ ★ ½
Season 3 (22 episodes on 5 discs): ★ ★ ★ ½
Season 4 (22 episodes on 5 discs): ★ ★ ★
Season 5 (22 episodes on 5 discs): ★ ★ ★
Season 6 (22 episodes on 5 discs): ★ ★ ★
Season 7 (22 episodes on 5 discs): ★ ★ ½

Season 8 (22 episodes on 5 discs): ★ ★

Seasons 1–3 also released in five individual volumes per season, each containing three episodes.

MGM Grand Home Video

Video: Anamorphic Widescreen; Audio: Dolby Digital 2.0 (Season 1); Dolby Digital 5.1 (Seasons 2–8)

At nine years and counting, Showtime's *Stargate SG-1* is the longest-running sci-fi series in the history of American television. Obviously star Richard Dean Anderson and company are doing something right, though the show has gone largely unnoticed by the entertainment media, even after reruns reached a wider audience in syndication on the FOX network. But *Stargate* is huge in Europe and Australia, where perhaps they're more tolerant of recycled *Star Trek* clichés. To be fair, fans have heard that accusation before and don't buy it. They also point out that their fictional universe has remained comparatively free of the wormhole-sized canon inconsistencies of latter-day *Trek*. That's a debate to be settled in convention lines. What is clear is that the *Stargate* DVDs easily rate the edge over most sci-fi programs, with some season sets offering a commentary track on every episode.

S

GREAT MOMENTS: Season 1: The SG-1 crew tries to find a doctor who went through the Stargate in 1945 in "The Torment of Tantalus"; Season 2: The American Indians on an alien planet in "Spirits"; Season 3: The alternate-reality tale "Point of View"; Season 4: SG-1 team members acquire superpowers at a dangerous price in "Upgrades"; Season 5: Daniel's life is threatened by radiation poisoning in "Meridian"; Season 6: Jack is suspected in an assassination attempt on Senator Kinsey in "Smoke and Mirrors"; Season 7: Daniel returns in "Fallen"; a Goa'uld ambush leads to tragedy in "Heroes, Part 2"; Season 8: The Atlantis expedition in "Prometheus Unbound."

FAST-FORWARD: Season 1: "Emancipation."

EXTRAS: Seasons 1 and 2: Behind-the-scenes featurettes and character profiles; Season 3: "Secret File to the SGC" featurettes; Seasons 4–8 contain commentaries on every episode; Season 4: Secret File featurettes; "Stargate SG-1: Timeline to the Future—Legacy of the Gate" featurette; Season 5: Three video diaries (Amanda Tapping, Christopher Judge, and Michael Shanks); featurettes "Inside the Tomb" and "Dr. Daniel Jackson—A Tribute"; Season 6: Twelve "Directors Series" episode featurettes; Season 7: "Beyond the Gate" featurette; "Directors Series" featurettes; Season 8: Behind-the-scenes featurettes.

Star Trek (1966–1969)

Season 1 (29 episodes on 8 discs): ★ ★ ★ ★ ★
Season 2 (26 episodes on 7 discs): ★ ★ ★ ★ ★
Season 3 (25 episodes on 7 discs): ★ ★ ★ ★
Volumes 1–40 (2 episodes on 1 disc each): ★ ★ ★

Paramount Home Video
Video: Full-Frame; Audio: Dolby Digital 5.1

Not many television shows have had more impact on American popular culture than *Star Trek*. For all the grief that Trekkies take over their passionate devotion and their ability to quote the star-dates of episodes the way other people recall the birthdays of their children, the family of Trek fans is hardly limited to a small costume-wearing cult. This is a series that has added expressions to our language and inspired untold thousands of children to pursue careers in science and exploration. You don't see NASA naming space shuttles after the *Jupiter 2*.

The original *Star Trek* series debuted on DVD in forty individual volumes of two episodes each. It has since been repackaged into season sets, much to the consternation of those fans who had already bought the entire run. Having established a price point over $100 on the *Next Generation* sets released years earlier, Paramount wasn't about to offer the series that started it all for any less, even if the market had changed. Instead, the company has attempted to justify the higher price with hard-shell packaging in the colors of the *Enterprise* crew uniforms, and enough extras to fill two separate discs. Given the desire of many *Trek* fans to know everything about the show down to the smallest minutiae, there's little doubt the behind-the-scenes featurettes and interviews will bring them back to the store.

Audio and video quality have been cleaned up as much as possible, but there are still some problems with the special-effects shots, a result of the original film's having been degraded after being processed multiple times to achieve the visual effect.

GREAT MOMENTS: Season 1: Kirk matches wits with Khan Noonian Singh (Ricardo Montalban) in "The Space Seed"; the tragic fate of Edith Keeler (Joan Collins) in "The City on the Edge of Forever"; Season 2: The *pon farr* turns Spock into one randy Vulcan in "Amok Time"; the introduction of the mirror universe in "Mirror, Mirror"; the comic adventure "The Trouble with Tribbles"; Season 3: A classic *Enterprise*-versus-Klingons battle in "The Day of the Dove."

FAST-FORWARD: Season 3: "Spock's Brain" was the episode of *Trek* held in lowest regard until *Voyager* released "Threshold."

EXTRAS: Each season set offers several documentaries of varying length. Highlights include "The Birth of a Timeless Legacy" (Season 1) and "*Star Trek*'s Impact" (Season 3); the "Life Beyond *Trek*" featurettes—one per set—contain profiles of stars William Shatner, Leonard Nimoy, and Walter Koenig.

Star Trek: Deep Space Nine (1993–1999)

Season 1 (20 episodes on 6 discs): ★ ★ ½
Season 2 (26 episodes on 7 discs): ★ ★ ★
Season 3 (26 episodes on 7 discs): ★ ★ ★ ½
Season 4 (26 episodes on 7 discs): ★ ★ ★ ½
Season 5 (26 episodes on 7 discs): ★ ★ ★ ★
Season 6 (26 episodes on 7 discs): ★ ★ ★ ★ ½
Season 7 (26 episodes on 7 discs): ★ ★ ★ ★
The Complete Series: ★ ★ ★ ½

Paramount Home Video
Video: Full-Frame; Audio: Dolby Digital 5.1

S

A hierarchy has formed within the egalitarian ranks of *Star Trek* fandom. There are now self-described "discriminating" fans who celebrate *Deep Space Nine* as not only superior to other *Trek* incarnations, but the only *Trek* series that can accurately be described as true science-fiction. (The others are relegated to the less-impressive "science-fantasy" status, with *Lost in Space* and *Doctor Who.*)

Most of this *DS9* love emerged with Season 3, when the Dominion came into its own and Sisko was put in command of his own starship, the *Defiant.* These story threads would take precedence through the remainder of the series, by which time other fans, bored with the more stagnant stories of the earlier seasons, had given up.

GREAT MOMENTS: Season 1: A nasty reptile arrives from the Gamma Quadrant in "Captive Pursuit"; sexy Klingon sisters B'Etor and Lursa turn up in "Past Prologue"; Season 2: John Glover guests as a symbiont host who attacks Dax in "Invasive Procedures"; Odo solves a mystery in the fun flashback tale "Necessary Evil"; Season 3: Riker from *Star Trek: The Next Generation* appears in "Defiant"; the parallel-universe adventure "Through the Looking Glass"; Season 4: Worf begins his tour of duty on *DS9* in "Way of the Warrior"; Sisko is presumed dead, but Jake won't believe it, in "The Visitor"; Season 5: The extraordinary "Trials and Tribble-ations" puts Sisko and Dax aboard Captain Kirk's *Enterprise*; Season 6: Worf and Dax marry in "You Are

Cordially Invited . . ."; Season 7: The baseball game in "Take Me Out to the Holosuite."

FAST-FORWARD: Season 1: The crew members are turned into board-game pieces in "Move Along Home"; Season 2: Bashir and O'Brien play racquetball in "Rivals"; Season 3: Quark's mother shows up in "Family Business"; Season 6: "Resurrection" is the worst of the mirror-universe stories.

EXTRAS: Each season set contains five to seven featurettes exploring various aspects of the series. Among the highlights: the behind-the-scenes look at how "Trials and Tribble-ations" was put together in the Season 5 set, and the wrap-party footage included with Season 7.

Star Trek: Enterprise (2001–2005)

Season 1 (26 episodes on 7 discs): ★ ★ ★ ★
Season 2 (25 episodes on 7 discs): ★ ★ ★ ½
Season 3 (24 episodes on 7 discs): ★ ★ ★ ½
Season 4 (22 episodes on 6 discs): ★ ★ ★ ★ ★

S

Paramount Home Video
Video: Anamorphic Widescreen; Audio: Dolby Digital 5.1

It was a sobering thought: when *Enterprise* wrapped its four-year run in 2005, fans had to contend with the prospect of a future without new *Star Trek* stories for the first time in eighteen years. And it wasn't just Trekkies mourning the loss; even in its most disappointing episodes, the various incarnations offered an optimistic view of humankind, and held out hope that despite all of our global troubles, tomorrow would be better than today. Television is a better place when *Star Trek* is a part of it, and many of us are counting the days until its return.

That said, *Enterprise* took longer than it should have to realize its potential, and as a result became the first *Trek* series to fall short of seven seasons since Kirk was in the captain's chair. Hindsight reveals that the first two seasons aren't as bad as they're remembered, and the Xindi story arc in Season 3 might have been overrated. The final season represents not just *Enterprise* but *Star Trek* at its very best, but it was too little, too late.

GREAT MOMENTS: Season 1: The first of Jeffrey Combs's appearances as Shran in "The Andorian Incident"; Archer faces the kind of civilization-altering decision for which the Prime Directive was invented, in "Dear Doctor"; Season 2: Vulcans land on Earth in the 1950s in "Carbon Creek"; Archer takes a break from universal diplomacy to care for his sick dog in "A Night in Sickbay";

Season 3: The Old West adventure "North Star"; Trip is cloned in "Similitude"; Season 4: The Augments story arc, featuring Brent Spiner as Dr. Arik Soong; *Enterprise* crosses into *Trek*'s mirror universe in "In a Mirror, Darkly, Parts 1 & 2."

FAST-FORWARD: Season 1: Trip gets pregnant in the silly "Unexpected"; Season 3: A telepath develops a fatal attraction for Hoshi in "Exile"; Season 4: The awful, awful, awful series finale, "These Are the Voyages."

EXTRAS: As with previous *Trek* season sets, fans will find the full panoply of special features—documentaries, cast interviews, commentaries, and outtakes, all of which help reduce the sting of the asking price.

Star Trek: The Next Generation (1987–1994)

Season 1 (26 episodes on 7 discs): ★ ★ ★ ★
Season 2 (22 episodes on 6 discs): ★ ★ ★ ★
Season 3 (26 episodes on 7 discs): ★ ★ ★ ★ ★
Season 4 (26 episodes on 7 discs): ★ ★ ★ ★ ★
Season 5 (26 episodes on 7 discs): ★ ★ ★ ★ ½
Season 6 (26 episodes on 7 discs): ★ ★ ★ ★ ★
Season 7 (26 episodes on 7 discs): ★ ★ ★ ½
The Jean-Luc Picard Collection (7 episodes on 2 discs): ★ ★ ★ ★

Paramount Home Video
Video: Full-Frame; Audio: Dolby Digital 5.1

Some were thrilled. Others were horrified. Most were horrified and then thrilled. In the two decades since the original *Star Trek* had been cancelled, the series had become revered by its original fan base and embraced by subsequent generations. How could any attempt to revive the franchise hope to compete with the ghosts of Kirk, Spock, and McCoy? Thankfully, some would say miraculously, they got it right. The success of *Star Trek: The Next Generation* launched the greatest second act in television history, eventually encompassing a canon of more than 700 shows.

This series was Paramount's first foray into season sets of *Star Trek* material, in which they established the precedent of high-quality releases at an equally high price. All seven seasons were released during 2002, setting back Trekkies more than 800 bucks. Resistance . . . is futile. But for those who waited, prices on season sets from every *Trek* incarnation were cut in half in 2006.

GREAT MOMENTS: Season 2: Data's battle for android rights in "The Measure of a Man"; Season 4: Picard is abducted by the Borg in "The Best of Both Worlds"; Stephen Hawking appears in "Descent, Part 1"; the *Enterprise* crew takes on the most delicate of missions in "First Contact"; Season 5: Mr. Spock appears in "Unification, Part 2"; Season 6: Picard's battle of wills against a Cardassian inquisitor in "Chain of Command, Part II" makes a mockery of the Emmy Awards for overlooking Patrick Stewart's performance; Season 7: The awesome series finale "All Good Things."

FAST-FORWARD: Sadly, this wonderful series opened with a dreadful pilot, "Encounter at Farpoint" (Season 1); the Wesley-centric "The Dauphin" (Season 2). And just about every other Wesley-oriented show.

EXTRAS: Each season set includes several featurettes ("Mission Overview," "Departmental Briefing") with cast and crew interviews. Other special features include the tribute to Gene Roddenberry in the Season 5 set; and the Season 3 documentary that explains what happened to Dr. Crusher, and how Rosalind Shays from *L.A. Law* turned up in sickbay.

S

Star Trek: Voyager (1995–2001)

Season 1 (16 episodes on 5 discs): ★ ★ ★ ★ ½
Season 2 (26 episodes on 7 discs): ★ ★ ★ ★ ½
Season 3 (26 episodes on 7 discs): ★ ★ ★ ★
Season 4 (26 episodes on 7 discs): ★ ★ ★ ★ ★
Season 5 (26 episodes on 7 discs): ★ ★ ★ ★ ½
Season 6 (26 episodes on 7 discs): ★ ★ ★ ★
Season 7 (26 episodes on 7 discs): ★ ★ ★
Seasons 1–5: ★ ★ ★ ★
The Complete Series: ★ ★ ★ ★

Paramount Home Video
Video: Full-Frame; Audio: Dolby Digital 5.1

Voyager has, for too long, been the favorite dumping ground of hardcore Trekkers, at least until *Enterprise* came along. But viewed in retrospect the series emerges as a solid and frequently inspired addition to the canon.

No one's arguing that Neelix could work your last nerve, and that there was too much focus on Seven of Nine after Jeri Ryan spiked the ratings in Season 4. But between getting lost in the Alpha Quadrant and finding their way home seven years later, Captain Janeway and her crew turned out as many memorable episodes as *The Next Generation* and *Deep Space Nine*. In fact, its first episode is the best debut outing for a *Trek* series ever, and that includes the original series.

The *Seasons 1–5* and *Complete Series* collections shave a few dollars off purchasing each season individually, but you may still have to take out a bank loan before writing that check. As with every *Trek* DVD set, Paramount sweetens the *Voyager* collections with all the extra features that fans have come to expect.

GREAT MOMENTS: Season 1: The pilot episode, "Caretaker," is a thrilling movie-length adventure that establishes the series' lost-in-space premise; a wormhole raises crew hopes of getting home in "Eye of the Needle"; Season 2: Q meets Janeway in "Death Wish"; Tuvok and Neelix are merged into one being in "Tuvix," one of the series' most intriguing stories; Season 3: George Takei reprises his role as Captain Sulu in "Flashback"; Season 4: Seven of Nine beams aboard in "Scorpion, Part 2"; the two-part "Year of Hell"; Season 5: "Timeless," an all-too-rare memorable Harry Kim episode; the Doctor develops feelings for Seven in "Someone to Watch Over Me"; Season 6: "Fair Haven," along with Paris's Captain Proton adventures, is the best holodeck-themed show; Season 7: Dwight Schultz appears as his *Next Generation* character, Reg Barkley, offers *Voyager* a way home at last in "Inside Man."

FAST-FORWARD: Season 2: A poorly timed Kes romance in "Elogium"; "Threshold" has been accurately described as the worst episode from any *Star Trek* franchise.

EXTRAS: Each season features a full array of behind-the-scenes documentaries, cast interviews, and featurettes. One highlight is footage of Genevieve Bujold, the first actress cast as Janeway, in the Season 1 set.

S

Starsky & Hutch (1975–1979)

The Complete First Season (23 episodes on 5 discs): ★ ★ ★ ★

The Complete Second Season (25 episodes on 5 discs): ★ ★ ★ ½

The Complete Third Season (23 episodes on 5 discs): ★ ★ ★

Columbia Tristar Home Video

Video: Full-Frame; Audio: Dolby Digital 2.0

They weren't TV's first buddy cops, and heaven knows they won't be the last, but Detectives Dave Starsky and Ken Hutchinson set the standard for this familiar formula, as two cops so close there were probably a few "Don't ask, don't tell" rumors floating around the precinct. *Starsky & Hutch* offered a reliable mix of laughs, drama, action, and tire-screeching car chases in that famous Gran Torino; the chemistry of stars Paul Michael Glaser and David Soul carried the bad episodes, and the good shows speak for themselves. All this, and Huggy Bear, too. The DVD quality is what you'd expect for late-'70s TV, no better, no worse.

GREAT MOMENTS: Season 1: The detectives deal with an armored-car heist gone awry in "The Hostages"; Season 2: Lynda Carter appears as a Las Vegas showgirl targeted for murder in "The Las Vegas Strangler, Parts 1 & 2"; the heartbreaking "Starsky's Lady"; Season 3: Hutch is accused of murdering his ex-wife in "Hutchinson: Murder One."

FAST-FORWARD: Season 2: Starsky and Hutch go undercover as cruise-ship entertainment directors Hack and Zack, in the two-part *Love Boat*–style "Murder at Sea"; the racially insensitive (even for the 1970s) "Huggy Bear and the Turkey."

EXTRAS: Season 1: Featurettes "It's Harder than It Looks," "The Third Star," "Behind the Badge," and "The Making of *Starsky & Hutch*, the Movie."

Strangers with Candy (1999–2002)

Season 1 (10 episodes on 2 discs): ★
Season 2 (10 episodes on 2 discs): ★
Season 3 (10 episodes on 2 discs): ★

S

Paramount Home Video
Video: Full-Frame; Audio: Dolby Digital 2.0

Comedy, like beauty, dwells in the eye of the beholder, which is why some will celebrate *Strangers with Candy* as a raunchy masterpiece (you know who you are), and others will just be revolted. Amy Sedaris plays forty-six-year-old "boozer, user, and loser" Jerri Blank, who embarks on a new life as a high school freshman.

GREAT MOMENTS: Season 3: Winona Ryder appears in "The Last Temptation of Blank."

FAST-FORWARD: For those who find John Waters–style comedy entertaining, none of it. Everyone else won't be buying these anyway.

EXTRAS: Season 1: Commentaries by Sedaris and costar Stephen Colbert; the original, unaired pilot; Season 2: Commentaries; a Museum of Television and Radio interview with the cast and creators; Season 3: Blooper reel; dance-sequence compilation.

Studio One (1948–1958)

Boxed Set (6 episodes on 3 discs): ★ ★ ★ ½

Sentence of Death/The Night America Trembled: ★ ★ ½

The Defender 1 & 2: ★ ★ ½

The Laughmaker/Square Pegs: ★ ★ ½

Goldhil Media

Video: Full-Frame; Audio: Mono

Ancient television that survives only in kinescope rarely cracks the home-video market, and when it does it's usually in cheap public-domain sets with broadcast quality comparable to what your grandparents enjoyed on their Sylvania Halo Light consoles. So what a treat to see the effort exerted by Goldhil on *Studio One*, a fifty-year-old dramatic anthology that boasted such writers and directors as Rod Serling, Gore Vidal, Sidney Lumet, and John Frankenheimer. The kinescopes have been cleaned up and digitally re-mastered, and though the results are still inferior to '50s-era TV that survives on videotape, the shows look better than they have in decades.

The boxed set contains all the episodes released in separate volumes listed above, which contain as-they-happened live performances from such luminaries as James Dean, Steve McQueen, William Shatner, Jackie Gleason, and Warren Beatty. Preserved with the episodes are original show bumpers and the Westinghouse commercials starring Betty Furness, one of the era's busiest and most beloved TV personalities.

GREAT MOMENTS: *Honeymooners* costars Jackie Gleason and Art Carney show off their dramatic chops in "The Laughmaker"; "The Night America Trembled," a look at the panic caused by Orson Welles's *War of the Worlds* broadcast, stars Warren Beatty, Edward Asner, and James Coburn, with television news pioneer Edward R. Murrow serving as narrator; a pre–*Rebel Without a Cause* James Dean stars in "Sentence of Death."

FAST-FORWARD: Nothing.

EXTRAS: Boxed set: A ten-minute documentary isn't much for a series that ran ten years.

The Super Friends (1973–1980)

Challenge of the Super Friends (16 episodes on 4 discs): ★ ★ ★ ½

The All-New Super Friends Hour (16 episodes on 2 discs): ★ ★ ★ ½

Warner Home Video

Video: Full-Frame; Audio: Dolby Digital 2.0

Meanwhile, at the Hall of Justice . . .

If you're a male, age thirty-five to forty-five, then the Super Friends were as much a part of your childhood as Pac-Man and sugar-coated cereal. Superman, Batman and Robin, Wonder Woman, and Aquaman join forces to battle various super-villains, and put up with annoying sidekicks and their cape-wearing pets. The two seasons released thus far on DVD feature our heroes squaring off against Lex Luthor's Legion of Doom (*All New* is just Season 2 of *Challenge*), and being joined by the Wonder Twins instead of Wendy, Marvin, and Wonder Dog. Both sets offer more extras than many of Warners' higher-profile primetime series sets. Among the highlights—baby-boomer celebrities reflecting on Saturday mornings in front of the TV.

S

GREAT MOMENTS: C'mon, it's *Super Friends*. Live it. Love it. All of it.

FAST-FORWARD: Gleek.

EXTRAS: *Challenge*: "Saturday, Sleeping Bags, and Super Friends" featurette; *All-New Super Friends*: Commentaries; "Pajama-Rama Super Friends Retrospective" and "The Wonderful World of the Wonder Twins" featurettes.

Superman: The Animated Series (1996–2000)

Volume 1 (18 episodes on 2 discs): ★ ★ ★

The Last Son of Krypton (3 episodes on 1 disc): ★ ★ ★

A Little Piece of Home (4 episodes on 1 disc): ★ ★ ★

Warner Home Video

Video: Full-Frame; Audio: Dolby Digital 2.0

While *Superman* was not as popular or creatively satisfying as their animated take on Batman, producers Bruce Timm and Paul Dini offer a version of the Man of Steel that honors the traditions of its many predecessors. They also found some terrific voice talent to tell the stories, from Tim Daly as Big Blue and Dana Delany as Lois Lane to married actors Mike Farrell and Shelley Fabares as Jonathan and Martha Kent.

GREAT MOMENTS: Volume 1: Superman races the Flash in "Speed Demons"; *The Last Son of Krypton*: The retelling of the origin.

FAST-FORWARD: Nothing.

EXTRAS: Volume 1: Commentaries by producers Bruce Timm, Paul Dini, and Alan Burnett, directors Dan Riba and Curt Geda, and art director Glen Murakami; featurettes "Superman: Learning to Fly" and "Building the Mythology: *Superman*'s Supporting Cast"; pop-up trivia feature on the episode "A Little Piece of Home."

Survivor (2000–)

Survivor 1 (13 episodes on 5 discs): ★ ★ ★ ½

Survivor II: The Australian Outback (15 episodes on 6 discs): ★ ★ ★ ★

Survivor All-Stars (18 episodes on 7 discs): ★ ★ ★ ½

Survivor: Pearl Islands (15 episodes on 5 discs): ★ ★ ★ ½

Season 1: The Greatest and Most Outrageous Moments: ★ ★

Season 2: The Greatest and Most Outrageous Moments: ★ ★

Paramount Home Video

Video: Full-Frame; Audio: Dolby Digital Surround

Reality shows thrive on unscripted drama, so it's intriguing to observe how a show like *Survivor* sells on DVD, given that all of its secrets have long been revealed. No effort was made to hide the results of each season-long elimination tournament from potential buyers who missed the original broadcasts—the box art for Season 1 lists Richard Hatch as the winner of the $1 million prize.

Bereft of their most compelling revelations—the twists in the game hatched by creator Mark Burnett, the formation of alliances, the winners of tribal and individual challenges, the elimination order—*Survivor*'s season sets attempt to compensate with a wealth of additional materials that enrich the viewing experience, including bonus footage, commentaries, and background features.

The presentation of nudity is an interesting issue; censorship is understandable when episodes must conform to broadcast standards, but there's no need for such restrictions on home video. Richard Hatch's tax-evading fat ass is still blurred in Season 1 episodes but is revealed in all its glory in the "Outrageous Moments" features, which are available with the season sets or as a separate purchase.

GREAT MOMENTS: Season 1: Sue's "Snake and Rat" speech at Tribal Council; Season 2: Rodger's reluctant cliff dive, Jerri's scheming, Elisabeth's cuteness, Colby's studliness, and the shocking turn of events that put Tina in the final two over the more beatable Keith Famie. *All-Stars*: Boston Rob securing a victory for his girlfriend, Amber, by convincing a gullible Lex to keep her around; *Pearl Islands*: The wonder that is Rupert Boneham, Osten getting trashed at Tribal Council, and Fairplay's "dead grandmother" story.

FAST-FORWARD: Season 1: Richard Hatch's nakedness; *All-Stars*: Sue quitting, and Jerri's meltdown at the reunion.

EXTRAS: Season 1: Commentaries by host Jeff Probst, Richard Hatch, Gervase Peterson, and Rudy Boesch; "Most Outrageous Moments" documentary, which includes all exit interviews and voting confessions; the Survivors' Top Ten List appearance on *The Late Show with David Letterman*; featurettes; Season 2: Commentaries by Probst, Colby, Alicia, Amber, Kimmi, Mike, Rodger, and Keith; "Most Outrageous Moments" documentary; four featurettes; reunion special; *All-Stars*: Four featurettes, bonus footage, commentaries from Rob C., Jenna Morasca, Jenna Lewis, Rudy, Tina, Lex, Alicia, Kathy, Shii Ann, Rob M., Amber, and Rupert; two reunion shows; *Pearl Islands*: Bonus footage and commentaries from Rupert, Sandra, Christa, Fairplay, Ryan, Burton, and Andrew.

S

SWAT (1975–1976)

The Complete First Season (13 episodes on 3 discs): ★ ★ ★ ★

See also: *The Greatest '70s Cop Shows*

Columbia Tristar Home Video

Video: Full-Frame; Audio: Dolby Digital 2.0

How could any show featuring characters with such cool names as Hondo, Street, Deacon, and Luca, who raced into action to one of the most pulse-pounding theme songs ever, get bounced from the schedule after just one season? It was violence that did in *SWAT*; never mind that the series was about the LAPD's Special Weapons and Tactics unit, which is called in on situations that the regular police can't handle. A little gunfire comes with the territory, but when the team blasted through urban locales with enough firepower to start a revolution, the ABC network lost its nerve in the face of a worried press and a few sensitive but vocal viewers.

The DVD set brings back great memories for everyone except perhaps cast members Steve Forrest and Mark Shera, who should still be bitter about what might have been. The episodes look and sound great for disco-era TV, but the set does not include the *SWAT* pilot, originally aired as a two-hour spin-off from *The Rookies*.

GREAT MOMENTS: The race-against-time climax, and the early-career appearance of Annette O'Toole in "The Killing Ground"; three of the most gorgeous blondes of the 1970s—Farrah Fawcett, Loni Anderson, and Lara Parker—all appear in "The Steel-Plated Security Blanket"; the all-criminal SWAT team in "Sole Survivor."

FAST-FORWARD: Nothing.

EXTRAS: None.

Sweet Valley High (1994–1997)

The Complete First Season (22 episodes on 3 discs): ★ ★ ★

Buena Vista Home Entertainment

Video: Full-Frame; Audio: Dolby Digital 5.1

What do you get if you mix *Saved by the Bell, The Patty Duke Show,* and *Archie* comics? Probably something like this adaptation of Francine Pascal's popular series of books about beautiful twins Elizabeth and Jessica Wakefield. *Sweet Valley High* isn't as saccharine as the name might suggest, but the sunny California setting and the series' focus on the pretty and popular kids results in a largely angst-free look at adolescence, which makes for a refreshing change from most contemporary high school shows.

GREAT MOMENTS: Jessica tries to steal Elizabeth's college boyfriend in "Dangerous Love"; Todd leaves Sweet Valley in "Say Goodbye."

FAST-FORWARD: It's all sweet.

EXTRAS: None.

T

Tabitha (1977)

The Complete Series (13 episodes on 2 discs): ★ ★

Columbia Tristar Home Video

Video: Full-Frame; Audio: Dolby Digital 2.0

Nobody really needs this short-lived sequel to *Bewitched,* cannily released as an impulse buy in conjunction with the first season of the original series. And yet . . . Lisa Hartman is awfully cute as the all-grown-up Tabitha Stephens, and she and Robert Urich make a photogenic couple. But Aunt Minerva pales in the mischievous mentor role next to Endora, and who knew Adam would turn out to be such a stiff? *Bewitched* completists, '70s-nostalgia lovers, and relatives of cast members will enjoy these twelve episodes, plus the original pilot starring Liberty Williams as Tabitha. The rest of you, move on.

GREAT MOMENTS: Dr. Bombay makes a house call in "Tabitha's Weighty Problem"; Mr. and Mrs Kravitz visit Tabitha In "Arrival of Nancy."

FAST-FORWARD: Minerva's in love (who cares?) in "Minerva Goes Straight."

EXTRAS: None.

Taxi (1978–1983)

The Complete First Season (22 episodes on 3 discs): ★ ★ ★ ★
The Complete Second Season (24 episodes on 4 discs): ★ ★ ★ ★ ★
The Complete Third Season (20 episodes on 4 discs): ★ ★ ★ ★ ½

Paramount Home Video
Video: Full-Frame; Audio: Dolby Digital Mono

Taxi was the last great sitcom of the 1970s, but though it's now remembered as a contemporary of such distinguished peers as *The Mary Tyler Moore Show*, *The Bob Newhart Show*, and *M*A*S*H*, it was never as popular in its original run. The series was cancelled by ABC after just three seasons, and though NBC picked it up for two more years it never found the audience it deserved. None of which matters now, as the show is just as entertaining today as it was nearly thirty years ago.

An amazing ensemble cast (Judd Hirsch, Danny DeVito, Tony Danza, Marilu Henner, Jeff Conaway, Christopher Lloyd, and Andy Kaufman) elevated stories both bitter and sweet at the Sunshine Cab Company. You never knew what you were going to get from week to week; *Taxi* strayed frequently from its standard workplace-comedy roots into flashback stories, flights of fancy, and surrealism, especially when producers allowed Kaufman to explore different sides of the eccentric foreign mechanic Latka, who, like Chris Lloyd's Reverend Jim, was a wholly unique and wonderful creation.

Though the season sets are disappointing in their lack of extras, the episodes themselves are essential. The second season rates an edge over the first, with the addition of Lloyd and Carol Kane as Simka, and the addition-by-subtraction loss of bland cabbie John Burns.

GREAT MOMENTS: Season 1: The first appearance of Reverend Jim in "Paper Marriage"; the two-parter "Memories of Cab 804," with guest stars Tom Selleck and Mandy Patinkin; Season 2: Reverend Jim's driver's test in "Reverend Jim: Space Odyssey"; Louis and Elaine's date in "Shut It Down, Part 2"; the "Lullaby of Broadway" musical number in "Fantasy Borough, Part 2"; Season 3: "Call of the Mild," a rare episode set far away from the garage; the two-part "On the Job" finds the cabbies looking for other work when Sunshine goes belly-up.

FAST-FORWARD: Season 1: The John Burns–centric episode "Money Troubles."

EXTRAS: None.

Teen Titans (2003–)

The Complete First Season (13 episodes on 2 discs): ★ ★ ½
Volume 1: Divide and Conquer (6 episodes on 1 disc): ★ ★
Volume 2: Switched (7 episodes on 1 disc): ★ ★
Volume 3: Fear Itself (6 episodes on 1 disc): ★ ★

Warner Home Video
Video: Anamorphic Widescreen; Audio: Dolby Digital 2.0

This kiddy-land take on DC Comics' junior crime-fighting squad is too anime-style for those who don't care for that stuff, and not anime enough for fans of the genre. But it was a breakout hit on the Cartoon Network, partly because of the insanely catchy theme song, and partly because the characters are so good that even a second-class cover has its moments.

GREAT MOMENTS: The theme song!; Volume 1: the Raven-centric "Nevermore"; Volume 2: Starfire and Raven switch bodies in "Switched."

FAST-FORWARD: Volume 2: "Car Trouble," featuring the ever-annoying Gizmo.

EXTRAS: Volume 1: Theme-song music video; Volume 2: Interview with theme-song performers Puff Ami Yumi; Volume 3: "Inside Titans Tower" featurette.

T

That Girl (1966–1971)

Season 1 (30 episodes on 4 discs): ★ ★ ★ ½
Volume 1 (9 episodes on 1 disc): ★ ★ ½

Shout! Factory (Season 1); Anchor Bay (Volume 1)
Video: Full-Frame; Audio: Mono

The first *That Girl* release was a set of nine shows that collected milestones in Ann-Marie and Donald's romance, Ann's most bizarre job auditions, and some of the series' memorable guest stars. Fans paid $60 and up on the secondary market after its surprise disappearance from stores, and then felt kinda silly when Season 1 debuted in a far superior package with lots of extras.

GREAT MOMENTS: Season 1: Ann and Donald first meet in the pilot, "Don't Just Do Something, Stand There"; Ann doesn't choose Donald when they appear on a *Dating Game*–style show in "The Mating Game."

FAST-FORWARD: Nothing.

EXTRAS: Season 1: Commentaries by Marlo Thomas and series co-creator Bill Persky; original promos and pilot episode; "That Girl, That Woman: The Creation of *That Girl*" and "*That Girl* in New York" featurettes; Volume 1: None. Oh, Donald!

That '70s Show (1998–2006)

Season 1 (25 episodes on 4 discs): ★ ★ ½

Season 2 (26 episodes on 4 discs): ★ ★ ★

Season 3 (25 episodes on 4 discs): ★ ★ ★

Season 4 (27 episodes on 4 discs): ★ ★ ★ ½

20th Century-Fox

Video: Full-Frame; Audio: Dolby Digital 2.0

As *Happy Days* portrayed the 1950s, *That '70s Show* transformed the music and fashions and pop-culture passions of a previous era into ready-made punch lines. Anyone who lived through leisure suits and "Farrah" hair might experience some embarrassing flashbacks, but the stunt casting of stars from the era—Danny Bonaduce, Lyle Waggoner, Eve Plumb—offered a more comfortable nostalgic buzz. The first season may have relied too heavily on eight-track and Tab references, but a strong cast allowed the series to move away from doing the time-warp every moment, and to tell funny stories that could be set in any era. The DVD sets likewise improved after a lackluster Season 1 offering.

T

GREAT MOMENTS: Season 1: "Eric's Buddy" is a surprisingly substantive look at homosexuality in an era when the closets were finally opening; Season 2: The Hanna-Barbera-style animation in "Afterglow"; the James Bond–girl reunion (including Maud Adams and series regular Tanya Roberts) in "The First Time"; Season 4: Eric discovers how life without Donna would have turned out in "It's a Wonderful Life"; the cast sings in "That '70s Musical."

FAST-FORWARD: Depends on one's tolerance for Ashton Kutcher.

EXTRAS: Season 1: "Hello, Wisconsin" featurette; "That '70s Tribute Show"; Season 2: Six behind-the-scenes featurettes; commentaries; Season 3: Commentaries and introductions by the cast and creative team; Season 4: Four David Trainer commentaries.

That's My Mama (1974–1975)

The Complete First Season (26 episodes on 3 discs): ★ ½

The Complete Second Season (13 episodes on 2 discs): ★ ½

Sony Pictures Home Entertainment

Video: Full-Frame; Audio: Dolby Digital 2.0

Often hailed as a hidden gem of the 1970s and the precursor to the hit *Barbershop* films, *That's My Mama* might have been a delightful sitcom to rediscover on DVD—had Sony not opted to release syndicated cuts of the episodes. And while I'm complaining, why not a single "complete series" package, since there were only thirty-nine shows in the run?

GREAT MOMENTS: Season 1: Comedian Slappy White appears in "Song and Dance Man."

FAST-FORWARD: Nothing.

EXTRAS: None.

3rd Rock from the Sun (1996–2001)

Season 1 (20 episodes on 4 discs): ★ ★
Season 2 (26 episodes on 4 discs): ★ ★
Season 3 (27 episodes on 4 discs): ★ ★
Best Episodes in the Universe, Really (4 episodes on 1 disc): ★ ★ ½

Anchor Bay
Video: Full-Frame; Audio: Dolby Digital 2.0

There was an innocence about the Solomons' adventures on a brave new planet that harkened back to an earlier era in situation comedies, when strange beings of all sorts found their way into America's suburbs. But *3rd Rock from the Sun* also made canny observations about the times we live in now, and proved a surprise hit for NBC after cracking the schedule as a midseason replacement. It's still hard to believe they pulled thirty-one Emmy nominations in five years, sometimes stealing statues from more significant shows, but the better episodes continue to hold up. Unfortunately, episodes appear on DVD in their syndicated cuts, hence the lower ratings here.

GREAT MOMENTS: Season 1: The aliens arrive in "Brains and Eggs"; *Gilmore Girls* star Lauren Graham attends "Dick's First Birthday"; Season 2: Sally meets Mark Hamill in "Fifteen Minutes of Dick."

FAST-FORWARD: Season 1: John Lithgow in drag is not a pretty sight in "I Enjoy Being a Dick."

EXTRAS: Each season set includes cast interviews, blooper reels, and behind-the-scenes featurettes.

This Is Your Life (1952–1961)

The Ultimate Collection, Volume 1 (18 episodes on 3 discs): ★ ★ ★ ★ ½

Respond 2

Video: Full-Frame; Audio: Dolby Digital Mono

Sometimes a television show can, fifty years later, take on the significance of a historic document. In *This Is Your Life*, host Ralph Edwards surprised someone every week with a retrospective of his or her life, featuring appearances by family, friends, and former associates. The series honored screen legends such as Boris Karloff and Bette Davis, then-contemporary pop stars Bobby Darin and the Carpenters, and other notable figures from politics, sports, and the classical arts. The footage in *The Ultimate Collection, Volume 1* of frank confessions by stars rarely glimpsed without a script, once-in-a-lifetime reunions, and stories of triumph and tragedy, offers insights that a three-hundred-page biography cannot provide.

GREAT MOMENTS: Stan Laurel and Oliver Hardy, moved to tears in their only live television appearance; honoree Bette Davis and guest Paul Henreid re-create a classic moment from their film *Now, Voyager*; the tribute to Holocaust survivor Hanna Bloch Kohner.

T

FAST-FORWARD: Nothing.

EXTRAS: Show introductions by creator-host Ralph Edwards; collector's booklet and photo gallery.

Three's Company (1977–1984)

Season 1 (6 episodes on 1 disc): ★ ★ ★ ½
Season 2 (26 episodes on 4 discs): ★ ★ ★
Season 3 (22 episodes on 4 discs): ★ ★ ★ ½
Season 4 (25 episodes on 4 discs): ★ ★ ★
Season 5 (22 episodes on 4 discs): ★ ★
Season 6 (28 episodes on 4 discs): ★ ★ ★ ½

Anchor Bay

Video: Full-Frame; Audio: Dolby Digital 1.0 (Season 1); Dolby Digital 2.0 (Seasons 2–5)

In the 1970s, Jack Tripper's cohabitation with two attractive women was considered scandalous, while his masquerading as a gay man, complete with lisping voice and limp wrist, was just an easy punch line. Today, it's the stereotyping that would get them in trouble, while the shacking up wouldn't raise an eyebrow. Times change, as do perceptions: back then we were so busy leering at the girls that we didn't see *Three's Company* for what it was: a drawing-room farce with a slapstick chaser. Critics thought it pushed the envelope on content, but the show was really a throwback to a comic form with its roots in Shakespeare, Oscar Wilde, and Noel Coward. Lucille Ball, who knew a thing or two about comedy, certainly noticed—*Three's Company* was one of her favorite shows.

GREAT MOMENTS: Season 3: "The Bake-Off" is classic *Three's Company* farce; Season 6: The arrival of Priscilla Barnes as Terri Alden marked a return to form after two disappointing seasons.

FAST-FORWARD: All of the Roper- and Furley-centric stories; the trio's landlords are best relegated to the supporting ranks.

EXTRAS: Season 2: Original series pilot; John Ritter documentary "Always Leave Them Laughing"; bloopers; clip packages; commentary by *Three's Company* book author Chris Mann; Season 3: Previously unaired pilot; "Remembering John Ritter" documentary; bloopers; Chris Mann commentary; interviews with actor Richard Kline and director Dave Powers; Season 4: Interviews with actors Don Knotts, Richard Kline, and Ann Wedgeworth; interview with Nancy Morgan Ritter; Season 6: "Lucille Ball Presents the Best of *Three's Company*" special; commentary on "Jack Bares All" by Dave Powers.

Thunderbirds (1965–1966)

Thunderbirds Megaset (32 episodes on 12 discs): ★ ★ ★

The Best of Thunderbirds (6 episodes on 2 discs): ★ ★ ½

Also available as individual sets:

Volumes 1–12 (each: 6 episodes on 2 discs): ★ ★ ★

A&E Home Video

Video: Full-Frame; Audio: Dolby Digital 5.1

Television's most exciting puppet show looks pretty antiquated now, but those of an earlier generation, especially in the United Kingdom, probably still thrill to the adventures of the International Rescue Team, as they battle the forces of evil in the year 2065. The digital remastering on these vintage shows is superb. "Videcolor" and "Supermarionation," two of creator Gerry Anderson's memorable hyperbolic boasts, have never looked better. As with all A&E sets, you're better off in for the full run than for the individual volumes; by doing so you'd nearly save enough money for one of Anderson's other creations now on DVD, including *UFO* and *Captain Scarlet.*

GREAT MOMENTS: Volumes 1 and 2: The introduction of the Firefly and the Thunderbird hoverbikes in "City of Fire"; Volumes 3 and 4: Lady Penelope outruns evildoers with fancy driving in "Brink of Disaster."

FAST-FORWARD: Volumes 9 and 10: The flashback episode "Security Hazard."

EXTRAS: *Megaset*: "Making of" documentary and behind-the-scenes featurette; *Best of*: A profile of Gerry Anderson, a Gerry Anderson interview, and a pop-up version of "Trapped in the Sky."

Thundercats (1985–1988)

Season 1, Part 1 (33 episodes on 6 discs): ★ ★ ★
Season 1, Part 2 (32 episodes on 6 discs): ★ ★ ★
Season 2, Part 1 (34 episodes on 6 discs): ★ ★ ½

Warner Home Video
Video: Full-Frame; Audio: Dolby Digital 1.0

T

Children's programming in the 1980s produced several half-hour toy commercials masquerading as animated series. But even with its stigma of rampant consumerism, *Thundercats* was an imaginative fantasy adventure. Twenty years after the series' original release, when nostalgia has prompted renewed interest, the stories still hold up.

Warner Home Video gave Lion-O and the gang the deluxe treatment on DVD; though sound and video quality aren't perfect, they're better than one could have managed from an antenna in 1985. Cheetara's curves never looked more alluring, but then you also have to stomach a sharper image of Snarf.

GREAT MOMENTS: Season 1, Part 1: The Thundercats start the series naked! Well, sort of, in "Exodus."

FAST-FORWARD: Silly characters like Snarf, Hammerhand, and the kindly "Ro-bears" make this otherwise interesting series seem pretty childish.

EXTRAS: Part 1: *Thundercats* fans, including the Wil Wheaton of *Star Trek* fame, are interviewed in a special featurette.

The Tick (1994–1996)

The Entire Series (9 episodes on 2 discs): ★ ★

Columbia Tristar Home Video
Video: Anamorphic Widescreen; Audio: Dolby Digital 2.0 Surround

A superhero send-up that was either too hip for the masses or too dumb even for FOX, *The Tick* was a live-action adaptation of a character that had already gathered a following through comic books and an animated series. Patrick Warburton, best known as Puddy on *Seinfeld*, donned the bulky blue suit and threw himself completely into the role, a true Adam West for the twenty-first century. But despite a colorful supporting cast and clever writing from *Tick* creator Ben Edlund, the show slipped through the network cracks and was cancelled after just eight of its nine episodes aired.

GREAT MOMENTS: Christopher Lloyd as Mr. Fishladder in the pilot episode; a *Weekend at Bernie's* moment with a deceased superhero ironically dubbed "The Immortal" in "The Funeral."

FAST-FORWARD: Some would say nothing, some would say the whole series.

EXTRAS: Commentaries by Barry Sonnenfeld and Ben Edlund.

The Time Tunnel (1966–1967)

Volume 1 (15 episodes on 4 discs): ★ ★ ½

20th Century-Fox

Video: Full-Frame; Audio: Dolby Digital 2.0

Another one of Irwin Allen's sci-fi cheese fests, brought to DVD with a plethora of fun extras. But why use double-sided discs on a four-disc set with just fifteen episodes?

GREAT MOMENTS: Tony meets his father on the eve of the Pearl Harbor attack in "The Day the Sky Fell In"; Tony and Doug set sail on an ill-fated ocean liner in "Rendezvous with Yesterday."

FAST-FORWARD: Nothing.

EXTRAS: Alternative version of the pilot; original radio and TV promos and trailers; an Irwin Allen home movie, taken on the *Time Tunnel* set; photo galleries of related comic books and articles.

T.J. Hooker (1982–1987)

The Complete First and Second Seasons (27 episodes on 6 discs): ★ ★

Sony Pictures Home Entertainment

Video: Full-Frame; Audio: Dolby Digital 2.0

When William Shatner has great material, he's an amazing actor, and don't let anyone tell you otherwise. From early guest spots on shows like *The Fugitive* and *The Twilight Zone* to *Star Trek* and *Boston Legal*, he commands your attention like the silver screen stars of yore. But when he's in bad material, watch out. His desperation to sell a defective product results in the scenery chewing and chaotic cadence in line readings for which he's become famous. And that's what you get in *T.J. Hooker*, an uninspired cop show that even Heather Locklear can't make watchable.

GREAT MOMENTS: Leonard Nimoy makes the illogical decision to guest-star in "Vengeance Is Mine."

FAST-FORWARD: When Hooker gets into one of his "I'm going to clean the scum off the streets" diatribes, watch out.

EXTRAS: None.

The Tonight Show (1962–1992)

The Ultimate Carson Collection: ★ ★ ★ ★ ★

T

Respond 2

Video: Full-Frame; Audio: Dolby Digital Mono

How do you encapsulate more than 4,000 hours of Johnny Carson *Tonight Shows* into one seven-hour "best of" collection? An impossible task, especially considering the debatable decision to include Carson's final two shows in their entirety, when choice clips might have sufficed. Still, it's hard to argue with a set that offers so much to treasure. Carson remains the gold standard to which all talk-show hosts are doomed to fall short, a gentleman of modest charm and rapier wit who seemed at ease with presidents and potato-chip collectors. He is the bridge between the golden-age sophistication of Jack Paar and the modern-day sarcasm of David Letterman, and for thirty years he brought his best game every night. Just hearing the first five brassy notes of his *Tonight Show* theme transport viewers back to the era of Ed and Doc, Carnac and Art Fern, bickering with Charles Grodin and flirting with Dyan Cannon. It's all here, it's all great. Go buy it now.

GREAT MOMENTS: All of 'em.

FAST-FORWARD: The "Danger Johnny" clips from the 1960s do not measure up to the rest of the collection.

EXTRAS: *The Johnny Carson Story*; the 1982 primetime special *Johnny Goes Home*, in which Carson escorts viewers on a tour of Norfolk, Nebraska;

behind-the-scenes footage; Johnny's script notes; a selection of "More to Come" art.

Tony Orlando & Dawn (1974–1976)

The Ultimate Collection (11 episodes on 3 discs): ★ ★ ★

Respond 2

Video: Full-Frame; Audio: Dolby Digital 2.0

Tony Orlando & Dawn sold seventy million records, which is probably hard for anyone to believe now. Looking back at their short-lived variety series, the group's "Brill Building meets English dancehall" songs hold up better than you'd expect, but the comedy skits fall flat.

As with its *Captain and Tennille* set, Respond 2 took a B-list series and gave it an A-list treatment on DVD, with well-selected episodes and a few unique extras that probably couldn't have surfaced anywhere else. Now that the video company has found its niche in old variety shows, let's see a Starland Vocal Band collection.

GREAT MOMENTS: Performances of such hits as "Tie a Yellow Ribbon 'Round the Ole Oak Tree" and "Knock Three Times."

FAST-FORWARD: The comedy segments.

EXTRAS: Tony Orlando on *The Tonight Show* with guest host Freddie Prinze; Telma Hopkins and Joyce Vincent on *Fridays* with Don Novello as "Father Guido Sarducci & Dawn"; A *Carol Burnett Show* parody with Harvey Korman as "Tony" and Carol Burnett and Vicki Lawrence as "Dawn"; Tony Orlando & Dawn Video Jukebox.

Too Close for Comfort (1980–1983)

The Complete First Season (19 episodes on 3 discs): ★

The Complete Second Season (22 episodes on 3 discs): ★ ★ ½

Rhino

Video: Full-Frame; Audio: Unknown

Actually, it's not the "Complete First Season" unless you're just counting episodes. Rhino opted to offer syndicated cuts of the shows, and the "it's better than nothing" argument doesn't work because *Too Close for Comfort* is hardly some long-lost television treasure. There aren't that many fans clamoring for the Rush family on their DVD shelf, but those that do certainly deserved to have the episodes preserved as they were originally aired. Fortunately, Rhino learned its lesson with the Season 2 set, which offers not only uncut shows but a nice mix of extras.

GREAT MOMENTS: None spring to mind.

FAST-FORWARD: Every moment of Cousin April, who actually made Munroe less annoying by comparison.

EXTRAS: Season 2: Commentaries by Nancy Dussault, JM J. Bullock, Lydia Cornell, and Deborah Van Valkenburgh; cast-reunion featurette.

Top Cat (1961–1962)

The Complete Series (30 episodes on 4 discs): ★ ★ ★ ★

Warner Home Video

Video: Full-Frame; Audio: Dolby Digital 2.0

The Flintstones belonged to the past and *The Jetsons* to the future, but *Top Cat* lived in the real world of New York City. This was the most sophisticated of Hanna-Barbera's '60s-era primetime series; in fact, it's hard to imagine kids having any interest in a character like Top Cat, a fast-talking, streetwise hustler inspired by Phil Silvers's Sergeant Bilko, and voiced to perfection by Arnold Stang. T.C. and his gang hung out at the pool hall and the racetrack, and spent their days scrounging for deli food and tormenting Officer Dibble, the dim but earnest cop that patrolled Hoagy's Alley. It's surprising that more attention was lavished on the DVD set for *Top Cat* than on more popular Hanna-Barbera series like *Scooby-Doo*, but then maybe it's about time this underrated series got the respect it deserves.

GREAT MOMENTS: Top Cat masquerades as royalty in "The Maharajah of Pookajee"; the gang convinces Benny's mother that her son is the mayor of New York in "A Visit from Mother"; a cameo appearance from Fred Flintstone and Barney Rubble in "Rafeefleas."

FAST-FORWARD: Even Dibble in drag can't save "The Case of the Absent Anteater."

EXTRAS: Commentaries by cast and animation historians; interviews with the cast, including Arnold Stang; a collection of art, stills, sketches, and backgrounds; documentaries "The Making of *Top Cat*" and "Back to Hoagy's Alley"; vintage commercials.

Touched by an Angel (1994–2003)

The Complete First Season (11 episodes on 4 discs): ★ ★ ★ ★

The Complete Second Season (24 episodes on 6 discs): ★ ★ ★ ½

The Third Season, Volume 1 (16 episodes on 4 discs): ★ ★ ★ ½

Paramount Home Video

Video: Full-Frame; Audio: Dolby Digital 2.0

There's no middle ground with *Touched by an Angel*; depending on who's offering an opinion, its stories are inspirational or sappy, the show's approach to religion either profound or simplistic, its morals uplifting or preachy. Even proponents must acknowledge an elevated cheese content, as when Satan was portrayed by *The Dukes of Hazzard*'s John Schneider. But even in a lesser episode, the series could orchestrate a moment of compassion and hope that might gut you with its beauty. It also helped that Roma Downey was TV's cutest angel since Cheryl Ladd, and the scripts always found ways for Della Reese to show off her jazz pipes about every fourth episode. In Season 2, the show's predominantly female viewing audience got its own heavenly eye candy when John Dye joined the cast as Andrew, an angel of death to die for.

Thus far only the first-season DVDs have been touched by any extras, though given what a blessing the show was to its creators, the fans who stayed loyal through nine seasons and more than 200 divine interventions have a right to expect some goodies on future boxed sets.

GREAT MOMENTS: Season 1: Alyson Hannigan guest-stars as a teenager in trouble in "Cassie's Choice"; Season 2: A surgeon faces a devastating decision in "Interview with an Angel"; Monica becomes the first angel arrested for drug trafficking in "Jacob's Ladder"; Season 3, Volume 1: "Promised Land," the pilot for the Gerald McRaney series; Kirsten Dunst appears in "Into the Light."

FAST-FORWARD: Season 2: "Unidentified Female," a failed attempt at more sophisticated, nonlinear storytelling.

EXTRAS: Season 1: An extended version of Executive Producer Martha Williamson's *60 Minutes* interview; Martha Williamson talks about *Touched by an Angel*; the series' two-part final episode; cast/crew commentaries.

Tour of Duty (1987–1990)

The First Season (21 episodes on 5 discs): ★ ★ ½
The Second Season (16 episodes on 4 discs): ★ ★ ½

Columbia Tristar Home Video
Video: Full-Frame; Audio: Dolby Digital 2.0

After the 1986 film *Platoon* won the Academy Award and returned Vietnam to the public discourse, CBS debuted a ground-level look at the war as seen through the eyes of Company B, led by Sergeant Zeke Anderson (Terence Knox). *Tour of Duty* was harsh and brutal and critically acclaimed, and also scheduled opposite *The Cosby Show* and *A Different World.* As a result, the war on CBS didn't last nearly as long as the one in Southeast Asia.

The Rolling Stones' "Paint It, Black" set an appropriately somber tone for the first-season episodes, which two supporting characters did not survive. On the DVD release you won't hear the song, or any of the other period music that helped define the war era in American history. For *Duty*'s original viewers, that alone might be enough to discourage purchase of the season sets. Season 2 introduced Kim Delaney as journalist Alex Devlin, and devoted several stories to the mental and emotional turmoil experienced by soldiers.

T

GREAT MOMENTS: Season 1: A newborn baby, the sole survivor of a massacred village, is protected by Zeke in "Brothers, Fathers, and Sons"; Zeke deals with pressures from the home front in "Roadrunner"; Taylor and Ruiz discover what Americans think of the Vietnam War in "Soldiers"; Season 2: Michael Madsen plays a sniper on the edge of sanity in "Sleeping Dogs."

FAST-FORWARD: Only the substitute music.

EXTRAS: None.

Tru Calling (2003–2004)

Season 1 (20 episodes on 6 discs): ★ ★ ½
Season 2 (6 episodes on 2 discs): ★ ★ ★

20th Century-Fox
Video: Anamorphic Widescreen; Audio: Dolby Digital 2.0

Eliza Dushku plus supernatural premise should have equaled compelling television, but *Tru Calling* didn't have Joss Whedon's ear for dialogue, or the humorous counterpoint to its creepy premise that made Dushku's work in *Buffy the Vampire Slayer* so memorable. The Faith-no-more actress plays a morgue attendant who communicates with the dead, reliving the last day of their lives in the hope of postponing the funeral. Mostly mediocre, but it gets better as it goes on, especially after Jason Priestley debuts as someone who shares Tru's gift but not her benevolence.

GREAT MOMENTS: Season 1: Jason Priestley joins the cast in "Daddy's Girl."

FAST-FORWARD: Nothing.

EXTRAS: Season 1: Deleted scenes; commentaries by creator Jon Harmon Feldman and star Eliza Dushku; audition reels; featurettes "Finding the Calling: The Pilot," "The Tru Path: Season 1" and "Evil Come Calling: A Late-Season Twist."

21 Jump Street (1987–1990)

Season 1 (13 episodes on 4 discs): ★ ★ ½
Season 2 (22 episodes on 6 discs): ★ ★ ½
Season 3 (20 episodes on 6 discs): ★
Season 4 (26 episodes on 6 discs): ★

Anchor Bay
Video: Full-Frame; Audio: Mono

Only the oh-my-god-he's-so-cute appeal of Johnny Depp could turn a show about high school narcs into must-see viewing among teenagers. *21 Jump Street* was an early hit for the fledgling FOX network and a star-making launch for Depp, but the DVD season sets suffer from the absence of original music. While this book has not issued a blanket condemnation for every set that opted for substitute tracks, clearly some shows are more adversely affected than others. This one really takes a hit.

Fans expecting tracks by U2, Depeche Mode, Concrete Blonde, and REM will be disappointed by their absence. The first-season episode "My Future's So Bright, I Gotta Wear Shades," named after the Timbuk 3 song that played under several scenes, now only uses the song once. Another drawback is the use of a syndicated cut on the pilot, and the presentation of episodes in the Season 4 set out of order. It's a lot to overlook, but less-discriminating fans might still enjoy catching up with Hanson and Penhall and Ioki, as well as the variety of guest stars in early-career roles that pop up in the first two seasons, among them Christina Applegate, Jason Priestley, and Brad Pitt.

GREAT MOMENTS: Season 1: The two-part pilot; Season 2: The conflicting loyalties after Adam Fuller is arrested for DUI in "Two for the Road"; the Harry Ioki showcase "Christmas in Saigon"; Season 3: The introduction of Booker in "Fun with Animals."

FAST-FORWARD: The music substituted for the original soundtracks.

EXTRAS: Season 1: Commentaries with star Peter DeLuise; interviews with creator Stephen J. Cannell and stars Holly Robinson Peete, Dustin Nguyen, and Steven Williams; Season 2: Peter DeLuise commentary.

24 (2001–)

Season 1 (24 episodes on 6 discs): ★ ★ ★ ★ ½
Season 2 (24 episodes on 6 discs): ★ ★ ★ ★ ★
Season 3 (24 episodes on 7 discs): ★ ★ ★ ★
Season 4 (24 episodes on 7 discs): ★ ★ ★ ★

20th Century-Fox

Video: Anamorphic Widescreen; Audio: Dolby Digital 2.0 (Season 1); Dolby Digital 5.1 (Seasons 2–4)

24 is a series ideally suited for DVD. The real-time stories told at a breakneck pace are best enjoyed in multiple doses, rather than waiting a week between installments. Which makes the absence of a PLAY ALL feature on the sets' MENU screens extremely inconvenient. Maybe Federal Agent Jack Bauer can find out where it went, soon as he's done racing against time to save his daughter or find a missing nuclear device.

T

GREAT MOMENTS: Season 1: The first assassination plot reaches its climax in "7:00 AM–8:00 AM"; the explosive season finale "11:00 PM–12:00 AM"; Season 2: The CTU tries to decide how to get rid of a bomb in "10:00 PM–11:00 PM"; Season 3: Another memorable series finale—"12:00 PM–1:00 PM."

FAST-FORWARD: Kim's clueless antics in Season 2, especially the infamous cougar scene, detract from the main storyline, and can be skipped by anyone but guys with a crush on Elisha Cuthbert.

EXTRAS: Season 1 offers only a Kiefer Sutherland introduction and alternate series ending, but Seasons 2–4 feature multiple commentary tracks, featurettes, and deleted scenes.

The Twilight Zone (1959–1965)

Definitive Editions: Season 1 (36 episodes on 6 discs): ★ ★ ★ ★ ★
Season 2 (29 episodes on 5 discs): ★ ★ ★ ★ ★
Season 3 (37 episodes on 7 discs): ★ ★ ★ ★ ★
Volumes 1–43, plus *Treasures of the Twilight Zone* and *More Treasures of the Twilight Zone* (each: 3 episodes on 1 disc): ★ ★ ★ ½

Collection 1 (35 episodes on 9 discs): ★ ★ ★ ★
Collection 2 (34 episodes on 9 discs): ★ ★ ★ ★
Collection 3 (33 episodes on 9 discs): ★ ★ ★ ½
Collection 4 (28 episodes on 9 discs): ★ ★ ★ ½
Collection 5 (29 episodes on 9 discs): ★ ★ ★ ★
Fortieth Anniversary Gift Pack (19 episodes on 6 discs): ★ ★ ★ ★

Image Entertainment

Video: Full-Frame; Audio: Dolby Digital Mono

The Gold Collection (156 episodes on 49 discs): ★ ★ ½

V3 Media

Video: Full-Frame; Audio: Dolby Digital Mono

1985–1989 Series: Season 1 (24 episodes on 6 discs): ★ ★ ★
Seasons 2 & 3 (41 episodes on 6 discs): ★ ★ ★

Image Entertainment

Video: Full-Frame; Audio: Dolby Digital 2.0

2002 Series: The Complete Series (43 episodes on 6 discs): ★ ★ ½

New Line

Video: Anamorphic Widescreen; Audio: Dolby Digital 5.1

The question is not whether the original *Twilight Zone* series is worth owning on DVD, but which of the many editions and repackaged collections offer the best quality at the best price. Image Entertainment got it right with its *Definitive Editions* only after several previous efforts, forcing thousands who already picked up various sets and individual volumes to pony up one more time. Consumer frustration should be short-lived, however, after taking a gander at the marvelous digital restorations and incredible extras in these must-have releases.

The five numbered *Collection* sets mix random episodes from the show's five seasons. *The Gold Collection* offers the entire series in chronological order in one package, but jacks up the price because of its "limited edition" status of only 2,500 sets; however, the episodes have not been remastered as well as in the *Definitive Editions*. You do get a certificate of authenticity, for what that's worth.

While the 1980s *Twilight Zone* revamp boasted contributions from such writers as Harlan Ellison and Philip DeGuere, and the 2002 series cast flavor-of-the-month guest stars like Jessica Simpson, Dylan Walsh, and Usher, neither is essential to a classic-TV collection.

GREAT MOMENTS: Too many to mention from the original series, which offered such classic supernatural tales as "Time Enough at Last" and "The Monsters Are Due on Maple Street" (Season 1), "Eye of the Beholder" (Season 2), and "To Serve Man" (Season 3).

FAST-FORWARD: The sixty-minute stories from the series' later seasons seem padded out to fill the running time.

EXTRAS: For the original series, the *Definitive Editions* have all the bells and whistles, from commentaries with surviving stars to isolated music scores, plus rare promos, an alternate pilot for "Where Is Everybody?", Rod Serling guest appearances on other series, and even an odd blooper or two; 1985 series: Both sets offer audio commentaries with Wes Craven, Harlan Ellison, Philip DeGuere, Alan Brennert, James Crocker, Bradford May, and J.D. Feigelson.

Twin Peaks (1990–1991)

The Complete First Season (7 episodes on 4 discs): ★ ★ ★

The Pilot: ★ ★ ½

Artisan (First Season); Catalyst Logic (Pilot)

Video: Full-Frame; Audio: Dolby Digital 5.1 (boxed set); Mono (Pilot)

T

What's the last thing you want to hear after purchasing Season 1 of *Twin Peaks* and pressing PLAY for the first episode? A "Previously on *Twin Peaks . . .*" voiceover. Quite possibly the most idiotic decision yet made in the annals of TV on DVD was the release of the series' first seven episodes without the brilliant pilot movie that sets in motion every story arc explored throughout the season, including the murder of Laura Palmer. The result is a five-star series trapped in a three-star box.

Newcomers to *Twin Peaks*, already upset at coming in late, also won't like getting drawn into the show's central whodunit, only to have the mystery remain unsolved. Since there were just seven episodes in the first season, why not add Season 2's twenty-two episodes and release a complete series set? Yeah, I know, rights issues. The pilot episode is currently available only on a poorly produced (and out-of-print) Asian import DVD, and Season 2 is owned by Paramount, which is planning its own release. Perhaps in this case it might have been wiser to iron out all the legalities first, and then unveil a collection worthy of David Lynch's masterpiece.

GREAT MOMENTS: Season 1: The arrival of Albert Rosenfeld (Episode 2); the Bookhouse Boys visit One-Eyed Jacks (Episode 6).

FAST-FORWARD: Any appearance by Johnny Horn.

EXTRAS: Directors' commentaries; cast interviews; episode introductions from the Log Lady; "Learning to Speak in the Red Room" featurette; "17 Pieces of Pie" featurette, set in the original Mar T Diner.

227 (1985–1990)

The Complete First Season (22 episodes on 3 discs): ★ ★ ★

Columbia Tristar Home Video

Video: Full-Frame; Audio: Dolby Digital 2.0

In which the housekeeper from *The Jeffersons* moved on up, but not quite as far as her former employers. Marla Gibbs went from serving dinner to serving set-up lines for Jackée Harry in this moderately successful sitcom that lasted five seasons. What began as an ensemble piece built around the tenants in Gibbs's apartment complex evolved into a showcase for Jackée as man-hungry Sandra. First-season guest appearances by Run-DMC and Bobby Brown speak less to the show's early popularity than to the deficiency of successful African-American series.

GREAT MOMENTS: The tenants believe they've won the lottery in "Pick Six"; Brenda asks Sandra for advice on winning Calvin's heart in "A Daughter Is a Precious Thing"; Sandra poses as Mary to flirt her way out of an auto repair bill in "Honesty."

FAST-FORWARD: Still all good, as Jackée hadn't taken over the whole show yet.

EXTRAS: Featurettes "Stories from the Stoop," "Three Ladies Remember *227*," and "From Stage to Screen: *227*."

UFO (1970–1973)

The Complete UFO Megaset (26 episodes on 8 discs): ★ ★ ★ ★

A&E Home Video

Video: Full-Frame; Audio: Dolby Digital 5.1

As with all of Gerry Anderson's shows, *UFO* was a sensation in Britain and a minor cult hit in the colonies, though it got a stateside boost from debuting in 1969, shortly after the cancellation of *Star Trek*. In the US markets where it was syndicated, the series provided solace to Trekkies who felt right at home with its combination of intelligent sci-fi storytelling and cheesy sets and costumes. This was Anderson's first foray into live-action TV. The stories of an Earth under attack by organ-harvesting aliens were more thoughtful than his "super-marionation" outings, and the idea of having the headquarters of SHADO (Supreme Headquarters Alien Defence Organization) located beneath a movie studio was inspired. But you could only take the show so seriously when all the girls on the Moonbase were garbed in go-go boots and purple wigs.

GREAT MOMENTS: Straker must choose between his mission and the life of his son in "A Question of Priorities"; A flashback to the beginnings of SHADO in "Confetti Check A-OK"; the UFO-attack sequence in "Reflections in the Water."

FAST-FORWARD: "Ordeal," an alien-abduction story that employed the dream-sequence reset button two decades before Bobby Ewing.

EXTRAS: Commentaries by actors Mike Billington, Wanda Ventham, and Ed Bishop, creators Gerry and Sylvia Anderson, and director Alan Perry; outtakes.

Underdog (1964–1973)

Boxed set (12 episodes on 3 discs): ★ ★ ★ ½
Chronicles (3 episodes on 1 disc): ★ ★ ★
Collector's Edition (7 episodes on 1 disc): ★ ★ ★
Nemesis (2 episodes on 1 disc): ★ ★ ½

U

SonyWonder
Video: Full-Frame; Audio: Mono

The best choice is the boxed set, which collects the three individual *Underdog* releases plus extras, and is priced to move. I wonder if Sony realizes how many people have been waiting for this show, after being deprived of their hero for decades once *Underdog* was blackballed from syndication. As every fan knows, one of this powerful pup's most potent weapons in the fight against crime was a vitamin pill he kept in his ring. As with Roger Ramjet, some parents thought a pill-popping superhero was a bad influence on their kids. The less said about such foolishness, the better.

Fortunately, the episodes selected for the set are among the best of the run, and while the quality of the animation makes *Rocky & Bullwinkle* look like a Pixar release, the stories are clever and funny, and Wally Cox was a perfect choice to give the hero his famed rhyming couplets ("When Polly's in trouble I am not slow, it's hip-hip-hip and away I go!"). Awesome theme song, too.

GREAT MOMENTS: *Collector"s Edition*: Underdog's evil twin, Tap Tap, debuts in "From Hopeless to Helpless"; the Earth's milk supply is threatened by alien felines in "Underdog vs. Overcat"; *Chronicles*: Mad scientist Simon Bar Sinister unveils his most deadly invention yet in "The Ticklefeather Machine"; King Klobber blackmails Underdog into marrying his daughter in "Zot."

FAST-FORWARD: Nothing.

EXTRAS: *Boxed Set*: Interview with *Underdog* co-creator Joe Harris; archival series introductions; bonus shorts featuring Tennessee Tuxedo, Klondike Kat, Commander McBragg, the Hunter, King and Odie, Tooter Turtle, and the Go Go Gophers.

Upstairs/Downstairs (1971–1975)

The Complete Series Megaset (68 episodes on 20 discs): ★ ★ ★ ★ ★
The Complete First Season (13 episodes on 4 discs): ★ ★ ★ ★
The Complete Second Season (13 episodes on 4 discs): ★ ★ ★ ★ ★
The Complete Third Season (13 episodes on 4 discs): ★ ★ ★ ★ ½
The Complete Fourth Season (13 episodes on 4 discs): ★ ★ ★ ★ ★
The Complete Fifth Season (16 episodes on 4 discs): ★ ★ ★ ★

A&E Home Video
Video: Full-Frame; Audio: Mono

One of television's first cult hits was not a sci-fi series or a cutting-edge sitcom aimed at alienated teenagers, but a fifty-five-part serial drama set in Edwardian Britain, that originally aired in America on *Masterpiece Theatre*. It's not an exaggeration to say that *Upstairs/Downstairs* put PBS on the map. Long before *Dallas* and *Dynasty*, audiences were obsessed with the goings-on in the stately drawing room and servants' quarters at 165 Eaton Place. The series earned nine Emmys and has been enjoyed by more than a billion people worldwide. Fans can save money by purchasing the *Complete Series Megaset* over the five season sets, for which pricing starts at eighty bucks for thirteen episodes each.

GREAT MOMENTS: Season 1: Elizabeth's flight in "The Path of Duty"; Season 2: King Edward visits Eaton Place in "Guest of Honour"; Season 4: Gordon Jackson's Emmy-winning performance in "The Beastly Hun."

FAST-FORWARD: "The Swedish Tiger" (Season 1).

EXTRAS: *Megaset*: "*Upstairs/Downstairs* Remembered: The Twenty-Fifth Anniversary Special."

V (1984–1985)

The Original Miniseries (1 disc): ★ ★ ★ ★

The Final Battle (2 discs): ★ ★ ★ ★

The Complete TV Series (19 episodes on 3 discs): ★ ★ ½

Warner Home Video

Video: Anamorphic Widescreen (*Miniseries*, *The Final Battle*), Full-Frame (*The Complete TV Series*), Audio: Dolby Digital Stereo (*Miniseries*); Dolby Digital Mono (*The Complete TV Series*, *The Final Battle*)

Intelligent science-fiction was in short supply on American TV between *Star Trek* and *Star Trek: The Next Generation*, but for a brief moment in the 1980s *V* filled the gap quite nicely. Clever promotion turned the original miniseries into event television, and tens of millions tuned in to watch the alien invasion (among them the creators of the film *Independence Day*, who ripped off *V*'s images of giant spaceships hovering over Earth's major cities). The collective audience gasp was practically audible when the humanoid Visitors revealed their true reptilian appearance, and when their glamorous leader Diana, memorably played by Jane Badler, indulged her affection for devouring live critters.

A second miniseries, *The Final Battle*, continued the story, and like its predecessor drew much of its inspiration from World War II and the Holocaust for its depiction of a planet subjugated by a totalitarian regime. After the final episode delivered another huge rating, NBC debuted *V* as a regular series in 1984, with Badler still in fine form as the only woman on '80s TV to have bigger hair than *Hunter*'s Sergeant Dee Dee McCall. But even Diana was no match for J.R. Ewing; scheduled opposite *Dallas*, the show was cancelled after nineteen episodes.

Though the special effects won't impress anyone now, everything else about *V* holds up, and the anamorphic-widescreen transfer used for the *Original Miniseries* on DVD is an unexpected surprise, especially for a show that's more than two decades old.

GREAT MOMENTS: *Miniseries*: The motherships arrive; Jane Badler swallows a rat. *The Final Battle*: The birth of the twins, and the capture of Juliette Parish.

FAST-FORWARD: *The Complete TV Series*: The dreadful episode "The Secret Underground."

EXTRAS: *Miniseries*: Commentary by director Kenneth Johnson; "making of" featurette.

Veronica Mars (2004–)

The Complete First Season (22 episodes on 6 discs): ★ ★ ★ ½

Warner Home Video

Video: Widescreen; Audio: Dolby Digital 2.0

Veronica Mars became UPN's first mainstream, non-science-fiction, non-reality critically acclaimed hit. Kristen Bell stars as a young girl who helps her father out at his private detective agency between high school classes, but it's not all adolescent angst and Nancy Drew: Veronica must solve the mystery of who killed her best friend, Lilly Kane, and piece together the murky events of a night when she believes she may have been raped.

In addition to critical acclaim, *Veronica Mars* was a hit on the Internet, where it inherited many *Buffy the Vampire Slayer* fans who were going through blonde butt-kicker withdrawal. But for a series with so much buzz, it's unfortunate that the first-season DVD set features no commentaries at all.

GREAT MOMENTS: Veronica and Wallace go undercover *Alias*-style in "The Wrath of Con"; *Buffy*'s Alyson Hannigan appears as Logan's older sister, Trina, in "Russkie Business"; Logan and Veronica finally kiss in "Weapons of Class Destruction"; Veronica learns who killed Lilly in "Leave It to Beaver."

FAST-FORWARD: Some "mysteries of the week," like the one in "Lord of the Bling," are less engrossing than others.

EXTRAS: An extended cut of the pilot episode; bloopers; deleted scenes.

The Vicar of Dibley (1994–2005)

V

The Complete Series 1 (6 episodes on 1 disc): ★ ★ ★ ★ ½

The Complete Series 2 and Specials (4 episodes on 1 disc): ★ ★ ★ ★ ★

The Complete Series 3 (4 episodes on 1 disc): ★ ★ ★ ½

BBC Video

Video: Full-Frame; Audio: Dolby Digital Mono

British television has always had fun with the clergy, and one of the UK's best holy sitcoms is *The Vicar of Dibley*, which surprised stateside Britcom fans by placing third in a BBC poll of the country's top 100 situation comedies of all time, ahead of such classics as *Fawlty Towers* and *Absolutely Fabulous*. The saga of Geraldine Granger, the first female vicar in a rural town of eccentrics, is not as gleefully blasphemous as *Father Ted* or *Dave Allen at Large*. Indeed, much as Geri's chief nemesis David Horton grumbles about a woman in the pulpit, most parishes would be delighted with such a spirited down-to-earth shepherd, especially as played with bubbly charm by Dawn French. Don't shut off the episodes too quickly or you'll miss the tag scene that follows the closing credits.

GREAT MOMENTS: Series 1: The choir auditions in "Songs of Praise"; Kylie Minogue visits Dibley in "Community Spirit"; Series 2: The season-long romance arc between Hugo and Alice; Mrs. C.'s last request in "The Easter Bunny"; Geri's mirror dance with Royal Ballet star Darcey Bussell in "Celebrity Vicar." Series 3: Geri's chocolate-fueled recovery from a broken heart in "Autumn"; "The Red Nose Special," featuring appearances from the Duchess of York (Fergie to you) and Johnny Depp.

FAST-FORWARD: Nothing.

EXTRAS: Series 3: A documentary on real female vicars; two holiday shorts.

VIP (1998–2002)

The Complete First Season (22 episodes on 5 discs): ★ ★ ½

Sony Pictures Home Entertainment

Video: Anamorphic Widescreen; Audio: Dolby Digital 2.0

Some bad TV should be avoided, and some bad TV should be embraced. *VIP* lands (barely) in the latter category, propelled by the appeal of star and Executive Producer Pamela Anderson. Forget the stories, about a valley girl who winds up as a bodyguard to the stars. There are no big action scenes, no great performances, no memorable lines of dialogue; the show exists only to revel in the charms of America's favorite ex-centerfold. On the grading scale of Pam's biggest hits, *VIP* is better than *Stacked*, but falls short of the bouncy standard set by *Baywatch*.

GREAT MOMENTS: The just-plain-weird sight of Marie Osmond and Pam Anderson together in "Bloody Val-entine"; Val and her team go undercover (but not much cover) as "The Double-D Girls" in "Val the Hard Way."

FAST-FORWARD: Pauly Shore's appearance in "What to Do with Vallery When You're Dead."

EXTRAS: Cast/crew commentaries (but not from Pam); two featurettes; a pop-up trivia track on the pilot episode.

Wacky Races (1968–1970)

The Complete Series (34 episodes on 3 discs): ★ ★ ★ ★

Warner Home Video

Video: Full-Frame; Audio: Dolby Digital Mono

It doesn't make you an awful person if you wished that, just once, Dick Dastardly and his snickering canine Muttley had found a way to drive the Double-Zero to a checkered flag. Dastardly obviously had the best car, as he was always ahead before stopping to play a dirty trick on the rest of the field, which inevitably cost him the race. Some of Hanna-Barbera's cleverest visual gags found their way into *Wacky Races*, a series of ten-minute cartoon shorts with a blissfully simple premise: eleven bizarre cars compete in a series of races around the world. While kids in the '70s laughed at the antics of the Slag brothers, Peter Perfect, and Professor Pat Pending, their older brothers were probably wagering on the results, which were always a surprise every week.

GREAT MOMENTS: The introduction of the racers at the start of each show by narrator Dave Willock. How many can you still name? Penelope Pitstop's clothing line drifting from the back of her Compact Pussycat (including her unmentionables! Oh, Dee-yah!) in "By Rollercoaster to Upsan Downs"; the pint-sized gangsters in the Ant Hill Mob go undercover as Snow White's dwarves in "See-Saw to Arkansas"; Dastardly's hurricane machine costs him yet another victory in "Overseas Hi-Way Race."

FAST-FORWARD: If you like one, you'll like 'em all.

EXTRAS: Commentaries by production designer Iwao Takamoto, character designer Jerry Eisenberg, and animation historians Earl Kress and Scott Shaw; on-screen factoids that list each driver's first, second, and third place finishes; featurettes "Rearview Mirror: A Look Back at *Wacky Races*" and "Spinout Spin-offs," a look at spin-off shows *Dastardly and Muttley in Their Flying Machines* and *The Perils of Penelope Pitstop.*

Walker, Texas Ranger (1993–)

The Final Season (23 episodes on 6 discs): ★ ★

The Complete First Season (26 episodes on 7 discs): ★ ★ ½

Paramount Home Video

Video: Full-Frame; Audio: Dolby Digital 2.0

According to the Internet (so it must be true), Chuck Norris can hit you so hard that he can alter your DNA. Decades from now your descendants will occasionally clutch their heads and yell, "What the hell was that?"

That's one of hundreds of "Chuck Norris Facts" that have made the rounds online, elevating the star of *Walker, Texas Ranger* to the pantheon of tall-tale legends. (My favorite: "There is no theory of evolution—only a list of animals that Chuck Norris allows to live.") Hopefully Paramount hasn't provoked the almighty wrath of Chuck by releasing the eighth and final season of *Walker* before the debut of Season 1. Not that you'll be lost in any complex character development or lingering plot threads by coming in late; the show never wavered from its "See Chuck, see Chuck kick somebody's ass" formula, and that was enough for the fans even if Norris was the most wooden leading man since Pinocchio.

The Season 1 set contains the two-hour TV movie that introduced the show, and sports one of the better-looking boxes of any DVD release, and that's just as well, cause you'd hate to make you-know-who angry. After all, crop circles are Chuck Norris's way of telling the world that sometimes corn needs to lie down.

GREAT MOMENTS: The fight scenes—come on, you watch for the plots?

FAST-FORWARD: All that stuff between the roundhouse kicks.

EXTRAS: None.

The Waltons (1972–1981)

The Complete First Season (24 episodes on 5 discs): ★ ★ ★ ★ ½
The Complete Second Season (24 episodes on 5 discs): ★ ★ ★ ★ ★
The Complete Third Season (25 episodes on 5 discs): ★ ★ ★ ★ ½
The Homecoming: A Christmas Story: ★ ★ ★

Season sets: Warner Home Video; *The Homecoming*: Paramount Home Video
Video: Full-Frame; Audio: Dolby Digital Mono

W

Even back in the 1970s, when television was a much tamer place than it is now, critics predicted *The Waltons* would be too square and too goody-goody for enlightened viewers of the day. What happened instead was that Americans weary from Vietnam headlines embraced this loving portrait of a rural family. Though the series had a warm and nostalgic feel, the Waltons were certainly not without hardship—the Blue Ridge Mountains during the Great Depression weren't a happy place. The fact that millions of viewers still enjoyed *The Waltons* as escapist entertainment speaks volumes about what their lives were like at the time. The video quality of the DVDs is slightly below that of other shows from the era, though it's not distracting enough to recommend passing on the season sets.

The Homecoming was the TV movie that inspired the series, and is most interesting now for the original casting of Andrew Duggan and Patricia Neal as Ma and Pa Walton, and Edgar Bergen as Grandpa.

GREAT MOMENTS: Season 1: The family enjoys a private circus performance in "The Carnival"; Olivia copes with a frightening diagnosis in "The Easter Story"; Season 2: John-Boy's selfless acts in "The Journey"; John and Olivia enjoy a long-overdue romantic getaway in "The Honeymoon"; Season 3: A land dispute spirals out of control in "The Conflict, Parts 1 & 2"; and, of course, the oft-parodied "Good night's" at the end of every episode.

FAST-FORWARD: Season 1: Zeb gets scared by a meteorite in "The Star."

EXTRAS: None.

Wanted: Dead or Alive (1958–1961)

Season 1 (36 episodes on 4 discs): ★ ★ ★ ½

New Line

Video: Full-Screen; Audio: Mono

Back in the days when more than two dozen Westerns rode tall in the saddle in primetime, *Wanted: Dead or Alive* emerged as one of the most popular. Steve McQueen launched his career as gentleman bounty hunter Josh Randall, a character introduced on another Western, *Trackdown.* That episode would have made a great extra in the Season 1 box set, but given the age of the material and the dearth of classic Westerns on DVD, it's hard to complain about the job New Line did with this vintage series.

GREAT MOMENTS: Josh has a "Wanted" poster on future *Star Trek* doc DeForest Kelley in "Secret Ballot"; Michael Landon guest-stars in "The Legend."

FAST-FORWARD: The colorized episodes, which fortunately are also here in their original black-and-white. Didn't we get all this colorization nonsense out of our system a decade ago?

EXTRAS: "Life in the Fast Lane," a documentary about Steve McQueen, and series featurettes.

The West Wing (1999–)

The Complete First Season (22 episodes on 4 discs): ★ ★ ★ ★ ★

The Complete Second Season (22 episodes on 4 discs): ★ ★ ★ ★ ★

The Complete Third Season (23 episodes on 4 discs): ★ ★ ★ ★ ★
The Complete Fourth Season (22 episodes on 6 discs): ★ ★ ★ ★
The Complete Fifth Season (22 episodes on 6 discs): ★ ★ ★ ½
The Complete Sixth Season (22 episodes on 6 discs): ★ ★ ★

Warner Home Video
Video: Anamorphic Widescreen; Audio: Dolby Digital 2.0

Any television show that can make Americans feel good about their federal government deserves every accolade it receives. Aaron Sorkin's take on the Josiah Bartlet presidency is certainly idealistic, which in Hollywood means Democratic, but *The West Wing* transcends party lines with characters that even a Conservative can embrace. If Bartlet actually ran for office, a lot of GOP loyalists would switch parties.

Rob Lowe's Season 4 departure did some damage, but the biggest loss was that of Aaron Sorkin, whose smart, sharp scripting of nearly every episode of the series' first four seasons ranks among television's most impressive achievements. Warner Bros. did right by this magnificent series with its DVD sets, which sport outstanding tech credits and a wonderful assortment of extras, including a fascinating look at how real White House veterans view *The West Wing*'s take on their service (Season 3).

GREAT MOMENTS: Season 2: The assassination attempt on Bartlet and its aftermath in "In the Shadow of Two Gunmen 1 & 2"; Season 3: The President calls the Butterball Turkey hotline for Thanksgiving cooking advice in "The Indians in the Lobby"; Season 4: The post–9/11 treatise "Isaac and Ishmael," much maligned at the time, remains a powerful examination of the issues that explores a profound moment in US history like no other series could.

FAST-FORWARD: Nothing.

EXTRAS: All seasons sets have episode commentaries by Aaron Sorkin and cast members, as well as gag reels and behind-the-scenes featurettes. Among the highlights are "*The West Wing* Inauguration" (Season 1), "Reel-Life to Real-Life" (Season 3), and "Behind Every Good Man . . . Is the First Lady" (Season 4).

W

What's Happening! (1976–1979)

The Complete First Season (21 episodes on 3 discs): ★ ★ ★
The Complete Second Season (22 episodes on 3 discs): ★ ★ ★ ½
The Complete Third Season (22 episodes on 3 discs): ★ ★ ★

Columbia Tristar Home Video
Video: Full-Frame; Audio: Dolby Digital 2.0

Unlike *Good Times* or *The Jeffersons, What's Happening!* didn't have an agenda beneath its comedy; there was no attempt to shed light on the African-American experience, or to confront political or social issues. The show just wanted to be funny. The closest contemporary comparison is *Welcome Back, Kotter*, and while that series is more easily recalled thirty years on, *What's Happening!* was better. I'd rather hang with Raj and Rerun than with Horshack and Barbarino any day.

GREAT MOMENTS: Season 1: Former Lockers dancer Fred Berry shows off his moves in "My Three Tons"; Raj torments a humorless history teacher in "The Sunday Father"; Dee reveals the heart that lies beneath her sarcasm in "The Hospital Stay"; Season 2: Dwayne's performance of "Handyman" in "Rerun Sees the Light"; Raj arranges for Dee's classmates to appear on *The Gong Show* in "Going, Going, Gong."

FAST-FORWARD: Even the lesser episodes offer a few laughs.

EXTRAS: None.

What's New Scooby-Doo? (2002–)

Volume 1: Space Ape at the Cape (4 episodes on 1 disc): ★ ★ ½
Volume 2: Safari, So Goodi! (4 episodes on 1 disc): ★ ★
Volume 3: Halloween Boos and Clues (4 episodes on 1 disc): ★ ★
Volume 4: Merry Scary Holiday (4 episodes on 1 disc): ★ ★ ½
Volume 5: Sports Spooktacular (4 episodes on 1 disc): ★ ½
Volume 6: Monster Matinee (4 episodes on 1 disc): ★ ★ ½
Volume 7: Ghosts on the Go (4 episodes on 1 disc): ★ ★ ½
Volume 8: Zoinks, Camera, Action! (4 episodes on 1 disc): ★ ★

Warner Home Video
Video: Full-Frame; Audio: Dolby Digital 2.0

While it's oddly reassuring to have the Scooby gang back in new stories, with upgraded animation from the Hanna-Barbera originals, there's something missing from these latter-day mysteries, and it's not just the right voice actors (only Frank Welker as Fred and Casey Kasem as Shaggy return from *Scooby-Doo, Where Are You?*). Maybe an audience that didn't grow up with these characters won't care, but it's jarring for us old-timers to see seatbelts in the Mystery Machine and Velma using a laptop.

GREAT MOMENTS: Volume 4: Scooby finally gets to visit the Scooby Snacks factory in "Recipe for Disaster"; Volume 6: The anything-for-a-buck band KISS meets Scooby in "A Scooby-Doo Halloween."

W

FAST-FORWARD: Nothing.

EXTRAS: Volume 1: Music videos; "Backstage with Simple Plan" featurette; Volume 2: "Road Trip" and "Velma Translates Scooby Talk" featurettes; Volume 3: Warner Bros. back-lot tour with Scooby and Shaggy; "Scooby-Doo's Famous Foes" and "Shari, the House of High Technology" featurettes; Volume 4: Music video; "Toy Designer's Story" featurette.

The White Shadow (1978–1981)

The Complete First Season (15 episodes on 4 discs): ★ ★ ★ ★
The Complete Second Season (24 episodes on 4 discs): ★ ★ ★ ★

20th Century-Fox
Video: Full-Frame; Audio: Dolby Digital 2.0

Timing was a problem for Ken Reeves. He played professional basketball in the era before multimillion-dollar contracts, and he played for the Bulls before Michael Jordan was drafted. That's why, when injury forced Reeves out of the NBA, he got stuck taking a coach's job at a high school in Los Angeles, where he taught life lessons as well as lay-ups. *The White Shadow* could have drifted into sappy *After School Special* territory, but avoided those clichés in favor of an honest depiction of inner-city life, the allure of sports as a ticket out of poverty, and the struggle to survive long enough to achieve that dream. Ken Howard was perfectly cast as the best coach and best friend these kids ever had.

GREATEST MOMENTS: Season 1: Coach Reeves meets his team in the pilot episode; the team forms a singing group in "LeGrand Finale"; Season 2: The coach teaches his team a lesson in humility when they play a game against the Harlem Globetrotters in "Globetrotters."

W

FAST-FORWARD: Nothing.

EXTRAS: Season 1: Cast/crew commentary; featurette "More than Basketball"; Season 2: Cast/crew commentaries; "A Series of Memories" and "Director's Debut" featurettes.

Who's the Boss? (1984–1992)

The Complete First Season (22 episodes on 3 discs): ★ ★ ★

Columbia Tristar Home Video
Video: Full-Frame; Audio: Dolby Digital 2.0

Cute guy and cute girl? Check. Sexual tension expressed via family-hour-friendly banter? Check. Precocious kids and an eccentric parent? Check. *Who's the Boss?* was a by-the-numbers series that followed a familiar pattern for eight seasons, right down to the awkward introduction of a new moppet when the originals passed puberty. And that's fine—not every sitcom has to be *Seinfeld.* Tony Danza and Judith Light never took home an Emmy (though costar Katherine Helmond did), but *Who's the Boss?* proved once again that likable leads and comfortable stories can be more precious television commodities than innovation—see *Arrested Development.*

GREAT MOMENTS: Tony Danza's *Taxi* costar Jeff Conaway appears in "First Kiss"; "Mona Gets Pinned" is a memorable showcase for Katherine Helmond.

FAST-FORWARD: Nothing.

EXTRAS: Six short featurettes, most devoted to individual characters, plus "Brooklyn Meets Connecticut." It would have been fun if Columbia had added an episode from *The Upper Hand,* the British adaptation of *Who's the Boss?* with Honor Blackman in the "Mona" role.

The Wiggles (1991–)

Wiggle Bay: ★ ★ ★
Wiggle Time: ★ ★ ★
Wiggly Safari: ★ ★ ★
Hoop-Dee-Doo! It's a Wiggly Party!: ★ ★ ★ ½
Toot-Toot: ★ ★ ★
Yummy Yummy: ★ ★ ★ ½
Top of the Tots: ★ ★ ★ ½
Live Hot Potatoes: ★ ★ ★ ★
Wiggly Wiggly Christmas: ★ ★ ★
Yule be Wiggling: ★ ★ ★
Santa's Rockin': ★ ★ ★
Cold Spaghetti Western: ★ ★ ★ ½
Whoo Hoo Wiggly Gremlins: ★ ★ ½
Sailing Around the World: ★ ★ ★

Lyrick Studios
Video: Full-Frame; Audio: Dolby Digital 2.0

The Wiggles, as any five-year-old can tell you, are four guys in brightly colored sweatshirts who like to sing and play with their friends, including Captain Feathersword and Dorothy the Dinosaur. Their best songs, "Fruit Salad," "Hot

Potato," and "Hoop De Doo," are so devilishly catchy that they'll stick in your mind for weeks. The DVD releases are fairly interchangeable, though for more mature Wiggles fans (yes, I know you're out there), *Live Hot Potatoes* is the best place to start.

GREAT MOMENTS: Naomi Wallace plays Magdalena the Mermaid in "Wiggle Bay"; the live performances in every release.

FAST-FORWARD: A little of Henry the Octopus goes a long way.

EXTRAS: None.

The Wild, Wild West (1965–1970)

The First Season (28 episodes on 7 discs): ★ ★ ★ ★

Paramount Home Video

Video: Full-Frame; Audio: Dolby Digital 2.0

Mixing the Western and secret-agent genres with a healthy dose of tongue-in-cheek humor, *The Wild, Wild West* was unlike any other show on television before or since. The series was blessed with a dynamic duo of leading men in Robert Conrad and Ross Martin, and one of the coolest opening-credits sequences in TV history. Fans should appreciate Paramount's surprisingly lavish seven-disc set for Season 1, and be grateful that they didn't include the dreadful movie version, featuring Will Smith as a rappin' James West.

GREAT MOMENTS: The first appearance of Dr. Loveless in "The Night the Wizard Shook the Earth"; Yvonne Craig plays Ecstasy La Joie, a sexy assassin who packs an exploding garter, in "The Night of the Grand Emir."

FAST-FORWARD: Nothing.

EXTRAS: Commentaries by Robert Conrad; promos for the pilot; alternate versions of the theme song and the opening-credits sequence.

Will & Grace (1998–)

The Complete First Season (22 episodes on 4 discs): ★ ★ ★ ★ ½

The Complete Second Season (24 episodes on 4 discs): ★ ★ ★ ★ ½

The Complete Third Season (25 episodes on 4 discs): ★ ★ ★ ★

The Complete Fourth Season (27 episodes on 4 discs): ★ ★ ★ ★

Lions Gate

Video: Full-Frame; Audio: Dolby Digital 2.0

It's a sign of societal progress that the step from *Ellen* to *Will & Grace* was a short one. Beyond its pro–alternative lifestyle stance, however, *Will & Grace* is the ultimate blue-state show, at least as the red states see blue: anti-family, anti-kids, New York is the only civilized place in the world, and there's no more egregious sin than a cheap haircut. The millennium-era message at NBC, also home to *Friends* and *Seinfeld*, was that relationships come and go, but friendships are forever. Apparently there were once many unhappy marriages at the Peacock network.

But one need not read between the lines to marvel at a perfectly cast lead quartet, and a barrage of pop-culture references worthy of a Dennis Miller monologue (Will to Grace: "You are so Markie Post in every single Lifetime movie"). Eric McCormack, Sean Hayes, and Megan Mullally earned their critical raves early on, but reexamining the series on DVD provides renewed appreciation for Debra Messing, the last of the four to win an Emmy, despite the fact that no one's done gorgeous and goofy this well since Elizabeth Montgomery. The guest-star infestation got to be a bit much after Season 3, but at its best, as in the final scene of the first-season episode "My Fair Maid-y," the amazing chemistry between Will and Grace rivals the rarified sparkle of Steed and Mrs. Peel. Higher praise is not possible.

GREAT MOMENTS: Season 1: Jack and Karen first meet in "A New Lease on Life"; a medley of quotable scenes in "The Truth about Will and Dogs"; Karen's withering criticism of Grace's fashion sense in almost every episode; Debbie Reynolds debuts as Grace's mother in "The Unsinkable Molly Adler"; Season 2: Grace wears a defective "Hydra-Bra" in the classic "Das Boob"; the return of Molly Shannon as Val in "Girls, Interrupted"; Season 3: Jack meets Cher in "Gypsies, Tramps, and Weed"; the '80s fashions in "Lows in the Mid-'80s"; Season 4: Will's magic act and Glenn Close's guest appearance in "Hocus Focus."

FAST-FORWARD: The Woody Harrelson episodes in Season 3.

EXTRAS: Season 1: Cast interviews; clip-package featurettes; Season 2: Outtakes and more featurettes, similar to Season 1; creator commentaries; Season 3: More of the same, marred by terrible MENU screens that are a challenge to negotiate.

W

Wings (1990–1997)

Seasons 1 & 2 (28 episodes on 4 discs): ★ ★ ★ ★

Paramount Home Video

Video: Full-Frame; Audio: Dolby Digital 2.0

There once was a show from Nantucket . . . that was consistently overshadowed in its original run by an amazing streak of popular Thursday-night situation comedies, from *The Cosby Show* and *Cheers* to *Seinfeld* and *Friends.* But in retrospect, one can better appreciate the clever writing and superb ensemble cast of what many used to call the weak link in NBC's "Must See TV" schedule. What a difference a few years makes—if *Wings* were airing now, it would be celebrated as TV's finest sitcom.

GREAT MOMENTS: The Trivial Pursuit game in "Sports & Leisure"; The Hackett brothers try to impress Helen on her birthday in "It's Not the Thought, It's the Gift."

FAST-FORWARD: Nothing.

EXTRAS: None.

The Wire (2002–)

Season 1 (13 episodes on 5 discs): ★ ★ ★ ★
Season 2 (13 episodes on 5 discs): ★ ★ ★ ★ ½

HBO Home Video
Video: Full-Frame; Audio: Dolby Surround 5.1

Nothing about *The Wire* can be summarized in brief. Its multilayered plots, its shifting perspectives, its complex investigations and subtly drawn characters (more than forty of them) require close attention over a full season to appreciate the series' dramatic depth and precision. Which makes the show ideal for discovery on DVD, where back-to-back episode viewings clarify Detective Jimmy McNulty's attempts to clean up Baltimore's housing projects and cargo docks through endless hours of surveillance.

GREAT MOMENTS: Season 1: The ambiguous finale, "Sentencing"; Season 2: McNulty gets revenge for his demotion in "Ebb Tide."

FAST-FORWARD: Season 1: The language-sensitive might want to skip past the investigation of a murder in a vacant apartment in "Old Cases," which contains more than thirty F-bombs.

EXTRAS: Each season set features commentaries from key creative personnel.

Wiseguy (1987–1990)

Volume 1 (13 episodes on 4 discs): ★ ★ ★ ★ ½
Volume 2 (11 episodes on 4 discs): ★ ★ ★ ★ ★

Volume 3 (13 episodes on 4 discs): ★ ★ ★
Volume 4 (13 episodes on 4 discs): ★ ½

StudioWorks Entertainment
Video: Full-Frame; Audio: Dolby Digital 5.1

Wiseguy fans, like *Crime Story* fans, are faced with the dilemma of wanting to buy the show on DVD, but worrying about the quality of the releases, and whether something better might be forthcoming. The four StudioWorks volumes seem "official," with participation from series creator Stephen J. Cannell and episode commentaries from star Ken Wahl. But widely reported quality-control issues, on Volume 4 in particular, are enough to make one hesitate. Music alteration is another drawback—don't expect to hear "Nights in White Satin" at the end of the Sonny Steelgrave saga on Volume 1. On the plus side, many retailers have cut the original issue price of $80 by as much as sixty percent, which makes it easier to take a chance. Some magnificent stories are here, especially in the first two sets, but if you buy you might want to save the receipt.

GREAT MOMENTS: Volume 1: The fate of Sonny Steelgrave in "No One Here Gets Out Alive"; Volume 2: The Proffit arc, featuring an unforgettable Emmy-winning performance from Kevin Spacey.

FAST-FORWARD: Nothing.

EXTRAS: All four volumes offer commentary on selected episodes by Ken Wahl; Volume 1 also contains an interview with Stephen J. Cannell and a gag reel.

Without a Trace (2002–)

The Complete First Season (23 episodes on 4 discs): ★ ★ ★ ½

Warner Home Video
Video: Anamorphic Widescreen; Audio: Dolby Digital 2.0

For any crime-drama airing between 2000 and 2005, half the battle is just standing out among all the other urban cops and crooks shows up and down the dial. (Do TVs still have dials? Sorry—your host is showing his age.) *Without a Trace* has two effective selling points: a cast full of Emmy and Oscar nominees (Anthony LaPaglia, Poppy Montgomery, Marianne Jean-Baptiste), and the wisdom to stick to a very specific format of missing-persons cases that are solved through psychological profiling.

GREAT MOMENTS: Charles Dutton's Emmy-winning guest appearance as a distraught father in "Between the Cracks" and "Hang on to Me."

FAST-FORWARD: Nothing.

EXTRAS: Deleted scenes; director's cut of the final episode, with previously unseen footage; commentary on the pilot; featurettes "The Motive" and "Fingerprints."

Wonder Woman (1976–1979)

Season 1 (13 episodes on 3 discs): ★ ★ ★ ½
Season 2 (22 episodes on 4 discs): ★ ★
Season 3 (24 episodes on 4 discs): ★ ★ ½

Warner Home Video
Video: Full-Frame; Audio: Dolby Digital Mono

It's hard not to view *Wonder Woman* as a missed opportunity. In Lynda Carter, the series found a heroine that fulfilled every expectation of a character already famous and beloved for generations. Carter had the dazzling looks, the regal bearing, and the right mix of confidence and naïveté to play an Amazon princess experiencing a "man's world" for the first time. Unfortunately, there wasn't much else to the show: scripts were unimaginative, Lyle Waggoner was a stiff as Steve Trevor, and Wonder Woman was never pitted against any of her more colorful comic-book adversaries. Still, the show has become something of a classic thanks to a leading lady who seems to have emerged, as shown in the series' opening credits, right from the pages of a DC comic.

Season 1 is set during World War II, with our super-heroine battling Nazis and saboteurs; subsequent seasons were moved into the present day, with Waggoner playing the son of the original Steve Trevor. In either era episodes are hit-and-miss, but for those who grew up on Lynda Carter, the box-cover art alone will probably get your money.

GREAT MOMENTS: Season 1: Lynda Carter first dons the iconic Wonder Woman costume in "The New Original Wonder Woman"; Debra Winger debuts as Wonder Girl in "The Feminum Mystique"; WW goes west with cowboy-star Roy Rogers in "The Bushwhackers"; Season 2: Steve Trevor II meets WW in "The Return of Wonder Woman"; the first appearance of the Wonder wetsuit in "Bermuda Triangle Crisis"; Season 3: *Behind the Music* poster-boy Leif Garrett plays a dual role in "My Teenage Idol Is Missing."

FAST-FORWARD: Season 1: WW faces a super-gorilla, played by a guy in a bad monkey suit, in "Wonder Woman vs. Gargantua!"; Season 2: The two-part "Mind-Stealers from Outer Space," a *Mystery Science Theater 3000* episode waiting to happen.

EXTRAS: Season 1: The documentary "Beauty, Brawn, and Bulletproof Bracelets: A *Wonder Woman* Retrospective"; commentary on the pilot with Lynda Carter and producer Douglas Kramer; Season 2: The documentary "Revolutionizing a Classic: From Comic Book to Television"; Season 3: Commentary on one episode by Lynda Carter; "Wonder Woman: The Ultimate Feminist Icon" featurette.

Wonderfalls (2004)

The Complete Series (13 episodes on 3 discs): ★ ★ ★ ★

20th Century-Fox

Video: Anamorphic Widescreen; Audio: Dolby Digital 5.1

When the quirky *Wonderfalls* was cancelled after four critically acclaimed but apathetically received episodes, fans rallied for a DVD release. The *Complete Series* box set represents a triumph for those who hoped their strange little show would not be forgotten. Newcomers who take a chance on the set, the first ever to contain more unaired shows than episodes that anyone actually saw, may wonder what the fuss was about. The premise: Jaye, an aimless slacker, takes a job at Wonderfalls, a Niagara Falls gift shop filled with trinkets that send her out on assignments. After questioning her sanity, Jaye begins to embrace her missions, and winds up helping others in unexpected ways. Minor music alteration, acknowledged in the commentary tracks, mars an otherwise excellent set.

GREAT MOMENTS: The lion speaks for the first time in "Wax Lion"; a cow creamer instructs Jaye to help the deported family housekeeper in "Crime Dog."

FAST-FORWARD: The series didn't last long enough to jump any sharks.

EXTRAS: "Greetings from Wonderfalls" featurette, and commentaries from Caroline Dhavamenes, Katie Finneran, Todd Holland, and Bryan Fuller.

W

The World of Sid & Marty Krofft (2002)

(13 episodes on 3 discs): ★ ★ ★ ★ ½

Rhino

Video: Full-Frame; Audio: Mono

Like the value packs of cereal once enjoyed by Krofft fans with their Saturday-morning TV, this three-disc set is an ideal sampler of nearly every series unleashed by the Krofft brothers in their '60s and '70s heyday, including such little-seen treasures as *Wonderbug*, *Dr. Shrinker*, and *ElectraWoman and DynaGirl*. One could argue with some of the episode selections—*H.R. Pufnstuf* is represented by its worst show—and they might have worked a Kaptain Kool and the Kongs appearance into the mix, but for anyone who grew up on this stuff and lived to tell the tale, *The World of Sid & Marty Krofft* is indispensable.

GREAT MOMENTS: Episodes of *The Bugaloos*, *Dr. Shrinker*, and *ElectraWoman and DynaGirl*.

FAST-FORWARD: *Far Out Space Nuts* and *The Lost Saucer* haven't aged well.

EXTRAS: The TV Land network commercials for their Saturday-morning retro-TV block.

The X-Files (1993–2002)

The Complete First Season (24 episodes on 7 discs): ★ ★ ★ ★ ★
The Complete Second Season (24 episodes on 7 discs): ★ ★ ★ ★ ★
The Complete Third Season (24 episodes on 7 discs): ★ ★ ★ ★ ★
The Complete Fourth Season (24 episodes on 7 discs): ★ ★ ★ ★ ½
The Complete Fifth Season (20 episodes on 6 discs): ★ ★ ★
The Complete Sixth Season (22 episodes on 6 discs): ★ ★ ★
The Complete Seventh Season (22 episodes on 6 discs): ★ ★ ½
The Complete Eighth Season (21 episodes on 6 discs): ★ ★
The Complete Ninth Season (19 episodes on 7 discs): ★ ★
Seasons 1–7: ★ ★ ★ ★ ★
The Mythology Collection, Volume 1: Abduction
(15 episodes on 4 discs): ★ ★ ★ ½
The Mythology Collection, Volume 2: Black Oil
(15 episodes on 4 discs): ★ ★ ★
The Mythology Collection, Volume 3: Colonization
(15 episodes on 4 discs): ★ ★

20th Century-Fox
Video: Full-Frame (Seasons 1–4) Anamorphic Widescreen (Seasons 4–9); Audio: Dolby Digital 2.0

The success of *The X-Files* on DVD, one of the first series to be collected in season sets, was confirmation of how many consumers would pay a premium price to own their favorite TV shows, prompting studios to begin cleaning out their vaults. The series once rivaled *Star Trek* in the obsessive zeal of its fans, though it hasn't retained much of that devotion, after two Mulder-less final seasons and a stubborn refusal to satisfactorily answer any of the questions that fueled Mulder's search for the Truth. Still, the sad fact that they squandered an ingeniously developed mythos of government conspiracy and alien invasion should not obscure the impact of those amazing early episodes. The DVD sets also helped establish the variety of special features that buyers anticipate, including commentaries and behind-the-scenes featurettes.

GREAT MOMENTS: Season 1: Scully meets Mulder in the pilot episode; the mythology is established in "Deep Throat"; the first appearance of Tooms in "Squeeze"; the brilliant "Ice"; Season 2: The debut of Alex Krycek in "Sleepless"; the season-closing cliffhanger in "Anasazi"; Season 3: Peter Boyle's Emmy-winning appearance as a reluctant psychic in "Clyde Bruckman's Final Repose"; Mulder is smitten with entomologist Bambi Berenbaum in "War of the Coprohages"; the comic flashbacks in "Jose Chung's 'From Outer Space'"; Season 4: Mulder believes a serial killer may have murdered his sister in "Paper Hearts"; Mulder races to save a terminally ill Scully in "Memento Mori"; posing as Mulder, a shape-shifter puts the moves on Scully in "Small Potatoes"; Season 9: Mulder returns in "The Truth," a valiant but flawed attempt to tie up nine seasons of confused mythology.

FAST-FORWARD: Season 4: "Home," unless you've got a very strong stomach; only the most devoted *X*-Fans may want to watch the final two seasons, following David Duchovny's departure.

EXTRAS: Seasons 1–4 feature Chris Carter interviews, deleted scenes, promotional TV spots, "Behind the Truth" segments originally aired on FX, and "The Truth About . . ." featurettes; episode commentaries, always with writers and never with cast, begin with Season 3; Season 5 includes the "Inside the *X-Files*" documentary; beginning in Season 7, the sets offer International clips; Season 9 includes two forty-five-minute documentaries, "Secrets of the *X-Files*" and "More Secrets of the *X-Files*," as well as a "Tribute to the *X-Files*" featurette.

The X-Men (1992–1997)

Legend of Wolverine (4 episodes on 1 disc): ★ ★ ★
The Phoenix Saga (5 episodes on 1 disc): ★ ★ ½
Reunion/Out of the Past/No Mutant is an Island (5 episodes on 1 disc): ★ ★
Sanctuary/Weapon X, Lies, and Videotape/Proteus
(5 episodes on 1 disc): ★ ★

Universal Home Video (*Reunion* and *Sanctuary*); Buena Vista Home Entertainment (*Legend of Wolverine* and *The Phoenix Saga*)

Video: Full-Frame; Audio: Dolby Digital 2.0

While it was exciting to have animated adaptations of the Chris Claremont stories that propelled *X-Men* to comic-book sales figures that outstripped Superman, Batman, and Spider-Man in the 1980s, the multiple liberties taken with the original stories will disappoint comic fans.

GREAT MOMENTS: Despite drastic changes from the comic, *The Phoenix Saga* still packs a wallop.

FAST-FORWARD: *Legend of Wolverine*: "Nightcrawler" doesn't do right by one of the New X-Men's founding members.

EXTRAS: The Buena Vista releases include a bonus episode, plus interviews with Stan Lee and Chris Claremont.

X-Men: Evolution (2000–2003)

Season 1, Volumes 1–4 (each: 4 episodes on 1 disc): ★ ★ ★
Season 2, Volumes 1–4 (each: 4 episodes on 1 disc): ★ ★

Warner Home Video
Video: Full-Frame; Audio: Dolby Digital 2.0

While the animation has improved from the previous *X-Men* cartoon series, these teenage versions of the familiar heroes will mainly be of interest to the preteen set.

GREAT MOMENTS: Season 1, Volume 1: The debut of Kitty Pryde in "The X Impulse"; Season 2, Volume 2: The first appearance of the Angel in "On Angel's Wings"; Season 2, Volume 3: Nick Fury and Captain America join forces with Wolverine in "Operation: Rebirth."

FAST-FORWARD: The "Apocalypse" stories don't work any better here than they did in the comic.

EXTRAS: Episode introductions with producer Boyd Kirkland.

Xena: Warrior Princess (1995–2001)

Season 1 (24 episodes on 7 discs): ★ ★ ★
Season 2 (22 episodes on 7 discs): ★ ★ ★ ★
Season 3 (22 episodes on 8 discs): ★ ★ ★ ★ ★
Season 4 (22 episodes on 10 discs): ★ ★ ★ ★
Season 5 (22 episodes on 10 discs): ★ ★ ★
Season 6 (22 episodes on 10 discs): ★ ★ ★ ★

Series Finale: Director's Cut: ★ ★ ★

Anchor Bay

Video: Full-Frame; Audio: Dolby Digital 5.1

"She was Xena, a mighty princess forged in the heat of battle . . ." A spin-off of the moderately successful *Hercules: The Legendary Journeys*, *Xena: Warrior Princess* surpassed its parent series in the quality of its acting, writing, and directing, as well as in longevity and viewership, becoming one of the most popular syndicated series of all time.

Whereas *Hercules* remained a light, goofy show throughout its run, *Xena* balanced camp with darker, more mature themes. Even the sillier aspects of Xena's pseudo-mythological world were always grounded by the depth of the central relationship between Xena, a warrior woman constantly atoning for past misdeeds, and her plucky sidekick, Gabrielle, a peaceful bard who developed into a seasoned warrior by the end of the series. The spirited performances of Lucy Lawless and Renee O'Connor inspired a massive cult following, and not just among geeks and lesbians, as reported in the popular press.

The picture quality improves in each DVD release, from dark, grainy, and smudgy in the first season to almost completely pristine in the later sets, with strong, solid colors and little to no digital artifacting, particularly in the last three seasons.

GREAT MOMENTS: Season 1: The introduction of the series' greatest villain in *Callisto*; Season 2: The extended flashbacks of Xena's dark past in *Destiny*; Season 3: *The Debt—Parts 1 & II*; the "Rift Saga" that temporarily split up Xena and Gabrielle and culminated in *The Bitter Suite*, the first original, full-length musical written for a one-hour drama, beating *Buffy the Vampire Slayer*'s "Once More, with Feeling" by three years; Season 5: The final episodes, in which Xena and Gabrielle are frozen in ice and awaken after twenty-five years to find the world changed around them and Xena's baby, Eve, grown into a fierce warrior woman in her own right; Season 6: the "Ring Trilogy" that turned Gabrielle into Sleeping Beauty and Xena into her prince; the alternate universe of *When Fates Collide*.

FAST-FORWARD: *Forgiven* (Season 3), introduces the most irritating character in the entire run of the series, Tara; the fifth season's *Married with Fish Sticks* has the unique distinction of not only being the worst episode of *Xena* but one of the worst episodes ever in the run of a good series; *Lifeblood* (Season 5) is a pilot episode from the same production company, *Amazon High*, that never went to series, so they reworked the footage into a *Xena* episode.

EXTRAS: There's nothing on Season 1 besides an informational CD-ROM which is also included with each subsequent season, and there are three audio commentaries on Season 2. But they pulled out all the stops for the final four seasons, which contain companion featurettes for nearly every episode, including cast and production crew interviews, as well as a few additional hour-long documentaries on some of the series' most notable episodes. The last season also offers footage from a Xena convention. Note that the commentary track on the single-disc release of the series finale is different from the one included in the final-season set.

You Bet Your Life (1950–1961)

The Best Episodes (18 episodes on 3 discs): ★ ★ ★ ★ ★
The Lost Episodes (18 episodes on 3 discs): ★ ★ ★ ★ ½

Shout! Factory
Video: Full-Frame; Audio: Mono

With 423 shows in the can it's unlikely we'll ever see a full run of this delightful game show, in which the game itself was almost incidental to the repartee between the contestants and host Groucho Marx. But these two highlight sets more than suffice, especially when accompanied by the extra features collectors have come to expect from a Shout! Factory release. The *Lost* box offers episodes that were not part of the syndication package, including Groucho's meeting with Pedro Gonzalez-Gonzalez, which is still almost unbearably funny.

GREAT MOMENTS: *The Best Episodes*: Miss Finland visits the show; the debut of the Duck; *The Lost Episodes*: Groucho meets Pedro Gonzalez-Gonzalez; comedian Ernie Kovacs and Groucho ogle a comely young lass.

FAST-FORWARD: The vintage commercials are fun, but after a while you might want to skip past the plugs for your neighborhood DeSoto/Plymouth dealer.

EXTRAS: *Best Episodes*: Three Groucho pilots; outtakes; bloopers; *Lost Episodes*: "The Making of *You Bet Your Life*"; outtakes; Groucho's original 1947 radio audition, "A Holiday Message from Groucho."

APPENDIX A

Merry Christmas, You Big TV Geek

No holiday plans again? Of course not—you have no friends because you spent the whole year watching television. Wait, did we say no friends? What about your TV pals? They celebrate the holidays every year, just like real people! Here are all the shows you'll need to get through the season, divided by decade.

Sleigh Bells Ring in the '60s:

ADAM-12: "Log 122"—Malloy and Reed search for a stolen car containing a needy family's holiday gifts. (*Adam-12: Season 1*)

THE ANDY GRIFFITH SHOW: "Christmas Story"—Local Scrooge Ben Weaver has a harmless bootlegger thrown in jail, so that's where the Mayberry townsfolk spend the holiday. (*The Andy Griffith Show: The Complete First Season*)

THE AVENGERS: "Too Many Christmas Trees"—Steed and Mrs. Peel attend a Charles Dickens–themed Christmas party, where there's murder afoot. (*Avengers: 1965, Set 2*)

BEWITCHED: "A Vision of Sugar Plums"—Sam flies problem child Billy Mumy to the North Pole to meet Santa. (*Bewitched: The Complete First Season*)

THE BIG VALLEY: "Judgment in Heaven"—The girl Jarrod brings home for Christmas is wanted by the law and her ex-boyfriend, who just broke out of jail. (*The Big Valley: Season One*)

THE DICK VAN DYKE SHOW: "The Alan Brady Show Presents"—All singing, all dancing, all wonderful—except for Richie's off-key performance of "The Little Drummer Boy." (*The Dick Van Dyke Show: Season 3*)

THE FLYING NUN: "Wailing in a Winter Wonderland"—Sister Bertrille tries to make it snow—in Puerto Rico. (*The Flying Nun: The Complete First Season*)

GILLIGAN'S ISLAND: "Birds Gotta Fly, Fish Gotta Talk"—The Skipper plays Santa—or does he? (*Gilligan's Island: The First Season*)

GREEN ACRES: "An Old Fashioned Christmas"—Oliver defies the Hooterville law against chopping down Christmas trees. (*Green Acres: The Complete Second Season*)

THE MONKEES: "The Christmas Show"—The Monkees teach a spoiled rich kid the true meaning of Christmas, and perform a beautiful a cappela rendition of the carol "Riu, Chiu." (*The Monkees: Season 2*)

THAT GIRL: "Christmas and the Hard-Luck Kid"—Ann gives up her holiday to spend it with a lonely boy whose parents are out of town. (*That Girl: Season 1*)

THE TWILIGHT ZONE: "Night of the Meek"—A department-store Santa Claus is cheered by a bottomless sack of toys. (*Twilight Zone: Season 2*)

Dreaming of a '70s Christmas:

ALL IN THE FAMILY: "Christmas Day at the Bunkers"—Archie's bitterness over not getting a Christmas bonus threatens to spoil the holiday. (*All in the Family: The Complete Second Season*)

THE BOB NEWHART SHOW: "His Busiest Season"—Bob's patients celebrate the season—sort of. (*The Bob Newhart Show: The Complete First Season*)

THE BRADY BUNCH: "The Voice of Christmas"—Cindy asks a department-store Santa to cure her mommy's laryngitis in time for her to sing at church on Christmas morning. (*The Brady Bunch: The Complete First Season*)

THE JEFFERSONS: "A Christmas Wedding"—Lionel and Jenny finally tie the knot. (*The Jeffersons: The Complete Third Season*)

LITTLE HOUSE ON THE PRAIRIE: "Christmas at Plum Creek"—The Ingalls spend their first Christmas on the prairie. (*Little House on the Prairie: Season 1*)

THE MARY TYLER MOORE SHOW: "Christmas and the Hard-Luck Kid"—Mary has to work on Christmas Eve, thanks to mean old Lou Grant. (*The Mary Tyler Moore Show: The Complete First Season*)

M*A*S*H: "Dear Sis"—Father Mulcahy writes a letter to his sister, reflecting on Christmas in Korea. (*M*A*S*H: Season 7*)

THE PARTRIDGE FAMILY: "Don't Bring Your Guns to Town, Santa"—The bus breaks down in a ghost town on Christmas Eve, but an old prospector helps the family pass the time with a tale of Christmas past. (*The Partridge Family: The Complete Second Season*)

THE SONNY & CHER SHOW—Cher sings "Oh, Holy Night"! (*The Sonny & Cher Christmas Collection*)

THREE'S COMPANY: "Three's Christmas"—The party's at Norman Fell's. So how do we get out of it? (*Three's Company: Season 2*)

THE WALTONS: "The Homecoming: A Christmas Story"—America meets the Waltons. (*The Homecoming: A Christmas Story*)

WHAT'S HAPPENING!: "Christmas"—Raj and Dee prepare to celebrate with their Dad, unaware that Ma has taken the day off from work. (*What's Happening!: The Complete First Season*)

WONDER WOMAN: "The Deadly Toys"—Wonder Woman meets the Riddler when Frank Gorshin guests as an evil toy maker. (*Wonder Woman: The Complete Second Season*)

Deck the Halls with '80s TV:

ALF: "Oh, Tannerbaum"—ALF and Willie head for the mountains to find a Christmas tree. (*ALF: Season 1*)

CHARLES IN CHARGE: "Home for the Holidays"—When a blizzard ends Charles's holiday plans, he finds himself stuck in the Pembroke home with their visiting Grandma Irene, played by Rue McClanahan. (*Charles in Charge: The Complete First Season*)

THE COSBY SHOW: "Father's Day"—The Huxtable kids give their dad a great Christmas, to make up for years of lousy Father's Day presents. (*The Cosby Show: Season 1*)

A DIFFERENT WORLD: "The Gift of the Magi"—Dwayne schemes to become Denise's "secret Santa," and Whitley meets her father's new, young girlfriend. (*A Different World: Season 1*)

DOOGIE HOWSER, M.D.: "Doogie the Red-Nosed Reindeer"—Doogie fakes being sick to get out of working the night shift on Christmas Eve. (*Doogie Howser, M.D.: The Complete First Season*)

THE DUKES OF HAZZARD: "The Great Santa Claus Chase"—Boss Hogg tries to corner the market on Christmas trees, but them Duke boys aren't going to let him. (*The Dukes of Hazzard: The Complete Third Season*)

THE GOLDEN GIRLS: " 'Twas the Nightmare Before Christmas"—The girls plan to spend the holiday with their families, but inclement weather brings them back together. (*The Golden Girls: Season 2*)

GROWING PAINS: "A Christmas Story"—Jason counsels a depressed department-store Santa. (*Growing Pains: The Complete First Season*)

HIGHWAY TO HEAVEN: "Another Song for Christmas"—A used-car dealer is shown the error of his ways. (*Highway to Heaven: Season 1*)

KNIGHT RIDER: "Silent Knight"—En route to a Christmas banquet, Michael helps a gypsy boy who witnessed a bank robbery. (*Knight Rider: Season 2*)

MARRIED . . . WITH CHILDREN: "It's A Bundy-ful Life, Parts 1 & 2"—Al gets a visit from his guardian angel (*played by Sam Kinison*). (*Married . . . With Children: Season 4*)

MOONLIGHTING: " 'Twas the Episode Before Christmas"—Richard Belzer slides down the chimney. (*Moonlighting: The Complete First and Second Seasons*)

MURPHY BROWN: "Murphy's Pony"—Murphy becomes a temporary mom to three abandoned kids. (*Murphy Brown: Season 1*)

PUNKY BREWSTER: "Yes, Punky, There Is a Santa Claus, Parts 1 & 2"—Henry searches for Punky's mother, with a little help from St. Nick. (*Punky Brewster: Season 1*)

XENA: WARRIOR PRINCESS: "A Solstice Carol"—Lucy Lawless plays the Fates, who bear a resemblance to Dickens's ghosts of Christmas past, present, and future. (*Xena: Season 2*)

Jingling All the Way to the '90s and Beyond:

ER: "A Miracle Happens Here"—Nobody likes to spend the holidays in a hospital, but the docs at County General make the best of it. (*ER: The Complete Second Season*)

EVERYBODY LOVES RAYMOND: "The Ball"—Ray tells Allie "the Truth" about Santa Claus, just before Santa shows up—twice. (*Everybody Loves Raymond: The Complete First Season*)

FRASIER: "Miracle on Third or Fourth Street"—Frasier works the holiday and consoles the lonely over the radio. (*Frasier: The Complete First Season*)

THE FRESH PRINCE OF BEL-AIR: "Deck the Halls"—Will decorates the mansion; his neighbor, Evander Holyfield, doesn't approve. (*The Fresh Prince of Bel-Air: Season 1*)

FRIENDS: "The One with the Holiday Armadillo"—Santa meets Superman! (*Friends: The Complete Seventh Season*)

GROUNDED FOR LIFE: "I Saw Daddy Hitting Santa Claus"—Sean puts a smack down on Santa, while Lily tries to figure out who sent her boxer shorts for Christmas. (*Grounded for Life: Season 2*)

HOME IMPROVEMENT: "Yule Better Watch Out"—Tim competes with his neighbor for best holiday light display, while Mark wonders if Santa is real. (*Home Improvement: Season 1*)

JUST SHOOT ME: "Jesus, It's Christmas"—The night custodian has a crush on Maya, and Finch dreams of a Caribbean Christmas. (*Just Shoot Me: Seasons 1 & 2*)

THE KING OF QUEENS: "Net Prophets"—Carrie and Doug fight over what to do with his Christmas bonus. (*The King of Queens: The Complete Second Season*)

NEWSRADIO: "Xmas Story"—Bill is stalked by a psycho Santa. (*NewsRadio: Seasons 1 & 2*)

THE O.C.: "The Best Chrismukkah Ever"—Seth invents a new bi-religious holiday. (*The O.C.: Season 1*)

THE OFFICE: "The Office Special"—A Christmas party packed with uncomfortable silences. (*The Office Special*)

SAVED BY THE BELL: "Home for Christmas, Parts 1 & 2"—Zack dates a girl from the streets. (*Saved by the Bell: Seasons 3 & 4*)

SEINFELD: "The Pick"—Elaine's overexposure in her Christmas card photo earns her the nickname "Nip." (*Seinfeld: Season 4*)

SOUTH PARK: "Mr. Hankey, the Christmas Poo"—Kyle sings the classic "A Lonely Jew on Christmas." (*South Park: The Complete First Season*)

TOUCHED BY AN ANGEL: "Fear Not!"—Monica brings a message of hope to a small town in mourning. (*Touched by an Angel: The Complete First Season*)

THE VICAR OF DIBLEY: "The Christmas Lunch Incident"—Geri accepts three holiday dinner invitations, and hears the world's worst knock-knock joke. (*The Vicar of Dibley: The Complete Series 2 and Specials*)

THE WEST WING: "Noel"—President Bartlet decides to sign his Christmas cards personally—all 100,000 of them. (*The West Wing: The Complete Second Season*)

WILL & GRACE: "Jingle Balls"—Grace decorates the windows at Barney's, and Will dates a ballet dancer who's hopefully not a nutcracker. (*Will & Grace: The Complete Fourth Season*)

WINGS: "A Terminal Christmas"—Everybody gathers at Faye's house for a holiday dinner, but she's in no mood to celebrate. (*Wings: Seasons 1 & 2*)

APPENDIX B

Ten Retro Programming Nights

As more shows debut on DVD it becomes possible to recreate the network programming schedules of years past. It's the next best thing to a time machine. To really complete the illusion, pick up a collection of vintage commercials from the bargain rack at your DVD shop of choice, or from eBay. Better yet, make a party of the night—invite friends, dress in appropriate period costume, and fill the TV trays with vintage snacks, available from a variety of online sources, including groovycandies.com.

RETRO PROGRAMMING NIGHT #1: ABC, TUESDAY, 1958: *Cheyenne, The Life and Legend of Wyatt Earp, The Rifleman, Naked City*

RETRO PROGRAMMING NIGHT #2: CBS, WEDNESDAY, 1965: *Lost in Space, The Beverly Hillbillies, Green Acres, The Dick Van Dyke Show*

RETRO PROGRAMMING NIGHT #3: CBS, MONDAY, 1967: *Gunsmoke, The Lucy Show, The Andy Griffith Show, Family Affair*

RETRO PROGRAMMING NIGHT #4: NBC, WEDNESDAY, 1971: *Adam-12, NBC Mystery Movie* (choose from *Columbo*, *McCloud*, or *McMillan and Wife*), *Night Gallery*

RETRO PROGRAMMING NIGHT #5: CBS, SATURDAY, 1973: *All in the Family*, *M*A*S*H*, *The Mary Tyler Moore Show*, *The Bob Newhart Show*

RETRO PROGRAMMING NIGHT #6: ABC, TUESDAY, 1978: *Happy Days*, *Laverne & Shirley*, *Three's Company*, *Taxi*, *Starsky & Hutch*

RETRO PROGRAMMING NIGHT #7: CBS, FRIDAY, 1981: *The Incredible Hulk*, *The Dukes of Hazzard*, *Dallas*

RETRO PROGRAMMING NIGHT #8: NBC, THURSDAY, 1987: *The Cosby Show*, *A Different World*, *Cheers*, *Night Court*

RETRO PROGRAMMING NIGHT #9: NBC, THURSDAY, 1994: *Friends, Seinfeld, ER*

RETRO PROGRAMMING NIGHT #10: FOX, SUNDAY, 1998: *The Simpsons*, *That '70s Show*, *The X-Files*

Index of Personalities